A LIFE IN PEACE AND WAR

By the same author
HAMMARSKJOLD

Brian Urquhart

A LIFE
IN PEACE
AND
WAR

W. W. Norton & Company
New York • London

To Sidney

First published as a Norton paperback 1991 by arrangement with Harper & Row, Publishers, Inc.

Library of Congress Cataloging-in-Publication Data
Urquhart, Brian.
  A life in peace and war.
  Includes index.
  1. Urquhart, Brian. 2. Diplomats—United States—Biography.
3. World politics—1945–   4. United Nations—Biography. I. Title.
E840.8.U83A3 1987   327.2′092′4 [B]   87-45270

ISBN: 978-0-393-30771-9

W. W. Norton & Company, Inc.
500 Fifth Avenue, New York, N.Y. 10110
W. W. Norton & Company Ltd
10 Coptic Street, London WC1A 1PU

1 2 3 4 5 6 7 8 9 0

Preface
to the Paperback Edition

THE INTERNATIONAL SCENE has changed dramatically since this book first went to press early in 1987. The end of the Cold War has allowed the powers of East and West to cooperate in making the United Nations, and especially the Security Council, begin to work as it was originally intended to work. Thus some of the conflicts mentioned in this book—Namibia and the Iran-Iraq War, for example—have been resolved, largely through United Nations action. At the same time the approach of the UN's Third World majority has become notably more pragmatic and less confrontational.

Iraq's attack on Kuwait evoked unprecedented unanimity and willingness to act through the Security Council. This act of aggression gave the concept of collective security its first full-scale test, including the collective use of force to liberate Kuwait. There is also a new and concerted effort to mobilize the United Nations system to deal with global problems like the environment. With the end of the Cold War it seems possible that the whole concept of international organization may at last be moving forward.

Although the United Nations has been transformed since this book was written, its early history still has an important bearing on its future. I hope, therefore, that this personal account of that history, and of the war that gave birth to the United Nations, may continue to throw some light on the nature and evolution of the world organization.

Brian Urquhart
New York
April 1991

Contents

Illustrations

Unless otherwise indicated, all photographs courtesy of the United Nations.

These photographs will be found following page 150

Following page 278

Acknowledgments

I OWE A DEBT of gratitude to all the people who, by making my life so interesting and enjoyable, also made this book possible.

I have had especially valuable advice from my wife, Sidney, from Ed Burlingame of Harper & Row, Aaron Asher, and Michael Janeway. May Davidson, my assistant for many years at the United Nations, and Marcia Bikales and Barbara Nelson have been infinitely helpful. I thank Milton Grant for his help with the pictures.

When I was leaving the United Nations, Franklin A. Thomas, the president of the Ford Foundation, suggested that I might work at the Foundation as a Scholar-in-Residence. I am enormously grateful to him and to the Foundation for providing me with the facilities and the perfect atmosphere, at the same time calm and stimulating, in which to finish this book.

I

Beginnings

M<small>Y MOTHER'S FAVORITE WORD</small> was "worthwhile." It was a moral criterion applied to plans, books, entertainments, and distractions of all sorts, as well as to friends and acquaintances. It weighed pleasure against moral worth, and invariably came down on the side of moral worth. It expressed perfectly the ethos of the nonconformist, provincial, intelligent middle class from which my mother came. It was not wholly destructive, but it cast a shadow of moral judgment, a veil of doubt and caution, over the simplest matters, and to this day I sometimes have difficulty in enjoying unalloyed the pleasure of the moment. It certainly gave one a sense of purpose.

My father must have been increasingly worn down by my mother's stern character and approach. He was a deeply self-centered man, interested only in himself and in his avocation—painting. Any distraction was doggedly resisted. My mother once told me that he regarded sex as a distraction which weakened his artistic powers and therefore seldom engaged in it. My father was selfish and good-looking, with great charm. He was inspired by the harmless and satisfying belief that he would eventually be recognized as one of the world's greatest painters. My mother, although she admired his painting, regarded this as vanity and foolishness, but for someone who did absolutely nothing but paint I could never see what was wrong with it. He was a good but unoriginal painter, highly skilled in watercolor and drawing, too derivative in oils.

My father's family came originally from the Scottish Highlands north of Inverness. The Urquhart clan had produced a number of minor figures and one major eccentric, Sir Thomas Urquhart. Sir Thomas translated Rabelais in a brilliant and original style not seen again until James Joyce.

1

He invented a universal language, wrote the tale of the Admirable Crichton, and traced his pedigree back to Adam and Eve through almost every known celebrity of antiquity. Sappho was, it seems, a Miss Urquhart. Pamprosodos Urquhart was the husband of Princess Termuth, who found Moses in the bullrushes. Sir Thomas fought in the Civil War on the Royalist side with gallantry and great incompetence, losing most of his manuscripts at the Battle of Worcester. They were, he noted later, "used for inferior employments and posterior uses" by the Roundheads. He went into exile in France and died of laughing in 1660 on hearing that the King had been restored. What did him in is thought to have been the news that King Charles II, on being presented with a Bible by the Roundhead Mayor of Dover, pressed it to his lips with the remark that in exile it had always been his most intimate friend. The Urquharts were massacred along with the other Highland clans in the disastrous defeat of Bonnie Prince Charlie at Culloden in 1746. My father's ancestors went south in the nineteenth century, his father becoming the minister at Portpatrick in Kircudbrightshire. My paternal grandfather had died a few months after my father's birth, and his mother during it. He was brought up by adoring aunts in Edinburgh and had the delightful accent of that beautiful city.

My mother's family were from the small bourgeoisie of Bridport in Dorset on the south coast of England, sensible, solid, public-spirited, decent people with a streak of Celtic eccentricity. My mother had five sisters and one brother. It was assumed that the girls would be unlikely to marry, and only two of them did. The others went into teaching or nursing or stayed at home to look after the older generation. They were great believers in reason, education, and moderation. They were Unitarians, going each Sunday to the rational, unceremonial meeting in the white early nineteenth-century Unitarian chapel in Bridport. My grandfather never tired of extolling his version of the Unitarian creed, "One God, no devil, and twenty shillings in the pound." I was born in my grandfather's house in Bridport in 1919.

My earliest memory of my father is on a fine spring morning in the early twenties, singing in a hip bath outside the back door of the exceedingly primitive cottage we then lived in, Cherry Tree Cottage, on Newtown Common in Berkshire (the site, incidentally, much later on, of *Watership Down*). Soon afterwards he rode away on his bicycle and never came home again.

This was the central mystery of my young life. My mother would never admit that my father was gone for good and when questioned would say that he would be back soon. He was travelling with a circus which he was painting, or he was visiting unspecified relatives. Inquisitive neighbors and unkind schoolmates constantly asked the same question. This went on for seven years, from my sixth to thirteenth year, when it gradually became apparent to me that my parents were divorced. Even then my mother never referred to it, and for many years I regarded it as a terrible disgrace, to be concealed at all costs. In fact the decree nisi had come through as early as 1926, and a friend had taken my brother and me to see the Test Match at the Oval for the day to get us away while my mother went through the formalities.

Newtown Common, where we lived until I was six, is the scene of my earliest memories. Our nearest neighbor was Mrs. Bolton, our only domestic help. It was she who wrecked my mother's proudest possession, six of the new stainless steel knives, by trying to sharpen them on the stone sink. ("There now, I thought 'ee wouldn't sharpen.") She was also good at cautionary stories. Seeing my brother chewing wild watercress, she told him of a boy who had done the same and been carted off to hospital in agony. "And when they cut'n open, there were six girt toads ajumpin' on his gittels." No more watercress after that. Then there was Mrs. Gosling, married to Major Gosling, retired and childless after a lifetime in India. Her two passions were children and cooking, and we spent much of our time in her cottage consuming the ruins of rich fruit cakes that never quite rose and jellies and meringues that never quite set. I remember running down her garden path and hearing her scream in alarm because there was an adder in the path. I stepped on it and ran on, and she became hysterical. I have had a horror of snakes ever since.

More exotic were Mr. and Mrs. Behrend, rich cotton manufacturers, encouragers and generous patrons of contemporary painters and musicians. They lived in Grey House, an enormous modern mansion a mile away through a larch wood. We took lessons in their schoolroom with their children, Julie and George, and they took us on expeditions and holidays and were immensely generous and kind throughout my growing up. They built a memorial chapel at Burghclere for Mrs. Behrend's brother who had been killed in Salonika in the First World War. The inside was all frescoes by Stanley Spencer, and we used to tiptoe in to watch the tiny painter working away on his scaffolding and sliding down ladders. The Behrends' house was my first experience of affluent life, and I recall vividly the meringues, the fragrance of peat fires, and the chauffeur-driven Daimler that usually made their children car-sick. I first heard Benjamin Britten and Peter Pears perform, as young men, in their house.

My elder brother, Andrew, and I spent a lot of time playing in the gully behind our cottage and damming the stream that ran through it, bordered in spring and summer with golden kingcups, violets, and anemones. We were sometimes joined in this occupation by Betty Pink, the daughter of the Newtown vicar who lived in a cavernous rectory on the other side of the gully. My brother used to pump the organ in church on Sundays and was well thought of in ecclesiastical circles. Our greatest excitement was an occasional trip by pony trap to Newbury, our local town, where we would stand on the bridge over the railroad to watch the express trains thunder through in clouds of smoke and steam on their way to London or the West Country. Or we could walk a mile in the other direction to watch the local train clanking slowly through the cutting. My memories of Newtown Common are all of novelty and the enchantment of nature, clouded by the obvious estrangement of my mother and father. The upper floor of the cottage was a single continuous room on different levels with little privacy, and their conversations late at night left me perplexed and anxious.

Another of my early memories is what for my mother must have been a nightmare visit to Scotland in 1924. We stayed in the Victorian apartment of my father's recently deceased Aunt Effie in Edinburgh, waiting excitedly each day for the noon gun on the castle and admiring the flower clock in Princes Street, and then at the home of my father's Caird relatives, Cassencarie. In the best of circumstances this would have been a trial. The house was so haunted that the main staircase (where, according to legend, several had inexplicably died) was closed by permanently locked glass doors. Andrew and I lived in a turret. Between my father and mother there were silences, scenes, and unexplained absences. But the main theme, felt but not identified by a five-year-old, was my father's pursuit of his cousin, whom he finally married.

I can only imagine what that summer must have been like for my mother, for she has never spoken of it. Her marriage, the center of her life (she had been engaged to my father in 1908), and her escape from the closed circle of her family, was at an end, and she knew it. My father had finally met her opposite, a sycophantic, mealy-mouthed woman who uncritically adored him and believed him to be the genius he was convinced he was. Up to this time his painting had shown some character and interest, and he was technically very good indeed. After 1926 it was often insipid, and he took to painting portraits of minor establishment and society figures where his obvious desire to please the subject sometimes lay like a layer of treacle on the canvas.

My father was a convinced spiritualist and the close friend of innumerable ghosts. He constantly reported conversations with people long dead as if he had just met them in the street. The houses he stayed in swarmed with psychic phenomena, and skepticism irritated him. He let drop that he had spent some happy hours on the shores of Loch Ness with the Monster, and his favorite Cairn terrier, Judy, jumped up onto his bed and barked each morning until his dying day, although she had died in 1936. He was conservative and detested the left wing and any painters later than the Impressionists. He was a terrible snob—a "tuft hunter" was my mother's expression for this—relishing even the humblest title or most minor public figure. For all his failings, my mother adored him in her critical way and never took the smallest interest in any other man. To her death in her hundred and first year she spoke of him with affection.

When my father bicycled away, his paintbox and easel slung over his back and his trunk following by the local carrier, our life abruptly changed. We moved in 1926 from the rural delights of Newtown Common to a suburb of Bristol, Westbury-on-Trym. Andrew had already gone away to school and was only at home in the holidays.

To a child of six our little jerry-built, semi-detached suburban house seemed, after the rustic simplicities of Newtown, to be a technological marvel. It had electric light and running water dispensed in the only bathroom (a bathroom was a novelty anyway) through white ceramic taps which seemed to me the height of chic. It was here that we plunged into a bath of cold water every morning of the year—a regime considered by my mother to be essential to health. We even had, occasionally, hot water produced by a coal boiler in the kitchen which fed tepid water, a bathful at a time, to a tank in a cupboard in my bedroom. My mother was apprehensive of such new-fangled gadgets, and I had, unfortunately, heard her discussing with her sister Hilda its potential for exploding and spreading general devastation. The tank rumbled occasionally and ominously during the night, and for some years I used to lie trembling in my bed awaiting the disaster. I never spoke to my mother of this because she disapproved of a show of any emotion, especially fear. I had also overheard my mother say to my Aunt Margaret, apparently in response to a request for clarification, "If I am on my deathbed today, it means I shall die tomorrow." I took this absolutely literally and was filled for years with forebodings and nightmares of my mother's death.

Since we had no money, and my father was unlikely to provide any, my mother had taken us to Bristol so that she could be a teacher in the

Badminton School for Girls, founded and run by her eldest sister, Lucy, and her partner for life, Miss Beatrice M. Baker (BMB). They were a wholly admirable couple, tough, public-spirited, and the best possible joint headmistresses of an academically first-rate school. Aunt Lucy was outgoing, confidence-giving, and did the practical work. Miss Baker, skeptical and sometimes difficult, was the intellectual inspiration of the enterprise. Since the ethos of Badminton School had, as I later realized, a vast influence on me, I quote at length on the subject from Iris Murdoch, who was a pupil at the school in the thirties.

. . . We were Athenians of course, but we were Spartans too. B.M.B. was, and certainly intended to be, a major influence upon her girls. But with all this toughness, indeed somehow as part of it, there was, among us junior citizens, an atmosphere which outlawed malice as (I believe) it outlawed lying: a kind of strong lucid security which inspired faith and a sense of freedom. A strong positive innocence seems to belong to that time and to be connected with that remarkable woman.

The word "naive" is indeed not out of place. B.M.B. was a passionate lover of intellectual things, but she was not really an intellectual. This may have been one of the sources of her strength. Led by her we confidently did everything, we were athletes, craftsmen, scholars, practitioners of all the arts. . . . We were introduced to the whole of history, the Assyrians, the Egyptians, the Romans were our familiar friends, and most of all the Greeks. The cool drawing room light was soon transformed for me into the light of Hellas, the last gleam of a Victorian vision of those brilliant but terrible people. That we took so much "cultivation" in our stride was perhaps largely a result of B.M.B.'s immense *confidence*, based not upon any scholarship but on a strong enthusiastic intuition. She gave articulate expression to a kind of pure idealism which people of today are too embarrassed to utter and too cynical to conceive. . . .

Vulgar snobbery being of course absent, perhaps in some very high-minded way we thought well of ourselves in our city state. But we were not all that cloistered, since a political sense was taken for granted to be an important part of a moral sense, indeed one with it. . . . "Public service" was a natural ideal, and this went with a lively informed interest in contemporary politics. . . . Looking back, we see the thirties as a time of dangerously unrealistic political dreams. Yet *we* knew about the concentration camps considerably before this idea was taken seriously by the general public. Moral sense was political sense and was also more or less identical with religion; in the ordering of these things B.M.B.'s view of the cosmos was paramount, a simple certainty untroubled by dogma. . . . Jesus, as teacher, shared the stage in morning prayers with a large variety of other mentors, including Lenin. Yet some sort of moral force and deep sincerity conveyed to us, together with an ideal of lucidity and truthfulness, the reality of inwardness and prayer. . . .

. . . B.M.B. had her own sort of strong handsomeness. She was, one must add to this picture, a humorous happy person, very often laughing. I recall her in a pallid lucid light, dressed in pastel greens with white blouses, a black velvet band over her silver hair, always ageless. . . . I do not think that I idealise my old teacher and my old school. My school teachers have been among the best people I have known, and among them this commanding figure stands out, a powerful domineering brave woman, imbued with a kind of pure-hearted moral certainty which now seems, alas for our time, old-fashioned and far away.

Badminton was an excellent school with some very un-English characteristics. Of these one of the most important was a passionate anti-xenophobia. The daughters of people in trouble all over the world were welcomed with open arms at Badminton. Indira Nehru came there when her father was in a British jail. From 1933 on they took in numbers of Jewish refugees from Germany and Austria, so that our little house and every available space was filled with them. These girls mostly did very well, and after the war, in which the school was extensively damaged by bombing, many large anonymous donations arrived. I had no doubt where they came from, but when I told Aunt Lucy she was, for once, seriously upset. "That isn't at all why we took them in here," she said.

Aunt Lucy and Miss Baker were strong supporters of the League of Nations, and teaching about international affairs occupied a surprisingly large place in the school curriculum. Every summer they would despatch a team to the League of Nations Summer School in Geneva. This excursion, much sought after, added an incentive and a point to the teaching. (It was in the Summer School in 1935 that I first saw, under construction, the appalling Palais des Nations in Geneva.) I don't think my aunts thought the League would prevent another world war or that it would really work as it was supposed to. They just thought it *ought* to be able to do these things if only enough people supported it intelligently, and that one day an international peace organization would work because it had to work.

*   *   *

As a child of six, for financial reasons, I had found myself at Badminton—a lone boy among two hundred or so girls. When I was eight I was transferred to a boys' "prep school," Colchester House in Clifton, a mile or two from home. This Dickensian establishment was run by an elderly bachelor who was, I now see, homosexual, sadistic, and alcoholic—words not in general currency in those days. His passion was beating, and his method was to send for the victim to his study, a den reeking of cigarettes and an undefined odor I later identified as whiskey. Your trousers (usually gray flannel shorts) were then removed and you lay face down on a sofa while the Headmaster, with much wheezing and grunting, produced a hairbrush with a longish handle which he lovingly called "Tickle Toby." Then, fondling and grunting, he would deliver ten or twenty stinging strokes at his leisure. After this, trying to repress tears of pain and humiliation, you would dress and leave the sanctum. The Headmaster would beat boys for almost anything, a mistake in Latin verse, in which we were supposed to be perfect, or, on one occasion, the entire soccer team for losing a match against another local school. I don't know what other parents did—possibly nothing—but my mother, having observed the black and blue results of this treatment while I was having a bath, made very strong representations to the Headmaster. He evidently respected her for this, and I was never beaten again.

Although I was mediocre at soccer and bored stiff by cricket, I was in other ways a good student. I had a prodigious verbal memory and enjoyed French and, above all, Latin, which was the key subject in the Headmaster's eyes. I could write grammatical and correct Latin verse when I was ten and made few mistakes. The only subject at which I failed totally was mathematics, our weekends being regularly ruined by the Saturday maths paper, but the Headmaster sympathized with that, and the maths teacher, Miss Bevan, was so fossilized that she didn't mind either. Fossilized also was Miss Tompsett who taught English. Unfortunately far from fossilized was our French teacher, a dedicated pincher and fondler of small boys. Colchester House itself was a sepulchral villa with that mixed odor of disinfectant, scrubbed pine floors, and overcooked cabbage which characterized many schools at that time. It was, on the whole, a profoundly depressing establishment.

The Headmaster, for all his foibles, really did mind about his boys and took great pains to get them to good public (private) schools, if possible with scholarships. He was aware that we had no money at all and took special trouble over me. He put me down for the King's Scholarship examination at Westminster School late in 1930 when I was eleven years old. My mother and I travelled up to London, I in a fever of anxiety so great that we stopped at the Army and Navy Stores in Victoria Street for a sedative before I sat down to the exam in the great hammer-beamed Monk's Dormitory at Westminster. As we journeyed back to Bristol on the evening train, I was convinced of failure. A few evenings later my mother and I were surprised at our supper by the arrival of the Head-master in his open Essex motorcar. He was radiant with triumph, for I had won a King's Scholarship, the youngest of his boys ever to do so. Even my mother was elated at the news, not least because it assured me of a good education without a crushing financial burden on her, although she later made a show of wondering if the whole thing was really worth-while. For me it was a turning point because it gave me affordable access to an ancient and civilized school for the next six years. I was elated, and also somewhat intimidated, at the prospect. And I was grateful, in spite of everything else, to the Headmaster.

*   *   *

In those days a motorcar was still a fabulous thing, at least in our circle. My Aunt Lucy, who did not drive, had bought an open ("Touring") Standard motorcar when we had first moved to Bristol, theoretically so that my mother could drive her and Miss Baker about. "Going for a drive" was considered highly as a form of recreation at that time. The truth was, I think, that Aunt Lucy, who was warm-hearted and thoughtful, had figured out a form of distraction and status for my mother in her lowest and (for her) most humiliating hour. Thus my mother took driving lessons and finally mastered this formidable machine. The car had gate-gears (non-synchronized), and "double declutching" was a key art in changing gear, which was usually accompanied by tremendous grindings of metal. There were other complications, especially in starting the car by crank handle if the rudimentary self-starter failed, as it often did, or when the clutch began to slip on steep hills. These uncertainties made all outings an adventure. After some time we would venture as far as Bridport in Dorset (64 miles), where my mother's parents lived and where my brother and I spent all our holidays. We used to time the journey religiously and were elated when we could achieve it in less than two hours.

Dorset was, and remains, a magic land for me. My grandfather had owned and operated, jointly with his brother Henry, the rope factory of Rendall & Coombs, and Bridport, a small market town, had been En-gland's prime source of rope and fishing nets since the time of King Alfred. In fact, "struck with a Bridport dagger" had been a synonym for being hanged in the Middle Ages. The rope works was an almost unrecon-structed pre-Industrial Revolution factory when I first knew it. It lay in several acres of land at the edge of the town on the banks of the placid little River Brit, with chicken runs, orchards, and courtyards lined with magnolia and trumpet-ash vines in the midst of it. The two main centers of activity were the rope walks and the braiding shop. In the former, 100 yards long, the big ropes were spun behind trolleys pushed manually to and fro. In the latter, men and women operated by hand and foot the clattering braiding machines which made England's finest nets. Throughout the eighteenth-century complex there was an exhilarating smell of tar and hemp.

It was paradise for a child, and the factory hands were great storytellers. One of them claimed to have witnessed the last public hanging in England by walking—aged nine—to Dorchester in 1864. Another had miraculously survived a submarine sinking in World War I. Each morning you heard two hooters; one, a high note, at 6:00 a.m. to wake up the laborers, and a second, a deep note, at 7:00, to announce that work had started. In my mind they always figured as the red and the black hooters. The lamplighter bicycled past each evening with his long lamplighting pole to light the gas street lamps. And we would watch with excitement from my grandmother's windows, which looked onto the Bridport–Lyme Regis road, for the red Royal Mail truck that passed exactly at five each afternoon. There was also the rat-catcher's Model-T Ford with a huge brass rat on the radiator.

There were alternative ways of going from Bristol to Bridport, and each seemed an adventure. The car was exciting enough. The train, on which one changed at Castle Cary and Maiden Newton, was even more so, especially the last lap on a broad-gauge track with a saddle-tank engine through the miraculous Dorset countryside, with stops at Toller Porcorum, Powerstock, Bridport, and West Bay, our local port. It was a single-track line, and to avoid accidents the engine driver used to pick up at each station a sort of totem pole which he would hand over at the next, a symbol of his sole right to the track. We always got off the train at Bridport Station and took the Greyhound Hotel bus into the town. The bus was a Model-T Ford with a foot-operated gear shift and a hand-operated klaxon horn.

You could also bicycle the 64 miles, and Andrew and I increasingly did this. It was exhausting, but nothing ever tasted as good as the ginger beer or cider we drank along the way.

In Bridport, we used to live in my grandfather's house, Avalon, or sometimes in the larger establishment of my enigmatic Great-Uncle Henry, Allington House. My grandfather had not been on speaking terms with Uncle Henry for years and had left the rope business to become Mayor of Bridport. He was bearded and dignified and looked exactly right in the mayoral robes. My mother and her five sisters were not expected to take sides in the feud, although Aunt Margaret looked after Uncle Henry and Aunt Hilda looked after my grandparents. Aunt Mildred, the youngest of the sisters, had married an officer in the Indian Army and spent much of her time in India. Aunt Janet had an adventurous life as a nurse in Egypt and India, and ended up as the matron of Badminton School. In those days there was usually a spinster housekeeper who had become a part of the family. My grandmother had Miss Cracknell (Cracky), and Uncle Henry, Miss Smith (Smithy). They worked harder than anyone else.

Great-Uncle Henry was a bachelor with white hair and a choleric high color. He was thoroughly difficult in a rather touchingly ridiculous way and loved to try to frighten children, which he signally failed to do. He was prone to obsessions and bargains, one year buying two hundred crates of toilet paper, another five barrels of liquid soap, and once twenty barrels of ship's biscuits—hard tack. We were all exhorted to consume large quantities of these commodities. He was concerned with the erosion of the British coastline and formulated a plan to cover it entirely with a particularly strong fine-meshed net which he had designed and was prepared to manufacture. He habitually wore a high stiff collar and a bowler hat, protecting the latter annually with a coat of tar. He let his office, across the main street from Allington House, be run increasingly by a clever and good-looking young man who had started as his office boy. This, for one reason or another, was violently disapproved of by my grandfather. Uncle Henry was addicted to very hot baths after which he looked like a boiled lobster. He had no friends and few discernible interests. He died while walking on the Dorchester road—he lay down on a pile of gravel, bowler hat and all, and simply expired. He had many of the qualities of Hardy's Mayor of Casterbridge.

Bridport offered a wealth of expeditions, walks, and picnics. Apart from duty excursions to feed, and collect the eggs of, the chickens (Brown Leghorns) that members of the family seemed to keep in odd corners of the rope factory or in bits of other people's gardens, there were a graduated series of walks and seasonal expeditions. When I was very young we would walk on Allington Hill, behind Uncle Henry's house, or go through the fields to Simondsbury, approached on all sides by ivy-hung, sunken lanes. On the way we would cross a bridge with the notice: "Anyone who defaces this bridge will be subject to deportation for life." Sometimes we would take a picnic to the seashore at Eype, where the pebbles ground one's feet in the undertow and the blue clay of the cliffs got stirred up in a storm so that the sea looked like gray soup. There were rock pools with shrimps and sea anemones, and wonderful fossils.

My grandfather had for several summers in my early childhood taken the old coastguard station at Cleve End on the Chesil Beach, and there we would camp out, walking and bathing during the day and playing Happy Families, Patience, Halma, and guessing games by the light of an Aladdin lamp in the evening. The bathing on the Chesil beach, for all the beguilement of its beauty and its sea holly and sea pinks, was dangerous except in the calmest weather.

My grandfather had made a simple device for teaching children to swim—a long rope with a halter which went around your chest under the arms. Secured in this harness, you were exhorted to go beyond your depth over the lacerating pebbles of the steep beach into the cold, choppy sea which had a terrible undertow. If you stayed afloat, all right; if you sank, an aunt pulled you in. It was a very effective way of teaching swimming. Picnics, usually tea picnics, were an important part of the ritual, and were persisted in regardless of the weather. We thus became adept at lighting, in driving gales or pouring rain, the methylated spirit stove which heated the kettle.

Another expedition was to West Bay, the seaport of Bridport, with its little harbor protected by two stout piers of rock held in by wooden piles. West Bay was often battered by storms, and the steam-driven pile driver with its ascending and falling weight was an exciting spectacle, like a dragon emitting great puffs of steam and smoke. If you went to West Bay in the evening by the path along the River Brit through Palmer's Brewery, where the Brit turned the waterwheel, you might be lucky enough to watch the Bridport water polo team play in the inner harbor or to see the fishing boats landing their catch. If the shoals of fish were near the shore, as the mackerel often were, the boats—sailing boats with long oars—would make a circle of net and bring the shoal onto the beach. While the fishermen filled great baskets with the catch, you could collect a bucketful for nothing and have fresh fish for supper. In the little harbor were small coasters from Holland or France or Denmark, their crews providing a cosmopolitan touch in Dorset. The French boats would sometimes bring from Brittany an onion man, who would ride his bicycle festooned with strings of onions from village to village.

Another, longer walk was over the cliffs from West Bay to Burton Bradstock. My grandfather's parents had lived in this village, and my Great-Aunt Florence still lived there in a council house called Rossgarth. Until the year she died at eighty-three, she bathed in the sea every day, winter and summer, from the steep, pebbly beach at Burton. Her hair was snow white and her face dark red from exposure to the elements. She was a convinced Socialist and a devoted reader of the *New Statesman*. Like her brother Henry, she never married.

My grandfather's youngest brother, Athelstan, was quite unlike the rest. A late arrival, he had determined to strike out on a new route in life. He became a solicitor in Yeovil, a market town inland from Bridport, married Amy, the heiress of a local brewer, and set up in style in Branksome Park, a rich suburb of Bournemouth. He had servants, two cars, a chauffeur, a tennis court, and a billiard room. He also had Miss Brooke Smith, known perversely as Mousie, a statuesque lady who had been his only daughter's governess and with whom he and his wife lived in a ménage-à-trois until the wife died and he married Mousie.

Uncle Athel became a Liberal member of Parliament for a time and introduced a bill permitting a man to marry his deceased wife's sister. He was an enthusiastic atheist, engaging in endless public correspondence with bishops and deans. He used to eat his breakfast porridge on his knees to show that the origin of kneeling was purely gastronomical—"the best position for the digestion." Beneath his posturing he was a kind and thoughtful man. Having no sons of his own, he devoted much time and interest to Andrew and me, advised my mother about our education, and paid for a great deal of it. Since my mother earned, at a maximum, £280 a year, this help was absolutely crucial.

On Christmas Eve in Bridport there was a great family walk over Colmer's Hill (a perfect shallow cone with ten pine trees on top) to Simondsbury and its sunken lanes to collect holly and ivy to decorate the house. Each year we picked a sprig of mistletoe from the same apple tree in the rope factory. Christmas Day started with stockings full of trinkets and sweets, a breakfast of sausage rolls, and then a long walk before Christmas lunch, at which my grandfather carved the turkey, we were allowed to taste a drop of sherry, and the blazing Christmas pudding was full of silver charms and threepenny bits. My grandfather, who for some unknown reason always called me "Captain," had a comforting way of repeating exactly the same remarks at the same time each year. Thus, of the dark Christmas fruit cake that appeared before our gorged eyes at teatime, he would invariably say to my grandmother, "If the walls of Jerusalem had been made of that cake, my dear, it would never have been taken by the Turks."

On New Year's Day there was a competition to find, if possible, the first primrose. The likeliest place for this was on the south-facing lower

level of Golden Cap, the highest cliff on the Dorset coast.* The pleasure
of actually finding the flower so early in the year was acute and unfor-
gettable.

At Easter we would all go for a picnic to Marshwood Vale, inland on
the way to Beaminster, where, in fields well hidden from the road, wild
daffodils grew in profusion. A little later came the bluebell season, when
the floors of all the copses and woods turned sky blue. My mother had
a lifelong passion for wild flowers, which gave her far more pleasure than
garden flowers, and much of our childhood revolved happily about the
seasonal appearances of kingcups, cowslips, foxgloves, honeysuckle, sca-
bius, broom, the rare sun plant which was said to eat flies, wild orchids,
sea pinks, and hundreds of other species.

Another favorite outing was to one of the several Iron Age hilltop forts
in the area, great rings of fortification ditches defending the strategic
summit. Of these by far the grandest was Maiden Castle near Dorchester,
but it was far away, and we usually went to Eggardun Hill or Pilsdon and
had our inevitable picnic tea in the bracken on the top after racing up
and down the ditches.

From these childhood expeditions I came to love walking in Dorset,
and as I grew older I usually went alone. A walk along the cliffs to the
top of Thorncombe Beacon to watch the sun set over Lyme Bay was my
first aesthetic experience, and I knew every path, short cut, clump of
gorse or broom, and cliff profile for miles along the coast. There was a
medieval Pilgrims' Way that ran all along the south coast to Canterbury,
marked here and there with little ancient chapels or their ruins. One of
these was at the bottom of Golden Cap at Stanton St. Gabriel, an ancient
village on the sea which had dwindled to the farm of Mr. Chedd and a
small thatched cottage which my Aunt Mildred later rented for fifteen
shillings a year.

The Dorset coast was a marvel in itself, with its changing moods,
geological surprises, and infinite variety. On the top of the cliffs the turf
was springy and full of downland flowers and herbs, and the larks rose
singing into the sky as you approached. The weather on the coast was a
vital part of its magic. The southwest gales drove in a soft life-giving rain
and heavy crashing seas. On a bright spring morning the sea sparkled
blue and one could see right down the coast to Devonshire. On crisp,
still days in winter the sea and the cliffs seemed to be holding their breath
in the cold.

---

*Uncle Athelstan's will decreed that his ashes should be scattered from the top of
Golden Cap, which they were in a driving southwesterly gale.

Dorset is full of small wonders, ancient, surprising churches, exquisite small (and some large) country houses, an intimate but ever-changing landscape, delightful towns and villages, where the pubs were full of amiable country talk in the broad Dorset accent which is akin to Anglo-Saxon. It was the place I liked best, and I spent as much of my holidays there as I could.

*

II

School

I ARRIVED AT Westminster School on a dank, foggy evening in January 1931. As the day of departure drew near, and a school trunk, rug, and other necessary equipment and clothing were gradually assembled, I became extremely apprehensive.

We had received various preliminary communications from the school. The first of these was a list of the forms of dress required for the different occasions of school life. These included a school uniform of Eton jacket, black gown, stiff white collar, and white bow tie, sundry less formal items, and no less than five different forms of headgear—mortarboard, top hat, trilby (for weekends), straw boater, and a sports cap in the King's Scholars' colors, green and pale blue.

We had also received the vocabulary of special terms and words to be used by the King's Scholars, on which one was to be tested on arrival. These included "greaze" meaning crowd or scrum, "shagged" (tired), "pitch" (apprehensive or nervous), "Fields" (the athletic grounds), and the appellations of the school servants—"John" for the males and "nymph" for the females. This last epithet was followed by a subsidiary question: Who is the oldest nymph? Answer: Mrs. Gray. How old is she? Answer: Seventy-nine. One did not go *to* anywhere, but "up." *Up* School, *up* Fields, etc., with a single exception that one went *to* College Hall, the medieval beamed hall where we ate all our meals.

On that first foggy evening of my Westminster career my mother left me in the dusk at the front door of No. 3 Little Dean's Yard, the house of the Reverend Guy Pentreath, the Master of the King's Scholars. Before I rang the bell I watched with anguish her small, determined figure retreating into the fog across the courtyard toward the exit archway. Then I announced myself to Mr. Pentreath.

Guy Pentreath was a muscular Christian of the "I say, fellows," school, but he was a thoughtful and kindly man, and the fact that he himself was obviously inhibited and puzzled by life was disarming. His efforts, for example, to address the subject of sex were touchingly inept. "I say, fellows," he would blurt after evening prayers, "are you troubled by dirty thoughts?" On that bleak first evening he welcomed me warmly and led me into the dormitory where the thirty-nine other Scholars were unpacking, the new arrivals desolate and silent like myself, the old hands shouting greetings and exchanging in-house jokes.

*　　　*　　　*

Westminster School had been, before the Reformation, the Monastery of Westminster. It was grouped around the cloisters attached to Westminster Abbey and two courtyards, Dean's Yard and Little Dean's Yard. The main Hall (destroyed by German bombs in World War II) had been the monks' dormitory. The Scholars' house was built by Christopher Wren—the top, dormitory floor one vast long room divided by low wooden cubicles, and the lower divided into rooms for each class of Scholars, again with individual cubicles and a communal space and fireplace in the middle.

Westminster was a fabulous place. The tombstones and tombs in the Abbey and the Cloisters, through which, dimly gas-lit on winter evenings, we made our way to College Hall, were an encyclopedia of English history. Ghosts abounded, including a recumbent stone figure reading a book who had been seen to turn the pages. On foggy evenings we ran rather than walked to supper. The Abbey itself was a great old church stuffed with history and memories and objects. We went to morning prayers there every day and to services twice on Sundays. I came to love it and spent much of my spare time investigating its rich variety.

One of the star attractions of the Abbey was its virtuoso organist, Osborne Peasgood. With his shambling gait, his shoelaces undone, and his copy of the current *Motor* under his arm, Osborne looked more like a failed car salesman than a musician of genius. Indeed he professed to prefer motorcars to music, and if you tiptoed up the stairs to the organ loft, led on by the swelling excitement of a Bach fugue, you would usually find Osborne playing away with the *Motor* propped up on the music rack. As the fugue reached its climax, he might shout, above the glorious sound,

"Just look at that three-liter Bentley." His mastery of the organ was apparently effortless, but his virtuosity sometimes caused trouble. His rendering of Purcell's *Trumpet Voluntary* was banned because the Headmaster believed that it over-excited the boys, and he tended to shout orders or comments from the organ loft, like the captain of a ship in a storm, to the ecclesiastical hierarchy in full regalia down below. One of his finest efforts came with the Thanksgiving service for the Recovery of King George V, at which the organ voluntary which played the monarch out of the Abbey was particularly stirring. After the service, King George asked Peasgood what "that splendid tune" had been. Peasgood was evasive but finally had to admit that it was his own improvisation on "Pop Goes the Weasel."

Outside the gate-house of Dean's Yard lay the cities of Westminster and London, and we were free to roam around them in our spare time. It was a wonderful place for a school.

*   *   *

The first year Scholars were allotted as servants to seniors, who would summon them with the cry of "Elec!" to perform their menial duties. We waited on the seniors during meals, fetching them eggs or toast which had to be cooked to perfection on the large open coal fire in the middle of the Hall, and also functioned as human timepieces to alert the older Scholars that it was time to go to class or to Abbey or to prayers. For this purpose, a Scholar stood on the steps at each end of the stone corridor which ran the length of College building and sang out "White's—'ming," holding each syllable as long as possible, the second syllable being a third lower than the first. (Costley-White was the Headmaster's name.)

Other timekeepers were Big Ben, whose chimes could be heard every quarter hour, the Abbey clock and bells, and, last but not least, the School Sergeant, Sergeant Bowler, a veteran of the Boer War, who rang his bell furiously up and down the corridors to mark the changing class periods. Sergeant Bowler, in veteran's uniform with medals, white mustache bristling, also took the roll each morning, appearing ramrod straight in each classroom with the words "Absentees, please, Sir." Our absent-minded senior Classics master, Mr. Smedley, had been known to respond by saying, "Absentees, please stand up."

Life at school was finely regulated by such customs and by things you could, or mostly could not, do. Although the Cloisters were paved with gravestones, there was one, Flood-Jones, which you were on no account to step on. There were various places and times, some highly whimsical, at which you must have a hat (usually a mortarboard) on your head. If you were over five feet tall or fifteen years old or more, you wore a tailcoat instead of an Eton jacket. Members of the Seventh Form (the top one), or people who had won their school colors as athletes, wore butterfly collars and, for Scholars, butterfly white ties instead of straight ones. If you went out of the school bounds you took off your Scholar's gown and had to wear a top hat and carry an umbrella, except on Sundays when you wore a blazer and a trilby hat in winter or a straw boater in summer—and so on. All of this dressing up took a great deal of time, maintenance, and laundry.

An annual school tradition was the "pancake greaze" on Shrove Tuesday. Until 1930 the whole school had taken part in this very rough game in which a chef tossed a pancake high over a beam in the Monk's Dormitory, and the boy who managed to get the biggest piece won a set of Maundy money (coins specially minted for the monarch to give as alms on visits to the Abbey). The casualties caused by three hundred and fifty boys all heading for the same pancake were such, however, that by the time I got there each class elected its toughest member to take part in the scrum.

The Scholars had an even more lethal annual ceremony called "Declams" in which four tables were piled one on top of the other. Each junior had to make his way to the top of this unsteady tower and there declaim a perfect four-line Latin epigram of his own creation while being pelted with tennis balls. This also had caused serious casualties and was abolished after my first year.

British public schools used to be famous for bullying and the organized persecution of unpopular or nonconformist boys. There was relatively little of this among the King's Scholars, although I was beaten up several times in my early years for no apparent reason except that I tended, if insulted unnecessarily, to answer back. But on the whole people were friendly. It was a new experience for me to have friends of my own age, which, living at home alone with my mother, I had never had in Bristol.

At Westminster I came to love music. I had a good soprano voice and used it far too long in choirs and the madrigal society, so that I overstrained it and weakened my later adult voice forever. I also took up the oboe, largely on the advice of my first form master who was himself a fine amateur oboist. I took lessons each week with a tiny elderly man called A. J. Shorter, and became one of the stars at school concerts. I went to concerts on Sunday afternoons in the Queen's Hall (destroyed during the war), where Sir Thomas Beecham, and, on a few memorable occasions,

Toscanini, conducted the London Philharmonic Orchestra, and learned with rapture the symphonic and orchestral repertoire. I also began to be seriously interested in pictures, the turning point being my first sight of one of Cézanne's *Mont Ste. Victoire* series in the great Impressionist Exhibition at the Royal Academy.

The education at Westminster was fairly haphazard. I doubt if the Headmaster, the Reverend Dr. Harold Costley-White, knew, or cared, much about education, but in his mortarboard, gown, and clerical bibs, he did *look* like a Headmaster—of the eighteenth century. He spoke in a singsong voice aimlessly accenting particular syllables, apparently to give an impression of sincerity, and we derived infinite pleasure from imitating him. He was muddle-headed in the extreme, and specialized in contradictory statements. Thus when someone asked him about the Book of Kings, he replied, "It *is* ama*z*ingly interesting, my friends, and perhaps what you *might* call extre*me*ly boring." Eminent persons frequently gave lectures at the school—I remember Gandhi in midwinter sitting cross-legged on a radiator—and one of the joys of such occasions was to watch the Headmaster wrestling with sleep. He usually woke up partially stunned when the visitor stopped talking, sometimes with comic results. A typical result was his response to Lord Lloyd's lecture. "We are ama*z*ingly grateful to Lloyd Lord, not only bec*au*se he *is* Lloyd George, but also because he is Howell's uncle." Actually, Howell's uncle was Lord Moyne. Costley-White's sermons in the Abbey were equally foggy and elliptical.

Under this benign but scatterbrained direction the school was allowed to go its own way under a motley crew of masters. Major Troutbeck yelled in class and could be heard all over the school. Mr. Claridge, the Modern Languages master, terrified his pupils by making faces and by his ogreishness, but was in fact a shy and kindly man. Mr. Smedley, the chief Classics master, often could not remember where he was. Mr. Bonhôte, the French master, was an opera singer who had lost his voice in Switzerland. If you were lucky you got a sort of education, and if you were very lucky you received that intellectual stimulus, the essential shot-in-the-arm, that changes the way you think and look at life.

I was, to my eternal good fortune, in the latter category. Against the Headmaster's opposition, I had transferred, at the age of fourteen, to the Modern Language side and spent two years learning German and French. At sixteen, I reached the top form (VIIth) and took the Higher Certificate, doing so well that it was clearly pointless to try to go any further at Westminster with modern languages. I still had two years before I could go to University and contrived, once more against considerable opposition, to transfer to the History side, an area widely regarded as a disreputable demi-monde of dangerous and unorthodox ideas. The History side was a one-man show, a small elite chosen and run by John Edward Bowle.

John Bowle was a schoolmaster of genius. It was he who opened up the main avenues of interest along which I have since happily travelled, and it was he who began to change my immature scholastic precocity into something approaching discipline and constructive thought.

Bowle only accepted boys he approved of. He insisted on having all his classes in the two most beautiful rooms of the school's Library, Ash-burnham House, designed by Inigo Jones. One of these rooms was fur-nished with armchairs, and the classes became what are now called seminars. We did the necessary minimum of routine scholastic work, but the main emphasis was on ideas and history as related to real life.

John Bowle made us read and discuss provocative contemporary books, something unheard of in other departments of the school. He would also bring in the authors to talk to our class, a wonderful experience for sixteen-year-old boys. Thus we spent informal afternoons with Bertrand Russell, H. G. Wells, Gerald Heard, Arnold Toynbee, Julian Huxley, A. L. Rowse, and a number of other less well known but equally fascinating people. The Headmaster, who occasionally wandered in during these sessions, was mystified and disapproving. He was disturbed to find boys sitting in armchairs during class time and apparently being taught by unfamiliar outsiders. I doubt if he had heard of Bertrand Russell or Huxley, let alone the others.

John Bowle encouraged us to express ourselves in writing and to think about ideas and history in terms of our own experience. We wrote frequent "essays" on general subjects well outside the school curriculum. Striking personalities and turning points in history were favorite topics. The ex-communicated Holy Roman Emperor, Frederick II of Sicily ("Stupor Mundi"), the Renaissance man before his time, was our hero. Bowle took immense pains in going over these efforts, and his encouragement, his impatience, and his trenchant criticism were a great incentive.

Bowle was not popular with the other masters and made no effort whatsoever to be so. Indeed, he went out of his way to show his contempt for their limitations. His relations with the Headmaster were also a con-tinuous exercise in brinkmanship, but he was preserved by the fact that his boys got a far higher proportion of scholarships to Oxford and Cam-bridge than any other class. They were clearly thriving academically and intellectually and remained intensely loyal to him.

A few years later a new Headmaster decided that Bowle was too much and achieved his downfall. Evidently alerted by inside information, he swooped on Bowle's class one day as the weekly essays were being handed in. The subject assigned by Bowle was "Write a short, critical biography of one of the following: Jesus Christ; Hitler; the Headmaster." That was the end of Bowle's stint at Westminster. He went on to write a successful series of eminently readable and down-to-earth books on political thought and history.

John Bowle's Oxford friends from the twenties were my first introduction to a world of sophistication and high life unknown to us in Bristol. Bowle's tempestuous, abrasive character and the fashion for drunkenness of that period had turned his Oxford career into a disaster. Arriving at Balliol as a promising Scholar, he had gone down three years later with a disreputable Third in Schools, the final examination, thereby putting an end to any hope of a professorial career. He had kept in touch with his Oxford friends, and on weekends he would dine with them and sometimes take me along. These brilliant, witty, all-knowing people were a revelation. I could never, I was convinced, match their effortless talk, their knowledge, or their fantasy and humor, but their light-hearted seriousness was new and intoxicating.

Sometimes Bowle's acquaintances overdid it. Every year in December the King's Scholars performed the Latin Play, a cycle of relentlessly boring Roman dramas by Terence and Plautus. The Latin Play was performed on an eighteenth-century stage erected in the Scholars' Dormitory, which was converted into a theater for the occasion. The high point of the evening was the Epilogue, written in Latin by the masters, in which the play's characters reappeared in modern dress and spoke Latin lines containing topical puns *in English*, a literary form so intricate that the audience was given a printed Latin text with the puns in italics. The Latin Play was a grand occasion to which the British establishment, bishops, peers, members of Parliament, etc., as well as the parents of the performers, were invited. The tickets were in great demand.

An important feature of the Latin Play was the female lead, for which the prettiest boy in the class was selected. The sublimated homosexuality of some of the masters found an outlet in the costuming and make-up of the heroine, and the results were often spectacular. This was particularly so on the occasion when Bowle had unwisely invited Lord Alfred Douglas as his guest. Douglas, then living in the Royal Albion Hotel in Brighton, was principally famous as the love object, and later the nemesis, of Oscar Wilde. Since that historic episode he had occupied himself as a minor poet and in litigation against persons he believed to have wronged him.

On the night in question there was, at the first entrance of the heroine, an admiring silence and a sort of corporate intake of breath, which was broken when a voice was heard to say, in fluting Edwardian tones, "Gad, that's an attwactive boy." A growl of disapproval greeted this remark, and the Headmaster, shaking himself out of his habitual torpor, rose to his feet, an impressive figure in full canonical dress, to demand that the speaker of the offending words leave the theater at once. Lord Alfred was hustled out, and the episode added yet another strike against Bowle.

Sex was, of course, a major feature of school life. Where is it not? But to my mind the notoriety of British public schools for homosexual activity is largely misconceived. The conditions which led to much random homosexual activity when I was at school were somewhat similar to those of a men's prison or a navy ship at sea on a long voyage. If adolescents are segregated at the height of their new-found sexual urge, they will find the nearest available outlet for it, namely, each other.

The masters were something else. When I was at school many of them were bachelors and likely to remain so, and there was no doubt that they often took a romantic, if purely platonic, interest in the boys they taught. Any overstepping of this unwritten rule would have been regarded as outrageous. The romantic homosexual tradition in British education was particularly marked at Oxford, where again the same unwritten rules applied. Oxford and Westminster had, after all, both started as monasteries. On the whole this tradition was greatly to our advantage, for our teachers were devoted to us and to our welfare and success. What agonies of frustration, deprivation, and unrequited love it visited on the teachers I cannot tell.

In my last year at school (1936–37), we became increasingly aware of the disasters that would lead to World War II. Those of us who were interested in politics were strongly anti-Nazi. We were moved especially by the Italian attack on Abyssinia, the plight of Haile Selassie, the Spanish Civil War, and Nazi annexation in Europe. The pacifism fashionable in the early thirties was giving way to a more active response, based on the proposition that we should make common cause with the Soviet Union against the Nazis. This feeling was especially articulated by the Left Book Club, a series of topical books by well-known Socialists published by Victor Gollancz. An improbable organization called the United Front of Progressive Forces (known as Uffpuff) was active in schools. Many of us good-naturedly joined it, although it appeared to do little except circulate pamphlets written in turgid Marxist jargon. If Uffpuff was a Communist front, it was certainly not a very sinister one—and in any case an alliance with the Soviet Union against the Nazis seemed on the face of it to be an excellent idea. It was what happened anyway in the end by *force majeure*.

In 1937 the Nazis were not by any means generally unpopular in England. Many conservatives positively admired them for their discipline, for their harsh treatment of Communists, for making the trains run on time, and so on. At Westminster we had in our midst, in top hat and tails, a son of Joachim von Ribbentrop, then German Ambassador to the Court of St. James. Ribbentrop, quite apart from his provenance, was not an appealing boy. He was doltish, surly, and arrogant. But the last straw was that he arrived each morning in one of *two* plum-colored Mercedes-Benz limousines. On arrival in Dean's Yard, both chauffeurs would spring out, give the Nazi salute, and shout "Heil Hitler!" With this triumphal accolade, Ribbentrop would disappear through the medieval arch into the Little Dean's Yard. To offset this insult to an ancient and civilized institution, we took to witnessing Ribbentrop's arrival with loud laughter. Each day the crowd grew larger and the laughter louder, until the ritual became quite a well-known event. The German Embassy lodged a strong diplomatic protest with the Headmaster, who quickly discovered the organizer of the game and sent for me.

I was at that time in a fairly strong position, having already got a scholarship to Oxford, but I did not wish to be expelled, and the Headmaster initially adopted a tone of high outrage, speaking of "irresponsible troublemaking," "insults to a friendly power," and so on. My efforts to put him straight on this score were unavailing, and we were discussing whether I could appeal to the School's Board of Governors when I recalled his capacity for missing the point and took another tack. I mentioned that the Nazi Mercedes were painted plum color, the color at that time reserved in England exclusively for vehicles of the Royal Family. The Headmaster was thunderstruck. "My *dear* boy," he said in tones of sympathetic indignation, "why didn't you tell me this before?" The diplomatic protest was rejected, I was officially regarded as a savior of the national honor, and von Ribbentrop took to arriving at school on foot just like everyone else.

Westminster was a great place for ceremonies, religious, secular, and historical, and the ultimate ceremony descended upon us in my last summer in the form of the Coronation of King George VI and Queen Elizabeth. The previous year had been marked by the abdication of Edward VIII. We had all, quite wrongly, been violently in favor of the monarch, regarding him as the victim of a cretinous and reactionary establishment. Although his brother Albert, the new King, was a dim and pedestrian figure by comparison, the grandeur and drama of the Coronation ceremony soon overcame these perceptions.

From the time of Henry VIII the forty King's Scholars of Westminster have traditionally been the first subjects to greet the new monarch after the crown is placed on his or her head before the high altar in Westminster Abbey. This function is enshrined in the marvelous Coronation anthem which starts "I was glad when they said unto me, we will go into the House of the Lord." They do this, according, naturally, to long-standing tradition, from the triforium of the Abbey, the gallery which runs round the building above the main arches—a dizzy space where, incidentally, William Caxton operated his first printing press.

The great ceremonial occasions of British life are a compound of history, magnificent settings and objects, nostalgia, folk memory, and painstaking organization. The Coronation is the most complex and symbolic of all these occasions. To preserve the magic, everything and everyone has to perform perfectly, with apparent spontaneity and with complete punctuality. Considerable discipline is also required, for the participants have to arrive early and sit still for hours. Their costumes are of a fantastic and baroque complication. Such ceremonies are fairy tales of a perfect life in which nothing can go wrong.

For the Coronation, the actors went through weeks of drilling and rehearsal, becoming totally involved in the mystique of the occasion. The King's Scholars were dressed in black velvet knee breeches, black silk stockings and buckled shoes, black tail coats over stiff white shirts, butterfly collars and white bibs, the whole surmounted by a glistening starched white open surplice. Processing into the Abbey and then up the spiral stairway to our lofty station, we waited for our moment of glory while the incantations of organ, trumpets, and choir soared and resounded through the vast space. When the time came, we yelled with devoted enthusiasm: "Vivat Regina Elizabetha! Vivat Rex Georgius! Vivat! Vivat! Vivat!" For a skeptical, rather left-wing adolescent, it was a great corrective.

After the Coronation, our lives seemed to remain in a haze, and every occasion—the Henley Regatta, the expeditions with friends, the leave-taking ceremonies called "Election," the final concert at which I played a Handel Oboe Concerto—seemed to be bathed, in memory at any rate, in golden, slightly misty, sunshine.

After leaving school I went to Bavaria with friends. That I chose to go to Bavaria, the spiritual headquarters of Hitler's Third Reich, shows how very shallow my political feelings were at that time. We stayed in a pretty village called Obergrainau and walked and swam in the lake. The locals were in Bavarian costume, and the Nazis were only in evidence on the main roads. It was a singularly mindless holiday from which I took myself to Mauriac in the Auvergne to walk in the volcanic hills with my mother. Europe seemed to be sleepwalking. I certainly was.

I left school with a great deal more than I had hoped to get from it, and also a lot more than I realized at the time. I had had a good formal education and, from John Bowle, an exceptional degree of intellectual stimulus. I had learned to talk in company and to mix relatively easily with other people.

What I did not realize at the time, and what the experience of the war increasingly brought home to me, was the extent to which I had absorbed, without knowing it, the ethos and the standards of an ancient English school. Those daily services in Westminster Abbey with ringing Anglican church music and the superb language of the prayer book, the exhortations of the masters about conduct and civility, the spirit in which games were played, and the code of conduct which governed our relations with each other were all things we had mocked, but in the end the laugh was on us. Most of us went out from Westminster with an ingrained idea of the concept of service. A lifetime later I can still quote, at the risk of seeming priggish, the prayer of St. Ignatius Loyola which we said every week in the Abbey and which seems to me, even for the non-religious like myself, to state the concept of service in its best form:

> Teach us, good Lord, to serve thee as thou deservest;
> to give and not to count the cost;
> to fight and not to heed the wounds;
> to toil and not to seek for rest;
> to labor and not to ask for any reward,
> save that of knowing that we do thy will. . . .

I never thought about it when I was young, but later, in times of stress or trouble or danger, I heard the prayer in my head and took a lot of comfort from it.

III

Oxford

I WENT UP TO Oxford in September 1937 as the Hinchcliffe History
Scholar at Christ Church. The scholarship was worth £150 a year, which
went a long way toward paying my expenses at Oxford. It was acquired
by a simple, one-day examination and an interview. The process was
discussed in advance by John Bowle with the Christ Church examiners
so that the questions, of a broad and rhetorical kind, were no surprise to
the candidate and the candidate was no surprise to the examiners—in
fact there was sometimes only one candidate. In defense of this process,
it must be said that the ablest candidate was always selected by Bowle,
and the Christ Church people would, and sometimes did, reject anyone
they did not think good enough.

I arrived at Oxford on a mournful damp September day and settled
into rooms in the Old Library at Christ Church. This was not the smart
part of the college described in Evelyn Waugh's *Brideshead Revisited*
and other social chronicles, but it seemed like paradise to me—a large
sitting room with a coal fireplace and a bedroom of my own, the bells
and chimes of Oxford marking the hours and quarters, a scout (servant)
called Smith, and very little work. Breakfast was brought to one's rooms
and lunch too if required. Dinner was eaten in Christ Church Hall, a
magnificent chamber built, like the main Quadrangle, by Cardinal Wol-
sey. The food was good, and in winter the Hall was warmed by two huge
open fires. At the entrance to Hall was the Buttery, presided over by
Fred, the benevolent butler, who dispensed beer, Christ Church Audit
Ale (specially brewed for the college), and sherry to the hearties and
rowdies who got amiably drunk each night. Drunkenness was considerably

esteemed at Christ Church, and vomiting and passing out were regarded with benevolence as signs of incipient manhood.

The amount of academic work required at Oxford was minimal, and there was virtually no supervision of, and very little interest in, undergraduates. In the first term there was a qualifying exam called Pass Mods based on a Latin history of the Crusades, the "Gesta Francorum." After that the only target was Schools, the one-week marathon final examination nearly three years away. "Schools" loomed larger and more sinister as the dissipated years went by and in some cases ultimately induced a complete psychological collapse. In the meantime you were supposed to attend a number of lectures, some of them grotesque, like the series by an elderly canon of Christ Church on Pope Innocent III which had not changed by a single word or phrase since 1909, or the historian at Exeter who refused to start his lecture if female undergraduates were in the room. You had a tutorial once a week at which you presented an essay, usually rushed together in the small hours of the night before.

The dons at Christ Church were, by tradition, non-enthusiasts. The moving spirit of the place, if there was one, was R. H. Dundas, an ancient bachelor whose conversational gambits and high fluting voice were legendary—"Are you interested in disease?" He was one of a number of dons whose spirit had been broken by the 1914–18 war and the wholesale slaughter of the flower of Oxford youth.

My tutors varied from year to year. I first went to J. C. Masterman, an extra-dry historian who became known in World War II for the "double-cross" procedure of turning round German spies. His arid personality was perhaps better fitted for such a task than for encouraging insecure and immature young scholars. My second tutor was Noel Myres, whose father, the Greek historian J. N. L. Myres, had donned full hoplyte armor to run the distance from Marathon to Athens and had haunted the Greek Islands in search of intelligence in World War I. Noel Myres had chosen the less glamorous subject of the Anglo-Saxons, about whom he was said to possess all available information, a crushing achievement.

The most noticeable don at Christ Church was Professor Frederick Lindemann, who later, as Churchill's wartime scientific adviser ("the Prof"), became Lord Cherwell. His alleged Teutonic arrogance, his wealth, and his Rolls-Royce, which he persisted in driving into the college quadrangle, as well, no doubt, as his foreign origin, made him an object of suspicion, resentment, and gossip among the other dons. He was seen as a dangerous interloper in the charmed, Lewis Carroll world of Christ Church.

Our days, not too much occupied with desultory academic chores, were nonetheless full of random activity. My friend from school, Gus Bradford, was already a keen archeologist and would organize local archeological digs in which more or less unskilled labor was always welcome. These days were of a relentlessly boring nature—I recall the excavation of a possible Iron Age storage pit at Frilford—and I soon defected, but Gus continued with obsessive single-mindedness. He even turned the war to archeological purpose, amassing a vast collection of air photographs on which he based a pioneering book on the archeological interpretation of aerial photographs.

The year 1937 was one of disillusion and anger. Hitler and Mussolini continued their aggressive progress unchecked and even admired in some British circles. "Better Hitler than Stalin at the Channel ports" was not a joke with such people. The murderous tragedy of the Spanish Civil War also evoked strong emotions on both left and right. German Nazi, Italian Fascist, and Soviet involvement, and the pusillanimous "non-intervention" policy of France and Britain, aroused violent feelings in many young people. Our heroes were the fabulous few who had put their lives on the line by going off to join the International Brigade in Spain. Jewish refugees were also appearing from Germany in increasing numbers with stories of persecution and concentration camps which, though mild by the standards of the later "final solution," already seemed hard to believe of a Western European nation.

The weak reactionary governments of Britain and France, having failed to stand together in the League of Nations against the bandit regimes of Italy, Germany, and Japan when there was still time, were now drifting separately to perdition. At Oxford two political directions, both equally irrelevant, were available—sharp left or sharp right. On the extreme right, the British Union of Fascists under Oswald Mosley—a pathetic imitation of Mussolini's Fascists—attracted attention less by its program or numbers than through its silly uniforms,* the antics of its leader, and the fact that on more than one occasion it had made a disagreeable but abortive effort to use Nazi tactics in the Jewish East End of London. It had little support at Oxford, and when Mosley came to address the local chapter in the Carfax Rooms, the hall was empty except for a front row of organizing dignitaries and a back section of jeering left-wing demonstrators.

*There was a story that when Mosley asked Harold Nicolson for suggestions for the uniform of the British Fascist Youth Corps, Nicolson replied: "I always think that a white shirt, grey flannels and plimsolls [sneakers] are awfully attractive."

Initially Oxford's freedom, lack of program or discipline, and imitation of grown-up life was completely bewildering to me, and the University Labour Club, with its strong Communist cadre, was a welcome base from which to make friends and explore the University. I took the left turn.

In the Labour Club we were anti-Nazi, anti-Fascist, vaguely pro-Soviet, and in favor of peace and disarmament. It later became clear to me that this was a faulty and thoroughly self-defeating program, since only rapid rearmament by France and Britain, preferably in alliance with the Soviet Union, had any realistic chance of stopping Hitler. For the time being, however, we met, canvassed, coffee-housed, and sang Socialist songs. "The Man Who Does the Dirty Work for Hitler," sung to the tune of "The Man Who Broke the Bank at Monte Carlo," was a favorite. We also pursued the somewhat grubby Labour Club girls.

Within this amiable framework the British Communist Party—itself at best a semi-comic organization—was hard at work, although with far less success than it seems to have had at Cambridge. A friend from Westminster, Michael Dean, had already been a dedicated Marxist at school, where he had organized the United Front for Progressive Forces. At Oxford he had become a member of the Communist Party. A number of older and more admired undergraduates were also Party members. Of these, Philip Toynbee was conspicuous by his charm, drunken escapades, and dilapidated appearance. Philip impressed us by combining Communist Party membership with the presidency of the Oxford Union and a continuing relationship with smart establishment society.

The star turn of the Oxford Communist Party was Comrade Abe Lazarus, a shop steward at the Cowley Motor Works. He was a small, intense man with an incessant flow of what we took to be Party jargon. "We must put this question to ourselves sharply and bluntly, comrades. We must ask ourselves fearlessly and frankly how Comrade Lenin would have faced this question," etc. If Abe Lazarus was not perpetrating a running practical joke, he was untouched by any ray of humor, and it was for giggling at one of his weekly briefings that I was thrown out for "bourgeois dilettantism" and was thus no longer troubled by the very mild temptation to join the Communist Party.

By the end of my first year I had lost interest in Labour Club activities, which seemed increasingly irrelevant to the appalling developments in Europe. Thus my second year at Oxford was enjoyable and almost entirely pointless. We had parties, picnics, punting expeditions, and private jokes, and did the minimum work to get by. In the winter we spent long evenings in front of the fire, organized "sherry parties," the currently popular form of entertainment, and went for long argumentative walks in the mist and gloom of the Oxford countryside. By that time it was clear that sooner or later there would be war and that anything but the pursuit of pleasure was apt to be a waste of time. About the only thing I pursued seriously was music, playing the oboe in the Oxford Music Club, in the Cathedral with the organist, Thomas Armstrong, and in college concerts.

The Oxford summer term of 1939 concluded with the Christ Church Commemoration Ball, an all-night affair ending with the sunrise in Christ Church garden, swimming in the Thames and breakfast at Shillingford, and an all-day picnic in punts on the Cherwell. The weather was perfect, and the hock and strawberries never tasted better. That, as things turned out, was the end of Oxford for me.

I had intended to catch up during the summer vacation on all the work I hadn't done, but in the prevailing mood of uncertainty I went to St. Tropez with some friends instead. It was for me the first and last of those magical trips by car through prewar France—uncrowded roads, charming small hotels, and delicious, cheap, regional meals. We stayed in the Hôtel de la Poste in Ramatuelle above St. Tropez, looking down from the terrace over olive groves to the unspoilt sea, the Anse de Pampelonne. The hotel was primitive and cheap, and the cooking of Mme Battini, the proprietress, inspired. I concluded with a week in Cannes with an American couple, Hope and Dodo Coffey, whom I had met through my friend Chris Hildyard, a Minor Canon of Westminster Abbey. Hope had written a best-selling novel in 1933 and had been living in Cannes on the proceeds ever since. It was a decadent world of rich expatriates leading perfectly sybaritic lives in marvelous villas. Scandals, liaisons of all kinds, and endless and lavish parties were the only order of business. The climate, the food, and the sea were idyllic. An atmosphere of total unreality prevailed. It was a suitable place to spend the last days of peace.

*   *   *

I returned to England in the last days of August and went to stay with my mother at Morecombelake on the Dorset coast. It was impossible to concentrate or to make any plans, and the crisis, when it came on September 1, was almost a relief. On September 3 we sat through Neville Chamberlain's "We are at war with Germany" broadcast, after Hitler had failed to respond to the Anglo-French ultimatum over Poland. At 11:15 a.m. the London air-raid sirens sounded by mistake, and everyone was suddenly in a new and unknown world.

As soon as war was declared, I went to Oxford to see what was up. Several of us stayed at the Bell Inn at Clifton Hampden on the Thames, trying to resurrect the agreeable spirit of frivolity of the early summer. It was heavy going. Quite what I had originally intended to do in Oxford at this time I do not know, but in the end, after a bibulous lunch at the George, I went to Christ Church where a recruiting station had been established, and joined up. The sight of one of the stuffier young Christ Church dons in full uniform with a sword nearly deterred me, but I filled in a long form in the belief that I had joined the Royal Navy. I then went home to my mother's house in Bristol to await developments.

I had anticipated that my mother would be upset at my joining up, as I had not consulted her and could easily have stayed at Oxford for another year. I underestimated her, and she was as approving as she ever found it possible to be. I found out later that she had strongly disapproved of my father's avoidance of military service in World War I.

I did not have long to wait. Ten days later I was ordered to report immediately to the 164th Officer Cadet Training Unit in the Goojerat Barracks at Colchester. I had evidently filled in the wrong form.

IV

World War II

ENGLISH LIFE in the first days of the war was dominated by a number of misconceptions, some rooted in the works of sensational popular journalists, like Beverley Nichols's *Cry Havoc*, and in the film of H. G. Wells's *War of the Worlds*. It was assumed that there would soon be a massive aerial bombardment and that poison gas would be used on a large scale. Gas masks of a rudimentary design were issued to the population and were supposed to be carried at all times. There was a national obsession with the blackout. Motorcar headlights were reduced to a feeble slit with black paint or cardboard, heavy black curtains or boards covered windows at night, street lights went out, and the lights in trains dwindled to an eerie blue glow. Children were evacuated from the larger cities. Cigarette smoking increased dramatically; to me the prevailing smell of the war is the smell of all-night stale cigarette smoke and army blankets. The more confined the space, the more people smoked.

All of this activity soon gave way to a charade-like situation in Britain which became known as the "phoney war." The blackout, rationing, evacuation of city children, and Air Raid Precautions were the sort of inconveniences which the British thoroughly enjoy. What, to me at any rate, was unforeseen was the indefinite loss of freedom of choice and movement and the idea that one was stuck for an indeterminate period in a vast, inefficient, and unpredictable machine.

Goojerat Barracks in Colchester had been condemned and abandoned as inadequate in 1934 and suddenly brought back into emergency service in 1939. The fact that peacetime standards lingered on during the "phoney war" period only served to highlight the ridiculous physical discomforts of British Army life. You could still get excellent food and drink and perfect service not only in London but in the hotels of a provincial town like Colchester. By comparison, Goojerat Barracks was abysmal—cold, stuffy, and unsanitary. We lived twenty to a barrack room on old iron army cots with ill-smelling "palliases" (mattresses) and even worse smelling gray army blankets. The prevailing aroma was of sweat, stale cigarette smoke, dirty clothes, and Brasso. There was no privacy, no rest, and no hot water.

Such are the perversities of the English class system that the cadets who had been to public school and university were far better prepared for these conditions than the so-called working-class young men who had mostly lived at home. The latter were mortified, suspicious, and intensely embarrassed. The rest of us were overbearing, reassuring, and full of bogus bonhomie.

Initially the food was inedible, and we lived on chocolate and raisins and occasional meals in town. It was said, perhaps with truth, that the motor mechanics had been posted to the cookhouse by mistake. I was the unwitting agent of a dramatic change in the cooking arrangements about two weeks after our arrival. As the Officer of the Day, accompanied by our sergeant-major, was approaching our table to ask the routine question, "Any complaints?", I happened to notice, in the untouched plate of stew before me, a rubber object. My neighbor, a sophisticated man of the world, urged me to enquire about the foreign object in the stew. This I did, holding it up on a fork, and only then did I begin to suspect its true nature. The sergeant-major turned purple with an interesting mixture of rage and embarrassment, and, muttering that he would take care of it, hurried the puzzled Officer of the Day on to the next table. Later that day, after a half-hearted attempt to accuse me of a distasteful practical joke, the sergeant-major advanced the implausible theory that the rubber object was the protective cover of the detonator of an anti-aircraft shell. The incident was reported, and the cookhouse staff were reassigned.

Until this incident, I had been something of an outsider—a twenty-year-old undergraduate with intellectual and aesthetic interests, not at all sure of myself and intensely miserable with military life. I used to escape the ghastly intimacy of the barrack room to watch, from a derelict garden behind the parade ground, the sun rise or set, and to bewail alone the abrupt and brutal change in my circumstances. After the mess-hall affair, I began to see that army life could also have a funny side.

Our days began at 5:30 a.m. and ended at 10:00 p.m. They were physically hard, though nothing to the battle training that was developed later on. We would do drill and Physical Training for two hours, followed by weapon training and firing, a route march of five miles followed by a stint of trench digging and wiring, and then five miles home. We had all been brought up on tales of the First World War and of the horrors of the trenches. In 1939 these horrors were only twenty years away, and there were still large numbers of men, including serving soldiers, who had endured them. We took these experiences for granted as the normal state of modern war, and all training, with characteristic wrong-headedness, was centered on trench warfare. There were lighter moments. The weekly lecture on "Man Management and Hygiene" was a favorite—and then there were Staff Sergeant Benson's demonstrations of the 3-inch mortar.

Sergeant Benson, like most of the instructors, was a regular soldier of the old kind. The army was his life, and he had served in Palestine, India, and elsewhere in the British Empire. At first he and the other instructors did their best to trip us up and make life hell, as was the routine practice of drill sergeants and instructors, but they soon discovered that we had both physical and psychological stamina of an order they were unused to, and the balance of power shifted from a tyranny of sergeants to a cooperative and conniving spirit.

Sergeant Benson of the Queen's Regiment was famous for his infantry weapons lessons, of which the pearl was the 3-inch mortar lesson. This weapon, the only immediately available heavy weapon of the British infantry, did not yet exist in numbers large enough to equip the army, but training establishments had one each, jealously prized and guarded. As no live ammunition was available, all training was done with dummy bombs.

The charm of Benson's performance lay in his conjuror's dexterity in setting up the mortar on its baseplate and tripod, setting the sight, and juggling the bomb, accompanied by patter based on the *Infantry Weapons Manual*, and enlivened by sudden questions, jokes, and other interjections. The climax of the show was when the bomb was dropped, tail first, down the mortar barrel to strike the firing pin that would propel it toward the enemy. Then Sergeant Benson, looking more like a music hall conjuror than ever, would rest at last and take a bow. Months after we had left Colchester, live ammunition became available and mortars were actually fired in training on the range. By that time Sergeant Benson's virtuosity had got the better of him, and he had speeded up the procedure to a quite unrealistic pace. It was thus that one day he dropped a live bomb into the tube nose first, killing himself and three of his squad.

It is a miracle that any army whose officers were trained as we were should have survived, let alone won, a war. We learned the most obvious and elementary tactics, but gained no idea of battle, of leadership, or of the essential elements of surprise, imagination, and restraint. The need to outwit the enemy by superior guile, skill, nerve, and discipline was scarcely even hinted at. Minimal attention was paid to the vital subject of communications. Emphasis was more on correct behavior than on performance. We learned how to drill troops, how to behave in the mess and how never to use sarcasm to other ranks, how to dig dugouts and latrines and communication trenches, and how to put up wire, but we scarcely ever wondered how we were going actually to fight the Germans. The lessons we were busy learning from dawn till late at night were the lessons of 1917, and they soon turned out to be irrelevant to what Hitler had in mind. Meanwhile, happily ignorant of the Nazi war machine, we kept up our spirits on route marches by singing "We're Going to Hang Out Our Washing on the Siegfried Line," "Hitler Has Only Got One Ball," and other patriotic songs.

Apart from the rigors of barrack life and the complications of the blackout, it was often hard to remember the war. We spent our weekends either in London or in the Red Lion in Colchester, which had excellent food. Local people were not yet tired of soldiers, who were still in relatively small numbers. Everyone was very hospitable. In January 1940 our four-month course came to an end, and we were posted as second lieutenants to our regiments.

I had chosen the Dorset Regiment because Dorset was my birthplace and my favorite part of England. The four months of training had made great changes in my attitude, appearance, manners, and even interests. When the war started, I despised and hated military life and was terrified of the war. Now I was a keen young officer, proud of my first officer's uniform, made with loving care by Bernard Weatherill of Conduit Street, with its regimental badges and buttons of different sizes and the required eccentricities of cut and material. I was looking forward to regimental life, to commanding men, and even, if I didn't think about it too much, to getting to grips with the enemy—the Hun, brother Boche, them Nazis, or Jerry, as he was variously called. I no longer pined for the joys of Oxford and of the civilian life I had only just started to live. When I went back to Oxford in February while awaiting my posting, I felt an insufferable sense of superiority to my contemporaries who had stayed on at the University instead of volunteering for the army. It was a bitter winter, and we skated for miles on the frozen River Cherwell and had cosy alcoholic evenings in college. But Oxford seemed parochial and already belonging to the past.

I was posted to the Dorset Regiment Depot in Dorchester, a nineteenth-century fortress-like structure, whose towers and phoney battlements surrounded the parade ground. There I learned the intricacies of military etiquette, evolved during countless and interminable tours of duty in the remote fastnesses of the Empire. "Never wear a belt in the mess, old boy"—"Don't speak to the Colonel or the Majors unless they speak to you"—"Pass the port clockwise," and so on. It was like being back at school. Our duties were easy and the quarters comfortable. Half of the officers were regular soldiers whose whole adult life had been the Dorset Regiment. They looked down on the civilians who had temporarily joined them, and I learned only later what a stigma it was for a regular officer to be posted to the depot in time of war. It usually meant that he was either incompetent or over the hill. No wonder the regular officers took out their frustrations on insufferable youngsters like myself.

After a few weeks in Dorchester I was posted to the 5th Battalion in the little market town of Frome in Somerset. The 5th Battalion was a territorial unit which existed as a volunteer cadre in peacetime, coming together for three or four weeks' training and carousing each year. It was a delightful group, with a sense of cohesion and kindness, and a strong feeling of shared roots and shared interests. The officers were mostly from the county squirearchy or the market-town bourgeoisie, while the men were peasants or small-town artisans.

The Dorsets spoke a dialect of English which is beautifully and phonetically reproduced in the verses of the nineteenth-century poet William Barnes. It was broad, mellifluous, and almost unintelligible to outsiders. It had a unique comic charm and an extraordinary breadth of expression. Most of the soldiers had never been to London, but some of them had been to Bournemouth and affected to be deeply shocked at the sophisticated goings-on in that seaside town. One of the Dorsets' favorite marching songs went:

> I was walking one morning round Lei-ces-ter Square
> For to see all the folk and the sights that were
>   there.
> But to see all them ladies dressed up in their tights;
> Oh my missus don't allow me to look at such sights.

This was nonsense, for agricultural mores were far less inhibited than those of the cities.

In Frome we were billeted in private houses and ate in the George Hotel in the center of the town. The colonel was Sir John Lees, a landowner and former cavalryman in his sixties, who had built up and cherished the 5th Battalion in peacetime. Now he was too old for service overseas, but he was greatly loved and respected. His passion was fox hunting and, since fox hunting was not available in Frome, he had brought along a pack of beagles as a substitute. He could outrun us all in the pursuit of hares, lolloping along uttering weird falsetto cries and urging on the mindless beagles, all of whose names began with B—Belvoir, Beauchamp, Beauregard, Berkeley, etc.

As the youngest and newest officer, I had the doubtful honor of being made Battalion Beagle Officer, and was responsible for the welfare of these capricious and monotonous hounds, which had to be exercised every other day. I soon discovered that unless you knew their names and the ritual falsetto cries, they were virtually uncontrollable. During our first outing they took off into the town, infested a church where a christening was in progress, and ended up in the local butcher's shop. The colonel was not amused. Nor was he pleased when I asked him, in my capacity as Battalion Recreation Officer, if he would play soccer for the battalion in a match with the town team. "Hate games," the true cavalryman replied; "Spoil your leg for a boot."

I spent many pleasant hours drilling and training my platoon under the watchful eye of Sergeant-Major Johnny Trimarcho, a butcher from Wareham with a ferocious squint, who was reputed to have killed a man with a meat cleaver in a jealous rage. He endeared himself to me early on when we were being inoculated, by fainting dead away at the sight of the needle. "I come all over queer," he explained.

The Dorsets were delightful company—kind, amusing, and never dull. They took pleasure in everything, and their knowledge of the countryside was extraordinary. They could move silently and swiftly at night and were accomplished poachers, so that delicious and unexpected gifts of game and rabbits, in and out of season, constantly appeared. One glorious night later on, we bivouacked during an exercise in Six Mile Bottom, a legendary Edwardian pheasant shoot in East Anglia. My driver and batman appeared early next morning festooned with pheasants. I never again met soldiers, or indeed a group of any kind, whom I liked as much. My corporal, Sid Liddle, keeps the survivors of our group in touch to this day from his home in Portsmouth.

In the early spring of 1940 I was posted away from my battalion as Intelligence Officer to the Brigade Headquarters in a neighboring village.

This was supposedly a compliment to my acumen, knowledge of languages, and academic background. The brigadier was a Royal Engineer Officer called B. K. Young, a shy, morose, but decent man who had done well in World War I and was believed to have been crossed in love.

Never having been to war, it was hard to envisage the battle function of a Brigade Headquarters which, in training, did nothing but simulated exercises—tactical exercises without troops (TEWTS, as they were called), telephone battles, map-reading contests, and so on. We drove all over Somerset and Dorset in those innocent days, imagining battles and campaigns, and playing elaborate charades in uniform in the bewitching countryside of my childhood.

Going on training courses was an important part of military life, and there the world of make-believe was even more predominant. Because there was a residual obsession with poison gas (all of World War I vintage), I was sent to the Army Gas School in Tregantle in Cornwall to learn the folklore attached to dealing with lewisite, phosgene, and mustard gas. ("Lewisite has the odor of geraniums; phosgene smells like musty hay," the *Army Gas Manual* explains.) Luckily we did not know about nerve gas or any of the other nasty surprises the Germans had prepared but never used.

While I was at Tregantle, the Low Countries were overrun and the Battle of France began its disastrous course, and we were all ordered to rejoin our units immediately. Our brigade, as part of the 43rd (Wessex) Division, was first moved toward Southampton to be shipped to France and then, as the only fully equipped division remaining in the British Isles, we were recalled and put into General Headquarters Reserve north of London in Hertfordshire.

With the rapid German occupation of Denmark, Norway, Holland, Belgium, and France, the war had started at last, but after Dunkirk was over the immediate arrangements in Britain were more farcical than serious. The truth was that there simply weren't enough troops to be serious. The volunteer Home Guard were armed with pikes and patrolled the countryside on bicycles or horses. To foil parachutists, all signposts, railway station signs, and place names were removed or painted out, causing maximum confusion and loss of time to which a total blackout greatly contributed. German parachutists, who had been used in Holland, became an obsession, and it was believed that they usually wore disguise. Nuns and clergymen were especially suspect. Fifth-column activities were imagined everywhere, and we were constantly on night patrol tracking down unexplained lights, mysterious signs on the ground such as arrangements of agricultural implements or hay bales believed to be signals to hostile aircraft, and following up alleged spies and enemy agents, reports on whom proliferated in the countryside, especially when the pubs were open and any stranger appeared.

On patrol one night I was stopped by a member of the Home Guard on a bicycle. Dismounting and saluting smartly, he asked me to come to the local pub to receive a report on his section's activities. When we got inside into the light, I was surprised to see that this elderly Home Guard private had seven rows of medals, and I asked him his name. "Field Marshal the Earl of Cavan, sir," he replied. He was a former Chief of the Imperial General Staff.

In the early summer of 1940 we finally got all our equipment and vehicles, and, in between our nightly searches for parachutists and fifth-column activities, we began to train more seriously. This mostly took the form of lengthy movement exercises—40 VTM (vehicles to the mile) and 20 MIH (miles in the hour). As Brigade Intelligence Officer, I had the responsibility of leading the brigade convoy, which meant that if you lost the way in the dark (no headlights and no signposts) on the rural roads of Hertfordshire or Essex, you could find yourself in a cul-de-sac with one hundred or so large vehicles jammed up behind you. It was essential to memorize the map and the distances, to make a detailed list or route map, and, if in doubt, to stop. In distant places at night the Brigade Headquarters would sometimes find itself billeted in country houses where the more dashing middle-aged officers pursued every woman under sixty. I was impressed and surprised at their singleness of purpose.

A great deal of time was spent trying to make the British Army's rudimentary radio equipment work. The radios were mostly housed in the back of pick-up trucks, and the signalers could be heard endlessly calling other stations in the simplistic codewords used by the entire army. "Hello, Exray, this is Sunray, Over," etc., etc. At that time we had little idea of the life-and-death importance of communications or of how outmoded and incompetent we were in this vital area.

Toward the end of August 1940 I had a traumatic experience after we had gone virtually without sleep for three nights. In this pre-Montgomery period, ability to function without sleep was rated high. (Montgomery very sensibly made it a disciplinary offense not to seize every possible opportunity to sleep, and himself regularly went to bed at 8:45 p.m. each night, even during battles.) We were bivouacked in a wood somewhere in Suffolk and, as Brigade Duty Officer, I was seated uncomfortably in the back of a radio truck.

I suddenly found myself walking through a wood in the moonlight with no idea where I was or what I was doing. With a sense of helplessness and growing panic, I realized that I did not have my map case, pistol, equipment, or helmet, a serious offense under Army Regulations. I eventually reached a country road along which a military despatch rider was approaching. He took me a mile or two to a moving column of vehicles which turned out to be our headquarters. In my somnambulistic absence, codeword "Cromwell," the signal for the German invasion of Britain, had come through, and we were on the move south. So much for the merits of going without sleep. The Dorsets naturally assumed I had been off on a tryst and were admiring of my nonchalance at a time of national crisis, for we were, it transpired, being moved to the south coast to take up positions in Dover against the anticipated German invasion.

After nearly a year of playing soldiers we were about to be seriously, or almost seriously, employed at last. Codeword "Cromwell" meant that a German invasion was imminent, and no time could be lost in reaching our new positions in and around Dover, the nearest point in England to occupied France. It was therefore decided to take the 43rd Division, of which our brigade was a part, straight through the center of London.

The Metropolitan Police escorted us through the city by a secret route known only to them and at high speed, which for a large military convoy was a vertiginous 35 mph. All young officers, including myself, were assigned to shepherding the convoy on motorcycles to ensure that it kept together. The staff had either forgotten, or did not know, that while the leading vehicle of a convoy may go steadily at the designated speed, there is a kind of whiplash effect which means that the last vehicles, to keep up, may often have to go twice that speed in order to compensate for delays along the line. Our heavy repair vehicles were soon grinding along at 50 mph, some ominously belching smoke. Unexpectedly, the route led past Buckingham Palace, and my most vivid memory of our historic dash to Dover is the desolate spectacle of our main repair truck in flames outside the Palace gates.

In Dover we deployed to defensive positions, fully confident of dealing decisively with the Germans. Brigade Headquarters was in the casemates of Dover Castle, tunnels cut into the cliff face in preparation for the expected Napoleonic invasion one hundred and fifty years before. On a clear day we had a fine view of the French coast, and even on foggy days we felt a continual rapport with the enemy across the water, for German long-range guns intermittently shelled the town and its surroundings, making a tremendous noise with surprisingly little effect. There were also continuous bombing attacks, as well as attacks on shipping going through the Straits of Dover.

I spent the days, and especially the nights, moving around our area. We expected the invasion at any moment. Objects washed ashore attained a special significance in those anxious days, and even the most ordinary piece of flotsam was earnestly studied for signs of sinister enemy activity. Local eccentrics were assiduously harassed, and strange lights and other phenomena constantly reported. Overhead the Battle of Britain continued.

Two World War I 16-inch naval guns had been hastily installed outside Dover to show that Britain could retaliate to German cross-Channel fire. While these guns (known as Winnie and Pooh) were being installed with the help of an enormous crane, a guardian Spitfire squadron circled constantly overhead. The Spitfires vanished when the crane had finished its work, exposing the gun positions to unopposed German dive-bombing. The Spitfires had been there to protect the crane, which was irreplaceable. Winnie and Pooh fired occasionally and with disastrous results. One shell from them invariably called forth a riposte of twenty or more German shells on the town, and after representations from the mayor and aldermen of Dover they limited their firing to demonstrations for distinguished visitors.

What is striking in retrospect is how confident we were of repelling the expected German invasion and how totally unequipped we were to do so. The Germans missed an opportunity to wade ashore virtually unopposed. St. Margaret's Bay, for example, was a crescent-shaped beach about half a mile long just east of Dover. In the thirties it had been a fashionable place, with villas belonging to theatrical people. Noel Coward was said to have lived there.

St. Margaret's Bay was defended by a platoon of the 5th Dorsets, my old battalion, and I took a special interest in it. A second lieutenant and thirty men armed with twenty-eight Lee-Enfield .303 rifles, a Bren light machine gun, a 2-inch mortar which, due to shortage of ammunition, nobody had ever fired, and one Boys* anti-tank rifle, a grotesque weapon renowned for breaking the collarbone of the firer and having minimal armor-piercing capacity. We spent many happy hours arranging fields of fire, enfilades, barbed wire, minefields, sandbagged emplacements, and other ploys from the *Infantry Manual*. The beach was occasionally shelled

---

*Boys referred to the inventor, Colonel Boys.

or strafed by a passing German fighter, adding greatly to the soldiers'
sense of self-importance.

At the end of the war I saw the plan for Operation "*See-Löwe* (Sea-
lion)," the German invasion of England. At the beginning was a map of
the overall German strategy, on which St. Margaret's Bay was marked
by a large arrow as one of the main initial points of attack. Our happy
platoon was to be subjected to a mass bombing attack, parachute divisions
behind the beach, and a massive amphibious assault from the sea.

After the climactic September of the Battle of Britain, which apparently persuaded the Germans that they could not invade without control
of the skies, a new wind was suddenly felt in South Eastern Command
—a wind which soon blew away what was left of the comfortable trappings
of peacetime. The beagles had long since been left behind, but officers
still carried large quantities of gear (shotguns, fishing tackle, golf clubs,
and dress uniforms), discipline was leisurely, and serious battle training
almost nonexistent. Our first hint of the change was a summons to a
cinema in Folkestone where we found virtually every officer of South
Eastern Command assembled in one extremely vulnerable place. Although a squadron of Spitfires circled overhead, this was a dashing departure from our normally defensive attitude and was evidently designed
to mark a new spirit of defiance.

Inside the cinema we were "put in the picture" by a small, wiry,
highly idiosyncratic figure, Lieutenant-General Bernard Montgomery,
later to become "Monty." Later in the war I had bitter cause to doubt
Montgomery's judgment and to detest his egocentricity, but in 1940,
when the war seemed endless and unwinnable, he made a tremendous
impression. Whatever else he may have been, Montgomery was a genius
at morale-building and training, and we desperately needed both. I don't
remember exactly what he said, but he appeared to take us into his
confidence, and we left the cinema with a feeling of at last having a leader
in full charge. We also had the feeling that if we didn't shape up, he
personally would find out and ship us out.

Dover was a favorite place for a quick visit by VIPs. I was deputed
to be at the station to monitor Winston Churchill's first arrival, which
coincided with a German bombing attack on Dover Harbour. The railway
approached Dover from the west through a tunnel under Shakespeare
Cliff, and we had assumed that the prime minister would disembark
immediately on arrival. When the train drew up at the platform, however,
Churchill did not emerge; we were told that he was having his after-lunch

nap and could not be disturbed. After some argument the train went back into the tunnel until the great man awoke.

Atlantic convoys to the Port of London continued to go through the Dover Straits after the fall of France under a hail of bombing and shellfire from the French coast, often with terrible losses. The harbor of Dover was considered unusable except for a few embattled minesweepers and small naval craft which sallied forth to escort the hard-pressed convoys through the Straits. Since these small ships were constantly under fire, their skippers tended to lose their crews and were always short-handed. In a pub one night I volunteered to go as a deck anti-aircraft gunner on his next escort job with Lieutenant Commander Kaye, the skipper of the minesweeper escort *Stella and Orion*.

It was cold and dark early next morning when I stumbled aboard the *Stella and Orion*. Skipper Kaye was warming up with rum and hot chocolate, and soon we were out to sea taking up station with the convoy. Having been sunk twice in the previous six weeks, Kaye was obsessed with air attacks, and as the day dawned he scanned the French coast for the first bomber flights. At first light there was a brief attack on some of the ships ahead and a few random shells from the German coastal guns. It turned out, however, that Kaye was looking in the wrong direction.

About two hours out from Dover there was a tremendous crash, and I found myself lying on my back on the bridge next to Kaye. A heavy waterfall then descended on us, after which we arose to observe the bow of the *Stella and Orion* floating away. Our half of the ship was evidently sinking fast, but a small drifter (fishing trawler) had been following in our wake and picked us off the remains of the *Stella and Orion* just before it sank.

I had no idea what had happened. Having grown up in terror of the hot-water tank in a cupboard in my bedroom in Bristol, I first assumed that the ship's boilers had burst. In fact Skipper Kaye's obsession with the Luftwaffe had been our downfall, for it had caused him to overlook the lurking peril of the magnetic mine. He had forgotten to switch on his anti-magnetic-mine gear, and we had blown up on a mine over which a fifty-ship Atlantic convoy had just safely passed.

Drying out aboard the drifter our day was not yet over. Off Deal a heavy German air attack sank some eighteen of the fifty ships in the convoy ahead. The succeeding lull was disturbed by an old-fashioned droning, and flying low across the sea came fifty biplanes, most of which were quickly shot down by the anti-aircraft escorts around the convoy. On our drifter we blazed away with every available weapon and claimed one enemy aircraft. This curious action turned out to be the only attempt by Mussolini's air force to attack Britain. One of the Italian airmen we picked up out of the water was indignant that he had been left behind and betrayed by the Luftwaffe. The scales had fallen from his eyes, he said, and he only longed for captivity in England. We finally put ashore at Sheerness, while the remains of the convoy steamed on to the battered Port of London.

Although he had agreed to my going, Brigadier B. K. Young was far from pleased at my day's outing and he forbade any of us to go to sea again. He was particularly displeased that my service pistol, which had been in the cabin with my equipment and had not been accessible after the explosion, had gone down with the ship. "You don't seem to realize," he kept saying, "that it is an offense under Army Regulations for an officer to lose his personal weapon."

The following week I was about to leave our Headquarters Mess in the Constable's Tower after lunch when sounds of enemy aircraft flying low drew me to the bay window with a stained glass St. George and the Dragon in the center that looked out over the harbor. A shrieking crescendo and whistle was followed by an explosion which blew me, and St. George and the Dragon, all the way across the hall. The dive-bombing attack I thought I was watching was aimed at the Constable's Tower. I was streaming with blood from deep cuts on the face and hands and lucky not to have been blinded, but apart from being severely shaken up, I had only superficial wounds. The next night a parachute mine was dropped just outside the castle walls. One of the Dorset sentries on the wall took it for a German parachutist and cried out, " 'Alt—'oo goes there?" before being blown off his post. The explosion was tremendous, and after it I began to jump at even relatively distant noises. This irritated Charles Mackenzie, the Brigade Major, a very decent Scot, and he sent me home for a few days' rest.

My mother's house in Bristol was the last place to go for this purpose. The city was raided every night by the Luftwaffe, and my mother made things worse by resolutely not hearing the air-raid warning siren or the sounds of approaching aircraft, anti-aircraft fire, and bombs. I was vastly relieved to get back to Dover.

I realized then how much easier it is to be a soldier than a civilian in time of war. A soldier in uniform is at least an integral and organized part of the nightmare. The civilian wanders in and out of it with no allotted role, subject to many of the dangers and discomforts but with none of the support of camaraderie, discipline, and esprit de corps, and with no hope at all of striking back against the enemy. My mother's fortitude astonished me. She was left in charge of the evacuated buildings of Badminton School and ran a small all-purpose class for the few children who were left in the city. About half the school buildings were damaged in the air raids, but she appeared to remain unmoved. She showed no fear, although alone in her flimsy little house at night with the sirens wailing, the ominous crescendo drone of approaching bombers, and the whistle and crash of bombs and anti-aircraft fire, she must have been terrified. She certainly made us temporary soldiers seem rather inadequate.

Back in Dover our duties were becoming routine. The Battle of Britain, mainly fought in daylight, had ended, and was succeeded by night raids on London and other cities. The Dorsets were becoming bored with what had become ordinary coastal defense duties. After Christmas we were moved back into the Kentish countryside to retrain as a field division and as an emergency reserve in case of invasion.

The long haul was only just beginning. Britain and the countries of the British Empire, with the battered expatriate remnants of the armies of Poland, Norway, Belgium, Denmark, Holland, and France, had to fight their way back to a point where the offensive could eventually be taken against Nazi Germany. At the time this seemed such a lengthy and desperate task that it was better not to think about it at all. It occurred to no one I knew that we might still lose the war—only that the rest of our lives might be spent fighting it. We spent our time training, doing exercises especially at night, and wondering where we would be going next. The people of Kent were hospitable and the girls friendly. London was not far away if one didn't mind air raids, and there were still concerts and theaters and quite good food. But there were always two nagging questions—how long? and how?

Part of the answer came in June 1941. We were at that time stationed in an evacuated school, Milner Court, in a pretty village just outside Canterbury. We had arranged a picnic in punts on the river on a perfect midsummer evening, and, in these idyllic surroundings, we heard over the radio the news of the German invasion of Russia and Churchill's declaration of support for the Soviet Union. It seemed totally illogical and too good to be true. All through the spring and early summer of 1941 the news had been disastrous—retreat in the Western Desert, ignominious defeat in the gallant effort to aid invaded Greece, and a hazardous evacuation from Crete after the hard-fought battle against German parachute and glider troops. Why on earth would Hitler, with all Europe and half of the Mediterranean in his grasp, open up a huge new front against his former ally, the Soviet Union? Had he never read *War and Peace* or heard of Napoleon?

Although the Nazis decimated the Russian Army in the first weeks of the invasion, the knowledge that another, and a huge, power was engaging and absorbing the Nazi war machine with its hitherto unbroken series of victories gave a new dimension of hope.

V

Airborne Forces

IN AUGUST 1941 my brigadier received a call from Brigadier F. A. M. ("Boy") Browning, who was then commanding a sister brigade in the Wessex Division. Browning had just been appointed Major-General, Airborne Forces, to develop the parachute and glider-borne troops of the British Army, and he was asking whether I would be available to join his staff as Intelligence Officer. I was delighted at this opportunity to leave the by now somewhat humdrum life of an infantry brigade for a new and dashing branch of the service. I was also flattered to have been asked for by Boy Browning.

Browning was a spectacular figure, cool and impeccable in his Grenadier Guards uniform. He had fought gallantly in World War I and had retained the slim figure, light movements, and boyish good looks of someone half his age, which accounted for his nickname. He was very much the dashing, romantic fighting officer of fiction. In fact he was married to the writer Daphne du Maurier.

Once you got used to Browning's mannered arrogance—wearing his cap at meals in the mess and always slightly aloof and challenging—you found a delightful and imaginative man and a loyal friend. It was from Browning's batman, Guardsman Johnson, who was his butler in civilian life, that I learned the infinite expressiveness of the word "sir." In fact it was the only word that Guardsman Johnson was ever heard to utter. "Sir" affirmative, "Sir" questioning, "Sir" enthusiastic, "Sir" grateful, "Sir" acknowledging, and so on.

Browning was an ambitious soldier, and all of his enthusiasm was directed into his new task. It is ironical that the German airborne attack on Crete, which caused the Nazi authorities to decide that large-scale airborne operations were costly and impractical, was a major incentive for the development by Britain and the United States of large airborne formations. We were starting out at exactly the point where the Germans had decided to stop. Over the next three years I was intimately involved in an airborne experiment of increasing scale and cost, only to learn, at Arnhem, the same basic lessons the Germans had learned in Crete in 1941.

In 1941, however, we were all imbued with the conviction that airborne troops would be the spearhead of the counteroffensive that would eventually end the war. Technically there was almost everything still to be done. The existing parachute facilities had so far been used mostly for training agents to be dropped in Occupied Europe. There was a parachute school at Ringway, the Manchester Airport, and a dropping ground equipped with a capricious balloon on a winch at Tatton Park outside Manchester. The 1st British Parachute Battalion had been formed, and French and Polish parachute battalions were envisaged.

In 1941 Britain had no transport aircraft suitable for parachute dropping. The authorities had therefore selected for this purpose the Whitley, an obsolete bomber, the distinguishing feature of which had been its retractable under-fuselage gun turret, a trashcan-shaped container which made the aircraft unstable without noticeably improving its defenses. When the turret was removed a circular hole was left in the floor, and it was through this hole, feet first, that Britain's first military parachutists dropped. It was a most inconvenient arrangement for getting out quickly and close together, and you were lucky if you didn't bang your head when the slipstream hit your emerging feet. The aircraft had no windows and reeked of glycol fluid, sweat, and other unwelcome smells. Until you jumped the world was completely cut off, and in rough weather when people were air-sick, the smelly darkness was particularly depressing. The parachute was attached to the dropping aircraft by a static line which automatically pulled it out as you left the aircraft. The parachutist tended to swing like a pendulum in any but the calmest weather, making landing full of unpleasant surprises.

Gliders, again in imitation of the Germans, were greatly valued although, apart from a small training glider, the only existing model was the Horsa (named after the brother of Saxon King Hengist), a wooden troop-carrying machine which looked very stately on the ground but veered and yawed sickeningly in the air. There was also on the drawing board a tank-carrying monster, the Hamilcar. The Americans were said to have a mass-produced aluminum glider, the WACO, which in the end proved to be the most serviceable of all.

In our pristine enthusiasm we overlooked—perhaps deliberately—the evidence of what had happened even to the redoubtably professional Germans in Crete. Gliders flying in tow at low altitudes and low speeds were sitting ducks for even the most mediocre gunner. It was difficult to set them down in the right place, and they tended to break up on landing, damaging or stunning their occupants. It was difficult to assemble a glider-borne force on the ground, especially under fire. Vehicle-carrying capacity was in the future, but it was hoped that a new American vehicle, the Jeep, if and when it became available, would fit into the Horsa.

At that time nothing heavier than the Sten gun—a mass-produced submachine gun just then coming into use—could be carried by a parachutist, although bags were later developed which could be lowered on a rope after jumping so that the bag landed separately but attached to the man. All heavier equipment was dropped in parachute containers which had to be located and opened on the dropping zone. This was bad enough in daylight, and in the dark it was even worse. No transport heavier than a folding bicycle could be dropped by parachute, and it was said that the army's folding bicycle was more dangerous than parachuting since it tended to fold while being ridden. There was also a new toy, the Welbyke—a forerunner of the Vespa and Lambretta—which had tiny wheels and a tiny motor and could be dropped in a container.

There was at that time considerable reluctance to question whether lightly armed, footbound soldiers scattered from the sky by parachute or in gliders, no matter how tough and aggressive they might be, were necessarily a sound military concept. Certainly small groups of parachutists or glider troops aiming at specific targets could be very effective, as they had been in the German invasion of the Low Countries and France. But organized in large fighting formations—brigades, divisions, and corps, such as existed later in the war—airborne forces were a dubious military proposition, redeemed time and again by the courage, fighting spirit, and skill of the officers and men.

Headquarters Major-General, Airborne Forces, or MGAF, as our group was called, started off modestly two floors underground below the Air Ministry in Whitehall. It was called the "Dungeon Party." It was not clear what exactly we were supposed to do from our subterranean headquarters. As a new outfit in a new field we were generally viewed with suspicion, particularly since we had no actual troops or military units under our command.

Our original group consisted of Colonel Gordon Walch as Operations Officer, another Grenadier, Colonel Johnny Goschen, as Logistics Officer, Wing Commander Nigel Norman as Air Adviser, and myself. We were later joined by others, including Major Dickie des Voeux, yet another Grenadier with whom I used to fly about the country in a Gypsy moth biplane visiting secret military establishments and who was killed at Arnhem. Nigel Norman, who was killed in an air crash on the way to North Africa, was a delightful companion, a marvelous pilot, and a talented light poet.

I was Browning's Intelligence Officer, but at such an early stage normal intelligence work was irrelevant. I therefore concentrated on getting to know the existing military and other agencies which would be able to help us when we started operations and on developing the contacts which might be useful in mounting airborne operations.

The Special Operations Executive (SOE), which was in the agent-dropping and Resistance business, was naturally reluctant to provide much information. Their equipment section was like a grown-up toy shop. Tiny radios, magnetized fly buttons that could serve as compasses, handkerchiefs that became maps when soaked, luminous balls to mark a track through thick country, tiny hacksaws to be sewn into hems of clothing, highly compressed foods, invisible inks, explosive paper, and countless other gadgets, including some very fancy weapons and explosives, were only a few of the items available. I wonder how many real agents ever used most of them.

Lord Louis Mountbatten's Combined Operations Headquarters, also in London, had a colorful cast of characters—adventurers, novelists, specialists in arcane subjects, aesthetes, ideologues of both left and right, the manager of the Curzon Cinema—presided over by the master showman of the British war effort. Being new themselves, they were much nicer to us than more established institutions and were anxious to cooperate in all kinds of madcap schemes. I recall an idea for destroying the U-boat bases at the French ports of Brest and Lorient. The French Resistance would collect enough French fire engines to carry a British parachute battalion. The RAF would drop incendiary bombs to set fire to the towns of Brest and Lorient. The British parachutists, dressed as French *pompiers*, would land, board the fire engines, and, bells clanging, would drive to the submarine bases and destroy them.

The Inter-Services Topographical Unit could provide topographical details of places all over the world. Among other resources it had a vast collection of picture postcards sent by holiday makers abroad (the Germans had a similar collection). The messages on these cards were of great sentimental interest and nostalgia, but the pictures tended to be too old and fuzzy to be of much use.

Our most important intelligence resource was aerial photographs, which were just beginning to be used on a large scale for intelligence purposes. For airborne troops they were especially valuable because they gave an accurate visual picture of an area which the soldiers would see for the first time as they descended on it, probably in the dark. The photographic interpretation center at Medmenham, in the Thames Valley, was staffed mostly by Women's Auxiliary Air Force officers renowned for their glamour as well as for a remarkable record of discoveries. The experimental German rockets and buzz bombs on the Baltic island of Peenemünde were first spotted on photographs at Medmenham. Medmenham also had a model section which constructed beautiful and accurate models of target areas. These were of immense importance in familiarizing airborne troops with their targets in advance.

The photographic interpretation course I attended at Farnborough early in 1942 was the most useful course I ever took. During it I caught my first glimpse of a jet aircraft in flight, one of two secret experimental models then in existence. It appeared at first to be an aircraft which had lost its propeller, when it suddenly soared effortlessly upward in a steep climb. It was the first time I heard the dynamic roar which later became so familiar.

On December 7, 1941, we heard, in our Whitehall bunker, the news of Pearl Harbor and the emergence at last of the United States as a full-fledged war ally. It seemed incredible that the other member of the Axis should have deliberately brought into the war the world's greatest industrial power. Although the war would still be long, the balance had been decisively tipped, and the final result could no longer be in doubt.

In our little world the major result of Pearl Harbor was the prospect of all sorts of American equipment and techniques. General Browning made a visit to the United States and came back greatly heartened by the scale and promise of American technology. The DC-3 (Dakota in British parlance) would allow parachutists to jump from a door in close formation and in far greater numbers, as well as being a far more reliable glider tug. The miraculous Jeep, with trailers, would become the standard unit of airborne transport. Above all, our efforts would now be supported by the vitality, the almost limitless resources, and the ingenuity and productive capacity of a great nation. We were no longer alone on a shoestring.

Soon after Christmas we moved our expanding staff to Salisbury Plain in Wiltshire, choosing as headquarters a small country mansion, Syrencote House, which was conveniently situated near the airfields of Upavon and Netheravon, on which our aircraft were based. Netheravon was one of the oldest airfields in Britain and still had grass runways. Why the site had been selected in the first place was a mystery since it was fairly hilly. Viewed from the end of the field, a departing aircraft would disappear downhill into a small valley and reappear accelerating up the other side to take off, with a bit of luck, on the crest. The lumbering Whitley, with its turned-down nose giving it a look of pessimism, extracted the maximum drama out of these unusual conditions.

Around us in Wiltshire the elements of the 1st Airborne Division were being assembled—a Parachute Brigade and an Air-Landing (glider) Brigade, and various engineer, artillery, and reconnaissance units.

As soon as we had settled in Wiltshire, each billeted in a different farmhouse, I went on a parachute course. This consisted of a week's toughening up in the grounds of Hardwick Hall in Derbyshire—long marches, violent gymnastics, learning to fall by jumping out of a moving truck, and so on. The second week was spent at Ringway, near Manchester, doing the actual jumping. The first four jumps, from the balloon at Tatton Park, were extremely disagreeable. The balloon itself, swaying and bobbing about, did not inspire confidence, and the winch was always going wrong. I once got stuck halfway up with a group of Welshmen. It was too low to jump, and we were there for four hours on a wooden platform with a hole in the middle and only a flimsy single strand of wire as a barrier. The Welshmen sang hymns about death throughout. The balloon, being attached to the ground, gave one an unpleasant sense of vertigo, as an airplane did not, and the effort of will required to jump in total silence was far greater than in the noise and bustle of an aircraft.

I did not mind the fairly rough training, but in my heart I hated and dreaded jumping. I was terrified that something would go wrong, leaving one hurtling helpless to the ground, and in any case the whole thing seemed profoundly unnatural. The more I jumped, the earlier I would wake up on the morning of the jump, and I would go to great lengths to find other matters to occupy my attention. The actual descent was a wonderful sensation, peaceful, solitary, and serene after the hurly-burly and noise of the aircraft, but from 1,200 feet (in order to minimize the time during which one was a target in the air) it was all too short, and ended in the crash and bump of an unpredictable landing.

I jumped whenever I could because I thought I would become less scared of it, but I didn't. I jumped with the Poles and French, sometimes as a sort of deputy supervisor in their first jumps, and they always seemed much more self-possessed and fatalistic than I was.

Our activities attracted increasing numbers of eminent visitors. Mr. Churchill liked to come down to Salisbury Plain for demonstrations of parachuting and gliding, bringing with him senior colleagues and distinguished guests. These occasions did not always go smoothly. I remember a demonstration of "Britain's Airborne Might" (as the *Daily Express* persisted in calling it) for Churchill and a newly arrived American major-general, Dwight Eisenhower. The appointed day was cold and blustery, with a wind well above the maximum speed for safe and orderly parachuting. Although the Royal Air Force warned that in these conditions the drop would be ragged and quite possibly in the wrong place, it was impossible to disappoint the distinguished audience, which at that very moment was making its way to a windswept row of chairs on Salisbury Plain.

We lumbered down the grass slope at Netheravon and up the other side, boosted into the air at the crest by the strong wind. After half an hour the red warning light went on, giving us two minutes to get into the correct sitting position to go out through the hole in the floor when the green light went on. Some of the original parachutists had volunteered in exchange for a commutation of army detention sentences and were in fact convicted felons. I always found these men—rapists, burglars, confidence men—to be particularly friendly and reliable, but the higher authorities felt they might prove untrustworthy under pressure and refuse to jump. For this reason the officer jumped last and was even supposed, if necessary, to draw his pistol, a practical impossibility in any case.

Emerging last from our aircraft, I could easily see that the situation was not promising. The line of seated VIPs, which was supposed to be at a safe distance, seemed rapidly to get nearer as I descended and the wind blew our little group off course. At about 300 feet I could sense the distinction of the lonely line, the prime minister, the air minister, Sir Archibald Sinclair, the sinister Lord Cherwell, the Chief of the Imperial General Staff, and the American general, as well as our own General Browning. Shouting a warning and trying to side-slip, I landed with a sickening bump just in front of General Eisenhower. The wind then took my parachute and dragged me at 30 miles an hour straight through the

VIP line. Detaching my parachute harness, I came to a halt, stood up and, for want of anything better to do, saluted.

The British, except for Browning, behaved badly, muttering "Disgraceful," "Damned poor show," and so on, and looking embarrassed. General Eisenhower, on the other hand, was perfectly charming. "Are you all right, son?" he asked. "You shouldn't be jumping in this wind anyway." He looked quizzically at the cylindrical cardboard container around my neck. I explained that it contained two carrier pigeons for communicating with Headquarters, and I extracted one, attached a message cylinder to its leg, and threw it into the air to launch it on its mission. The pigeon had evidently had enough nonsense for one day and flew to the top of a nearby bush, where it sat cooing and eyeing the company with an evil look. "I see we shall have to do something about your communications," Eisenhower said.

The Americans became more and more central to our lives as 1942 progressed. Brigadier-General James Gavin established a Parachute Brigade that was to be the first element of the U.S. 82nd Airborne Division. Gavin was an impressive figure—modest, taciturn, and tough. He seemed to have great reserves of judgment, courage, and wisdom. We also acquired a United States Liaison Officer, U.S. Air Force Colonel Anthony B. Harris, a much decorated flier from World War I and a public relations man in civilian life. Wherever we were, Anthony B. Harris, though bilious and raffish in appearance and far from young, would immediately acquire a beautiful girlfriend and would beguile our days with vivid accounts of their nocturnal activities. "She knows more tricks than a monkey on a ten-foot pole," he would tell us. He had a genius for making himself, and us, comfortable, and gave me my first experience of the generous and lavish conditions of United States military service.

It was on a jump in early August 1942 that my career as a parachutist abruptly ended. We flew longer than usual before the jump, apparently in order to acclimatize the troops to long flights in preparation for operations in North Africa. We were still in gloomy Whitleys, although American DC-3s were to be used for future operations. As usual I was dreading the jump and doing my best not to show it. The moment I left the aircraft I knew something was wrong, for I was rapidly overtaking the "stick" of parachutists who had preceded me. Looking up I could easily see the problem—a parachute looking like a budding tulip instead of a mushroom.* I hit the ground with a sickening crash.

*We did not pack our own parachutes, which were prepared by the Women's Auxiliary Air Force.

By the time I recovered some degree of consciousness, my "stick" had gathered. I was unable to move at all and lay rooted to the ground looking up at the towering bodies of my comrades. Nobody dared move me until Brian Courtney, our Australian parachute doctor, who had jumped from a different aircraft, arrived. I was enormously reassured by his presence. He gave me a shot of morphia, and the next thing I remember was being wheeled along a corridor in a military hospital. There had been a very bad glider accident just before our drop, and the meager resources of the hospital were entirely taken up with the resulting casualties. I therefore lay in the reception room for what seemed an eternity. Shock and extreme pain had now taken hold, and only the stolid presence of Brian Courtney provided any comfort at all.

I next regained consciousness in a bed in the hospital ward. Two English military doctors were discussing my condition and agreeing that it was hopeless and that scarce resources would be better used elsewhere. Even in my semi-comatose and drugged state this struck me as outrageous, but I passed out again before being able to communicate my outrage to anyone else. The night passed in spasms of pain and semi-consciousness. It seemed impossible to attract attention. I could hear the American nurses who manned the wards gossiping in the sluice—a hell-hole where in British military hospitals nurses gathered to wash out various containers and drink tea—but the doctors' view that my situation was hopeless and not worthy of attention seemed to have been generally accepted.

There is nothing worse than being angry in a state of extreme physical weakness. The doctors I had overheard were officers of the Royal Army Medical Corps which had, probably wrongly, a grisly reputation for incompetence and worse. It seemed to me clear, as far as anything was clear, that I was going to die in the foul-smelling military hospital at Tidworth Pennings in Wiltshire because I couldn't attract anyone's attention. Much of this, no doubt, was pain- and morphine-induced paranoia, but not all of it.

In a spell of consciousness next morning I opened my eyes to see General Browning beside my bed and I tried in a confused way to express my feelings. Whatever it was that I said, Browning evidently acted at once, as was his habit. Severe parachute accidents were of considerable medical concern at that time, and I was quite an interesting case. I had a broken femur (thigh), three compacted vertebrae in my lower spine, very badly damaged ankles, and undiagnosed internal injuries, as well as extreme shock.

Later in the day my alarm increased during another talk between the doctors, who again assumed that I was unconscious. This time, evidently spurred on by a blast from General Browning, their indifference had turned to misdirected zeal, and they were discussing putting me in plaster from head to foot. In deep shock and with the sort of injuries I had, this would, I was told later, have probably been lethal, but once again fate, spurred on by General Browning, intervened—this time in the reassuring figure of Major-General Rowley Bristow, the Chief Orthopedic Surgeon to the British Army, peering keenly at my recumbent form over half-moon spectacles.

Rowley Bristow was a superb doctor. As a young regimental medical officer in World War I, he had noticed that shrapnel wounds resulted in the permanent paralysis or atrophy of limbs if the nerves had been severed and no effort had been made to reconnect them. Under fire in the trenches, therefore, with a watchmaker's loup (glass) he began to knit nerves together before casualties were evacuated. Since nerves grow back very slowly, he was widely regarded as crazy until some eighteen months later when his patients began to show results.

Bristow quickly revolutionized my situation. He ordered a halt to all medical treatment in the military hospital and my immediate removal to St. Thomas's Hospital, then evacuated to a former lunatic asylum called Botley's Park near Chertsey on the Thames. When it was pointed out that such a long move would probably kill me, he announced that a new and experimental piece of equipment, the Jones Abduction Frame, specially designed to move patients with multiple fractures, was already on its way by air. After giving precise instructions, he left.

I remember very little of my transfer to Botley's Park. Three of the nurses at Tidworth, in a touching last-minute effort to ease my journey, had separately given me three unrecorded and maximum doses of morphia. They had omitted to observe the army rule that if you gave an unconscious person morphia, you were supposed to inscribe an "M" on his forehead with ash, mud, lipstick, or whatever pigment was available. My arrival at Botley's Park was therefore something of a fiasco. A large group of doctors and medical students had gathered, not to see me, but to see the Jones Abduction Frame. They were enthusing about it when the head nurse, Sister Saxby, took my pulse and announced that I had none. My mother, who had been alerted to be on hand, was told that I was clinically dead. Characteristically, she refused to believe it.

In MLG Ward (Males Lower Grade), I slowly regained consciousness, not without some hallucinations, including the conviction that General

Bristow was the gardener and should not be allowed in the ward. My new situation was very different from the soggy, sweat-soaked, neglected bed at Tidworth Pennings. I was now poised on my back at an angle of 30 degrees head down, a heavy weight on pulleys attached to a pin through my left knee to provide traction for my broken thigh. A cord through pulleys over my head connected another weight with a sling under my impacted back. I was more or less immobile except for my head and arms. The St. Thomas's nurses were professionals—kindly, tough, knowledgeable, and always available.

As soon as the shock wore off and the doses of morphia were being reduced, a formidable young woman, Miss Walker, came into my life. I was at that time deeply depressed—even lachrymose—at the thought of missing the first active operations of our airborne enterprise. Two operations were then being considered—Dieppe and the capture of Tunis. Miss Walker would hear no nonsense of that kind. "You came in here completely fit," she said in one of those totally inaccurate statements which are so hard to challenge, "and you will work to maintain that degree of fitness." Since I was unable to move my lower limbs at all, and any movement caused agonizing pain, I inquired with some emotion how this was to be done. "We shall exercise your muscles constantly," replied Miss Walker, and that is exactly what she did. First, by relatively gentle electric treatment, all the muscles were made to move. Then I learned to tense and relax all the muscles without moving my body at all. I became addicted to this new way of life and spent several hours a day at it. It worked. I was originally told that I would probably be on my back for seven or eight months, and in hospital for a year. I was determined, with the aid of Miss Walker, to cut the time in half.

Once I ceased to repine for the joys of military life, I began to enjoy the hospital routine. General Browning had thoughtfully provided a case of whiskey, a rare commodity in those days, and the nurses would dispense it to me and to visitors and other patients in the most charmingly discreet fashion. For the rest of the time I read and read, trying not to listen to Tommy Handley in a show called ITMA ("It's That Man Again") and to the *Warsaw Concerto*, which were the dominant fare on the radio.

By the end of November 1942, Miss Walker's and my efforts began to show results. The weight and pin were removed from my leg, and my bed was lowered level with the floor, causing me to faint from the drainage of blood from the brain. I graduated from a wheelchair to crutches, and at Christmas I was released, slightly lame but all in one piece. The only piece of equipment I took from the hospital was a steel brace for my back.

In order to get me through the period of convalescence with something useful to do, General Browning had arranged for me to attend the Staff College at Camberley, although at twenty-three I was far below the normal age. This was an intensive four-month course (telescoped from the two-year course of peacetime). We attended lectures, wrote papers, did endless TEWTS (Tactical Exercises Without Troops—"You are the Divisional Commander of a Redland Division which has been surrounded by Blueland forces—you are being heavily bombed—your Chief of Staff has been killed/gone crazy, etc."), and took complicated tests. Being good at examinations, I found it all relatively easy except in one respect.

At Camberley I learned that it is unwise to make jokes to people who are earning their living. The instructors were exceedingly hard-working and serious-minded, and the deputy commandant, Brigadier Kit Huxley, was even more so than most. It did not go over well to start a paper on the duties of the military staff with a bad joke such as "Bread is the staff of life; the life of the Staff is one long loaf," or to make up fantastic extra situations on outdoor exercises. Had I not been good at the work, and if people, knowing of my spectacular accident, had not made allowances and been kind, I would not have done well.

On leaving the Staff College in April 1943, I happily rejoined General Browning's staff as GSO 2 Intelligence with the rank of Major. During my stay in the hospital and the Staff College, the tide of war had turned. The Dieppe raid, in which we might have taken part, and the Tunis expedition were bloody and costly disasters, but at El Alamein the British Eighth Army had reversed the situation in the Western Desert and inflicted on the German Army its first major defeat. The Eighth Army was now advancing along the North African coast toward Tunis, Algeria had been taken over by the Allies, and the German Army was bogged down in the wastes of Russia. In the Pacific the Japanese were still inflicting defeats on the Allies, but there too the tide was slowly turning.

In my absence we had acquired from the United States Air Force a symbol of the new optimism, a personal DC-3 aircraft for General Browning. Its captain, Joe Beck, and navigator, George Parkinson (Parky) Denny, were my first personal experience in a long and happy relationship with the United States. They had christened the aircraft "Boy's Boys," which was proudly painted on the nose—an informal, egalitarian gesture which seemed amazing to those of us schooled in the stiffness and formality of British Army life.

In April it became clear that we were going to North Africa on some undisclosed business. I was by now fairly mobile and, in terror of being left behind, made great demonstrations of physical fitness. I even volunteered to jump again, praying that nobody would take me up on it.

We left for Algiers in two aircraft. The first, a Hudson, crashed in Cornwall just after takeoff. Nigel Norman, alone of the passengers, was killed. This darkened all our lives.

We took off, also from Cornwall, in *Boy's Boys*. Two extra gas tanks were installed inside the fuselage to give the necessary range to reach Gibraltar with a sufficient loop out into the Atlantic to avoid German fighters from France. We flew all night in the fumes of gasoline and were much relieved to land in Gibraltar at dawn. As usual, the admiral, the Governor-General, and everyone else of any consequence had been to school with, played polo with, sailed with, or fought in World War I with Browning. We took off late in the evening for another night flight to Algiers.

We were quartered in La Marsa outside Algiers as part of an organization with the cryptic title of Headquarters 141 Force. It was clear to all of us that we were planning and preparing for the next step after the capture of Tunis, the jump across the Mediterranean to Sicily and Italy. Algiers seemed very exotic after Syrencote House.

Once again our precise role was somewhat uncertain. The 1st Parachute Brigade and the Air-Landing Brigade were shortly to come out from England to the area around Kairouan in Tunisia, an ancient city of mosques. The American 82nd Airborne Division (General Ridgeway), with Gavin in command of the Parachute Brigade, was to be stationed in Mascara in the hinterland of Algeria, with its Glider Brigade at Oujda. The theater commander was General Harold Alexander, the British troops being commanded by General Bernard Montgomery and the Americans by General George Patton.

I gained a small insight into the personalities of two of the top men late one evening when I arrived by air from Tunis at the Maison Blanche airfield in Algiers. It was dusk, and the airfield was nearly deserted. I had a heavy pack, a bad case of what was then called Gippy Tummy, and no idea of how to get into town. I began to walk disconsolately toward the airfield gate when a jeep already fully occupied pulled up and the driver, wearing goggles against the dust, asked if I wanted a ride. I gratefully accepted and climbed aboard. We had scarcely started again when the sound of sirens was heard approaching at speed from town. We quickly pulled off the road and were covered with dust by a convoy of motorcycle outriders, an armored car, and two large Cadillacs flying enormous flags. It was Patton.

As we pulled back onto the road, our driver turned to the officer beside him and said, "Reggie, I believe I ought to get a slightly larger flag." I then noticed that at the top of the jeep's radio aerial there flew a small Union Jack, the flag of the commander-in-chief, General Alexander, who was our chauffeur for the evening.

I visited General Ridgeway's headquarters in Mascara, a hot inland town. The American Army seemed incredibly luxurious. Their rations were far more lavish than our endless round of porridge, corned beef, stew, hot sweet tea, strawberry jam, and tinned peaches, but in the long run I found U.S. rations even more monotonous. The U.S. Army took salt tablets in hot climates, something unheard of in the British Army where generation after generation of soldiers had suffered and died from heat prostration and dehydration.

At this time a difference arose between our two armies on the matter of tropical shorts. The British Army in the tropics traditionally dressed in shorts of a comically ambivalent cut. Coming down to the knee, they had the worst qualities of both long and short trousers. I always refused to wear them on the grounds that they were uncomfortable, no protection against mosquitoes, and ridiculous. The belt arrangement alone, three little straps and buckles, was enough to get you killed if in a hurry. In the mid-eighties they briefly became a fashionable item, and I gave mine to my daughter Rachel.

Presumably because these shorts were about the only war supply which Britain then possessed in excess quantities, the British offered to supply them to the U.S. Army recently arrived in North Africa. The British evidently felt that the Americans were new and inexperienced and needed to be shown a thing or two. The Americans were not receptive to this point of view, and many regarded the British as a bunch of stuffy, outmoded, amateur ex-colonialists with a deplorable military record in the war so far. They were quite polite about it, but the offer of shorts was too much.

As soon as our parachute and glider troops had arrived in North Africa, I spent more and more time in Tunisia. The troops were encamped around a series of dusty temporary airstrips in the desert outside Kairouan. Tunis itself had fallen to the Allies earlier in the summer, and relics of the recently defeated Germans were all around—wrecked vehicles, German Army road signs, and a distressing local tendency to greet one with "Heil

Hitler." In one cactus thicket I found a toilet constructed from a bomb casing with the inscription: "Mach Fenster auf, Lass Luft Hinein. Dann wird der Nächste Dankbar sein. (Open the window, let in the air. The next person will be grateful.)"

We had a small planning headquarters in the enchanting seaside village of Sidi bou Said. When there was nothing to do, we went to bathe at Hammamet—then a tiny village with a marvelous beach—or at Sousse or Sfax, or made expeditions to the Roman remains, of which the most striking was the intact Colosseum at El Djem, rising like a great cake out of the flat desert. It was hard to believe that this dusty, gritty, arid land had once been the cornbelt of the Roman Empire.

Our task was to assemble the airborne component of the invasion of Sicily which was to take place early in July. It was obviously going to be a difficult operation, and the air photographs showed a land almost totally unsuited for the landing of parachute and glider-borne troops.

There were more immediate problems. Various forms of dysentery were rampant, and we were all yellow anyway from the anti-malaria specific of the day, Mepocrin. The Tunisians, though friendly, were not much help either. A train, supposedly bringing military supplies from Algiers, had run out of fuel. The crew solved this problem by using successive trucks on the train for firewood, so that when it arrived in Kairouan it consisted of two intact railway trucks and thirty sets of wheels with no superstructure.

One night an enterprising Tunisian shepherd got into the main ammunition dump and twisted the nosecap of a 20mm shell. The resulting explosion detonated the entire dump, and we all lay on our faces until the firework display finally came to an end. As the day of the invasion was near, this was serious, and I was sent to Algiers to see how quickly our losses could be replaced.

The invasion of Sicily took off on schedule, with the Americans taking on the southwestern coast and the British the eastern coast and the ports of Syracuse and Catania. The glider-borne troops were to capture the main bridge and hinterland outside the port of Syracuse where the main British landing was to take place, followed in a day or two by the 1st Parachute Brigade, which was to perform a similar operation outside the port of Catania further up the coast.

The invasion of Sicily provided the opportunity for the first major Allied airborne operation. It was a disaster. The night takeoff, which I witnessed, with loaded gliders from the desert airstrips round Kairouan, was in itself a challenging operation, complicated by darkness, dust, and flying sand, but this was about the only unqualified success. Many of the gliders were cast off too soon and landed in the sea, drowning many soldiers. The landing zones were so rough that the gliders broke up on landing or were widely dispersed. Only eighty men were available to capture the main target, the Ponte Grande, and they ran out of ammunition and lost it again. The brigade ceased to exist as a fighting formation. The operation was not a good advertisement for glider-borne operations.

The ensuing parachute operation to capture the Primosole Bridge at the approaches to Catania did not go smoothly either. Some of the aircraft flew over Allied naval vessels and were shot down by mistake. The drop was at night, and the troops were badly dispersed, less than a third arriving at their planned locations and nearly all the vital equipment missing. Although they fought magnificently, Catania finally fell to the Allies many days after the remnants of the Parachute Brigade had been shipped back to Africa.

Our headquarters took no active part in these doings, and I finally managed to get to Syracuse by sea on a landing craft with Johnny Goschen. We pushed forward as far as possible and found the Eighth Army fighting its way north from Catania. We had no business to be there and soon returned to Bizerta and Tunis.

After the Sicilian operation, there were no more airborne expeditions in prospect in the Mediterranean. In England, however, other and larger plans were being discussed. Getting back to England reasonably quickly presented a problem. Almost all troops going to the Mediterranean in those days went by sea, and aircraft doing the long and hazardous trip were relatively rare except for VIPs. I finally hitched a ride from the Tunis airfield on a Halifax four-engined bomber which was returning to England having landed in North Africa after a raid on southern Germany. We took off confidently enough for Gilbraltar, but something went wrong and we did a forced landing in Fez, Morocco, where we spent an idyllic week at the Palais Jamai, formerly the Vizier's palace, where we were the only guests.

We took off at last in the middle of the night for England, the idea being to cross the danger area of the Bay of Biscay in darkness. It was cold and uncomfortable in the Halifax and our mood was not improved when, as dawn broke, the navigator announced that we were low on fuel. The sea stretched away, sullen and stormy in all directions with no hint of land. Surplus equipment was jettisoned to lighten the load, and we were just preparing to dump our personal gear when a cry of joy went up from the cockpit. Land's End was in sight dead on target. It seemed an eternity before it got near enough to be clearly visible, but at last we landed. The pilot, sweating, pointed to his fuel gauges, all registering empty.

It was a pleasure to be back in England, or indeed back on the ground at all. The moist Atlantic air, the green grass, the drinkable water and untreacherous food all seemed a luxury. We called our headquarters and were angrily informed that we had been given up for lost. A Whitley was sent to collect us, and for once it was a pleasure to travel in that depressing aircraft.

Back at Syrencote House, the invasion of France was already the main preoccupation, and General Browning was determined that airborne forces would play a major role in it. He was agitating for the establishment of an Airborne Corps of two divisions, presumably with himself in command. A similar arrangement on the American side would then make up the First Allied Airborne Army, a grandiose conception that even the Nazis in their heyday had never attempted. Browning was very ambitious for his airborne army and perhaps for himself as well, and he was extremely well connected. He pursued his ideas relentlessly at the top military and political levels, and eventually got what he wanted.

At this time I had begun to have serious doubts about the soundness of what we were trying to do. The experience in Sicily had been discouraging. Airborne troops in battalion or even brigade strength could be very effective for surprise attacks on specific targets. But composed as major formations, divisions, corps, or army, they suffered severe shortcomings. To fly them to their targets took huge numbers of transport aircraft which, except at night, were slow and extremely vulnerable. The range of these aircraft was limited. The troops tended to be dispersed on arrival. Once on the ground a large formation of airborne troops, although of elite quality, was something of a white elephant. It had no heavy weapons, very little transport—and that only jeeps—and no logistical back-up. If in action, it was likely very soon to run out of ammunition. It had to be sustained by air and defended by air until it was relieved by advancing ground troops. An airborne formation could not be maneuvered and fought like an ordinary mobile ground formation. It was essentially light and static.

Enthusiasm and the formidable fighting qualities of the officers and men tended to veil these awkward and unpopular facts. Airborne troops were already legendary fighters and had been christened by the press "The Red Devils" because of their maroon-colored berets. At the outset General Browning had tried for sky blue for the airborne beret, only to find, much to his disgust, that the color had been preempted by the Royal Air Force Regiment which guarded airfields, so we had to settle for maroon. The reputation of the British Parachute Regiment was such that paratroops in armies all over the world subsequently adopted the red beret. Along with the Pegasus badge, also conceived by Browning, and the parachute wings, it was worn with pride and swagger.

Much organizational work was needed to fill in the grandiose design of the Allied Airborne Army. My task was to be prepared at short notice to supply comprehensive intelligence about a wide range of possible targets. The first and main preoccupation was D-Day itself.

In November we sadly left Wiltshire for London to be near the new Headquarters 21 Army Group, Montgomery's headquarters for the Allied invasion. 21 Army Group was forming in the old buildings of St. Paul's School in Hammersmith (now torn down), an unlikely place for a military headquarters planning a secret operation on which hundreds of thousands of lives would depend. Its echoing classrooms could not house most of the staff, and much of the headquarters was accommodated in the rows of little houses surrounding the school. A number of friends were to be found in this warren. Kenneth Younger was in some arcane branch of intelligence, as was Stuart Hampshire. Montgomery's Chief of Intelligence was another young Oxford don, Bill Williams, who later became Warden of Rhodes House. It was more like being in a displaced university than in the army. We lived in requisitioned apartment buildings nearby, and could spend the evenings in London. I spent many of mine with Alfreda Huntington, whom I married the following year.

In the early months of 1944 we had become Headquarters British Airborne Corps which, with the United States Airborne Corps, would make up the First Allied Airborne Army, and we began to put together a headquarters as if we would operate in the field like a normal corps headquarters. This in itself was a dangerous self-deception. As the GSO 2 (Intelligence), I developed a staff of my own. Our work was vital to the planning stage of operations and for assembling all possible information about their mission for the airborne troops.

Alfreda Huntington and I were married in St. Stephen's Chapel, Westminster Abbey, at the end of March 1944. The occasion was notable for the absence of Alfreda's parents, Constant and Gladys Huntington. The Huntingtons were American expatriates of the post-Henry James vintage and had higher expectations for their only daughter. Their opposition was an important factor in Alfreda's determination to marry me, and a considerable insult as far as I was concerned. Alfreda was a member of a group then known as the "Liberal girls." These were for the most part the highly intelligent daughters of the Liberal establishment. Most of them had, in the custom of the English upper middle class, been given no higher education except a sort of Grand Tour in France or Italy. They were original, emancipated, broad-minded, and very good company, but in Alfreda's case the lack of the discipline of higher education was a shocking waste of a lively and original intellect.

After a very brief honeymoon in the Lake District, I returned to Headquarters Airborne Corps, which moved in April to Moor Park, an eighteenth-century house converted into a golf club near Rickmansworth, just outside London. The other units and formations of the First Allied Airborne Army were scattered around the area, the headquarters being in Ascot and the fighting units near airfields in Berkshire and East Anglia.

D-Day was an immensely complex operation requiring huge logistic support, complicated timing, and an armada of different and often exotic vessels. The airborne part of the plan was relatively simple, the Americans landing behind the western beaches at the base of the Cherbourg peninsula and the British 6th Airborne Division securing the eastern flank along the River Orne. Air photographs, constantly updated, were the basis of most operational planning, and I spent much of my time at the Medmenham Photographic Interpretation Centre. We were also concerned to make the Corps Headquarters operational in the conviction that it would take to the field in subsequent operations after D-Day. From the luxury of our billets in Rickmansworth and the spacious halls of Moor Park this was impossible, and I moved our group into tents on the golf course. Even then we had a formidably unmilitary appearance.

In this attempted transformation, my batman/driver, Mike Stannion, played an essential role. Stannion was by trade a poacher and part-time truck driver in Norfolk. He had been with the 1st Parachute Battalion in Sicily, and finding himself badly wounded in the battle for Catania had decided, in the manner of a born countryman, to crawl up the slopes of Mount Etna and find a friendly farm to recover in rather than risk the attentions of the Royal Army Medical Corps. This seemed to me to show both independence and common sense, but when Stannion, fully recovered after an eventful stay at his Sicilian farm during which the farmer had tried to make him marry his daughter, reported back for duty, he was charged with desertion, the most serious possible offense. I heard of his case, and, stripped of his corporal's stripes, he was posted to me as batman. This may have been intended as a punishment, but it didn't work out that way. I found Stannion invaluable in the confused conditions in which we were living and took a great liking to him. He was an open and kindly adventurer, a terrific fixer, and intensely loyal. He stayed with me until the end of the war.

In May the first German V-1 "buzz bombs"—the original Cruise missile—began to fly over London. They were certainly a novelty. Alfreda, who was expecting our first child, was still working at the American Embassy and had taken two floors of a house in Oakley Gardens in Chelsea. I could still occasionally get to London for the night, and it was on such an occasion that the first V-1s arrived, a throbbing sound of a small jet engine getting louder and louder and then a complete and eerie silence as the engine cut out, followed by a tremendous explosion. It was a most unnerving weapon until the anti-aircraft defenses, using proximity fuses, got the measure of it, and the RAF discovered that they could shoot the "buzz bombs" down by diving to get up speed. In the safety of Moor Park I worried about my pregnant wife in the danger zone.

At Moor Park, apart from the preparations for the invasion, we were giving thought to what would happen afterwards. If the initial invasion was successful we would still have the 1st Airborne Division, not to mention the Corps Headquarters, uncommitted and impatient to join in. The troops taking part in the invasion were confined to camp before the actual briefing on the operation began. The security risks were immense, and it was a miracle that the Germans remained uncertain of the actual location of the invasion up to, and even after, D-Day. The whole south of England was packed with troops, vehicles, and supply dumps. The ports were full of landing craft, many of new and strange design, and the vast collection of paraphernalia to build the artificial harbor called "Mulberry" off the invasion beaches. I have always wondered how Eisenhower, Montgomery, and Bradley could have slept at night with their responsibility for this huge and precarious enterprise, vulnerable as it was to weather, breaches of security, untried new equipment, and the possible failure of a vital unit to fulfill an essential task.

As usual, General Browning's headquarters had no operational role except to prepare for someone else's operations and to worry about possible imperfections. We were once again relegated to the role of elderly relatives seeing the young folk off on a great adventure. The general's scarcely concealed frustration certainly stemmed from this condition, and this was to have important consequences later on. I saw our parachutists off at Brize Norton airfield in the Cotswolds late in the evening of June 5 and returned, with a great sense of anticlimax, to Moor Park to await developments. The beachhead was established, in some places with great difficulty and great heroism, and the return to Europe had started. The 6th Airborne Division, in spite of considerable casualties, did well and held the flank.

We were all desperately anxious to get to Normandy as soon as possible to see the battle for ourselves, although we really had no serious business there. I finally managed to get over six days after D-Day on a DC-3 to an airstrip near Lisieux on the American side. From there I made my way across to the 6th Airborne Division, which was being desultorily shelled by the Germans. After three days I was brusquely ordered to return to work at Moor Park.

The work in hand was the preparation of the first of a series of airborne operations that did not take place, and the consideration of various options. One of these was an assault on the V-1/V-2 terror weapon launching sites in the Pas de Calais, which had, even by German standards, exceptionally heavy anti-aircraft defenses. Incessant strafing and bombing had little effect on these immense concrete structures. The V-2 rocket—the original ballistic missile—had now joined the V-1 "buzz bomb" in the attack on London. The V-2 carried a heavier warhead and gave no warning of its approach. The first one knew of it was a tremendous explosion followed by a strange, cosmic, whooshing sound. Many of these rockets, which had hundreds of electrical connections, failed to function due to sabotage by the forced laborers in the under-mountain concentration camp factory at Nordhausen where they were assembled. In the end it was decided that airborne troops would have no chance against the defenses of the launching sites and that the only solution to the V weapons problem was to break out from the beachhead and capture the north coast of France as soon as possible.

The first major airborne plan to be considered seriously after D-Day was a descent by the British Airborne Corps in the plain between Paris and Orléans, misleadingly christened the "Paris–Orléans gap," to disrupt the retreating German Army and to assist the advance of Patton's Third Army. General Patton, who did not like the British anyway, had made his feelings about this operation clear from the start. "If I find any Limeys in the way," he was reported to have said, "I shall shoot them down." We actually got as far as loading up in gliders before this operation was called off because General Patton's troops had got there first.

The breakout from the Normandy bridgehead, which Montgomery had so longed to achieve, was not carried out by the British Army. A hard tank battle with very heavy British and American air support was fought by the British for the town of Caen, where the Germans had concentrated their toughest opposition to the invasion, but the British did not surge forward. With less serious immediate German opposition, Patton's U.S. Third Army did. Flooding out of the Cherbourg peninsula, they became a military and logistical legend, powerfully orchestrated and inspired by their capricious but charismatic leader. It was a splendid performance—a cavalry charge by armor on a vast scale.

The German Army was caught and mangled in the pincer movement of the Argentan–Falaise pocket, the U.S. Army pressed on, and Paris was liberated. The British, battered at Caen, re-formed and advanced less spectacularly. Patton got the headlines. This was to have important psychological repercussions.

After the breakout from the beachhead and the carnage of the Argentan–Falaise pocket, the German Army in northern France collapsed and retired in disorder, and the British 21 Army Group at last surged forward. Brussels fell in August but the port of Antwerp, captured on September 4, was not opened up because its sea approaches remained in German hands, leaving the now enormous Allied military expedition with no major European supply port nearer than Cherbourg. This was an inexplicable strategic failure by Montgomery. Patton was still plowing on in the south and had reached Metz. Otherwise there was, after the capture of Brussels, a general slowing down.

At Moor Park this situation gave rise to all sorts of frenetic planning as we studied various operations to break the logjam. Liège, the River Meuse, and other points were scrutinized to see where the by now impatient British and American airborne divisions, withdrawn and re-formed in England, could be deployed to end the war. Nowhere did the desire for action burn more steadily than in the breast of Boy Browning, who had not yet commanded troops in battle in World War II. Holland was the limit of the range of transport aircraft stationed in Britain. The pressure to get into action intensified.

Elsewhere similar sentiments were taking hold. Montgomery, chagrined by the spectacular successes of Patton, was seeking, contrary to his reputation for caution, a British masterstroke to end the war.

Out of these and other elements the idea of Operation "Market Garden" was born. By mid-August we had researched and planned just about every remotely practicable airborne operation in Northern Europe within the range of our DC-3s. The idea of an operation across the Rhine delta, which consists of three major rivers (Maas, Waal, and Rhine), was therefore in the nature of a desperate last throw. At that time 21 Army Group was stalled on the Albert Canal in Belgium and at the sea approaches to Antwerp. It had failed, like Hitler in 1940, to press on in the moment of victory, and the German Army had rallied in ideal defensive terrain, the canal-intersected Low Countries.

From the first inkling of it, an operation to take the great bridges across the Rhine delta at Arnhem, Nijmegen, and Grave had seemed to me strategically unsound. Patton was going forward in the south against only moderate opposition and would reach the Rhine where it was one river instead of three. His tanks used enormous quantities of fuel which would have to be cut off if another large mobile armored operation were to be undertaken in the north, since Cherbourg could not put through enough gasoline to supply both operations. An advance through Holland would take the Allied armies far north, quite apart from its probable effects on the fate of the Dutch population. The area between the existing British forward positions on the Albert Canal and the bridges was more than 60 miles of flat land intersected by canals and traversed by roads which were essentially causeways—ideal country for holding up an armored or motorized formation. Even supposing the German Army was completely demoralized, it seemed unlikely that they would fail to put up a strong resistance on the borders of the Fatherland.

Apart from strategic considerations, the main question was whether the relieving British ground forces could advance and secure the bridges captured by the airborne forces before the latter were overwhelmed by the German counterattack. Anti-aircraft defenses on the air route into the landing zones were also a serious problem. The airborne troops would have to be supplied and reinforced by air until they were relieved by the ground troops. Surprise and fighter strafing might allow the first waves to get in relatively easily, but after that the anti-aircraft problem would almost certainly become severe.

We concentrated through the last days of August and the first days of September on preparing the best possible plans for "Market Garden." As the days wore on, the operation steadily expanded until two American and one British airborne division were involved. General Browning was to be in command at last, his Corps Headquarters landing by glider outside Nijmegen in the first wave. We were all suitably gratified at this prospect so long deferred.

As I worked day and night on the information available on the topography of the area, the aerial photographs showing German positions and anti-aircraft emplacements, the information coming in from various sources, including the Dutch Resistance, and the mounting evidence that the

German Army routed in Normandy was re-forming itself, I became increasingly anxious.

I was also worried by the state of mind of General Browning and my brother officers. There seemed to be a general assumption that the war was virtually over and that one last dashing stroke would finish it. The possibility of German opposition was scarcely considered worthy of discussion. The "Market Garden" operation was constantly referred to as "the party." It was said that Colonel John Frost, the gallant commander of the 1st Parachute Battalion, was considering taking along his golf clubs and ceremonial mess uniform.

This attitude struck me forcefully on a day when Prince Bernhard of the Netherlands came to Moor Park for a briefing. General Browning described the forthcoming operation as "laying a carpet of airborne troops" over which the Allies would pour into Germany. I muttered to Gordon Walch that I wondered if the carpet would consist of live or dead troops. He was not amused. There seemed to be a feeling that the Dutch population should have a chance to take part in "the party" and should be called out early on to harass the Germans. This seemed to me appallingly irresponsible. Civilians, however brave or well intentioned, are an impossible handicap in military operations, and should the operation fail, they would be beyond help. These views, when I tried to express them, were received in hostile silence. It was very clear to me that I was beginning to be regarded as a spoilsport or worse.

I do not know what the Americans thought of the plan, although I suspect that Generals Ridgeway and Gavin were less than enthusiastic, but on the British side I found few people to whom I could talk rationally. One was Brigadier John (Shan) Hackett, the commander of the 16th Para Brigade. Shan was a much-decorated officer with a keen mind and an extraordinary fighting record in the Middle East and North Africa, but as the commander of 3,000 men whom he was about to lead into battle, it was obviously impossible for him to express doubts about the wisdom of the plan.

I was increasingly unable to hide my own feelings and became obsessed with the fate of "Market Garden." I was desperately anxious to go on the operation, but I was even more anxious for it to be reconsidered carefully.

I had to drive by jeep incessantly between Moor Park, Allied Airborne Army Headquarters at Ascot, Medmenham Air Photo Centre, and the 1st Airborne Division, collecting, analyzing, and disseminating the latest intelligence. On these long drives I agonized over the situation, sometimes wishing the jeep would crash and take me out of it all. My short nights were sleepless.

On about September 10, after the date of "Market Garden" had been set for September 17 and Browning had been appointed the overall commander, I noticed a more or less casual remark in a 21 Army Group Intelligence Summary that elements of the Second SS Panzer Corps, the 9th (Hohenstaufen) and 10th (Frundsberg) SS Panzer divisions, were reported to be refitting in the Arnhem area. This was confirmed by the Dutch Resistance. This was appalling news. Even if these formidable fighting units had been badly mauled in Normandy and were short of armored vehicles, they were a deadly threat to lightly armed airborne troops landing in their vicinity.

When I informed General Browning and Colonel Walch of this development, they seemed little concerned and became quite annoyed when I insisted on the danger. They said, as I remember, that I should not worry unduly, that the reports were probably wrong, and that in any case the German troops were refitting and not up to much fighting. This reaction confirmed my worst suspicions about the attitude of Browning and his staff, and I concluded that Browning's ambition to command in battle was a major factor both in the conception of "Market Garden" and in his refusal to take the latest news on German opposition seriously.

In this I did Browning a grave injustice. I did not fully realize until more than thirty years later, when Cornelius Ryan published his masterly account of the Arnhem battle, A Bridge Too Far, that "Market Garden" was the offspring of the ambition of Montgomery, who desperately wanted a British success to end the war. In fact Browning himself, in expressing his doubts about the wisdom and scope of the operation, had used the phrase which Ryan took as the title of his book.

It seemed to me essential to try to convince Browning of the appalling risk to which he was subjecting the 1st Airborne Division. The risk that the relieving ground troops would not arrive in time was bad enough for the whole operation, but 1st Airborne Division was dropping north of the northernmost of the three great bridges and would have to hang on the longest. For all the courage, fighting skill, and spirit of its officers and men, how could it hope to do this in the presence of two of the best armored divisions of the German Army?

To convince Browning of the danger, I decided to try to get actual pictures of the German armor near the 1st Airborne Division's dropping zone, and asked for oblique photographs to be taken of the area at a low altitude by the acknowledged experts in this art, an RAF Spitfire Squadron stationed at Benson in Oxfordshire. Oblique photographs taken at low altitude were as good as, or better than, pictures taken on the ground, and any danger of security leaks could be handled by including the photographic aircraft in one of the myriad Allied fighter-bomber strikes which swarmed across Holland to the Ruhr each day.

The pictures when they arrived confirmed my worst fears. There were German tanks and armored vehicles parked under the trees within easy range of the 1st Airborne Division's main dropping zone. I rushed to General Browning with this new evidence, only to be treated once again as a nervous child suffering from a nightmare. Even in my overwrought state I got the message very clearly. I was a pain in the neck, and only our long association and his natural kindness prevented the general from saying so.

Later in the day Colonel Eggar, our chief doctor, came to visit me. He informed me that I was suffering from acute nervous strain and exhaustion and ordered me to go on sick leave. When I asked him what would happen if I refused, he said, in his kindly way, that I would be arrested and court-martialed for disobeying orders. I begged him to let me go on the operation in any capacity. He refused. I tried to explain the cause of my anxiety and asked if there was no way of stopping, or at least reshaping, the operation. He again said no, but I had the feeling he understood me better than discipline allowed him to say.

Thus at 5:00 p.m. on September 15, two days before Operation "Market Garden," I handed over to my deputy, David Ballingall, and drove down to Amberley in Sussex where Alfreda, expecting our first child, was now living. She was surprised to see me and even more surprised at my gaunt and haunted appearance. Since I could not, for security reasons, explain what had happened, she very sensibly set about trying to cheer me up. Nonetheless it was a desolate and miserable time.

This interlude did not last long. On Sunday, September 17, the air armada carrying Operation "Market Garden" aroused southeast England from its weekend torpor, and the landing was triumphantly announced the same day. On Monday the newspapers trumpeted success—"Operation Goes Off Without a Hitch" (*Daily Herald*). On Tuesday the communiqués remained optimistic but had become muted. On Wednesday it was clear that something was seriously wrong, and at the end of the week I was called by the War Office and told to report at once to Northolt airfield outside London where arrangements would be made for me to rejoin Headquarters Airborne Corps in Nijmegen, Holland. I was unworthily relieved at this order. It had been unbearable to have nothing to do as the news got worse, and I left Amberley within the hour.

From Northolt, Stannion and I flew to Brussels where we stayed the night. There were alarming stories about the plight of the 1st Airborne Division. The southernmost bridge over the Maas at Grave had been captured early on in the operation by the Americans, but the Nijmegen bridge over the Waal had only just been captured by the American 82nd Airborne Division in an incredible assault river crossing, and the congested road to the "Market Garden" area from the south was constantly being cut by the Germans, impeding the advance of the relieving armored force upon which everything depended. Ryan has given a meticulous account of all this.

My own problem was to get to Nijmegen and rejoin Browning's headquarters as ordered. I finally found a friendly artillery spotter who was prepared to fly me there, and this, at treetop height, he did, Stannion following on later by jeep.

I do not know why I was ordered to return at this juncture and can only assume that in the debacle that Operation "Market Garden" had become, it looked odd for the Airborne Corps Chief Intelligence Officer to be absent on sick leave. I was greeted warmly by Browning and my old friends, but I could not help noticing that talk about the current military situation was kept to a minimum. The atmosphere was very different from the triumphant and confident tone of the previous weeks.

The situation was indeed abysmal. After the 82nd Airborne Division's heroic capture of the Nijmegen bridge, the Guards Armored Division's tanks were soon stopped again on the other side several miles from Arnhem. The beleaguered 1st Airborne Division had held the Arnhem bridge against enormous odds for five excruciating days, but when it became clear that they were not going to be relieved, what was left of the division was ordered to get out across the river by night, leaving the wounded behind. Out of 10,005 men, only 2,163 were evacuated in this way; 1,200 men were dead and 6,642 were missing, wounded, or captured, among them Shan Hackett who, badly wounded, was hidden by the Dutch and escaped months later, as did many others.

The operation which was to end the war in Western Europe had been an unmitigated disaster, almost certainly destroying all possibility of an early victory. It had diverted essential support from Patton when he was forging ahead, given the Germans a success on the eve of their total defeat, made a nightmare of the last months of war for the Dutch, and landed the British Army in a riverine swamp for the winter. The casualties, both military and civilian, were appalling—more than 17,000 Allied soldiers killed, wounded, or missing in nine days of fighting, no possible reckoning of civilian casualties, and all for nothing or worse than nothing. Much of the town of Arnhem was destroyed, and after the battle the Germans forcibly evacuated the entire population for the remainder of the war. Small wonder that Prince Bernhard later remarked, "My country can never again afford the luxury of another Montgomery success." A number of my friends were killed, notably Dicky des Voeux with whom I had started in the airborne business, and many were missing.

Airborne Corps Headquarters had virtually nothing to do in Nijmegen. We lived on the outskirts of the town in a villa which was periodically shelled by German 88mm guns and tried to keep ourselves busy, but nobody's heart was in it. From Nijmegen we could, on a clear day, see the German V-2 rockets taking off for London and Antwerp from the Hague, and this increased our sense of impotence and frustration.

My own situation had become an embarrassment to me and to everyone else. After ten days, I suggested to Browning that I be posted out of the Airborne Corps as soon as possible. He said that he regretted my desire to leave but fully understood it. He thanked me for my years with him, regretted our recent disagreements, and undertook to have me posted immediately. As usual he was as good as his word. In a letter he wrote to me on my departure Browning repeated all this, adding that it might be as well if our disagreements remained a private matter between us.

I heartily agreed with him. I was sickened by the disaster, the loss of so many good men, the idiocy of the enterprise, and my own complete failure to do anything about it. The last thing I wanted was to talk or write about it. The men of the 1st Airborne Division, as is the British custom in military disasters, had become heroes in a great cause. This at least was some consolation for the bereaved families—a small solace which I had no wish to spoil.

It was, of course, inconceivable that the opinion of one person, a young and inexperienced officer at that, could change a vast military plan approved by the President of the United States, the Prime Minister of Britain, and all the military top brass, but it seemed to me that I could have gone about it more effectively. I believed then, as most conceited young people do, that a strong rational argument will carry the day if sufficiently well supported by substantiated facts. This, of course, is nonsense. Once a group of people have made up their minds on something, it develops a life and momentum of its own which is almost impervious to reason or argument. This is particularly true when personal ambition and bravado are involved. In this case even an appeal to fear of ridicule and historical condemnation would not have worked. The decision had been taken at the highest level, and a vast military machine had been set in motion. The opinions of a young intelligence officer were not going to stop it.

There is nothing like proving to be right for making a person unpopular. With the exception of Shan Hackett, I saw virtually none of my airborne colleagues again for forty years until the fortieth anniversary ceremonies at Arnhem. By that time, after all the books and movies, everyone was older and wiser, and I was glad to see my surviving friends again. John Frost, the hero of the Bridge, told me he had never been given the information about the Germans which I had provided. He observed that General Browning should have stayed in England backstopping the operation, rather than masquerading as the Airborne Corps Commander in Nijmegen where he was cut off and could do nothing to influence the battle.

The failure of "Market Garden" was underplayed in the media. A halfhearted attempt was later made to attribute it to betrayal by a Dutch double agent called King Kong. This was self-serving nonsense. The Germans were in church or relaxing when the first landing took place and simply couldn't believe it was happening. The fact was that an unrealistic, foolish plan had been dictated by motives which should have played no part in a military operation that put so many lives and the early ending of the war at risk. All I wanted to do was to shut it out of my mind.

The Arnhem tragedy had a deep and permanent effect on my attitude to life. Before it I had been trusting and relatively optimistic, with a self-confidence that was sometimes excessive. After it I doubted everything, tended to distrust my own as well as other people's judgment, and became deeply skeptical about the behavior of leaders. I never again could quite be convinced that great enterprises would go as planned or turn out well, or that wisdom and principle were a match for vanity and ambition.

VI

War's End

SOON AFTER MY LAST talk with General Browning, I received orders to report to the G (CW) (Chemical Warfare) branch of 21 Army Group Headquarters, then located in a vast apartment complex on the Avenue Louise in Brussels. This appeared to be a backwater of backwaters, chemical warfare having long since been disregarded as a practical weapon. Nonetheless I reported to the brigadier in charge immediately, grateful to get away from the stultifying atmosphere of Airborne Corps Headquarters.

The brigadier was a birdlike, exceedingly diffident man who treated me with embarrassing deference as one who had been through hell in battle, knew what war was like, and so on. This was, of course, nonsense, but he was so sincere about it that I did not like to disillusion him. It then transpired that he had recently been given a new task for which his own deskbound staff were unsuited. This was to set up a group called "T" Force.

"T" Force was to proceed with the advance units of the Allied sweep into Germany to secure strategic intelligence targets. These included industrial plants, laboratories, caches of documents, certain headquarters and, if possible, eminent German scientists. The innocent assumption of the War Office was apparently that such persons would make all possible efforts to escape from the Allies and go East to join their comrades in the Axis, the Japanese, in order to continue the struggle. I doubt if the British authorities really believed this. The sole desire of the distinguished Germans I met later was to go West, preferably to California, as soon as possible. A more cynical interpretation of our task was that Britain was anxious to get hold of as many German industrial and technological secrets as possible for its own future benefit.

It crossed my mind from time to time that "T" Force was an elaborate hoax set up to mask some other purpose. This was partly true of a parallel American group, the United States Strategic Bombing Survey (SBS), a lavishly established organization with which we cooperated. The SBS, ostensibly studying damage caused by strategic bombing, was particularly preoccupied with finding what the Germans had done in the nuclear field.

In Brussels we made detailed preparations for the day of the Allied advance. We compiled intelligence target dossiers, studied photographs, and contacted all the various formations with which we had to work. Even so, our time was scarcely filled.

There was plenty to do outside. I had many friends in the Army and Air Force. Philip Toynbee was then masquerading as a Field Security Officer, looking even less military in uniform than he did in civilian clothes. John Bury, from Westminster, was on the intelligence staff, and Michael Judd, a Greek scholar from Wadham College, Oxford, turned up as a much-decorated wing commander in command of a Typhoon fighter-bomber wing.

I became friends with an exiled Spanish Republican minister, Juan Ortega, who lived with his Belgian wife, Denise, and family at 10, Rue des Drapiers, and we spent most of our evenings with the Ortegas and their demi-mondaine Belgian friends. They were the constant victims of misunderstandings. Juan was wrongly arrested at various times as a diamond smuggler, a collaborator, and a black marketeer. We always managed to get him out and I am sure that none of the charges were true. Food and drink were short in Brussels, and our contributions were gratefully received.

Stannion was greatly admired by Philip Toynbee and John Bury as a sort of noble savage. My airborne jeep, so that it could be more easily loaded into aircraft, had a detachable steering wheel. This was a godsend in Brussels where the rate of vehicle theft was high. The picture of Brussels that stays in my mind is of Philip, John, Stannion, me, and the steering wheel drinking Gueuze (Belgian sour beer) in small bars late at night, while Philip got steadily drunker and Stannion told us about his new friend, "the Countess," who seemed to have strange and exigent tastes.

I remember Christmas 1944 for two reasons. One was the Ardennes offensive. This final spasm of Hitler's war effort did not affect us too much in Brussels, although it was surprising to look out of the window and see a squadron of German fighters coming in at rooftop height. We were sent

in jeeps to patrol the outskirts of Brussels for the German paratroops who
were reputed to be on their way to assassinate Eisenhower and Montgomery. They were supposed to be wearing American uniforms, and we
were to unmask them by asking arcane questions about baseball. It was
bitterly cold and snowy, and we didn't find much of interest.

The other event that Christmas was the birth, on December 22, of
our son Thomas. I had made elaborate plans to get news of this event
through Norman Field, a friend at my old headquarters which was now
back in England. The codeword was—God knows why—"Mauser" for a
boy and "Ratter" for a girl. Norman's Telex message read: "Mauser dropped
safely at 0425 hours on 22 December. All parties well." This was inter-
cepted by the Intelligence Branch, and I had some difficulty in explaining
the prosaic truth. In January I managed to get home for a few days to
see Alfreda and Thomas in Amberley.

In February, the Army began to move again. I had got the brigadier
to agree that I could run "T" Force operations from the field. I had at
my disposal a battalion of the King's Regiment, four Pioneer Smoke Companies, and a Bomb Disposal Company. These units were supposed to
secure and guard our targets. We also had a group of technical experts
in Brussels whom we could call forward as necessary. Stannion and I
moved by jeep.

After the massive airborne crossing of the Rhine in March, we crossed
the border into Germany. This was the country that for nearly five years
had seemed invincible. Now it was a place of ruins and ghosts and pa-
thetically ingratiating people. The destruction in the Ruhr was tremendous, and we mostly camped out. It was like a macabre holiday.

As we moved steadily east with the advancing 21 Army Group, the
stench of defeat lay heavy over the towns and countryside. We had a
number of targets in and around Hanover, including the Hermann Goer-
ing Aeronautical Research Institute—a place where all sorts of ideas,
some crazy and some visionary, had been pursued by the increasingly
cranky scientists favored by the Nazis. There was a project, for example,
to produce space mirrors which were supposed to deflect and concentrate
the sun's rays on England, thereby scorching it up.

Hanover was very badly damaged, but the municipal cellar, well underground, had been intact until Russian forced laborers got into it. They
had turned the vaults into a scene out of Hogarth or Hieronymus Bosch.
Hundreds of Russians had smashed vat after vat of wine and spirits so
that the floor was six inches deep in mixed alcohol. Kneeling down to
drink this powerful draft, the Russians soon began to collapse into it, and

many drowned before the military police closed the entrance and evac-uated those inside. Forced laborers were everywhere in town and country, wandering aimlessly in search of a way home.

Looting had been strictly forbidden in France and Belgium, but in Germany it was covered by euphemisms such as "liberating" or "phasing out." My only real coup in "T" Force was due directly to Stannion's insatiable appetite for loot. We had reached a small town called Celle late one afternoon and, since our radio was not functioning well, I was not sure where we were in relation to the advancing Allied troops. I therefore decided to spend the night in the town, which seemed quiet enough. Stannion returned from taking a look round with his eyes glowing with excitement. There was, it seemed, a silk factory a block away full of real and artificial silk ready to be "liberated."

I was impressed, from the outside, by the size of the silk factory, but when we got inside and were greeted by an extremely nervous German manager, the place seemed rather small. I was not particularly interested in silk, but told the manager to show us round. The tour did not take long and stopped at a large steel door which I told him to open. He refused, saying he was not authorized to do so, and became so agitated that I began to wonder what German forces were still in Celle.

Stannion, a born romantic, suggested we should shoot the lock out, a movie procedure that I had always had doubts about. It seemed as good a time as any to try it, so I fired my pistol at the lock. The door was instantly opened from within by a distinguished-looking man in a white coat who asked in perfect English what he could do for us. I explained that we were interested in what was going on in the factory, and he ushered us into what seemed to be a very sophisticated laboratory. The manager disappeared.

When I asked the purpose of the laboratory, the scientist, Doktor Professor Groth, took me aside and said he could only tell me if he could leave the place with me and stay under my protection until the Allied troops took him over. I had already learned that he had spent some years in California—at Berkeley, I think—which accounted for his perfect En-glish. I readily agreed to his request, whereupon he informed me that the purpose of the laboratory was "to isolate isotopes of uranium."

A few months later this news would have electrified me, but this was before the Hiroshima bomb. The word "uranium" did ring a distant bell, for I remembered a novel by Harold Nicolson called *Public Faces* pub-lished in 1933, which had revolved around the invention of a uranium bomb so powerful as to revolutionize international relations. I thought about this as we escorted Professor Groth back to our little encampment, which evidently disconcerted him by its smallness and vulnerability.

When I told the Intelligence Branch at 21 Army Group Headquarters on the radio about "isolating isotopes of uranium" there was a long silence after which a new voice peremptorily ordered me to stay where I was and keep everyone and everything under guard until further notice.

We spent a rather uneasy night in Celle. I was aware that we had stumbled on something much more interesting than our usual industrial plants or caches of documents and I was uncertain exactly who was in control of Celle. The following morning some British armored cars showed up and headed for the small airfield, at which several DC-3s then landed. The passengers were dressed as captains, majors, and colonels in the U.S. Army, but the newness of their uniforms and the self-conscious way they wore their military caps labelled them beyond doubt as civilians.

I was anxious to do the honors and make the introductions. I need not have bothered. The visitors fell on Dr. Professor Groth like a long-lost brother, and soon they were happily dismantling and crating the laboratory. My questions were turned aside with patently false answers. I was somewhat irritated. After all, we had found the isotope laboratory —admittedly for the wrong reasons. The experts hadn't even known it was there.

With the frustrating feeling of having taken part in an important event without really knowing what it was, we packed up and got on the road again. Our next stop was an even greater, and far more unpleasant, surprise.

In the general excitement over the isotope affair, I had missed an order over the radio to all British troops in our area not to advance until further notice. The reason for this order was the Bergen-Belsen concentration camp, which presented immense humanitarian and medical problems, and had to be taken over systematically.

In 1945, little was generally known in the Army about concentration camps or even about the Nazi policy of exterminating the Jews and some other ethnic groups. We were thus almost totally unprepared for the horrors that we saw in Germany. I had been aware of Nazi anti-Semitism because my aunts, from the earliest days of Hitler, had taken in German Jewish girls at Badminton School, and I had had several Jewish refugee friends at Oxford. Even so, the "final solution," the actual extermination of millions of people, was simply unimaginable. We were completely unprepared for Belsen.

My first intimation of the Bergen-Belsen concentration camp was a high barbed-wire fence along the road with what from a distance appeared to be logs stacked inside it. On a closer view the logs turned out to be neatly stacked corpses. We soon arrived at the main gate of the camp where the prospect was indescribable, a desolate litter of human beings, mostly dehumanized to a point just short of death. Many were in fact dying, and there were corpses as far as the eye could see.

I was at a loss as to what to do. There were about twenty of us in four vehicles. The camp was obviously vast and contained some thousands of people in critical condition. We had no facilities at all to deal with such a situation, even supposing we had known what to do.

Our arrival had caused the nearest thing to excitement possible for people so totally debilitated, and a strange and fantastic crowd began to assemble. It was the first warm day of spring and some of the walking skeletons were naked, but most wore the striped pyjamas which were the uniform of the concentration camp. I went inside the gates with Stannion, but left everyone else outside to avoid arousing false hopes. Most of the crowd seemed beyond articulate speech, even supposing we had found a common language. There was, however, a group of doctors and nurses from Vienna who were in better psychological shape, and from them I learned a little of the situation.

The Bergen-Belsen camp was built quite late in the war and had grown and got steadily out of hand as the end of the war approached and conditions inside Germany became more chaotic. My camp informants, when I inquired where the staff and guards were, indicated that they had not been inside the camp for some days, although guards could still be seen in the watch towers around the perimeter—low-grade Hungarian troops sunk in apathy and hopelessness.

The distribution of food and water in the camp had long since broken down, and cholera, typhus, smallpox, and dysentery had added additional suffering. The heroic Vienna doctors had established a small compound for the camp children and had sidetracked as much food and water as they could for them. These children alone had a remotely normal physical appearance, although one side of their playground was the wall of corpses I had seen from the road.

The huts of Belsen, designed to hold only thirty or forty people, gave a horrible meaning to the word "concentration." In many huts there were a hundred or more, several to a bunk, the dead, the moribund, and the living mixed up together. The daily mortality rate from starvation, disease, and dehydration was in the hundreds. One thing struck me forcibly. The dead on a battlefield fill the air with the sickly, clinging, sweet-sour smell of death and putrefaction. In Belsen, with its thousands of corpses, there was no such smell. The dead were literally skin and bone.

Belsen was so overwhelmingly monstrous that it was hard to feel any of the normal emotions of horror or distaste—only a consuming rage at this vast spectacle of deliberate human degradation. I learned over the radio that massive convoys of ambulances and doctors were being organized and that a team from British Second Army was on its way to take over the camp. Down the road outside the main gate was the SS barracks, where many of the SS guards, as well as the commandant, Krämer, who was subsequently christened the "Beast of Belsen," were still residing. Any normal person would have put as much distance as possible between himself and the scene of so monstrous a crime, and one can only assume that in their bestial way they had believed in what they were doing.

This was certainly borne out by the conduct of Oberstürmbannführer Krämer, who stated that under the Rules of War he could not surrender to a junior officer. Stannion volunteered to shoot him on the spot as we had too few men for guard duty, but in the end he was locked up in a roomy refrigerated meat locker at the barracks. The electricity in the area had been off for some time.

We then ordered the SS guards, including some women, into the camp to start digging mass graves. It was a futile gesture, but it seemed to have some symbolic point. (There is a picture at Yad Vashem, the monument to the Holocaust in Jerusalem, of these SS women so employed.) The inmates seemed oblivious to their former guards in their new capacity as gravediggers.

Next day the first official visitors began to arrive, including General Brian Horrocks, commander of the British 30th Corps. When he asked for the SS commandant, someone went to fetch Krämer from the meat locker. Inexplicably, the electricity had gone on during the night, and Krämer was chilled and extremely surly. He conducted the general round the camp in a jeep almost with pride, pointing out with Teutonic meticulousness its salient features. After that he was immediately and permanently confined.

I should not have been at Belsen in the first place, and now that the specially organized convoys were arriving there was nothing I could do anyway. As we were leaving the area, a German farmer and his family stood across the road to stop our little convoy. The farmer indignantly explained that the "barbarians" (Russian forced laborers) were looting his property and demanded the protection of the British Army and the punishment of the "barbarians." I asked him if he had noticed the Belsen camp up the road. He said he had not. I told him it was high time he found out about it, and we took him to the main gate of Belsen to join the gravedigging squad.

The Belsen experience had a stunning effect on all of us. British soldiers are by nature kindly, even about their enemies, and at this late stage of the war the Germans were still "old Jerry" to them. After Belsen, the men never used that phrase again and treated the Germans they met with disgust and contempt.

General Patton marched units of the U.S. Third Army through the Nordhausen concentration camp to show them what they had been fighting against. In its own way Nordhausen, which I visited a few days later, was even more grotesque than Belsen. The V-2 rocket and the ME-163 rocket engine were both assembled at Nordhausen in two parallel tunnels running right through the mountain and connected by bays full of machinery. The tunnels ran through limestone with very little ventilation or safety devices of any kind. From the camp on the mountain above, the workers descended to the hell below in cagelike elevators. They worked twelve hours a day seven days a week, until they collapsed from exhaustion or lung disease, when they were put out to die in a special part of the camp. In spite of these conditions, they found the will and the way to sabotage a large number of the V-2s. I found this more moving than any feat of courage on the battlefield.

Montgomery's forward HQ was located in tents and caravans of all sizes in the middle of a sandy heath. I was called in to report on our recent activities and was driving away when the military police suddenly ordered everyone off the road to make way for two battered German Army Mercedes staff cars. They contained the German generals coming to negotiate the surrender on the Western Front with Montgomery.

I returned as fast as I could to the little town outside Hamburg where we had stopped, and arrived just in time to hear the official announcement. We gathered in a courtyard at the back of a farmhouse to hear over the radio Montgomery's message to the Army, and then uncorked whatever we could lay hands on to celebrate. Stannion found some Nazi flags which he laid down as a carpet along the main street of the little town.

It is difficult to reconstruct what I actually felt at the time on such an overwhelming occasion. Nearly six years from despair to victory, many friends gone, fantastic waste and destruction, many things seen and experienced, much learned and much already forgotten. I remember thinking particularly of my Oxford friends, Michael Brodrick and Merlin Montagu Douglas Scott, who were killed in the desert early in the war, of Dickie des Voeux dead at Arnhem, and my fellow officer-cadet Andy Whately Smith, now missing with the French Resistance in the Vosges. I wondered about all those nameless faces in war photographs, refugees, prisoners, civilians under bombing, Russians in the snow and wreckage of their country, crewmen on sinking freighters—how many of them would their families see again? I tried to imagine what my wife and my mother would be thinking at that moment and how my brother Andrew was faring in Burma.

I did not meditate that things would never be the same. I hadn't had too much experience of the old order and did not feel I would really miss it. I *did* think that the greatest task at hand would be to help prevent such disasters from ever happening again.

We did not have much time for ruminating on the meaning of victory, for we were ordered to press on as quickly as possible to Lübeck and Kiel before the Soviet investigating teams could get there. Lübeck, a beautiful Hanseatic city, had been little damaged. As we were entering the city, our way was blocked by a resplendent German convoy coming in the other direction—twenty-six vehicles of the 1937 vintage, shining, immaculate, and bearing no scars of war.

I was tired and in a hurry and told the driver of the first vehicle to have the convoy pulled off the road. He said politely enough that this was impossible since the convoy had the highest priority. I told him to send for his commanding officer, and soon, mincing down the road in field boots and rows of decorations, came a German colonel out of a 1930s movie.

This apparition explained the high priority of his mission. For many years his unit had been the mobile back-up radio station for the Oberkommando der Wehrmacht, and now he was speeding to the assistance of Gross-Admiral Doenitz, who had succeeded Hitler but had no communications. The call had come at last. I pointed out that he was going in the wrong direction—Doenitz was to the north in Flensburg—and that there was really no great rush as Germany had just surrendered. He seemed downcast by this news. I asked him about his unit. It had been built, he said with pride, for "our little experiment in Spain. . . ." All my undergraduate feelings flooded back, and I told this elderly clown to pull his circus off the road at once. He seemed puzzled at my change of mood. I reported:

In Lübeck, the most important target was the great DWM works, the investigation of which by Ordnance experts still continues, and the most remarkable "Opportunity" target was a mobile transmitting station comprising 26 gigantic vehicles and worth several million pounds, whose director sought "T" Force protection on the grounds that his equipment was about to be looted by the demoralised German Army. He had, he said, been standing by for an emergency since the Spanish Civil War, in which his station had been tested, and evidently felt that he had missed his cue.

Kiel was near Admiral Doenitz's headquarters at Flensburg, now the seat of the German government, and the natives were not at all friendly. An American team had arrived there much better briefed than we were but with no military protection. My two companies of soldiers were better than nothing, and together we approached the naval research station where, we had been told, a revolutionary jet-propelled submarine was being constructed. This was presumably what we were supposed to reach before the Russians. The German guards did not seem to have heard about the surrender. Once that was settled I left the American experts and 30 Assault Unit, a British naval intelligence commando run by Major Tony Hibbert, to get on with it, whatever it was. On the way back through the dockyard, as I passed the German cruiser *Hipper* at anchor, a harassed German naval officer appeared in order to surrender the ship. I explained that this was quite unnecessary but as he insisted, proffering a receipt pad with duplicate carbon copies, I signed for the cruiser anyway.

My report on this recaptures some of the feeling of the time:

When "T" Force arrived in Kiel, the situation was somewhat Gilbertian. The garrison consisted of some 12,000 fully armed Germans, one cruiser in dry dock and one upside down in the harbour, and a number of U-Boats and smaller craft, and some 40,000 extremely rampageous displaced persons.

The German Naval Commander was at first inclined to be sceptical as to the opinion of the "T" Force Commander, backed by 200 men, that the German nation had surrendered, but a brisk telephone conversation with Admiral Doenitz, then at Flensburg, confirmed this opinion and both sides then set about producing an orderly situation in the port which was almost completely shattered by Allied bombing. The entire functions of garrisoning and military government devolved on these two coys [companies] until other troops arrived on 8 May. Many of these functions were then taken over and an Army Form B108 was received for the cruiser "Hipper."

The most valuable target in Kiel was the Waltherwerke, complete with Herr Walther. Although this character had been engaged in burning his documents for the past four days and had completed this task on the afternoon before the arrival of the troops, it subsequently transpired, when Herr Walther was convinced the Nazi Party was a thing of the past, that he had taken the precaution of micro-filming the most important documents, and that the prototype of his most important production, a jet-propelled submarine capable of 25 knots under water, was still intact in the works. This was taken care of by 30 AU.

There was really very little to do in Kiel for someone unacquainted with naval affairs, so I asked permission to move on to Denmark. This was slow in arriving, but in two days I was told to go ahead. I harbored romantic ideas of helping the Danish Resistance to finish the struggle. A parachute battalion had already been flown into Copenhagen.

Any notion that the Danes needed help was soon dispelled. Although we got a completely unjustified heroes' welcome everywhere, it was clear that the Danes had dealt with the Germans themselves and were now single-mindedly bent on celebrating. This they did twenty-four hours a day with relentless fervor, and the arrival of a small group of British soldiers provided the perfect excuse for another celebration. Thus we proceeded from village to village and farm to farm in the perfect spring weather in a haze of Alborg Akvavit and pickled herring, made much of, embraced by delightful girls, and invited to sing and dance all night by fathers of families. It was extraordinarily difficult to move on with the requisite speed.

We had arranged to meet a senior officer of the Danish Resistance, Dr. Halfdan Lefèvre, at dawn at Kørsø on the last part of the journey to Copenhagen. Dr. Lefèvre certainly looked the part, dressed in field boots, a short military coat, and fur cap, and he made it clear that there wasn't much left for us to do. The Resistance had dealt with the Germans, and they were now engaged in dealing with Danes suspected of collaboration.

I had a list of Danes whose friends in England had lost touch with them and wanted news. When I showed this list to Dr. Lefèvre, I realized that we were on very delicate ground. As he perused the list, his face would darken and then, moving on, he would make an exclamation of approval. At the top of the list was Karen Blixen, author (as Isak Dinesen) of several books, including *Out of Africa*, which my father-in-law, Constant Huntington, had published. Dr. Lefèvre was horrified and said she was a collaborator. I said that I was convinced there was a misunderstanding. Karen Blixen was a singular and courageous woman. Her brother had been the only foreigner to win the Victoria Cross in World War I.

She was an old friend of my parents-in-law. She was a remarkable writer. Dr. Lefèvre, unconvinced, strongly advised against my visiting her. I replied that I would do so anyway.

By the time I got to Copenhagen and had seen a little of what the Danes were doing to each other, I decided that I should visit Karen Blixen right away. She lived in an old white wooden house called Rungstedlund, overlooking the Sound and across to Sweden. Stannion and I got very dirty looks when we asked the local Danes for directions, but they evidently did not wish to interfere with a British officer, and we finally drove up to the house. There was no sign of life at all. I knocked on the front door, making reassuring British sounds. Still no sign of life. We opened the door and walked through to the kitchen overlooking a lawn ringed with evergreens. There was a steaming cup of tea on the table. We went out to the lawn at the back, making further encouraging British noises. Suddenly I heard Stannion give an awestruck "Cor!", and from the evergreens stepped a figure in a black hood and cape.

Baroness Blixen behaved as if she had just been picking mushrooms in the shrubbery, but in fact she had been hiding on the offchance that we were emissaries of the Resistance coming to get her. She was overjoyed when I explained who I was, and told us of her tribulations, which stemmed apparently from a lecture she had given in Berlin early in the war and from a misunderstanding of her latest book *The Angelic Avengers*, which was, she said, an allegory of the German Occupation. Though having great doubts about her wisdom in having gone to Berlin, I promised to do what I could to clear things up.

When we made ready to leave, Karen Blixen announced that she must go with us. I wasn't too happy about this. There was a strict order against taking women in military vehicles, but I was mostly worried, unworthily, about what the Resistance might do. They had administered summary justice on lesser Danes. However, there was nothing for it but to agree, and with Stannion in the back, Sten gun at the ready, and the baroness in the front looking seigneurial, we swept into Copenhagen. We got some more dirty looks but nothing worse. That evening Karen Blixen went on Danish radio to explain all to the Danish people. In doing this she played heavily on her rescue, on higher orders, by a young British parachute officer.

I saw her again years later in New York at the height of her fame and reminded her of this episode, but she couldn't seem to recall it.

Another name on my list was Countess Moltke, a formidable American lady who was a friend of my mother-in-law, Gladys Huntington. She was definitely a "good Dane," in strong contrast to the several "bad Danes" on my list, and seemed to have survived very well. She too had a problem. She had buried some important and secret archives in her garden in 1940, but could not remember exactly where. Stannion and I spent a hot and sweaty afternoon under her direction, fruitlessly digging trenches across the lawn and removing a rock garden. I do not know if the archives were ever found.

It was time to return to Germany to see what postwar duties would be allotted to us. We were soon assigned to a small town called Goslar in the Harz Mountains. This was agreeable enough, and, like many of our missions, was based on a fantasy. It was believed that diehard SS troops were gathering in the Harz Mountains in an organization called the Werewolves to conduct guerrilla warfare against the Allies and keep the Nazi flag flying. We were supposed to deal with this menace. We never saw any evidence whatsoever of this organization, and as far as I know it didn't exist. We were billeted in a delightful hotel in the hills above Goslar and enjoyed a spring holiday doing very little.

I had found out that, due to my long service but young age, I could not be sent to the Asian theater of war but also had little chance of being demobilized for some years. I was therefore doomed to an indefinite spell in the occupation of Germany, an appalling thought after six years in the Army. I wrote to Alfreda and asked her to find out if there was any way I could get out of the Army and at last become a civilian.

My letter arrived in Amberley on a weekend when Professor Arnold Toynbee was staying to visit Philip and Ann Toynbee, who were then living in our cottage. Professor Toynbee was a shy but effective man. During the war he had become head of the Foreign Office Research Department, an institution designed to gather information about the situation in Occupied Europe. When told of my problem, he volunteered to request my services for this already moribund organization.

Professor Toynbee was as good as his word, and the results, in our sleepy sector in Goslar, were quick and impressive. An order arrived from the War Office requiring my instant repatriation for purposes which could not be divulged. My brother officers, deeply impressed, assumed I was joining the secret intelligence service. I was as ignorant as they were. Special air transport was provided, and after a spectacular and sentimental farewell dinner, Stannion delivered me to a waiting DC-3 which took me to London.

VII

Peacetime and the UN

My ARRIVAL in England, after all the excitement and anticipation at
Goslar, was a considerable anticlimax. To the movement control officers
at Northolt airfield, I was just another statistic. No one was there to spirit
me away to secret, high-level interviews in Whitehall—"We need your
help, Urquhart"—and instead, encumbered with my valise and kitbag,
I made my solitary way down to Sussex and started to become a civilian,
leaving behind with little regret the army world I had lived in for nearly
six years. This transformation was slightly impeded at first because lack
of any respectable civilian clothes caused me to dress for some weeks as
a major of the airborne forces.

My entire adult life so far had been spent in the Army. To live with
Alfreda and our son, Thomas, to come home after work each evening,
and to be free to make my own arrangements and plans was an intoxicating
new experience. Initially at any rate, I tended to be patronizing and
intolerant of civilians, judging them by absolute standards and criteria
which had little or nothing to do with the difficulties or limitations of
ordinary life. I read now with acute embarrassment some of my efforts
to advise my civilian superiors in the early stages of my career. The words
of F. M. Cornford in his *Microcosmographica Academica* are exactly right:
"You think (do you not?) that you have only to state a reasonable case,
and people must listen to reason and act upon it at once. It is just this
conviction that makes you so unpleasant. . . ."

My work as head of the Low Countries Section in Arnold Toynbee's
Foreign Office Research Department (FORD) was not exacting. Indeed,
it was something of a formality since our principal function of collecting
information on the German-occupied territories had, by definition, lapsed

with the liberation of Europe. This essential fact had not yet sunk in with most of my colleagues in FORD, and one was not encouraged to mention it. I made a show of information-gathering and reported once a week to my frankly skeptical co-workers, most of whom were in normal life the very competent staff of the Royal Institute of International Affairs, of which Toynbee was the director.

After three weeks of this charade, I felt both bored and out of place. As I was agonizing over my sense of obligation to Arnold Toynbee for having got me out of the Army, that shy but perceptive man remembered —did he ever forget anything?—that I had once told him of my prewar ambition to work for the League of Nations. Now his friend, Gladwyn Jebb of the Foreign Office, had been appointed Executive Secretary of the Preparatory Commission of the United Nations, which meant in effect that he was in charge of organizing and setting up the new world organization. Jebb was about to start recruiting his staff in Church House, Westminster.

I lost no time in visiting Jebb at the Foreign Office. He had a reputation for being supercilious and overbearing, but I soon discovered that his manner concealed an essentially kindly and humorous nature. Apart from my war record I had virtually no qualifications for a civilian job of any kind, but Jebb took me on at once as his private secretary. This was a decisive stroke of good fortune. Within a month of leaving the army I had not only entered the vocation I had always aspired to but had entered it in a position with unequaled possibilities both for learning the job and for advancing in it.

In the months I worked for Gladwyn I learned a great deal—about civilian life, about diplomacy, about people, and about how to get things done. Gladwyn deliberately cultivated his aloof image. His most famous performance came in 1950 during the Korean crisis in his verbal battles with Andrei Vishinsky, the notorious Soviet prosecutor and deputy foreign minister. I remember Andrei Gromyko scowling and pontificating, "I have a formal complaint to bring against the Executive Secretary" (Jebb), and Gladwyn responding blithely, "I tremble."

Gladwyn had views about many things, especially diplomacy and international affairs. He had played a leading role in the British team which had worked on postwar reconstruction, of which the United Nations was an important part. He believed deeply in the importance of these arrangements while being very much aware of the problems and obstacles that would make it so difficult for them to work in practice. He was both imaginative and realistic and knew better than most people that while a perfect international organization was impossible, an imperfect one was a great deal better than nothing and might well be the indispensable factor in avoiding a nuclear world war. Twenty-five years later he summarized his feelings about the United Nations thus:

> Among men, struggle is inevitable—if only because life is a struggle. . . .
>
> . . . So in order that mankind should not destroy itself totally in its struggles, it is essential to have some place . . . in which reason, or law, can be brought to bear on conflicts, either for preventing them, or for ending them in accordance with certain generally accepted rules. We must not despair if these rules are often violated, or, more frequently ignored, or even if the Super-Powers sometimes fail to make use of the machinery altogether. The great thing is that it should be there. And when the abyss really yawns before them I believe that this time . . . it is to the United Nations that the nations will turn.

Dag Hammarskjold, in rather the same vein, once commented that the United Nations was created not to bring mankind to heaven, but to save it from hell.

Gladwyn was a skilled draftsman and was good at dealing both with the national representatives on the Executive Committee and with his own staff. He was lucky to have as his first recruit—I was the second—David Owen,* who became his deputy. David was the opposite of Gladwyn in many ways—an unpretentious Welsh-Yorkshireman—and they made a splendid partnership. David was resourceful and innovative. He was a scholar and an omnivorous reader. He had a quiet passion for the work and was a great organizer. The apparent ease with which, in the early stages, we put together an international staff and made the initial arrangements for the world organization was in large part due to him.

David and I did a wide variety of jobs—moving furniture, allotting office space, setting up meeting rooms, preparing for and writing minutes of meetings, drafting documents, dealing with crackpots, alloting duties to the staff as they arrived, and receiving ministers, ambassadors, and other distinguished visitors. There was no formality. Our first office, which we shared, had, for some forgotten ecclesiastical reason, three doors, and I recall an occasion when they opened simultaneously to admit, respectively, two London charladies, a consignment of typewriters, and the Foreign Minister of Yugoslavia. We also dealt with the press.

After forty years it is hard to recapture the freshness and enthusiasm of those pioneering days. The war was still vivid in everyone's mind and

*Not to be confused with the British Foreign Secretary in the late 1970s.

experience. Many of us had been in the armed forces, and others had only emerged from underground resistance movements a few months before. To work for peace was a dream fulfilled, and the fact that everything had to be organized from scratch was an additional incentive. Nothing seemed too much trouble and no hours too long. Bureaucracy, frustration, routine, empty rhetoric, political pettiness, and disillusionment were still in the future and had not yet dulled the feeling of elation and adventure.

Although I had started the war with a dread and hatred of military life, I had soon become accustomed to it and quite good at it, but I never lost my revulsion at violence and destruction or my fear of bombs, bullets, and death. As the war continued this revulsion had increased, reaching a peak at the sight of the atrocities, the misery, and the ruin of Europe, and the incomprehensible monstrosity of the concentration camps. The pointlessness and essential idiocy of war had also been brought home to me in a particularly painful way by my failure to do anything to ward off the disaster of Arnhem. To someone in such a frame of mind, to be directly involved in setting up the world organization which was "to save succeeding generations from the scourge of war" seemed too good to be true.

It is not easy to recall the conditions and the preoccupations of August 1945. The war had finished, surprisingly for most of us, with the Hiroshima and Nagasaki atomic bombs. Never in history had one era been so decisively closed and a new one so ominously begun by a single revolutionary act.

The United Nations Charter had been drafted and adopted at San Francisco some two months before the Hiroshima bomb in ignorance of this fundamental change in human fortune—the acquisition of a means of destruction capable of destroying human society. The Charter had been based on the concept of an extension of the wartime alliance into peacetime. The "United" in United Nations came from the Atlantic Charter of 1941 and referred to nations united in war, not in peace. The permanent members of the Security Council with the power of veto were the leaders of the victorious wartime alliance, and the Charter assumed, with a stunning lack of political realism, that they would stay united in supervising, and if necessary enforcing, world peace. Roosevelt's concept of the "Four Policemen," and the fact that the early outline of the Charter had been worked out exclusively between the major Allies, gave the permanent members of the Security Council a key position in the future world organization which they have never either relinquished or managed to live up to.* Thus from the outset, like the city of San Francisco in which it

---

*In 1987 they finally began to work together, with predictably satisfactory results.

was born, the United Nations rested on a permanent fault. In our case the fault was political.

*   *   *

The task of the fourteen-member Executive Committee of the Preparatory Commission of the United Nations was to make detailed specifications for the working organization of which the Charter was the blueprint. The United States was represented by Edward R. Stettinius, a man of theatrical good looks and unnaturally white teeth. Most of the work was done by his deputy, Adlai Stevenson, who eventually succeeded him and whose grace, eloquence, and humor lightened many a heavy debate. The Americans had a formidable delegation of experts and enthusiasts, including Leo Pasvolsky, who more than any other single person could claim authorship of much of the first draft of the Charter, Ralph Bunche, Alger Hiss, and a small army of specialists. They represented the new transatlantic order which was to make the UN everything the League of Nations, in the absence of the United States, had failed to be. They were dedicated believers in self-determination and decolonization, in international order and law, and in Human Rights, a then more or less novel preoccupation in the international arena.

In Britain a Labour government had succeeded Churchill's wartime government, and its main representative in the preparatory phase of the United Nations was the Minister of State, Philip Noel-Baker, an unrivaled champion of internationalism and disarmament. All the frustrations and lost opportunities of the League of Nations, of which he was a veteran, and all the tragedies of the thirties and of World War II had only confirmed in Phil's dauntless heart the conviction that we must build an international organization which would ensure peace. He was, and remained into his nineties, an undismayed and unapologetic evangelist, preserving into old age, together with a prodigious historical memory, the single-mindedness and dedication of youth. He was assisted by an eminent scholar, Professor C. K. Webster, who wore a tennis player's green eyeshade as a protest against photographers' lights to which, like all other manifestations of publicity, he objected in principle. Ernest Bevin, the massive Foreign Secretary, occasionally appeared, but Noel-Baker and Webster did all the work. They did not see eye to eye with Bevin on many matters and were regarded by him with ill-concealed impatience.

Noel-Baker and Webster represented the old tradition of Woodrow Wilson, Lord Robert Cecil, and Fridtjof Nansen, the saint of the League of Nations who first made refugees an international concern. For them the League of Nations was still an inspiring ideal which had simply gone into hibernation during the war. They believed that miracles—disarmament, for example—had nearly happened in the past and could, with the proper approach, happen in the future. They were determined to preserve the intimate atmosphere and privacy of the fledgling world organization, protecting it overzealously from the rude attentions of the press and from publicity. They doggedly resisted attempts to have meetings broadcast and believed that in a confidential and discreet collegial atmosphere all things were possible. The intimate rules of the British House of Commons were their inspiration.

Andrei Gromyko represented the Soviet Union—dour and gruff but with a wry humor occasionally showing through, like the sun through winter clouds. The Russians were reserved and formal, cautiously finding their way in a relatively new environment. In the UN as it was then constituted, the West enjoyed a large and unquestioned automatic majority. The Charter was basically a Western concept, taking for granted that democratic behavior would be the norm in the new international order, a proposition rendered even more unattractive to the Soviets by their minority status. The West's monopoly of nuclear weapons was an additional and forceful reason for Soviet caution. The great confrontation was still ahead, and a remnant of the spirit of wartime cooperation remained, but Soviet suspicion of the West was already very much in evidence. Nonetheless, the debates in the Executive Committee and Preparatory Commission were relatively harmonious.

The other representatives on the Executive Committee were also distinguished, and the meetings had style and interest. Among them was Lester Pearson of Canada, that informal and refreshing man who later contributed so much to the development of the United Nations, especially in peacekeeping. The Czechoslovak representative was Jan Masaryk, who became a figure of tragedy and died falling from a window after the Communist takeover of Prague in 1948. He was a charming man, outspoken, urbane, and funny. He had lived in the United States and had a fine transatlantic idiom of speech. At a meeting after what had evidently been a good dinner, Masaryk listened with growing impatience to an obscurantist statement by Gromyko with many "ifs" and "on the other hands," and finally, in exasperation, growled, "And if your aunt had balls she'd be your uncle."

China had a veteran of the League, Dr. Wellington Koo, small and polished, and Iran another supremely civilized diplomat, Nasrullah Entezam. Australia had Paul Hasluck, later Governor-General of Australia, and the Australian Foreign Minister, Dr. Herbert Evatt, unpredictable, ambitious, and later on an almost paranoid President of the General Assembly. It was said that Dr. Evatt had wished to become Secretary-General, first President of the General Assembly, and a Judge of the International Court, but in casting too wide a net had missed them all.

Meanwhile we, the nucleus of the future international civil service, had more immediate and mundane preoccupations. Our temporary headquarters, Church House in Dean's Yard, Westminster, an undistinguished neo-Georgian building, had become the temporary seat of the bombed-out House of Lords and had been radically rearranged for that purpose. Apart from its labyrinthine original design, it was obstructed with sandbags, barbed wire, blackout curtains, air-raid shelters, and all the clutter of wartime London buildings. Our first job was to prepare it for peacetime use.

We were all optimists and regarded the occasional cynic or "realist" with contempt. I have since often wondered whether in 1945 we were exceptionally naive, in the company of many others who believed in the possibility of organizing a peaceful and just world. Could the great powers of East and West, with inspired leadership, have realized the great vision they had set forth in the Charter and turned the historic corner to a world of peace and security, or was that always a quixotic fantasy? Instead, after the Allied victory, the residual distrust and ideological rivalry, which had been submerged in the common effort to beat Hitler, soon rose to the surface again. As we set up shop in London, the smiles of San Francisco were already giving way to a carping and suspicious mood.

In 1945 it was the general view that the functions of the Secretary-General and his staff would be primarily administrative and that political involvement would be the exception rather than the rule. The Russians in particular feared an independent or pro-Western Secretary-General who might stack the cards against them and were suspicious of any whiff of supranational authority or erosion of the sovereign rights of states. They made no bones about their skepticism of the concept of an impartial and objective international civil service.

From the beginning this was a matter of the highest importance for me. I was a determined internationalist and saw our work as a mission to bring objectivity and common sense to bear on problems of peace and war, as a national civil service does in a well-organized state. Although I have since had ample cause to realize the practical difficulties of this beguiling concept, I have never lost my belief in its ultimate validity and necessity.

Gladwyn Jebb and David Owen were, in their different ways, good examples for the aspiring international civil servant. Gladwyn's disciplined mind made it easy for him to take an objective international point of view and to oppose his own compatriots when necessary with ease and even enjoyment. David was a pragmatic idealist and was determined to exemplify the impartiality required by the Charter. The Soviets certainly viewed us as three plausible British agents carrying out the instructions of our government under the guise of UN officials. Personally, I was not yet bothered by the question of how effective objectivity, fairness, and impartiality would be as weapons in the rough and unscrupulous world of politics. I still had virtually everything to learn.

*   *   *

The meetings of the Executive Committee of the Preparatory Commission began in London on August 16—ten days after the first atomic bomb explosion over Hiroshima—and lasted until November 24. The Committee covered the whole range of activity and organization of the United Nations and was, by present standards, a model of precision and common sense. The habit of nitpicking and ideological confrontation had not yet taken hold, and a vast amount of work was accomplished in a short time. As Jebb wrote in the Introduction to the Committee's report:

> The Executive Committee believes that the Report which follows covers adequately the various problems which the Preparatory Commission will have to solve, if the principal organs of the United Nations are to constitute themselves and begin their work as soon as possible, and particularly if the first part of the First Session of the General Assembly is to be conducted with dignity and despatch befitting a great landmark in the history of the world.

One important and controversial matter was the Executive Committee's decision to locate the permanent headquarters of the United Nations in the United States, leaving it to the full Preparatory Commission to recommend a precise location on the advice of a special committee which would consult with the United States authorities. The European members, France, the Netherlands, and Britain, strongly favored Geneva, and Noel-Baker made an emotional speech for Geneva, rejecting the idea of it being haunted by ghosts of past failure. The majority favored the United States, and Gromyko, doubtless recalling the Soviet's expulsion from the League, stated: "The Soviet Government considers that the United States would be the proper place for the United Nations Organization. The

United States is located conveniently between Asia and Europe. The old world had it once, and it is time for the New World to have it."

By the end of December the Preparatory Commission, with the general agreement of its members, completed its proposals to the General Assembly on the establishment of the United Nations. It had sailed through its work, buoyed up by the prevailing optimism of the time. After the horrors of the previous six years, a chastened generation of leaders seemed not only to have learned its lesson, but to have agreed on a new system to "save succeeding generations from the scourge of war." In this bright new dawn, a world ordered by reason, law, and common interest seemed at last to be within practical reach. The final paragraph of the Commission's report reflected this atmosphere of hope:

> If the spirit in which this last task has been accomplished is any guide, the United Nations will be successfully and happily inaugurated; and if by its early actions the new Organization can capture the imagination of the world it will surely not belie the expectations of those who see in it the last chance of saving themselves and their children from the scourge of war. It is in this confident hope that the Preparatory Commission presents its Report to the United Nations.

It is evidently easier to agree on the design of a great political organization than to make it work in practice.

*   *   *

We had a peaceful family Christmas at home at Amberley in Sussex. The enclave in which we lived had been bought by Alfreda's grandfather, a Philadelphia tycoon with a passion for landscape painting, in the early years of the century. It comprised the end of the village street around the church and castle—a large house and a number of thatched cottages and barns, a picture postcard of an idealized English village. Amberley was bounded to the north by great marshes and to the south by the Sussex Downs. It was a lovely place with a dangerously relaxing climate—a wonderful escape from the toils of London.

On January 10, 1946, the first session of the General Assembly opened in the Central Hall, Westminster. Clement Attlee, the new British Labour Prime Minister, gave the inaugural speech, and Paul Henri Spaak of Belgium was elected President. A quotation from Attlee will suffice to convey the spirit of the occasion:

> The United Nations Organization must become the over-riding factor in foreign policy.

After the first world war there was a tendency to regard the League of Nations as something outside the ordinary range of foreign policy. Governments continued on the old lines, pursuing individual aims and following the path of power politics, not understanding that the world had passed into a new epoch. . . .

. . . Let us be clear as to what is our ultimate aim. It is not just the negation of war, but the creation of a world of security and freedom, of a world which is governed by justice and the moral law. We desire to assert the pre-eminence of right over might and the general good against selfish and sectional aims.

On the podium Spaak, a great orator of the old school, was flanked by Gladwyn Jebb and Andrew Cordier as procedural adviser. ("Monsieur Jebb, c'est la perle des Secrétaires-Généraux Provisoires," Spaak told the Assembly.)

The first meeting of the Security Council on January 17 was a historic occasion with its lighter moments. The president was the Australian Ambassador in Washington, Norman Makin, who had presented a duck-billed platypus to the Washington Zoo and was known as the Minister Platypotentiary. Ernest Bevin, not realizing his microphone was switched on, was heard around the world to rumble, "That bloody Chairman has double-crossed me again." Jebb describes Bevin's "mantic utterances which baffled his own side and the opposition alike."

The clouds were gathering fast. Two days after the Security Council's first meeting, the presence of Soviet troops in Iran was brought before the Council, quickly followed by a Soviet countermove complaining of British troops in Greece and Indonesia. On February 4, Syria and Lebanon complained to the Council of the presence of French and British troops in their countries. The pattern of the future was already in place.

On February 1 the Assembly appointed, as the first Secretary-General, Trygve Lie (pronounced Lee), the Foreign Minister of Norway. This appointment followed, as something of an anticlimax, the canvassing of various distinguished names, including those of Eisenhower, Anthony Eden, and Lester Pearson. It indicated, in a matter of the highest importance, the limitations that the adversary East-West relationship would impose on the effectiveness of the UN. There was no consideration of who might be best qualified for the job. As they could not agree on a winner, the undistinguished choice of Lie was regarded by both sides as politically a safe bet.

The cynicism of the selection process was brought home to me during Lie's nomination. I was at that time responsible, among other things, for the General Assembly speakers' list, and Ed Stettinius, the United States Representative, came up to my table in the Assembly Hall and inquired if I could identify Mr. Lie, whose name he mispronounced. I pointed out the substantial figure of the Foreign Minister of Norway, and shortly thereafter listened with some skepticism as Stettinius, in his nominating speech, referred to Lie as a household word, a figure known to all the world, a leader in the Allied struggle for freedom, etc. I was still unused to international political rhetoric and felt an indignant pang of anxiety for the future.

I was transferred to Lie as one of his personal assistants. Lie brought with him his Norwegian secretary, Ingrid Martius, who supported him superbly. He also brought in, as a speech writer and general adviser, a veteran war correspondent of the Chicago *Daily News*, William H. Stoneman, who married Ingrid soon after our arrival in the United States. Bill was a tremendous asset, sardonic, tough, and a man of great integrity. He was not in awe of Lie and was good at talking him down from his frequent rages. As a well-known war correspondent, he was also a great help in dealing with the press.

I felt sorry for Lie. He had had an honorable career in Norway as a labor leader and minister of justice and had gone into exile in England as foreign minister with King Haakon when the Germans invaded Norway in 1940. He was credited with having ordered ships of the Norwegian Merchant Marine at sea in 1940 to report to British ports. But as Secretary-General of the new world organization he was out of his depth. Lie was an unsophisticated man who relied more on peasant shrewdness and what he called his "political nose" than on intellectual effort or hard diplomatic work. He was, in public life at any rate, a naturally suspicious man with a hair-trigger temper. He was jealous of his position and at the same time nervous of it. He would leave a public event if he felt he had not been properly seated, and Gladwyn Jebb records a dinner for Anthony Eden at which Lie popped into the dining room before dinner to change the place cards, giving himself the place of honor.

Lie had the massive physique of an athlete who had run to seed in middle age. He was a great eater and drinker and, if the program permitted, went home each afternoon for a siesta. He was apt to go dark red in the face with rage and to utter, jowls quivering, complex and ominous Norwegian oaths. This usually made Ingrid and Stoneman laugh, which made things worse.

Lie has often been judged and found wanting, but this is scarcely fair. He did not, perhaps, have the ideal qualifications or the charisma for the job, but then who did? And, more relevant, who else could have been accepted by East and West? Lie himself was certainly aware of his own shortcomings. "Why," he asks in his memoirs, "had this awesome task fallen to a labor lawyer from Norway?" Nor had the way in which he came to the Secretary-Generalship been auspicious. He had originally been approached by the United States to be the first President of the General Assembly on Christmas Day 1945 in a telegram which had to be delivered to Lie in a remote log cabin high in the Norwegian mountains by a local farmer on skis. Having thus caused the maximum trouble to all concerned and apparently also got Soviet agreement, the United States switched its support to Paul-Henri Spaak of Belgium without ever telling Lie or anyone else of the change of candidate. Thus when Gromyko nominated Lie as President of the General Assembly, the United States Secretary of State, James F. Byrnes, said nothing. After much confusion, a secret ballot was taken, in which Spaak got 28 votes and Lie 23.

This performance was a grave embarrassment for Lie. Spaak was a wartime colleague with whom he had no desire to compete, and the silence of the United States which had so urgently wooed him made Lie appear to the public as Moscow's man. As a Norwegian Socialist, Lie had been both anti-Nazi and anti-Communist. As minister of justice he had given Leon Trotsky asylum in Norway and then expelled him after one year for breaking the rules of asylum. During the war his closest ties had been with the British, but now, even before his appointment as Secretary-General, he had been identified in the public mind as a Soviet-sponsored figure.

For me, the transition from Jebb to Lie was difficult. I always felt that Jebb knew exactly what he was doing. I could therefore concentrate on trying to help and on learning as much as possible. With Lie I did not have this reassuring sense of confidence. Rightly or wrongly, I felt that he was confused, temperamental, and insecure in his new and demanding job and was often carried away by the emotions of the moment. I doubt if Lie ever trusted me. He had, I learned later, checked up on me extensively through military back channels, but had only discovered that I had a reputation for being independent and sticking to my own opinion—presumably a reference to the Arnhem business. I had an uneasy time as his personal assistant, but this in no way diminished my eager anticipation of the work ahead.

VIII

New York and Trygve Lie

THE BRIGHT DAWN had passed, and the day was about to become increasingly cloudy and confused. Lie had been appointed on February 1, 1946. On February 14 the Assembly chose New York as the interim headquarters of the UN, and this determined, among other things, where I would live for the rest of my working life. Such was our state of enthusiasm in those days that the idea of leaving England, perhaps forever, to serve the United Nations seemed perfectly normal and very exciting. We sold our 1932 Chrysler two-seater, put things in order at Amberley, and departed for New York in mid-March, Alfreda and Thomas by sea on the SS *Gripsholm*, and I by air with Lie in a converted Lancaster bomber made available by the Royal Air Force. My first impression of New York was rushing through the Holland Tunnel from Newark Airport and surfacing in a brightly lit city where steam poured out of the roadway. We were all initially housed in the Waldorf-Astoria where the food, room service, and luxury were a stunning contrast to postwar England.

On March 21 the temporary headquarters of the UN was established at Hunter College in the Bronx. This unusual and inconvenient locale was dictated by the lack of any other immediately available premises in the New York area. The college buildings were temporarily adapted for UN purposes, the gymnasium becoming the Security Council Chamber. It was here, almost immediately after our arrival in New York, that Gromyko walked out when the Council refused to delay consideration of the continued presence of Soviet troops in Iran. This was the first public demonstration of the Soviet intransigence which later became the norm, but at the time it caused a sensation. Abe Rosenthal, then a junior *New York Times* reporter, had the wit to pursue Gromyko downtown by taxi and got a scoop by interviewing him. It was also in the gymnasium at Hunter, in June, that Bernard Baruch presented the plan for an international atomic energy authority.

Unlike the League of Nations, which had nearly two years to organize itself before starting work, the United Nations hit the ground running. It was operational almost before the task of organization had started, and this put tremendous pressures on Lie and his colleagues. In London Lie had already begun to assemble his team of senior officials, the eight Assistant Secretaries-General, and the process was completed soon after our arrival in New York. The results were not uniformly impressive.

The five great powers had agreed that the head of the Security Council and Political Affairs Department should be Russian, the Chief of Administration American, the Economic Department British, the Social Affairs Department French, and the Trusteeship Department Chinese. The Russians produced Arkady Sobolev, an electrical engineer who had turned diplomat during the war and had been in the Soviet delegation at Dumbarton Oaks. He managed with considerable style to walk the tightrope between being the senior Soviet official and being an international civil servant in a particularly sensitive post, and we all became very fond of him.

The American nomination was not so fortunate. Adlai Stevenson and Eisenhower's brother, Milton, both having turned Lie down, Secretary Byrnes lackadaisically produced John B. Hutson, a Southerner who had been an under secretary in the U.S. Department of Agriculture, which he had left for unspecified reasons. Hutson had little demonstrable administrative ability and a total lack of political sense. He did not stay long.

After Sir William Beveridge, Geoffrey Crowther (then editor of the *Economist*), and Sir Arthur Salter had all refused the post, David Owen became the British Assistant Secretary-General as head of the Economic Department, where he recruited a distinguished staff. His colleague in Social Affairs was Henri Laugier, a congenial French academic with a boundless contempt for the ways of international bureaucracy. Laugier was no organizer or operator and so was constantly frustrated.

The eight Assistant Secretaries-General constituted the nearest thing Lie had to a cabinet. They would meet each week with the Secretary-General, ostensibly to report progress and discuss serious problems. I was the secretary and minute-taker of these meetings, and they were a disillusioning experience. Most of the time was taken up with trivial and peripheral matters such as the allotment of office space and cars. We even had an interminable discussion over the final salutation in official correspondence, the Europeans championing "Your obedient servant," while the Americans, claiming this was undemocratic and servile, insisted successfully on the fatuous "Accept, Excellency, the assurances of my highest consideration." There was little sign of the high-level interplay of statesmanlike ideas that I had anticipated. Lie seemed more flustered than ever in these meetings, and I think he found them as irritating as I did.

A major figure in Lie's set-up was Andrew Cordier, who had succeeded David Owen as the Secretary-General's Executive Assistant. Cordier was a history professor from Ohio who had become the world's greatest expert on the Rules of Procedure of the General Assembly and the Security Council. He was a tough, bumbling figure who was always prepared to dive in, no matter how shallow or muddy the water might be. Cordier did a great deal to mitigate or short-circuit the confusions caused by the Assistant Secretaries-General.

I was the most influential of a group of young people in the Secretariat who had been active in the war. Christopher Burney, as a British agent in France, had been caught by the Gestapo, tortured, and put in solitary confinement for eighteen months, after which he had lived out the war in Buchenwald.* Stephane Hessel had been a French Resistance fighter who had also ended up in Buchenwald. Paddy Bolton had been private secretary in Russia to the wartime British Ambassador. Also in our office was the beautiful and tragic Jacqueline Nearne, another French Resistance figure, who had seen her fiancé shot by the Germans three days before the liberation of Paris.

We were the constituency of the highest good, and were incessantly critical of the bumbling and, to us, obfuscating methods of the emerging UN bureaucracy. We felt that Lie, Cordier, and the Assistant Secretaries-General were not imaginative, motivated, or uncompromising enough. We were constantly, and unsuccessfully, suggesting ways in which they could do better. Our criticisms were not altogether fair. The faults and omissions that we attributed to our senior colleagues were, at least in some part, the inherent faults of the political nature of the UN system.

*   *   *

On March 5, 1946, just before we left London, an event had taken place which came to symbolize the end of the wartime alliance and the beginning of what was to be the dominant postwar relationship in inter-

*His *Solitary Confinement* is one of the most remarkable books of World War II.

national affairs, the Cold War. This was Winston Churchill's "Iron Curtain" speech at Fulton, Missouri. Most people were still under the spell of the Allied victory, in which the Soviets had played such a vital part. It seemed impossible to believe that they would not continue to play a major role in the peace for which they had paid so much. Churchill's speech was greeted at the time with much criticism. Lie, for example, believed that it would inevitably result in a progressive hardening of the Soviet position and suggested that the British Labour government should dissociate itself from it. Churchill's prophetic declaration foreshadowed the negative trend which was soon to undermine the very foundations of the UN as a political institution.

Already, during the Preparatory Commission, the Russians had become more suspicious and less cooperative. They had been particularly reserved about the Military Staff Committee which many regarded as a key to the future effectiveness of the UN in keeping the peace, and appeared very negative on the idea of collective action which was the essence of the Charter concept of maintaining international peace and security. In October 1945 the Council of Ministers of the United States, the USSR, and the United Kingdom had broken down over the question of three-power control in Germany, causing Jebb to comment that if the *three* foreign ministers couldn't reach agreement on important issues, it seemed unlikely that the five-power system in the Security Council could work. Europe was becoming set in two opposing blocs.

It was already clear that the Soviet Union would devote its efforts in the UN to confining the organization to channels where the Soviet Union had the capacity to control and limit action. At San Francisco many governments had expressed fears about the paralyzing potential of the veto, but none of the five permanent members had been able to suggest acceptable limitations on its use. The conference had therefore made do with vague assurances to the effect that the veto would seldom, if ever, be used. The veto was the Soviet defense against the Western majority, and they used it frequently.

The Charter concept of maintaining peace was based on the power of the major states. The UN could only work properly if those states agreed to cooperate and could first come to a broad agreement on, and have mutual respect for, their own various interests. This they have so far signally failed to do.* The veteran French statesman Joseph Paul Boncour spoke prophetically at the last session of the Assembly of the League of

_____

*This was written in 1986. Since 1987 the permanent members of the Security Council have at last begun to work together.

Nations in 1946: "The strength and weakness—I repeat the strength and weakness—of the new institution is that it depends on agreement between the five permanent Great Powers."

The story of the political life of the United Nations has been, to a considerable extent, the story of a continuous effort to improvise around, and to sidestep, the obstacle of fundamental great power differences, and to find substitutes for the great power unanimity which had originally been intended to be the main driving force of the new organization.

In the belief that the Charter was going to work as it had been written, great efforts were made to get the best possible people for the Secretariat. E. T. (Bill) Williams, the brilliant young Oxford don who had been General Bernard Montgomery's Chief of Intelligence in North Africa and Europe, was appointed to head the Enforcement Division, which would be responsible for coordinating enforcement action by the Security Council. Bill's official functions simply never materialized and, as the months went by, it became clear that they never would. He finally left to become Warden of Rhodes House at Oxford. Other distinguished recruits also left.

In the absence of great power consensus, improvisation and an imaginative use of the powers of the Secretary-General soon became the key to any useful work on the political side. Since I worked for the Secretary-General, I did not feel so acutely the frustrations visited on Williams and many others.

*   *   *

Hunter College was due to revert to its academic function in September, a fact anticipated by numerous abusive letters from the vocal anti-UN forces in the New York area. The General Assembly was to meet in the fall and also had to be suitably housed. New temporary quarters therefore had to be found pending the Assembly's decision on the permanent headquarters. There was literally no suitable space to be had in New York City itself, although at one time or another the Villard Houses on Madison Avenue (now the Helmsley Palace Hotel) and the Carnegie Mansion on upper Fifth Avenue were suggested as possible sites for the United Nations.

From this unpromising situation a new and sublimely inconvenient temporary arrangement emerged. The Secretariat and the Councils would be housed in the Sperry Gyroscope plant at Lake Success on Long Island, forty-five minutes from the city, and the General Assembly in the skating rink at the former World's Fair Grounds in Flushing Meadows. We moved to Lake Success in mid-August. After two months in New York, Alfreda and I took a small house in Manhasset, Long Island, which was conveniently near to Lake Success, to which I used to walk each morning through the park of the Jock Whitney estate, Greentree.

Our daughter, Katie, was born in July 1946. As soon as Alfreda and Katie returned home from the hospital, I joined Lie in Europe. We attended the opening of the European Peace Conference in the Palais du Luxembourg in Paris and left before the conference degenerated into bitter and abusive wrangling. We moved on to Bern to pay a formal visit to the Swiss government and then to Geneva for the formal closing of the League of Nations and the transfer of its property and assets to the UN. This sad ceremony, presided over by the last League Secretary-General, Sean Lester of Ireland, and Lie, was enlivened by a parallel event in the Palais des Nations, the conference of the UN Relief and Rehabilitation Administration, that immense outpouring of American wealth, expertise, and good will which did so much to put the war-shattered world on its feet again.

The UNRRA Director-General, Fiorello La Guardia, formerly Mayor of New York, had become capricious. The Palais des Nations, an abominable and pretentious construction, has a number of peculiarities, including a private elevator for the presiding officer of the Assembly. At the opening of the UNRRA conference, both Lie and La Guardia claimed this small and uncertain vehicle as a personal right, and, against all advice, got into it together. When the doors closed on the competitive statesmen, the elevator, instead of ascending, sank slowly out of sight. From the depths came multilingual imprecations (La Guardia persisted, inexplicably, in addressing Lie in German). A Swiss engineer was summoned, and after a long pause the elevator was cranked up to ground level and its disheveled cargo released.

One result of our trip to Geneva was a new nickname for Lie. One morning I was visited by the admirable police chief of Geneva, who kept a watchful eye over important visitors and was dealing brilliantly with the problems of a small city afflicted with a turbulent population of political refugees. He inquired in the discreetest possible manner if we were having any security problems. Stoneman and I assured him we were not. Could we perhaps then explain why the Secretary-General of the UN went out at night in disguise? Stoneman undertook to solve this mystery, and it turned out that Lie, who liked the nearest thing to night life the city of Calvin would permit, had visited a nightclub under the name of Rodney Witherspoon. After that he was always "Rodney" to us.

An immense task of establishment was achieved in this first year by an organization which was still searching for a home, recruiting its staff, and establishing its methods of work. No less than twelve permanent international commissions and subcommissions as well as the Economic and Social Council, the International Court of Justice, UNICEF, and the International Refugee Organization were constituted and started their work during the remainder of 1946. The result of this tremendous burst of international procreation was a proliferating and overlapping web of activities and bureaucracies. Certainly an unprecedented range of human activity was covered, but the possibility that governments might not follow up, on the national level, these high-minded international activities was not considered. Nor did we suspect that our efforts to build a brave new world would, in some cases, soon degenerate into fixed and parochial bureaucracies repeating, year by year, in excruciatingly tedious inter-governmental meetings, ideas which had become almost meaningless clichés. The gap between international incantations and harsh national realities was still not apparent.

There is nothing intrinsically wrong with bureaucracy—quite the contrary; without bureaucracy, modern society would not run. But when bureaucracy becomes involved with more or less abstract ideas, a terrible elephantiasis often sets in, and this happened in the United Nations system. Cockeyed ideas from member states or other sources begot studies which produced reports which set up staffs which produced more reports which were considered by meetings which asked for further reports and sometimes set up additional bureaucratic appendages which reported to future meetings. The process was self-perpetuating. Few senior officials were able to resist the siren call of empire-building in their departments, and governments were insatiable in their thirst for jobs. Thus we soon began to lose the austere and slim figure on which we had prided ourselves in Church House.

In the optimism surrounding its birth, there was a popular impression that the United Nations would act on the international level as a government acts on the national level. For better or for worse, the UN is nothing like a government. It has no sovereignty or power of sovereign decision-making. It is an association of independent, sovereign states which depends for its effectiveness on the capacity of its members to agree and to cooperate, and on the ingenuity and dedication with which the Secretariat interprets and carries out their wishes. The capacity of governments to agree and cooperate has proved to be quite limited.

The uncontested right of all members to speak at all times has, over the years, turned many of the deliberative organs of the UN into a preposterous and repetitive bore. There were a few great orators—Paul-Henri Spaak, Léon Jouhaux, two or three of the older Latin American ambassadors, Andrei Vishinsky, Hector McNeil, the young British minister of state in the Attlee government, Senator Tom Connally of Texas, and Adlai Stevenson were memorable. They were, however, the exception, and the press and public galleries soon began to empty. The delegates themselves also soon ceased to show up for meetings in respectable numbers. There is a story of a foreign minister addressing the Assembly at lunchtime, with only one other foreign minister present. Deeply touched, the speaker thanked his stalwart colleague who replied, "Oh, not at all. I am the next speaker." It is a terrible system, but no one has ever succeeded in finding a substitute.

The UN has a seemingly limitless capacity to produce often lengthy documents in six languages and in immense quantities. Efforts to eliminate a document usually provoke a group of governments to demand its continued existence, and other governments will probably support them in case they wish to exert a similar privilege in the future. These reams of battleship-gray prose are a heavy burden.

The statesmanlike attitudes of the early meetings soon gave way to competitive point-scoring, and on many critical issues the level of debate sank to name-calling, polemics, and abuse, rendering a positive outcome precarious if not impossible. In 1946 these depressing tendencies were only just beginning to become apparent.

*　　　*　　　*

On a sunny late autumn day in October 1946 the United States formally welcomed the United Nations to its shores. The occasion was the opening of the General Assembly session. In the morning the delegates, in a ninety-six-car motorcade, preceded by detachments of the United States Army and Navy, drove to City Hall for the welcoming ceremonies. At a reception in the Waldorf-Astoria, Secretary of State James F. Byrnes told them, "Those whom war hath joined together let not peace put asunder."

In the afternoon President Truman opened the Assembly session in the converted skating rink at Flushing Meadows. The meeting symbolized, he said, "the abandonment by the United States of a policy of isolation." While admitting that "it is easier to get people to agree upon peace as an ideal than to agree to subject their own acts to the collective judgment of mankind," Truman declared, "To permit the United Nations to be broken into irreconcilable parts by different political philosophies would bring disaster to the world." He also spoke of the necessity of the industrial and agricultural progress of the less well-developed areas of the world. "The American people," Truman concluded, "look upon the United Nations not as a temporary expedient but as a permanent partnership, a partnership among the peoples of the world for their common peace and common well-being."

It was an inspiring address by the president of by far the most powerful country in the world. Unfortunately, strong currents were already beginning to flow in the opposite direction. The Baruch Plan for an International Atomic Development Authority, which had been tabled in the summer of 1946, had envisaged the cessation of the manufacture of nuclear arms and bombs, and the disposal of existing bombs. While the Baruch Plan may have been good propaganda, there was never the slightest chance that, pushed by the automatic Western majority, it would be accepted by the Soviet Union. The Soviet Union, racing to complete its own nuclear bomb, had counter-proposed a convention to outlaw the production and use of atomic weapons. The resulting deadlock gave the green light for the nuclear arms race to proceed at full tilt. The Military Staff Committee, the linchpin of the system of peace enforcement envisaged in the Charter, was already in difficulties on the essential question of the type and quota of forces to be made available by the great powers, and its work soon ground to a halt. These two developments, more than any other, signified the decline of the grand Charter design of collective security in which the Security Council, led by the great powers, would assure the stable international conditions in which disarmament and arms control could proceed.

Colonial problems, although a source of disagreement between the United States and its European allies, were not yet a dominant preoccupation. The Palestine question and the State of Israel were still in the future. The main emphasis in 1946 was on dealing with the political and material debris of the war. The focus was still on Europe. Disarmament, relief, reconstruction, refugees, and war crimes were the main preoccupations of the day. The West had a large and unassailable majority in the General Assembly. The United Nations was viewed with extravagant benevolence by its uncontested leader, the United States.

*   *   *

While invitations to establish the permanent headquarters of the UN on their territory flowed in from cities and localities all over the United

States, xenophobia and hostile reactions to the UN were also much in evidence. On their long triangular drives between Lake Success, Flushing Meadows, and Manhattan, delegates arriving for the first time in the United States were puzzled and distressed when the UN stickers on their cars provoked abusive comments from fellow drivers.

Lie believed strongly that the ultimate good of the UN would be best served by siting the organization in New York. The New York City authorities responded by offering the whole Flushing Meadows area, reclaimed land on a desolate inlet of Long Island Sound, which a British delegate compared to the coastal wastes of Southwest Africa. Lie, to the rage of rival claimants, persisted in championing New York City. The Assembly subcommittee on the question recommended Philadelphia or the Presidio in San Francisco, with White Plains, Westchester, in second place. The British and Soviets rejected San Francisco, even though President Truman had offered the Presidio to the UN without cost. By December, there was total confusion.

Lie told New York's Mayor William O'Dwyer and Robert Moses that, in the absence of a better proposal, New York City would be out of the running. Moses, a city planner of great vision, had earlier mentioned Turtle Bay, an area of slums and slaughterhouses bordering Manhattan's East River between 42nd and 48th Streets. It seemed a remote prospect and the probable costs prohibitive, but the challenge appealed to Moses, and he contacted the Rockefeller family, Wallace K. Harrison, the architect of Rockefeller Center in New York, and William Zeckendorf, a real estate tycoon. While intensive real estate and financial negotiations were undertaken, the wrangle at the United Nations continued aimlessly, gaining precious hours for Lie and the New York negotiators. On December 11, the United States Ambassador, Warren Austin, was able to read to the Headquarters Committee a letter from John D. Rockefeller, Jr., offering the UN $8.5 million to buy the Turtle Bay property on the East River between 42nd and 48th Streets for its permanent headquarters. The Assembly gratefully accepted the offer by 46 votes to 7 against (the Arab States, Australia, and El Salvador).

The vitality, the vibrant cosmopolitanism, the abrasive pressures, and the manifest and heroic imperfections of New York City, the communications center of the world, have provided a testing and stimulating environment for the world organization. Like all long associations, it has had its ups and downs and frictions, but by and large it is a mutually advantageous relationship. A provincial environment, lack of pressure, and excessive comfort and leisure bring out the worst in diplomats. I believe that if the UN eventually grows stronger and more important, New York City will have been a major contributor to the process.

The team of consultant architects proposed by Wallace Harrison contained some distinguished figures, notably Le Corbusier of France, Sven Markelius of Sweden, and Oscar Niemeyer of Brazil. The Chinese representative was said to be China's greatest exponent of building in wood, and Mr. Bassov of the USSR was believed to be primarily interested in foundations. Le Corbusier and Niemeyer had a great deal to do with the original architectural concept of the UN building, but Le Corbusier soon fell out with his colleagues, and Niemeyer appeared in New York less and less, so that in the end the main burden fell on Wallace Harrison. The present United Nations Headquarters is a highly successful functional building which is also an important architectural creation in its own right. Wallace Harrison was its main begetter.

Wally Harrison remained permanently concerned with the buildings he built. Having completed the UN building, with all its complications and exacting specifications, he kept a steady eye on its fortunes and its development. Later on I was responsible for dealing with acquisitions and works of art—sometimes entirely unsuitable gifts from governments—and it was my thankless lot to try to get the best and to discourage or conceal the worst. To the end of his life Wally was always ready to come across town to discuss the siting or the concealing of a new acquisition. Some things, the Chagall window outside the Meditation Room, for example, or the great Hepworth sculpture in the forecourt, neither of them governmental gifts, gave him great pleasure. I was sorry that he did not live to see the beautiful sculpture by Henry Moore in the forecourt. Over less agreeable offerings he grinned ruefully and helped to find the best way to minimize their impact.

The slums and abattoirs of Turtle Bay soon began to fall to the wrecking crews, and the UN Headquarters rose majestically from the rubble, coming into full use in 1952.

*   *   *

In the immediate postwar years the whipping boys of the international community were the old colonial powers. The Indonesians were fighting a war of liberation against the Dutch; the turn of the French and Belgians was yet to come. The British were the prime target, and the British Labour government, to its surprise, found itself assailed on all sides. Egypt was already complaining about the presence of British troops in Egypt, and the question of Palestine was about to become, and to remain, the most difficult subject on the UN agenda. A special session of the General Assembly on Palestine was called on the initiative of Britain at the end of April 1947 and set up the Special Committee on Palestine, which, in November, proposed the Partition Plan. Thus began a seemingly endless imbroglio in the Middle East.

In those early days the world was divided about the Palestine question along lines very different from now. The Soviet Union, for example, was an enthusiastic sponsor of the new State of Israel and was the first government to grant de jure recognition to it. In 1947 we were naively optimistic as to what could be done about this most complex and tragic of historical dilemmas, where two ancient peoples were in an unequal but deadly competition for a small but infinitely significant piece of territory, a struggle made critical by Hitler's annihilation of the Jews of Europe on the one hand and the emergence of Arab nationalism on the other. Britain must be enabled to relinquish the Mandate of Palestine with dignity. The Jewish refugees from World War II must be allowed to settle. The Palestinians' interests and rights must be protected. A plan must be found to accommodate the conflicting rights and demands of Arabs and Jews. The international community, through the United Nations, must restore peace and execute the plan. In our innocence, none of these things seemed to us impossible.

The British, in the throes of a severe post-war economic crisis, were under heavy attack from virtually all quarters for their handling of Palestine. Arabs resented the Balfour Declaration and Britain's sponsorship of the demand for a Jewish homeland in Palestine. Jews violently objected to British restrictions on the migration to Palestine of Jewish refugees from Europe. Menachem Begin in the Irgun Zvai Leumi, Yitzak Shamir in the Stern Gang, and many others were conducting an effective campaign of terrorism and harassment against the British Mandatory Power in Palestine—a campaign which was rapidly eroding British resolve to stay on. Segments of American opinion were passionately critical, while the Soviets launched massive denunciations of colonial repression. In Palestine itself violence steadily increased.

The formal departure of the British Mandatory authority and the announcement of the State of Israel took place within twenty-four hours on May 14–15, 1948. The armies of five Arab states invaded Israel on May 15. A crushing responsibility fell upon the United Nations and upon the United Nations Mediator, Count Folke Bernadotte, and his deputy, Ralph Bunche. In the beginning the emphasis was on the negotiation of a settlement of the Palestine problem, which, in our optimism, many of us believed to be a matter of a month or two.

As the summer of 1948 advanced, the Palestinian refugee problem became acute, while the prospects of a settlement receded in the face of adamant Arab refusal, backed with force, to accept the existence of the State of Israel. Only King Abdullah of Jordan was far-sighted enough to see that a settlement at this point would be the best the Arabs would ever get, and he paid for his vision with his life two years later. Bernadotte himself was assassinated by the Stern Gang in Jerusalem on September 17, 1948.

Bernadotte's assassination was a flagrant outrage. There was never much doubt as to who had killed him, but in all the subsequent indignation about terrorism he is rarely mentioned. His assassins went unpunished. Some of them became successful and respected members of society. Since his murder and the conspiracy of silence that followed it, I have had difficulty in joining without reservation in the hue and cry over "terrorism." Leaders of activist "liberation" movements, of which Shamir and Begin were two prominent examples, have seemed to me to be a category apart, not to be judged by conventional standards but rather for their persistence and ruthlessness in overcoming great odds in pursuit of a political goal.

After Bernadotte's assassination the emphasis in the UN shifted from negotiating a Palestine settlement to getting an armistice and containing the conflict in Palestine, and it never fully shifted back to the original objective.

The Palestine problem has haunted the development of the United Nations ever since 1948. It is a matter of such passion and partisanship, of convictions so deeply held on all sides, that those who become involved in it usually pay a heavy price. I do not mean to belittle the importance of the issues or the sincerity of the beliefs and aspirations of all those concerned, but the involvement of the United Nations in the Palestine problem over the years has twisted the organization's image and fragmented its reputation and prestige as no other issue has.

The UN as set up in 1945 was a diplomatic and bureaucratic organization. The Arab-Israeli War of 1948 projected it into operational activities which had to be improvised in response to a violent and dangerous situation. In Palestine we had to organize Military Observers to supervise truces and cease-fires and to act as go-betweens among the fighting parties. These soldiers and civilians, in small numbers in a violent situation, took on enormous responsibilities and behaved with great courage and resource. The Military Observers became the backbone of the subsequent Armistice arrangements.

Ralph Bunche, as Bernadotte's deputy, was the main architect and improviser of this pioneering operational activity. Although it is now a commonplace feature of the international scene, the use of military officers from many countries as impartial honest brokers in conflict situations was, in 1948, a novel concept. Bunche's extraordinary grasp both of principle and of practical matters, and his calm but dominating personality and leadership, were the key factors in developing this technique and securing for the observers the respect and confidence which are their only weapons. It was on the foundations laid by Bunche in Palestine in 1948 that we constructed the machinery of peacekeeping that has since proved useful in many different conflicts.

After Bernadotte's assassination, Bunche also assumed the function of Mediator, although out of respect for Bernadotte's memory he insisted on being called the "Acting Mediator." By dogged and imaginative negotiation on the island of Rhodes late in 1948 and early in 1949, he achieved what many considered impossible, the Armistice Agreements between Israel and its Arab neighbors. He thus established the only existing basis for a tenuous peace on the borders of the new State of Israel. Bunche was awarded the Nobel Peace Prize in 1950.

*   *   *

I arrived in Paris for the General Assembly session on September 15, 1948, two days before Bernadotte's assassination. I had unwisely taken a month's leave—my first since going to New York—and I came back to a mess of which I had been, with the best intentions, one of the originators. Almost since our arrival in New York I had been appalled by the disorganization and slipshod methods of the Secretariat and the lack of coherent direction from the Secretary-General's office. In this I may have been over-zealous, applying military standards to the far wider and foggier area of international affairs and bureaucracy. But there was certainly much room for improvement, and early in 1948 David Owen and I hit upon a plan to do something about it.

Robert Jackson—Commander Jackson, or Jacko, as he was known—was originally an Australian naval officer. He had first come to public notice early in the war as the organizer of the critical defense of Malta, and he was promoted to the supplying and feeding of the whole British-controlled Middle East which was being strangled by the German and Italian blockade of the Mediterranean. He then became the guiding spirit and chief executive officer of the United Nations Relief and Rehabilitation Administration (UNRRA).

Jackson was the most able and imaginative large-scale operator I have ever encountered. His capacity to work at full pressure, taking into account a large variety of economic, political, logistical, financial, and natural factors and making them into a coherent operational plan, was a marvelous thing to see.

To employ Jackson to organize Lie's office was my idea of the salvation of the UN bureaucracy, and I have seldom had a less happy one. David Owen and I persuaded Lie to take Jackson on in February 1948 as his coordinating executive, a job which Jacko, in his naval way, insisted on referring to, to the resentment of his colleagues, as Chief of Staff. Lie, in an inspired preemptive move, appointed me as personal assistant to both Jackson and himself.

Lie and Jackson, while maintaining a sickening degree of face-to-face cordiality, took an instant dislike to each other. Thus I would spend my days listening to each separately vilify the other, only to witness their bursts of forced bonhomie when they met. I doubt if Lie understood Jacko, who tended to talk to him in cricketing metaphors.

Jacko's high-pressure ability and wide experience also alienated his fellow Assistant Secretaries-General, a stuffy and insecure lot to begin with. I soon began to see that we had installed a racing engine in a family automobile and could expect trouble.

On my way from a vacation in Italy to Paris, I learned that Lie had fired Jackson. I was shocked and angry that a decision had been taken in my absence on a matter in which I was intimately concerned. This preoccupation was soon overtaken by the shock of Bernadotte's assassination in Jerusalem, but my relations with Lie deteriorated rapidly.

*   *   *

The Cold War had started in earnest; Western Europe, in the throes of reconstruction, was narrowly escaping a Communist takeover; the Berlin crisis was at its height; and Palestine had become a world problem. The French had made enormous efforts to house the UN General Assembly in spite of the rigors and shortages of postwar France. The meeting was psychologically important for France, still haunted by the horrors of war and its aftermath. The former Gestapo Headquarters in Paris and even residual German military directional signs were still visible, and controversies over resistance or collaboration were a painful reminder of the horrible choices that enemy occupation imposes on the citizens of a victim state.

The issues before the Assembly were important enough, and there was much of a less serious kind. There was a running feud between Lie and Herbert Evatt, the Australian foreign minister who was President of the Assembly. Evatt was a brilliant but insecure man, almost paranoid in his desire to dominate and in his suspicion of those around him. He was even jealous of Eleanor Roosevelt.

Evatt was acutely apprehensive of Lie upstaging him, and one bone of contention was their respective offices, two large temporary enclosures at the center of our headquarters in the Musée de l'Homme with a space between them in which Bill Stoneman and I, with various aides and secretaries, were bivouacked. Evatt had carefully measured these boxes to be sure that Lie's was not larger than his.

One day, after a furious row with Evatt, Lie emerged from Evatt's office purple with rage and slammed the door with all his strength. This caused the walls of Evatt's box to collapse, leaving the two statesmen glowering at each other over the ruins. This was too much for Stoneman and me, and our leaders, equally put out at being laughed at, joined forces in rebuking us, Lie going so far as to tell us that we were fired. At last they had something to agree on.

The British team at the Assembly comprised a wide variety of personalities and sexual preferences. Among them the most flamboyant was Guy Burgess, who had long been notorious, although not yet for his now best-remembered role as a Soviet agent. An evening meeting of the Balkan Subcommittee, which was trying to deal with the violent and chaotic situation on the northern borders of Greece, offered an excellent opportunity for Burgess's propensity to shock. The group consisted of the foreign ministers of Great Britain, Greece, and of Greece's Balkan neighbors, the latter being eminently conventional, old-fashioned Communists, and Burgess's appearance one evening, drunk and heavily painted and powdered for a night on the town, caused much outrage. When I mentioned this episode to Sir Alexander Cadogan, the head of the British Delegation, he replied icily that the Foreign Office traditionally tolerated innocent eccentricity.

If there was a star of the Paris session, it was Eleanor Roosevelt, whose particular triumph was to bring about the unanimous acceptance of the Universal Declaration on Human Rights, a landmark of incalculable importance in the struggle for human decency and mutual respect. Mrs.

Roosevelt's debates with Vishinsky on the fate of European refugees were one of the highlights of the session. "We here in the United Nations," she told Vishinsky, "are trying to develop ideas which will be broader in outlook, which will consider first the rights of man, which will consider what makes man more free. Not governments, but man." Mrs. Roosevelt had an extraordinary capacity for presenting complex ideas in simple language. She was a marvelous mixture of grandeur and modesty.

The first time I ever appeared before a television camera was, fortunately, with Mrs. Roosevelt. It was at the height of the McCarthy period and the rhetoric against the United Nations had reached an unprecedented level of nastiness. We were to discuss the United Nations with two of the UN's more fanatical opponents, and Mrs. Roosevelt noticed that I was extremely nervous. "Don't worry," she said, "just watch me." After listening to five minutes of vitriol, in which she and the United Nations were castigated for the presence of the Soviet Union in the world organization, her calm, sardonic counterattack was devastating. "I suppose," sneered one of the attackers, "you would have approved of having Hitler in the League of Nations." "Of course," said Mrs. Roosevelt, "then we might have avoided the Second World War." Her common sense and confidence in her convictions were great morale-builders.

*   *   *

I had strongly disagreed with Lie over his treatment of Jackson. After Bernadotte's assassination and Ralph Bunche's succession as Mediator in Palestine, I also became increasingly worried by Lie's attitude to Bunche and indeed to the whole Palestine question.

Bunche had inherited a dangerous and thankless task which he carried out with his usual integrity and single-mindedness. Lie in his memoirs generously recognized this, and so did the Arabs and Israelis. In fact when Bunche died twenty-three years later, Golda Meir waited in the rain until the doors of the funeral home in New York opened in order, as she explained when I hastened to rescue her from the downpour, to be the first to pay a last tribute to Bunche. It was a moving recognition from a very hard-headed national leader.

In 1948, things were not so easy for anyone. Lie was under relentless pressures from all sides on the Palestine issue and was rumored to have become biased in favor of Israel. I now doubt this allegation. When the Arabs, who had opposed the UN Partition Plan by military force, accepted the truce ordered by the Security Council on July 17, 1948, they gave up their last hope of eliminating the new State of Israel. The easiest individual on whom to focus their feelings of resentment against the United Nations was the Secretary-General, who was obliged to, and did, staunchly uphold the UN decision for partition which the Arabs had gone to war to negate. From the Israeli side, the efforts of the UN and the Mediator in making proposals for a settlement were regarded with suspicion and resentment born of a great feeling of insecurity. All of these pressures bore in on Lie. Palestine was the first great test of the United Nations as the international authority in a specific situation. Lie felt strongly that the decisions of the organization must be respected, and if possible enforced. In the circumstances, this was not likely to please either the Arabs or the Israelis.

Nor was it easy for Lie to accept that one of his officials had become the focus of world attention. I greatly respected and admired Bunche, and was troubled that while he was carrying out a lonely and hazardous task in the Middle East, he was being undermined and even put in danger by the goings-on at UN Headquarters. Lie was not happy when I said as much to him.

It was quite clear to me that I no longer enjoyed Lie's confidence, if indeed I ever had, and I myself was increasingly uneasy about him. I therefore suggested to Lie that I should work elsewhere. Nothing could be done until we returned to New York, so I determined to enjoy myself in Paris in the meantime.

After a family Christmas at Amberley, Alfreda and I left England for New York on the *Queen Mary* in a gale which blew the ship onto a submerged obstacle in Cherbourg harbor. This mishap caused us to return to Southampton for repairs which lasted, punctuated by optimistic reports from Cunard, for five days. We finally got to New York twelve days later. It was a stormy crossing, and three small children (our son Robert was born in February 1948) on a transatlantic liner were a considerable handful. The best thing about the voyage was the life-giving presence of Isaiah Berlin.

Our return heralded a singularly futile and bleak period in my career. I obviously could not go on working for Lie. Being British, I could not go to Palestine where the action was, since the British at that time were the arch-scapegoats. I had no desire to sink into a bureaucratic sinecure, and yet I wanted to go on working for the United Nations.

On our return to New York I was relegated to the part of the Secretary-General's office which was supposed to coordinate the work of the specialized agencies. Our work epitomized, in its futility, the built-in diffuseness of the United Nations system. There was, and is, as little chance of the Secretary-General coordinating the autonomous specialized agencies of the UN system as King John of England had of bringing to heel the feudal barons. Indeed, the situations are in some respects similar. The agencies each have their own constitutions, budgets, and national constituencies, and have no intention of being coordinated by the UN, although they must pretend to be in favor of it. In the coordination section our self-serving documents papered over this ambivalence by being skillfully drafted to give the appearance of saying something while giving offense to no one.

*　　　*　　　*

In 1950, North Korea invaded South Korea. Due to the absence of the Soviet Union from the Security Council in protest at the exclusion of Communist China, the UN actually went to war against aggression for the only time in its history. I was on holiday with Alfreda in Venice at this historic moment, and it is a measure of my complete separation from the serious business of the UN that I stayed on vacation for another four weeks. In any case, after the initial proceedings in the Security Council, in which the United States rushed through a decision for the UN to intervene with force before the USSR woke up to what was happening, the United States was designated as the Unified Command for the operation and took full control. The UN had little or nothing to do with the military action.

The main effect of the Korean War on the Secretariat was a complete break between Trygve Lie and the Soviet Union, which had been perceived, wrongly, as his chief original sponsor. Lie loyally carried out the decisions of the Security Council on Korea and was, as a result, excommunicated forever by the Soviets.

A simultaneous development on the American side compounded Lie's already considerable difficulties—the insidious smog of McCarthyism. The Secretariat, and especially its large American component, was a natural hunting ground for Senator Joseph McCarthy and his henchmen, Roy Cohn and David Schine, and Lie soon found himself in an extremely difficult situation.

McCarthy was reckless, unscrupulous, and had no interest in, or regard for, the truth. His antics put Washington and the American establishment in a state of defensive panic which closed many doors to his victims. I know of no case among the Americans then in the Secretariat where there was any real evidence for McCarthy's accusations of Communist treachery and betrayal.

This evil phenomenon threatened the career and sanity of one of my closest friends. Gustavo Duran was an authentic hero. Born of a well-to-do family in Madrid, he had been a professional pianist and composer, until, at the age of twenty-seven, he was called up as a reserve officer in the Spanish Army to resist the insurgency of Franco. He had fought for the Spanish Republic with heroism throughout the Civil War, becoming a corps commander at the age of twenty-nine. He was one of the last Spanish Republican generals to surrender. He appears by name in Ernest Hemingway's *For Whom the Bell Tolls.*

Gustavo had escaped from Barcelona on a British warship and went, with many other Spanish refugees, to England, ending up at Dartington Hall, a progressive school in an Elizabethan palace in Devonshire, where he met and married his American wife, Bonte. As the British military establishment showed no interest in taking on a foreigner with three uninterrupted years of battle experience against the Germans and Italians in Spain, Gustavo and Bonte soon left for the United States.

When the United States came into the war Gustavo, who had taken American nationality, went to Cuba to work with his old friend Hemingway in a bizarre naval intelligence operation in the Caribbean. They lived in Hemingway's famous house, the *Finca Vigía*, in macho style. Bonte's arrival there was evidently not altogether welcome to Hemingway. When she entered the drawing room on her first evening, she exchanged greetings with a large and friendly dog. "Leave the bitch alone!" Hemingway roared. This ambiguous remark set the tone for the rest of Bonte's stay.

When Gustavo came back to Washington toward the end of the war and began to hear distorted versions of his role in the Spanish Civil War, he asked for an official State Department investigation. The inquiry cleared him completely. In 1946 he joined the UN Secretariat.

Joseph McCarthy, at the outset of his anti-Communist rampage, accused Gustavo of being a Soviet agent and dredged up a libelous and derogatory version of his career published in the Franco press. Gustavo was, at first, unperturbed. He had, after all, asked for, and been cleared by, a United States government investigation and did not take McCarthy's reckless charges seriously. Nor did his friends.

We were badly mistaken. FBI agents conducted personal inquiries among his friends. At a rally in Madison Square Garden McCarthy, pointing to a blown-up photograph of Gustavo in his Spanish Army general's uniform, intoned, "It seems incredible that Duran is here dressed as a

Communist agent." As *Time* magazine commented, "He said it seemed incredible, and it was." Some former friends began to make themselves scarce.

Gustavo was a proud man, and he was humiliated and disgusted by this squalid episode, which also had practical consequences. He was due to go to Europe on United Nations business and could not extract his American passport from the State Department. He could have used his UN *Laissez-passer*, but would then have been unable to reenter the United States. The authorities evidently hoped that Gustavo would take this course. On the day of his scheduled departure for England, I took Bonte and her three daughters to the ship. Gustavo stayed behind. As we neared the gangplank, a man approached me and said, "Good morning, Mr. Duran. I see you are leaving us." Ignoring him, I went on board to install the Duran family. When I left the ship, the man again accosted me saying, "Ah, Mr. Duran, I see you have changed your mind." I then identified myself and demanded that he do the same. When he refused, I said that I would complain of his harassment to a nearby policeman. He begged me to go no further, explaining that he was an FBI agent. I suggested that he tell his organization to lay off Duran. Gustavo's passport arrived by special messenger the next day, too late for him to catch the boat. He was eventually once again fully cleared.

The case of Ralph Bunche, the most distinguished American member of the Secretariat, was even more absurd. On the fabricated evidence of government informers, Ralph was summoned before a grand jury to explain his alleged links with the Communist Party in the thirties. His hearing had to be adjourned on one occasion so that he could fly to Washington for dinner with President Eisenhower. After a long and involved hearing he was fully cleared.

The McCarthy witch-hunt played havoc with the morale of the Secretariat and with Lie's leadership. Lie tried to defend his American staff by cooperating with the American authorities in investigations to clear those who were under suspicion. In normal times this might have been the best course to follow, but times were not normal. Lie was caught in an impossible situation, for in cooperating with the procedures designed to clear the accused members of the Secretariat, he whetted the appetite of the witch-hunters, gave credence to their charges, and lost the confidence of his staff.

Politically the Soviet excommunication of Lie was a disaster; administratively and psychologically the McCarthy witch-hunt was immensely destructive. A great personal tragedy darkened the latter process. Abraham Feller, the Legal Counsel of the UN, was a brilliant man and a delightful and witty companion. After serving the New Deal with distinction, he had seen in the United Nations a chance to pursue its aims on the international stage. As Lie's chief legal adviser, Abe was regarded with suspicion both by the witch-hunters and by the hunted. The strain proved too much, and he jumped out of a window in his apartment in the autumn of 1952.

This was a time of frustration and disillusionment. After the Jackson episode I was viewed with considerable suspicion by Lie and the senior members of the confused bureaucracy which I had so unrealistically tried to shake up and revitalize and was sidelined in the Kafkaesque fantasy of the coordinating office.

Fortunately there were other demands on my time. The new UN Headquarters in Manhattan was ready in August 1950. The only reason for living in a Long Island suburb—to be near Lake Success—had vanished, and Alfreda and I decided to move to Manhattan. She found a superficially derelict but basically sound four-story house on East 70th Street which we bought for $38,000. This stretched our unstable finances to the limit, but we decided that we could swing it if we did all the renovating work ourselves and rented the top floor as a separate apartment. Thus my unused energies were fully employed as painter, plasterer, floor-scraper, paper-hanger, and odd-job man. We moved to Manhattan in the spring of 1951.

IX

Dag Hammarskjold

On November 10, 1952, Trygve Lie surprised everyone by announcing his resignation. He wanted, he said, to hand over to someone who could have the united support of the membership. In those days candidates did not campaign for the office of Secretary-General as they now, regrettably, do, but were designated by the Security Council, and a prolonged search for a successor began. In March 1953 the Council announced its agreement on Dag Hammarskjold of Sweden.

Although he had had a distinguished career from an early age in Sweden, Hammarskjold was not widely known outside his own country. It was generally felt that he was a cautious, safe, and non-political technocrat who might heal some of the rifts that had appeared under Lie and would avoid controversial political actions. In this belief the distinguished permanent members of the Security Council were delightfully mistaken, for Hammarskjold was an exceptional man with a strong and independent sense of mission.

Hammarskjold's election gave the United Nations eight years of dynamic, and often visionary, leadership. His advent signified a turning point in the affairs of the UN at a time when several other developments also gave grounds for optimism. Eisenhower became President of the United States in January 1953, giving hope for an end to the Korean War. Stalin died in March. There was a new sense of international purpose in the air.

Dag Hammarskjold initially appeared as diffident, quiet, and youthful for his forty-seven years. His informality and modest manner concealed a strong and determined nature and an almost evangelic passion for his work—a passion which increased over the years as he identified himself more and more with the objectives and ideals of the Charter. It also concealed a remarkable intellect and an extraordinary talent for administration.

Taking over his new office with a minimum of fanfare, Hammarskjold set about tackling the immediate problems by making, as was his habit, an intensive intellectual analysis of them. He attacked the "loyalty" problem not only by a much firmer line with the American authorities, but by asserting his leadership over the staff and reformulating much of the basic philosophy of the Secretariat. He established a forward momentum by himself taking initiatives, instead of simply reacting to events. He also reorganized the administration with impressive energy and expertise, reducing the budget and redeploying the members of the Secretariat. His papers and statements on these matters are masterly monographs on administration and management. Unlike most such documents, they are stylish, simple, and readable.

I first met Hammarskjold in May 1953 at a dinner given by Gladwyn Jebb (later Lord Gladwyn), who was then British Ambassador to the United Nations. I do not recollect what we said, but he evidently decided after that meeting, perhaps also at the urging of Gladwyn, that he would move me into his immediate circle.

One of Hammarskjold's organizational changes brought two senior officials, the American and Soviet Assistant Secretaries-General, into his own office as his chief assistants for active political assignments. The top American official was Ralph Bunche, and Hammarskjold assigned me to him as his chief assistant. Bunche, who liked to do things on his own, was not too keen on this arrangement at first, but he was soon reconciled and later came to like it. For me it was a summons back into the mainstream of UN political activity and effectively launched me on the work that I have been doing ever since.

My time with Bunche and Hammarskjold was by far the most rewarding experience of my career. Working up to fifteen hours a day and often through the night over a period of seventeen years, I must have spent more hours with Bunche than with anyone else in my life. It took time and effort to get to know him, to appreciate him and to gain his confidence and, ultimately, his friendship. I owe him an immense debt not only for that friendship but also for his example of integrity, clear thinking, and consistency, and for his demonstration of the art of negotiation.

Although I worked in Hammarskjold's office for eight years and saw a great deal of him, I never felt I knew him well. I doubt if more than a few Swedish friends ever really knew him—or he them. When I think of Hammarskjold—as I still often do, for he was the most memorable of men—the image of the unicorn comes to mind, an image which Hammarskjold himself uses in his book *Markings*. Although Hammarskjold was a public man of astonishing accomplishments, he had a striking innocence of mind and attitude and seemed remote from ordinary life. He exemplified the very Swedish characteristic of personal mystique—someone ostensibly private and mysterious who attracts constant attention and achieves great fame. He was the most unusual and striking personality I have encountered in public life.

Hammarskjold was not an easy man. His relentlessly high intellectual and ethical standards made him intolerant of incompetence and impatient with slow or confused performance. He was at the same time shy but demanding, modest but arrogant, quiet but with a formidable capacity for anger and indignation. I do not think he was accustomed to dealing with people at close quarters, and he did not encourage intimacy or familiarity. Indeed those who attempted it usually suffered painful rebuffs. However, because his other qualities were so impressive, his aloofness seemed entirely natural.

There was, and is, an enduring rumor that Hammarskjold was homosexual, which in the 1950s was a far more sensational allegation than it would be now. I worked closely with Hammarskjold for eight years, as did many others. None of us ever saw the smallest evidence or justification for this story, which was assiduously peddled by people who did *not* know Hammarskjold and who, for one reason or another, resented him. Hammarskjold himself was fully aware of the gossip and wrote a haiku about it:

> Because it did not find a mate
> They called
> The unicorn perverted.

My own impression was that Hammarskjold was unusually squeamish of all close personal contacts, was exceptionally jealous of his privacy, and could not envisage sharing his life with anyone else. I would guess that he was asexual, admittedly a rare condition. He was certainly a determined loner in his personal life. In *Markings* he himself, half disapprovingly, hints at a narcissistic tendency in his own character. There is nothing particularly novel or unusual about homosexuality, but the rumors about Hammarskjold have always struck me as vulgar, and sometimes self-serving, attempts to demean and diminish an exceptional and unusual person.

Hammarskjold was a deeply committed man. He believed in what he was doing in full knowledge of how difficult—even impossible—his task was. He knew more about each aspect of our work than we did ourselves and maintained a ruthlessly high standard of performance and behavior. He was supremely well qualified in a wide variety of disciplines—law, economics, diplomacy, and politics in particular. It was both fascinating and challenging to work for him.

In his first year at the UN, Hammarskjold effected an extraordinary transformation both in the attitude of the Secretariat and in the renewed interest and respect with which governments and outside observers began to treat the UN. It was a triumph both of personality and of intellect. In the sometimes almost unbearable frustrations of later years, I have often recalled that time and that slight, indomitable, strangely innocent figure as a reminder of what can be done through leadership and commitment to an idea.

When I went to work for Bunche and Hammarskjold, I realized how little I really knew of politics and diplomacy and how superficial my perceptions of our work had so far been. Bunche was a hard taskmaster and quite deliberately made life difficult for new recruits. I had known him since 1946 but had never worked with him or experienced at first hand the meticulous attention to detail and capacity for hard work which lay behind his remarkable achievements in Palestine.

Bunche never accepted propositions or information without testing them out. He was skeptical of facile formulations or slick ideas and profoundly suspicious of ostensibly plausible and smooth operators. He tended to question everything, including practical arrangements, a process which took up a great deal of time. This irritated people until they discovered that he was usually right. Bunche believed that any deviation from absolute intellectual or personal honesty was inadmissible. He was also the kindest and most compassionate of men, the indefatigable friend and champion of the weak and oppressed. Except for those that were obscene or merely abusive, he personally answered every one of the thousands of letters he received each year. He was a down-to-earth man who greatly enjoyed the more ludicrous and farcical aspects of the situations we dealt with.

As with many of Hammarskjold's concepts, the exact function of the office of the "Under-Secretaries-General without Portfolio" (as Bunche and his Soviet opposite number were originally called) was not clear at first. We had no fixed duties, staff, organization, or jurisdiction. We were to be assigned special political tasks, and the title was later changed to "Office of the Under Secretaries-General for Special Political Affairs." Bunche's Soviet colleagues suffered from the fact that Bunche was not only remarkable but permanent, whereas they only came for a year or two. They too were a distinguished lot, including Anatoly Dobrynin, who later served for more than twenty years as Soviet Ambassador in Washington, and our relations were cordial and cooperative.

Although the development of the conflict-control technique later called "peacekeeping," and the negotiations often associated with it, became the main business of our office, our first main assignment had to do with the peaceful uses of atomic energy.

*   *   *

In December 1953, President Eisenhower had presented to the General Assembly a far-reaching and imaginative international scheme for the peaceful uses of atomic energy which included a great international scientific conference "to study the development of atomic power and to consider other technical areas—such as biology, medicine, radiation protection and fundamental science—in which international co-operation might most effectively be accomplished." The Eisenhower proposals seemed to offer the possibility of a new era of East-West cooperation on this most sensitive and important branch of the technological revolution.

Hammarskjold insisted that the Advisory Committee for this conference, of which he was chairman, should consist solely of scientists of the highest possible standing. Thus there came into being the most distinguished committee in the history of the United Nations. Its members included I. I. Rabi of the United States and Sir John Cockcroft of the United Kingdom, both Nobel Prize winners, Soviet Academician D. V. Skobeltsin, Bertrand Goldschmidt of France, and Homi Bhabha of India, a brilliant mathematician, physicist, artist, and musician. Hammarskjold felt very much at home in this company of practical intellectuals, and his skill as a chairman and intermediary, his quiet but dominant personality, and his obvious intellectual powers soon welded the group into an effective team.

The organizing secretary of the conference was Professor Walter G. Whitman, Professor of Chemical Engineering at the Massachusetts Institute of Technology, and Hammarskjold put me in as his chief executive officer and assistant. Walt, with his goodness of heart radiating through his bifocals, and his scrupulous attention to detail, sometimes reminded me of Dr. Dolittle. He assembled a brilliant and diverse team of young scientists as the "scientific secretaries" of the conference, and we set to work, in January 1955, to stimulate and organize what we hoped would be the greatest exchange of previously classified scientific data in history. In the process Whitman and I visited Moscow, London, and Paris to elicit scientific papers to match the impressive lists already produced by the United States and Canada. In the end we had 1,067 scientific papers to work into a two-week program. We also had, with the help of the scientific secretaries, to try to explain the significance of this material to the press and public. Abdus Salam's press conference on the significance of pi mesons was generally considered to be a classic in this field.

The conference took place in Geneva in August 1955. It included a large scientific exhibition of which the highlight was a functioning American "swimming-pool" reactor. (I encountered this artifact again five years later during the uproar in the Congo. It had been given to the University of Lovanium in Leopoldville and played an unwelcome role as the first potential radiation hazard in Africa.)

The conference attracted a record number of mystified but respectful journalists. Every meeting began and concluded precisely at the advertised time. We had installed elaborate warning mechanisms—warning lights, bells, and gongs—to curb long-windedness but we never had to use them. We also installed a music room where the scientists could relax between meetings. They were the most disciplined and constructive group of people ever to attend a UN meeting.

The conference built a new bridge between East and West, and, to some extent at least, revived the concept of an enlightened world community of science and scientists which had been overshadowed by the war, the Cold War, and by the invention of nuclear weapons. It was a politically encouraging event in the most promising and constructive year for international peace since the beginning of World War II. On the scientific side it may also have contributed to the euphoria about nuclear energy—the patronizing phrase "non-renewable sources of energy" (meaning oil and coal) dates from this time—which has been rudely dispelled over the succeeding years.

The establishment of the International Atomic Energy Agency (IAEA) was the next phase of Eisenhower's 1954 initiative. Hammarskjold felt strongly that this Agency, above all others, must not be isolated from the political life of the UN by claiming purely technical status. It might—indeed should—play a key role not only in developing the peaceful uses of atomic energy but also in future systems of arms control, nuclear safeguards, and inspection for disarmament. He designated me, as the UN official with the most direct and detailed experience of these matters, to be the executive coordinator for the setting up of the future Agency, but before I could embark on this task a new crisis broke out in the Middle East.

X

The Suez Crisis

IN LATE OCTOBER 1956 Israel, Britain, and France invaded Egypt and precipitated a uniquely confused and dangerous international crisis. In the previous year Nasser had approached the Soviet Union for the arms the West had refused to provide him. The Egyptian-Czech arms agreement was a turning point for the Western powers, but their efforts to offset Soviet influence by setting up the Baghdad Pact and by initially offering massive financial aid for the Aswan High Dam further complicated an already explosive situation.

The situation between Israel and Egypt in Sinai and the Gaza Strip had also deteriorated. From February 1955 the Israelis launched a series of operations against Egyptian and Palestinian soldiers in the Gaza Strip. Egypt responded in August with the first raid on Israel by Egyptian-trained Palestinian "fedayeen" from the Gaza Strip, giving rise to heavy Israeli reprisals.

The "fedayeen" guerrillas (and later the PLO) were a new problem for the international community. No Arab government would admit direct responsibility for their efforts, which were usually against civilian targets. The Armistice Truce Supervision machinery was powerless to give protection against this clandestine and ostensibly unofficial activity. Israel's massive reprisals, on the other hand, were a clear violation of the Armistice Agreements and were usually condemned as such by the Security Council. Thus began a new and embittered phase in Israel's relationship with the UN, the organization which had given birth to it and protected it in its early struggles. The cycle of violent action and reprisal steadily escalated.

International tension over the future of the Suez Canal reached critical

dimensions in July 1956 with the abrupt cancelling of the Western fi-
nancing of the Aswan High Dam, to which Nasser responded by nation-
alizing the Suez Canal Company.

Israel invaded Egypt through the Sinai on October 29 with the avowed
intention of eliminating the "fedayeen" bases from which terrorist raids
had been launched. Two days later, working with Israel on a prearranged
plan, Britain and France, having given an "ultimatum" to Egypt and Israel
each to withdraw ten miles from the Suez Canal, began bombing Egyptian
airfields and other targets as a preliminary to invasion. All of this came
as a shock to most people—to the United States which had not been
informed in advance by its allies, to the other Western countries, and
even to the British ambassadors in Cairo and at the United Nations.
Hammarskjold felt doubly betrayed. He had been conducting apparently
promising negotiations over the future of the Canal with the British,
French, and Egyptian foreign ministers, and the talks were scheduled to
resume on the very day of the Israeli invasion. Britain and France were
the standard-bearers of that Western European civilization that he so
greatly admired. Hammarskjold's statement of principle in the Security
Council made such an impression on me at the time that I quote it at
length:

> The principles of the Charter are, by far, greater than the Organization
> in which they are embodied, and the aims which they are to safeguard
> are holier than the policies of any single nation or people. As a servant
> of the Organization the Secretary-General has the duty to maintain his
> usefulness by avoiding public stands on conflicts between Member nations
> unless and until such an action might help to resolve the conflict. How-
> ever, the discretion and impartiality thus imposed on the Secretary-
> General by the character of his immediate task may not degenerate into
> a policy of expediency. . . . A Secretary-General cannot serve on any
> other assumption than that—within the necessary limits of human frailty
> and honest difference of opinion—all Member nations honor their pledge
> to observe all Articles of the Charter. . . .
>
> The bearing of what I have just said must be obvious to all without
> any elaboration from my side. Were the Members to consider that another
> view of the duties of the Secretary-General than the one here stated would
> better serve the Organization, it is their obvious right to act accordingly.

The Anglo-French expedition was a fiasco from the start. Conceived
in anger and deceit, foolishly planned, and hesitantly carried out, it rapidly
landed both countries in an impossible situation, denounced not only by
their allies but by much of their own people as well. The fact that, due

to the long voyage from Malta, the seaborne landings in Egypt could only take place five days after the air offensive had started ensured failure, for in those five days all of the massive forces opposed to the expedition had time to rally. On November 4 Hammarskjold was authorized by the Assembly, since the Security Council was blocked by British and French vetoes, to negotiate a cease-fire and secure the withdrawal of all forces behind the Armistice Demarcation Lines. Although it was evident that the British and French Forces, still on their way from Malta, would have to land as scheduled on November 5, it was also becoming clear that the main task before the UN was to find a way to save their faces and to allow them to withdraw with what dignity they could salvage, as soon as possible.

The idea of a United Nations force had been discussed early in the crisis by Lester Pearson and Hammarskjold. The original idea had been that the Anglo-French forces would be subsumed into such a force, but this was soon dropped as politically out of the question. Hammarskjold was initially skeptical of the new concept of a United Nations force and doubted if it could work. However, by November 3 even Britain and France were taking the position that they would stop their own military action if Egypt and Israel would accept a UN force to keep the peace. Hammarskjold was therefore obliged to explore the idea, and he was formally asked to do this by the Assembly on November 4.

All this time Bunche and I had been more or less on the sidelines. Hammarskjold started writing his report on the establishment of the United Nations Emergency Force (UNEF) before lunch on November 5. He read the first three pages to Pearson and Cordier at lunch and dictated the rest between various other commitments during the afternoon. By late that evening, after a Security Council meeting, he appears to have felt the need for more support and advice, for at 10:30 p.m. he went over the text with Bunche, Cordier, and his Legal Counsel, Constantin Stavropoulos. The report was completed at 2:30 a.m. the following day and despatched to the British and French governments for whom it was the condition for agreeing to a cease-fire in Egypt.

Hammarskjold's report was a conceptual masterpiece in a completely new field, the blueprint for a non-violent, international military operation. The Emergency Force now had to be put together and deployed in Egypt as soon as possible in order to assure the withdrawal of French, British, and Israeli forces before some new complication, such as the deployment of Soviet forces in Egypt, emerged. General E. L. M. (Tommy) Burns, the Canadian Chief of Staff of UNTSO, was instructed to set up shop in

Cairo at once, while in New York we started to assemble and organize the first UN peacekeeping force.

I was the only person on the thirty-eighth floor with extensive military experience, and those six years of World War II and the arid hours at the Staff College now proved exceptionally useful. Literally everything about the new force had to be worked out from scratch. We established in our conference room on the thirty-eighth floor a group which met around the clock to tackle problems and resolve them as they came up. The group consisted of military representatives of countries which had troops immediately available—Canada, Colombia, Denmark, Finland, India, and Sweden—and two American officers to coordinate airlift and logistical support. Hammarskjold, Cordier, or Bunche appeared from time to time. I provided continuity and ensured that our discussions were followed up by action. David Vaughan, the head of our Department of General Services, was the moving spirit of our logistical improvisations.

We covered an extraordinary variety of ground in a very short time. One of the first problems was how to identify the UN troops. With three foreign armies fighting on Egyptian soil it was important that the UN Force should be clearly distinguishable, but its soldiers would be wearing their own national uniforms, some of them—the Canadians, for example—identical with the British Army. Distinctive headgear seemed to be the key, and we agreed on blue berets, only to find that it would take weeks to get enough of them made. There were large stores of American Army helmet liners readily available in Europe, and to spray-paint them UN blue was a simple matter. Thus the "Blue Helmets" ("Casques Bleus") came into being. Having no logistical pipeline, we solved the problem of initially supplying the UN Force by buying the supplies on the seventeen ships which had been blocked in the Suez Canal during the fighting. Our efforts were almost exclusively an exercise in improvisation.

Strong emotions were raised by the Suez affair. Virtually everyone I knew was violently opposed to the Suez expedition, which we regarded as a doomed, dishonest, and contemptible aberration by the British and French governments. It was therefore with some embarrassment that I greeted the British Foreign Secretary, my old wartime acquaintance Selwyn Lloyd, when he arrived in New York in November. His bantering style ("I remember you as an exceedingly insubordinate young officer," etc.) was more in evidence than ever.

As soon as the British and French were forced to recognize the folly of the Suez operation and agreed to withdraw, they began, as a face-saving policy, a maddeningly detailed and critical supervision of UN efforts clean up the mess they had created, questioning every step with a patronizing self-righteousness that was hard to take seriously. They concentrated particularly on the preparations for UNEF and on Hammarskjold's arrangements for clearing the Canal, which had been blocked by the Egyptians as soon as the French and British attacked.

Selwyn Lloyd brought with him a delegation—called a "specialist group"—to supervise, with a similar French group, our efforts. These Anglo-French "specialists" were dumped on me since no one else either wanted, or had the time, to deal with them. Their mission contained much comic material. They were masquerading as civilians, although the British colonel always called the brigadier "sir," and both called their naval colleague "sir." When I addressed the latter as "Admiral," he bridled and repeated that he was a civilian. I commented on his habit of standing in the window swaying gently to and fro with a roll of secret Admiralty charts under his arm, and also on the deference paid to him by his army colleagues, adding that I had looked him up in *Who's Who* anyway.

The British brigadier got into trouble, at our gruesome first meeting, with his French colleague, a very stuffy naval captain. The brigadier recounted how on the morning of the Anglo-French landing in Egypt, the Chief of the Imperial General Staff had opened his morning meeting by saying, "Gentlemen, after more than three thousand years Egypt has once again suffered a plague of frogs." The French captain left the room in a rage. "Oh dear," said the brigadier, "I seem to have put my foot in it."

In my indignation at my own country over Suez, I learned a lesson from Hammarskjold. He had been perhaps more outraged than anyone by the Anglo-French action, but when the balance tipped and everyone was hounding the British and the French, it was his tact and skill that helped them to withdraw and save face. Suez, taking place against the darker background of the Hungarian tragedy, was a traumatic experience for the West. Hammarskjold grasped this important fact long before most people and determined to do everything he could to re-knit the essential web of Western solidarity so badly torn by this ill-judged, ill-fated action.

The first units of the United Nations Emergency Force took to the field in mid-November. The troops were flown by Swissair charter to the Capodichino airport at Naples and thence to Egypt by Italian military "Flying Boxcars" (C-119s). The British and French troops left Egypt before the end of the year.

The problem of the Israeli occupation of Sinai remained and was the subject of a series of acrimonious negotiations at the United Nations. The matter was finally resolved, in March 1957, by President Eisenhower. At the time of the Israeli invasion on October 29, four days before the U.S. presidential election, Eisenhower had publicly denounced it, defying all conventional American electoral wisdom. Two days later, even more strongly, he had condemned the Anglo-French adventure. An electoral landslide put him back in the White House. Eisenhower viewed the necessity for Israeli withdrawal from Sinai as a matter of international principle under the Charter of the United Nations. He apparently told the Israelis that the United States would radically restrict its support of Israel if Israeli withdrawal from Sinai was further delayed. The Israeli withdrawal was completed in late March 1957.

The Israelis withdrew with a bad grace, destroying roads and railway communications and leaving uncharted minefields in their wake, all of which caused considerable grief and trouble to UNEF. They started a vitriolic propaganda campaign about Hammarskjold's and UNEF's alleged partiality to Egypt. Israel also refused to allow UNEF to be stationed on the Israeli side of the line, a grave weakness for a peacekeeping force. The Israeli attitude to UNEF changed a few months later when they realized that the force, in its impartial way, had achieved peace on what had formerly been their most violent and bloody frontier.

Although UNEF's establishment went comparatively smoothly, the novelty of the peacekeeping concept, and the lack of previous experience and of time to prepare the troops for service in a situation completely new to them, kept us all busy and, at times, anxious. When the force moved into Gaza in March 1957, the attitude of the inhabitants was uncertain, and the UNEF troops were correspondingly apprehensive. On the first evening, when the muezzin started the call to prayer, some UNEF troops sprayed the minaret with warning shots, believing that the unfortunate priest was inciting civil disorder. We were lucky not to have had more of this kind of misunderstanding.

UNEF lasted just over ten years. Scarcely anyone realized the basic value or importance of its presence in Sinai and Gaza until it was dramatically terminated in 1967. The disastrous results of that termination are still with us. In its later years, the force was steadily whittled down for financial reasons until it had about 1,400 effective soldiers on a front stretching 300 miles from Gaza to Sharm el Sheikh. I used to be sent out from time to time to reduce UNEF's strength still further, largely in response to the urging of the United States and Britain, which were paying much of the bill. Treasury officials especially questioned the presence of a Swedish company at the then remote and inaccessible seaside location of Sharm el Sheikh at the entrance to the Gulf of Aqaba. The Swedes were there to provide a pretext for the Egyptians not to reoccupy the coastal batteries commanding the Strait of Tiran. Their whole point was simply *to be there* as a symbol of international consensus. The conventional Treasury mind never quite grasped this concept even after we gave the Swedes the pointless task of counting and identifying ships going through the Strait. The dismal experiences of 1967 belatedly brought about a much wider understanding of the peacekeeping role.

The modus operandi of peacekeeping operations, now commonplace, was then a first experiment, a complete innovation. We were asking soldiers, against all tradition and training, to take part in non-violent operations in a critical situation—operations, moreover, which were not under the control of their own governments. The new peacekeeping operations touched on the most delicate issues of military psychology, national sovereignty, international politics, and national and international law. Hammarskjold balanced these delicate factors in a masterly display of negotiation, management, and diplomacy, which allowed this completely novel enterprise to take hold and become a historic success.

I only fully understood the meaning of this effort two years later, when Hammarskjold was asked to report to the General Assembly on the UNEF experience, the success of which had created a high degree of enthusiasm in unexpected places. John Foster Dulles, and the U.S. Congress in a unanimous resolution, for example, called for the establishment of a standing UN peacekeeping force. Hammarskjold displayed extreme reserve in responding to this enthusiasm. I was asked to prepare a first draft of his report on the subject and devoted my summer vacation to writing an account of the creation of UNEF, drawing optimistic conclusions for the future. This draft was received by Hammarskjold, who had not explained to any of us what he had in mind, in polite silence, and he then wrote his own analysis. His main object, he wrote, was to avoid on future occasions the degree of improvisation that had been necessary with UNEF. He also hoped that his report might make clear the "legal restrictions imposed on the Organization by national sovereignty, as recognized in the Charter," and especially the need for the consent and cooperation of the host country. "Our approach to this problem," he said,

> is guided by the strictest respect for the rules of the Charter. It is entirely pragmatic in nature. It does not involve, even by implication, the creation of any new obligations from Member Nations. It does not affect, or seek in any way to affect the competence of the UN organs or their interrelations under the Charter. It does not try to freeze a pattern of action, nor would

it give rise to arrangements conducive to a premature or inappropriate use of similar means in the future. It does not presume to lay down legal rules binding in all circumstances. But it does, I hope, create a preparedness for such action as may later be found necessary, in so far as our previous experience of more general application can be utilized.

In other words, no standing peacekeeping force.

As with the peaceful uses of atomic energy, we were in danger of being swept away by an ephemeral tide of success and optimism. The hard realities of international life lay in wait like treacherous reefs beneath the deceptively smooth waters of high tide. Hammarskjold knew this and never got carried away. In the Congo we would run into the very problems which he had foreseen in his 1958 report.

*   *   *

The unexpected success of UNEF was a turning point for the United Nations and for Hammarskjold. In a critical situation we had shown that we could improvise a new kind of military operation that could actually achieve important results. UNEF was a great victory for common sense, innovation, hard work, and intelligent leadership. This result would have been impossible without the voluntary cooperation, however reluctant, of all concerned, including the British, the French, and the Israelis.

The UNEF success was in dramatic contrast to Hammarskjold's inability to do anything about the Soviet repression of the Hungarian insurgency. The Hungarian revolt had started on October 23, 1956, and ran parallel to Suez, but with very different results. The Soviet Union had no intention of heeding the decisions of the United Nations or anyone else on events in a country within its sphere of influence, and the Western powers were perfectly aware, as Eisenhower pointed out in his memoirs, that any forceful action by them would risk nuclear confrontation. The United Nations was the ideal dumping ground for such an unmanageable problem, and the Secretary-General the perfect scapegoat for the international community's inability to act.

With the Security Council blocked by the Soviet veto, the Assembly condemned the Soviet Union by a large majority and passed the problem of getting the Soviet forces out of Hungary to the Secretary-General. All Hammarskjold's efforts on Hungary were rebuffed by the Soviet Union until it was far too late to do anything useful, and he was reduced to marginal humanitarian tasks. He was stridently criticized in the West for this failure. Western governments masked their own inability to act by publicly urging Hammarskjold on, knowing perfectly well that effective action was impossible. Hammarskjold, who was normally realistic about political expediency, found these strictures hard to bear, particularly when it was sometimes implied that in his anxiety to chastise Israel, Britain, and France, he had neglected to make sufficient efforts over Hungary. In Hungary there was no question of Soviet compliance with UN decisions, and, if no one was prepared to challenge the Soviet Union, the UN and the Secretary-General were impotent.

* * *

By April 1957 peace had returned to Sinai, and UNEF was becoming routine. I therefore spent the next six months on the establishment of the International Atomic Energy Agency (IAEA) in Vienna, working with a brilliant Swiss civil servant, Paul Jolles, who had been appointed Executive Secretary of the Preparatory Commission of the Agency.

The Soviets had just launched Sputnik, the first man-made object in space. In Vienna you could dial a special number and hear Sputnik beeping away triumphantly. With the often parochial wheelings and dealings of our work in Vienna I could not help feeling that the Atomic Energy Agency, for all the professed nobility of its objectives, was already old-fashioned. It seemed at that time that the Agency was likely, in the short term at least, to be mostly another sop to the conscience of the nuclear powers, a parochial sideshow while the real questions of the nuclear age were decided and dealt with elsewhere. Later on, the Agency safeguards systems became an important part of the Non-Proliferation Treaty, and it remains a valuable potential agent in future nuclear arms control arrangements.

In international affairs it often takes a major disaster to demolish nationalistic obstacles to progress. In 1986 one of the Soviet reactors at Chernobyl in the Ukraine exploded, blowing radioactive fallout over Scandinavia and Europe. In the storm of recrimination which followed, the IAEA Director-General, Hans Blix, was the first to go to Moscow and to treat the tragedy as a transnational technological disaster which had showed, if further proof were needed, that reactor accidents do not respect national frontiers. It remains to be seen whether the Agency will eventually fulfill the great ambitions that some of us had for it at its birth.

I was glad to return from Vienna to Ralph Bunche's office in New York in early November 1957.

XI

The Lull Before the Storm

In New York there was a strong and positive tide flowing under Dag Hammarskjold's leadership. He had been reelected unanimously for a second term by the General Assembly on September 26, 1957, giving notice that he would not serve if the vote was not unanimous. He planned to concentrate in his next five years on building up the active role of the UN in keeping the peace and, in so doing, to develop the role of the Secretary-General in filling vacuums created by disagreements among the great powers in the Security Council.

Although Hammarskjold was cautious and realistic on the sensitive issue of national sovereignty—his reaction to Dulles's suggestion for a permanent peacekeeping force was an example of this caution—he also believed that the time had come to take further steps to enhance the role of the United Nations as an active peacekeeping organization. I am not sure whether he realized at that time what dangerous territory he was entering, where a sudden change in the pattern of events could put him into direct confrontation with one or more of the great powers. In any case, in 1958 we were all very proud of our organization and believed that it was on the right track at last.

Hammarskjold was in many ways an unworldly man and often made mistakes in trying to judge quickly the character and capacity of others. He was always looking for the perfect colleague and, somewhat to the annoyance of his permanent staff, several jewels without price were imported, were given extravagant attention, soon proved to have feet of clay, and left, usually with much ill-feeling. The average cycle was about six months. By 1958 Hammarskjold had come to the conclusion—belat-

edly perhaps—that he was best served by his existing senior colleagues.
Thus the most important crisis assignments now tended to come our way.

I had concluded early on that Hammarskjold preferred his colleagues
to keep a dignified distance, but this did not mean that he was not an
important and ever-present feature of our lives. He was so interesting
and commanding a personality that we were happy to work for him in
whatever capacity and in whatever part of the world he might suggest.
This was terrible for family life, but irresistible. What none of us clearly
foresaw in 1958 was that a certain hubris was setting in.

In March 1957, I was asked by Bernard Moore, the BBC correspondent at the UN, to give some anecdotal background for a BBC portrait
of Hammarskjold. I answered that Hammarskjold was not a very anecdotal
man, nor was I, but that I would do my best:

". . . The most interesting thing about Hammarskjold," I wrote,

> is that he has by his own personal character and talents transformed the
> office of the Secretary-General into something much more important than
> it ever was before, and this has radically affected both the political position
> of the United Nations and also the position of the Secretariat. He has
> done this by slow and relatively quiet steps, spending the first part of his
> term of office in gaining the confidence of Governments, especially the
> major ones, which in turn has caused them to land on his shoulders a
> large number of problems to which they could find no solution themselves.
> Whether this is a desirable thing for the long-term development of the
> United Nations I am not quite sure, since it raises once again the old
> illusion that the United Nations is a sort of super-government, whereas
> it is, in fact, as is now very obvious, only a treaty backed by an admin-
> istrative organisation which happens to be directed by an exceptionally
> able man.

I do not recall what had already made me nervous of the dangers of
perceived supranationalism, but I suspect it was the slightly evangelistic
tone which had begun to creep into some of Hammarskjold's utterances
and attitudes.

By 1958 I was no longer the enthusiastic neophyte of 1945. In the ups
and downs of thirteen years, I had concluded that we could do a lot of
useful things for humanity, provided we were not deluded by grandiose
or simplistic ideas of an instant new world order. A dedicated international
staff led by an outstanding Secretary-General could certainly help to avoid
the worst, make a lot of situations better, and develop a more effective
international system, but I doubted if we would be privileged to usher

in the millennium. We just had to go on trying and keeping faith with the Charter. As a rational, international Whig, I was sometimes uneasy at the possibility that Hammarskjold might be beginning to hear voices.

*   *   *

The summer of 1958, much of which I spent in Geneva organizing the Second International Conference on the Peaceful Uses of Atomic Energy, was dominated by the crisis in Lebanon. Although this was a picnic compared to later Lebanese disasters, it had all the makings of the most dangerous possible situation—a regional and domestic squabble in an area where the Soviet Union and the United States had both interests and deep suspicions of each other's intentions, and where each had clients anxious to involve them actively in the conflict.

The basic element of the 1958 crisis in Lebanon was the opposition's resistance to President Camille Chamoun's determination to get a second presidential term by amending the Lebanese Constitution. Lebanon's pretext for bringing the crisis to the United Nations was the charge that the United Arab Republic (Egypt and Syria) was intervening in the internal affairs of Lebanon by infiltrating armed bands across the Syrian border.

Hammarskjold set up a three-man Lebanon Observation Group, Galo Plaza of Ecuador, Rajeshwar Dayal of India, and General Odd Bull of Norway, served by a large group of United Nations Military Observers. Hammarskjold, as usual, went to the area to install the Observation Group and conducted intensive talks in Beirut and in Cairo, where he aimed to pin Nasser down to a firm undertaking not to interfere in Lebanon. The British and American governments, who deeply distrusted Nasser, evidently hoped that massive infiltration from Syria would be confirmed. Certainly Chamoun's government was deeply disappointed and angry when the Observation Group, which could find no evidence of infiltration, refused to state, on the basis of its observations, that any such infiltration was taking place.

The Lebanese government increased its pressure on the United States to intervene in Lebanon and was backed up by Iraq, Turkey, Iran, and Israel. This pressure was being resisted in Washington when, on July 14, an unrelated event, the coup by Brigadier Kassem in Iraq, threw Washington's caution to the winds. Wrongly construing Kassem's coup as the beginning of the Nasser-led, Moscow-inspired takeover of the Middle East which had long been one of the CIA's favorite nightmares, Washington landed some 10,000 Marines in Lebanon, which is not contiguous to Iraq and had nothing whatsoever to do with Kassem's coup. Apart from being an illogical and precipitate move which risked a Soviet counter-move, the massive landing by the United States Marines on a popular bathing beach south of Beirut on a Sunday afternoon halted the process of domestic compromise in Lebanon. Hammarskjold's task thus changed to a rescue operation, the devising of a face-saving formula which would, as soon as Washington realized the risk and the irrelevance of its action, allow the Marines to be withdrawn with honor. Britain had simultaneously moved troops into Jordan and also had to be extricated.

The number of UN Observers was increased although their task did not demand it; the General Assembly held a special session at which Eisenhower put forward a program for peace in the Middle East; and on August 18 the British and U.S. governments announced that they would withdraw their troops from Jordan and Lebanon if the UN took steps to ensure the peace and security of those countries. Hammarskjold played along skillfully with this charade, and the Lebanese crisis ended to almost everyone's satisfaction with minimal bloodshed. Not unnaturally, Hammarskjold was not given too much credit in subsequent Western memoirs for what was certainly one of his better exercises in crisis diplomacy.

The 1958 Lebanese story was a good example of Cold War mythology obscuring the realities of a regional episode, and of the naiveté with which powerful governments can react to such a situation. It was also a foretaste of the Lebanese habit of seeking to involve outsiders in their internal political struggles and a reminder that powerful governments, if trapped by their obsessions or preconceptions, can sometimes be easily manipulated.

*   *   *

In 1959, the world, in the late sunshine of the old order, was on the brink of great and stormy events. Ghana had gained independence in 1957, and Guinea became the eighty-second member of the UN in 1958, after Sekou Touré's classic defiance of de Gaulle, heralding the avalanche of new independent African states; the Algerian civil war remained violent and indecisive; tentative moves and countermoves over Laos foreshadowed the wider tragedy of Vietnam and Cambodia; the spirit of detente appeared to set the tone of East-West relations. Cyprus, apartheid, and Southwest Africa were still distant rumbles of thunder on a summer night. It was still, if only just, the world of the powers of 1945, not yet directly challenged in the United Nations by the emerging Third World, but already on the defensive.

In late May 1960, an American U-2 spy plane was shot down over the Soviet Union, and the Soviet Union was rebuffed by the Security Council when it asked for condemnation of incursions by U.S. aircraft into Soviet airspace. The long-planned summit talks in Paris broke down when Khrushchev withdrew, and the United States–Soviet relationship sharply deteriorated. The clouds were gathering, but in that early summer no one was quite sure where the storm would break. Certainly none of us anticipated that it would eventually center on the United Nations and on our revered Secretary-General. In little more than a year the United Nations would be split down the middle and Hammarskjold would be dead.

XII

The Congo

THE BELGIAN CONGO became an independent state on June 30, 1960. Almost immediately, sensational stories of the abuse, harassment, rape, and murder of Belgian colonists sent a shock wave through the Western world, while the reintroduction of Belgian paratroops caused indignation in the Congo and Africa.

Hammarskjold had visited the Congo earlier in the year and had been impressed by its size, wealth, and complexity, but above all by the total lack of preparation for its impending independence. Foreseeing trouble, he sent Ralph Bunche to Leopoldville well before Independence Day and told him to stay on to be available to the new government for consultation and advice. The post-independence chaos greatly exceeded Hammarskjold's premonitions.

Bunche's first letters to Hammarskjold from the Congo gave no grounds for optimism. Joseph Kasavubu, the president-elect, and Patrice Lumumba, the prime minister, old antagonists, were already at loggerheads, and Bunche foresaw that they would soon fall out for good. The Belgians, believing that after independence the Congolese would need them and that nothing would be substantially changed, were openly contemptuous of the new Congolese leaders. Even the name of the new state was in doubt, since the French Congo across the river, also newly independent, was already called Congo.

Already during the independence ceremonies Patrice Lumumba's acid, hard-hitting speech in response to the paternalistic homily of King Baudoin of Belgium had set the tone for the drama that was soon to follow. Lumumba not only castigated the Belgians in emotive terms but scored a popular point over Kasavubu, who had made sycophantic references to them. The key figure in the country was unquestionably Lumumba, of whom Bunche wrote on July 4: "At times he resembles the most recent version of God's angry young man. But I have also seen him relaxed and laughing heartily, after being excitable and emotional only shortly before." We were to learn much more about Lumumba's volatile temperament in the weeks to come.

The Congolese, apparently believing that independence gave them the right to do as they had been done by, attacked Belgian settlers all over the Congo. The Force Publique, the Congo Army in which no Congolese held a higher rank than sergeant, mutinied and threw out its Belgian officers. The Belgians panicked and left in large numbers, and the Belgian government sent Belgian troops, mostly young paratroopers, back into the newly independent country to restore order and protect Europeans, causing the Congolese in their turn to panic. Public administration, business, and communications came to a standstill. In ten days the Congo, technically the most advanced of all African colonies, had crumbled into anarchy and chaos.

In this disastrous situation Kasavubu and Lumumba first appealed to the United States to intervene. Eisenhower politely turned this request down and suggested they go to the United Nations. This they did on July 10. Hammarskjold immediately set about consulting the members of the Security Council and the African states as to how best to respond. The situation was further complicated the very next day by Moise Tshombe's announcement of the secession of the Congo's richest province, Katanga. On July 12, in a further request, Kasavubu and Lumumba asked for United Nations military assistance. Fighting was now going on in most of the main towns of the Congo between Belgian troops and the mutinous Congolese Army.

Kasavubu and Lumumba's request was unprecedented, but Hammarskjold realized that an immediate and conspicuous UN intervention was the only hope of getting the Belgian troops out and of avoiding a complete breakdown of public order and administration. Outside intervention was another disastrous possibility, for both the United States and the Soviet Union were watching the situation closely. In these pressing circumstances there was no time to consider where this new expedition might lead the United Nations or what obstacles it might run up against a little further down the road. Thus, on the morning of July 13, Hammarskjold asked for an urgent meeting of the Security Council. At luncheon that day he briefed the members of the Council at length, proposing United Nations assistance in security and administration, the sending of

United Nations troops, and the shipment of emergency food supplies. The Council met at 8:30 p.m. on the hot, humid evening of July 13; when it adjourned at 3:25 a.m. the following day, the organization was committed to the most difficult and challenging task in its history.

Up to this point I had watched the proceedings from the sidelines. Bunche was in Leopoldville, and I was running his office, but during the night it became clear that some very urgent practical action was going to be necessary.

When the Security Council adjourned in the early hours, we went immediately to Hammarskjold's conference room on the thirty-eighth floor to discuss what had to be done. Hammarskjold, as usual, was the mainspring, telephoning all over the world for troops, aircraft, staging areas, and supplies, evolving instructions and directives, setting up a command and staff organization, and choosing a name for the new operation—ONUC (Organisation des Nations Unies au Congo). Three hours later, when we dispersed for breakfast, the operation was already under way. I was instructed to go to Leopoldville at once with my colleagues John Olver and Virgil de Angelis by whatever means could be found, in order to help Bunche organize and run his new command.

Thursday and Friday were filled with hectic preparations for a country and an operation about which we knew virtually nothing. By Friday it was only clear that the first troops would be from Ghana, Morocco, Tunisia, and Ethiopia, with a mixed bag of pilots for whom we still had to find aircraft. The United States and the Soviet Union were taking care of the initial airlift of troops and supplies to the Congo.

We left for London on Friday evening and I drove to Amberley from Heathrow to say goodbye to Alfreda and the children, whom I was to have joined for the summer holidays the following week. We took off the same evening for Kano in Nigeria, which was the staging point for U.S. transport aircraft running the emergency food lift into the Congo. As all commercial flights to the Congo had been suspended, we hoped to be able to hitch a ride on one of these aircraft.

Kano was full of terrified Belgian civilians evacuated from the Congo by returning American transport aircraft. They were a sorry sight. We soon located a C-124 bound for the Congo, and proceeded via Douala (Cameroun) to Leopoldville.

The pilot and the crew of our C-124 had come directly from a relief mission to the victims of an earthquake in Chile, and our arrival in the Congo was somewhat confused. The pilot's map only showed Ndolo, the old airfield of Leopoldville, which had been closed for some time. We landed on it nonetheless, and crowds of Congolese ran at the aircraft from all sides. The pilot, who had been talking to the Belgian refugees at Kano, did a quick turn and took off through the crowd which scattered like rabbits. We then located the new Ndjili airport where we should have gone in the first place.

Ndjili was all tension and bustle. It had recently been taken over by young Belgian paratroopers who were both aggressive and nervous, a terrible combination. They had already established a disastrous relationship with the Congolese at the airport and an uneasy one with the UN. An unending stream of American transport aircraft were flying in and out carrying food supplies or UN troops from Rabat, Tunis, Addis Ababa, and Accra. An aircraft from Jerusalem brought Lieutenant-General Carl Carlsson von Horn, the Swedish UN Chief of Staff in the Middle East whom Hammarskjold had appointed as commander of the UN operation. Von Horn was an unhappy choice. He was vain, arrogant, and jumpy. His arrival in the Congo was typical. We had told him from New York to fill his plane with all the things we needed urgently—flags, blue helmets, armbands and identifying insignia, communications equipment, and other essentials. Instead he had brought his personal automobile. (If there was one thing readily available in the Congo it was motorcars of all kinds, which had been abandoned by the hundreds by the departing Belgians.)

The American Military Air Transport Service aircraft which made our rapid deployment possible were in the capable hands of Major Steve Cuomo from New York. No task seemed to be beyond Steve's ingenuity, and he ordered his world-encircling fleet about the skies with breathtaking ease and speed. He also excelled in acts of kindness. Bunche, who was diabetic, was dependent on fresh milk, a nonexistent commodity in the Congo, so Steve flew it in daily from Germany. The U.S. Military Air Transport Service was a miracle of improvisation, flexibility, and common sense.

When I arrived in Leopoldville after two successive nights' flying, I was, unreasonably perhaps, looking forward to a shower and even a few hours' sleep. When, however, I called up Bunche from the airport to announce my arrival, he told me to stay where I was as he had an interesting assignment for me. I detected in his voice the note of glee which usually meant that he was about to hand you a hot potato.

Just before midnight, Bunche arrived at the airport. As acting commander of the UN troops pending von Horn's takeover, he had been given a hot, stuffy office in the control tower. Bunche's room attracted everyone with a problem or a complaint. It was also the headquarters of the Ghana contingent, then directed by a British general, Henry Alexander. It was surrounded, against our wishes, by heavily armed and tense young Belgian paratroops. It was here that incoming troops and personnel were given orders for their next move. It was all very informal.

The cradle of the mutiny of the Congolese Army was a large military camp at Thysville, halfway between Leopoldville and the Congo's main Atlantic port of Matadi. Both places had become ghost towns inhabited only by mutineers and terrified Congolese, and both were essential to restoring normal life. No trains had run to Matadi for two weeks, and the port was closed. The task Bunche had in mind for me was to take a detachment of troops, open up the railroad, and restore order in Thysville and Matadi. We were discussing what troops were available when the incoming transport planes began to disgorge the Moroccans. They looked tough and taciturn and marched off the runway preceded by a band and a venerable black goat, their regimental mascot. They were obviously just the thing for Thysville and Matadi. Their commander, a compact and urbane veteran, was Colonel Driss Ben Omar.

Our next problem was how to get a train and, more difficult, an engineer willing to drive it. We managed to locate an engineer and overcame his natural timidity by liberal administrations of beer. He was even induced to bring the train, an elegant white diesel affair, to a siding near the airport to pick us all up. We finally got the Moroccans mustered at 2:30 a.m. and drove to the siding where we found several journalists, including Henry Clay of NBC, who was later killed near Stanleyville. Although the United Nations was officially—and wrong-headedly—negative about the press at that time, I was delighted to have their company.

We draped a UN flag across the front of the engine, more for aesthetic reasons than practical ones since the Congolese had never heard of the United Nations. "L'ONU? C'est quel tribu? (The UN? What tribe is that?)" a local Congolese official inquired. We stationed a cooperative local businessman, Mr. Kernow, who had expressed a desire to help, in the cab to boost the engineer's morale, and embarked for our first mission.

Having no idea of the situation down the line, Colonel Driss and I agreed that we would stop at each station and formally address whomever happened to be on hand. If mutineers appeared, the Moroccans would detrain and look tough, and the mutineers would be told to report back to barracks. If this proved insufficient, limited forceful action would be taken. The colonel and I travelled in a first-class compartment with the goat, which smelled awful but was very dignified. The goat had a tremendous effect on the crowds along the way and probably did more than anyone else to secure respect for the United Nations. The colonel, an old campaigner, slept a good deal which was wise of him. It was cold, mosquitoey, and there was nothing to eat or drink.

The expedition was a great success and far less hazardous than we had foreseen. The inhabitants came running through the bush to greet our train and listened to our speeches at each station with wonder and incomprehension, their eyes on the goat and the band. At Inkisi, where the road and railway cross the Congo River, there was a large crowd, many Force Publique soldiers, and great excitement. The soldiers had just shot down a Belgian fighter which had been strafing the bridges, and its wreckage was still smoking at one end of the station.

The soldiers, dressed up for mutiny in full battle rig with all weapons loaded and camouflaged helmets, were edgy and suspicious. Never having heard of the United Nations or Morocco, they were inclined to assume that everything was a Belgian trick. Colonel Driss handled them with tact and just the right note of authority. While explaining that we came as friends, he insisted that discipline, order, and calm must be maintained. Soldiers should go back to camp and civilians to work. This did not go down too well at Inkisi, and there were angry protests. Driss responded by asking the local commander to mount a guard of honor for the raising of the United Nations flag while the Moroccan band played. This increased the local commander's prestige, and he suddenly became very friendly, his beaming smile visible for a long time as the train pulled away. We left a small Moroccan detachment behind anyway.

The word of our progress had gone ahead of us. We reached Thysville early in the afternoon and were greeted by a large crowd. The majority were mutineers in a hostile and suspicious mood. The Moroccans were light-skinned enough to pass, in Congolese eyes, for Belgians—in fact practically any foreigner of any color qualified—and the colonel and I were anxious to avoid a showdown. The goat and the band detrained ceremonially, the band playing while the battalion formed up on the station square. The audience were enchanted.

While the troops took control of the Thysville camp, Colonel Driss and I set off up the hill in a Force Publique jeep to meet the newly appointed civil administrator. The administrator seemed entirely at sea in an office which had never been handed over and where the desk was still piled high with the unfinished business of the colonial regime. He charmingly admitted that the situation was beyond his comprehension. He was also extremely nervous of the mutineers. They got drunk, he

My parents' wedding—Bridport, 1910.

With my mother and Andrew—1926

Badminton School directorate: Miss B. M. Baker (left), Aunts Lucy and Janet Rendall. The dog is "Major."

The King's Scholars of Westminster processing to the Coronation of King George VI—Westminster Cloisters, 1937. (BU is third in the nearest row.)

Oxford undergraduate—1938.

Jumping from a Whitley.

General Boy Browning dominates a group photograph of his original airborne staff—the "dungeon party"—1941. (BU in circle upper right.)

SS women at Bergen-Belsen bury the dead. (Photographs at Yad Vashem, Jerusalem.)

A battered Mercedes brings the German Commander in the West to surrender to General Montgomery—May 1945.

My driver, Mike Stannion, examines a V-2 rocket—Germany, April 1945.

With Halfdan Lefèvre of the Danish resistance—Denmark, May 1945.

First session of the United Nations Security Council. (At table, Andrei Gromyko, Ernest Bevin, Edward Stettinius. Among others present: Adlai Stevenson, Alexander Cadogan, Nicholas Henderson, and Andrew Cordier. David Owen and BU, top right in back.)

Trygve Lie supervises ballot counting in the General Assembly. At table: David Blickenstaff, Nasrullah Entezam, Abe Feller, Gunnar Hägglöff, and BU.

With Dag Hammarskjold—1955.

Setting up UNEF I—New York, 1956 (Ralph Bunche, General E.L.M. Burns, David Vaughan, BU and military attachés).

Congolese soldiers, during the mutiny, with Colonel Driss Ben Omar—Inkisi,
Congo, July 1960.

Hammarskjold with Bunche and BU—Leopoldville, Congo, August
1960.

With my mother, Alfreda, Thomas, Katie, and Robert—Amberley, 1956.

said, and looted and assaulted women. He begged Colonel Driss to station some of his men in the town.

The Force Publique mutiny was the key to the situation, and we got back to the military camp as soon as courtesy would permit. The Moroccans had already begun to establish order, and a rabble of mutineers was straggling back. Driss personally stopped the more disorderly of these and demanded a salute, rebuking them for their disarray at a time when they had just become the masters of their fate. He topped this off by organizing and commanding a mixed guard of honor for the raising of the United Nations and Congolese flags over the camp headquarters, personally drilling the guard for an hour, the Moroccan soldiers prompting and guiding the disoriented Congolese, until Driss was satisfied that their performance was good enough. It was a masterly show and had the effect of turning the mutineers back into soldiers again.

The Moroccans were especially effective in the Congo and later undertook the training of the Congolese Army. This effort, which would have made a vast difference for the future, had to be discontinued three months later for political reasons after the constitutional crisis.

Order had returned to Thysville, and reports from Matadi indicated that word of the Moroccans' imminent arrival had already had a salutary effect. Colonel Driss Ben Omar was obviously equal to any occasion and had taken to United Nations peacekeeping as if he had been doing it all his life. I therefore reluctantly took my leave of this admirable soldier of peace and returned by jeep to Leopoldville in the middle of the night. It was, unexpectedly, very cold, and the only covering I could find was a large UN flag. Swathed in pale blue I entered Leopoldville for the first time.

Bunche had established a temporary headquarters in the Stanley Hotel, a relatively comfortable establishment where his bedroom also served as our main office. I was glad to find a bed and my luggage and to get a few hours' sleep.

The violent interaction between the Belgian troops and the Congolese destroyed all hope of restoring calm and normality. Our most urgent task in the Congo was therefore to replace the Belgian troops as soon as possible. We also had to help the new and totally inexperienced Congolese administration to take hold of the reins of government in a chaotic situation. Being the sole source of protection and assistance in Leopoldville, our headquarters attracted everyone who was frightened or had a problem, a category which included a large percentage of the population and all foreign residents. We also received, night and day, urgent calls for help from all over the vast country.

The UN contingents, after a few hours' stopover at Ndjili, set off again to their appointed regions—the Ethiopians to Stanleyville, the Tunisians to Luluabourg in Kasai, the Irish to Kivu, and the Moroccans to Bakongo and Coquilhatville. The Guinean battalion, after many delays, set off by boat up the river to the steamy plantations of Equateur. They seemed to have more problems than anyone else, and the fact that the battalion commander was a four-star general was no help.

The Belgian exodus, and the breakdown of all normal communications except for a capricious telephone network, had left an almost total vacuum. The Leopoldville police station had been stripped and put out of operation by the departing Belgians. The control tower at the airport had to be manned by international personnel. The financial and banking institutions were in chaos and needed instant attention.

Efforts by newly appointed Congolese officials to fill such gaps were usually unhelpful. The new chief of communications in Coquilhatville, when asked for a working plan of the province's telephone system, proudly produced the local telephone directory. On arriving at the hospital in Matadi the Moroccans came upon the head male nurse, just promoted to director, in the operating room with his assistant, both brandishing scalpels and arguing, over the recumbent form of a terrified patient, as to where the first cut should be made for an appendectomy. Neither had been given any surgical training whatsoever.

My first morning in Leopoldville, Tuesday, July 19, was spent in a meeting with the Belgian military, the aim being to get them out by the following Saturday. "We want to show you how honest these silly Belgians can be," said the Belgian Commander-in-Chief facetiously, but it wasn't as simple as that, as we soon found out when Bunche told them they must also evacuate the strategic bases of Kamina and Kitona, as well as secessionist Katanga. All hell broke loose, the Belgian Chief-of-Staff spluttering, "If that happens we shall need a UN Force in Belgium to quell the revolution."

Lumumba himself was not much help either. On this particular day, for instance, he delivered an ultimatum to Bunche on Belgian withdrawal, withdrew it when Bunche pointed out that it would be entirely counterproductive, and then repeated it later on the radio. Lumumba was unquestionably intelligent and a demagogue of considerable powers, but he lacked stability or judgment. As prime minister he was, in any case, trying to deal with a virtually impossible situation. In 1957 he had written *Congo Mon Pays*, a sympathetic, perceptive, and often humorous book. When I reviewed it in 1962 I wrote of him:

> Lumumba was perhaps more misunderstood and more misinterpreted than any postwar nationalist leader. By his partisans he was depicted as a saint, a martyr, and a great revolutionary leader, and by his opponents as the devil incarnate. Somewhere in between the two the truth lies, of a courageous, unstable, inexperienced, imaginative, quicksilver, and patriotic man who went disastrously wrong and for whom the situation and his own personality finally proved too much. He was, at his best, a talented and intelligent man who had made an immense effort to analyse and understand the problems of his own unfortunate people. . . .
>
> The world would not let Lumumba alone, and he had none of the inherited resistance to flattery and self-delusion which is so essential for a public man. He was naive, however intelligent, and when power and celebrity came to him his naïveté turned to mania. At the end he was adulated, feared and fanatically attacked. His real public life lasted for just under two years. Whatever else he did, he certainly made an impression.

The Western press soon stereotyped Lumumba as "pro-Soviet" or "Red." Nothing could have done more to misrepresent the reality of Lumumba. His first international action as prime minister was to appeal for American intervention in the Congo, hardly the act of a "Soviet puppet." Lumumba, like many liberation leaders, was a nationalist and an opportunist who would demand or take help from wherever he could get it. He was forever appealing to the United Nations, the United States, the African countries, the Western Europeans, and the Soviets. Like most such leaders he casually used Marxist rhetoric. During the crisis in September, during one of his many rows with the United Nations, and sandwiched between appeals to us for assistance, he threatened in a public statement that in eight days' time Soviet troops would come to the Congo

> chasser brutalement l'ONU de notre République. . . . S'il est nécessaire de faire l'appel au diable pour sauver le pays, je le ferai sans hésitation, persuadé qu'avec l'appui total des Soviets, je sortirai malgré tout victorieux.
>
> (to expel the UN by force from our Republic. . . . If it is necessary to appeal to the devil to save the country, I shall do it without hesitation, persuaded as I am that, in spite of everything, with the full support of the Soviet Union I shall emerge victorious.)

This somewhat tactless statement epitomized Lumumba's attitude to out-side help and his hair-trigger and opportunistic nationalism.

Lumumba's attitude to us was relatively friendly most of the time. At one of our earliest meetings he had taken me aside to ask why Ham-marskjold had sent "ce nègre Américain" (Bunche) to represent the UN in the Congo. I told him brusquely that his remark was both offensive and absurd. Hammarskjold had simply sent the best man in the world for this impossible job. Lumumba apologized profusely, but the incident was a sad sidelight on racism, inverted racism, and the traumatized state of mind of many Congolese.

Lumumba knew nothing of orderly procedure and was surrounded by an unsavory crowd of hangers-on—a Yugoslav quack, a French renegade "political adviser," the Guinean femme fatale, Madame Blouin, and the Ghanaian Ambassador. There were also transient rogues—an American con-man, for example, to whom Lumumba was about to give a million-dollar advance for an unwanted and imaginary hydroelectric scheme. Whatever their relations with Lumumba, the Soviets certainly were no part of this raffish crew.

Our meetings with Lumumba would usually go, in a single hour, from cordiality, to threats, to grumbling, and back to cordiality and appeals for help. He worked in the old formal office of the Belgian Governor-General, which had about ten telephones dotted about the room. Whenever the telephone rang, which was often, Lumumba would rush from one in-strument to the other trying to locate the one that was ringing. If he succeeded in doing this, he would shout, "À qui j'ai l'honneur?" and then launch into a lengthy and emotional dialogue. It was extremely difficult to have a coherent conversation with him. It happened one day that his five-year-old son was in the room and, with his superior hearing, located the ringing telephone at the first try. It was valuable to have Patrice Junior around in the interests of saving time and the prime minister's temper.

Visiting Lumumba's residence was not always a pleasant experience. If you were not obviously Congolese, the guards tended to take you for a Belgian and arrest you. At night especially, primed on beer and "chanvre" (the local hashish), the guards could be extremely disagreeable. Our peo-ple were constantly being arrested by mistake, and it took hours and usually the intervention of Lumumba's military aide, Colonel Joseph Mo-butu, to get them released. In late July Lumumba conceived the idea of making a grand tour to New York and other places, which gave us a respite.

Another cross to bear was our own military organization. General von Horn had brought in cronies from the Truce Organization in Jerusalem to fill key posts, and they were mostly useless. They drank a lot and seemed strangely reluctant to go outdoors and get an idea of what was really happening. Since I knew something of military matters, I was detailed by Bunche to travel about as much as possible. This was resented by von Horn and his crew.

We also had difficulties with General Henry Alexander, the British Ghanaian Chief of Staff, who contrived at the same time to be a confidant of President Kwame Nkrumah and to hold old-fashioned colonial views about the Congo. He believed the Congolese Army should be disarmed, if necessary by force. "The nigger in the woodpile," he once said to Bunche, "is the ANC [Armée Nationale Congolese]." When I told Henry that he might have phrased this better, he was appalled and wanted to apologize. I assured him that he had given Bunche a story he would cherish all his life. Alexander was a courageous officer of the old school and a born leader of troops, but he simply could not swallow the idea that we refused to disarm the national army of the country we had come to help.

We soon moved from the Stanley Hotel to a block of apartments, the Royale, on the Avenue Léopold, the main boulevard of the city. We were still cramped for space, and the elevators were treacherous. F. T. Liu, who had come out originally with Bunche, and I shared a bedroom which also served as our office. Bunche presided day and night at a long table in the former salon of the apartment, which soon became known as the snakepit.

Since we were short of staff, this proved a surprisingly efficient way of dealing with the continuous series of emergencies and surprises which constituted daily life in the Congo. Bunche described a typical day:

. . . There is never a morning that does not begin without some new excitement—bayonetted Congolese at the door, trouble at the airport, UN staff arrested, a complaint also coupled with a new threat from the Prime- or Vice-Prime Minister, the military boys wanting to start shooting, etc. etc. The morning starts always this way and the day continues the same way, virtually, until the next morning . . . yesterday was about the quietest day in some time—we only had about three tough letters from Lumumba to answer, the commentaries on the SecGen's speech and the Alexander report to do, the mob to disperse in front of the French Embassy and the case of M. Dieu, and the assault upon and attempted rape of Bob West's wife. We got to bed early—about 3 a.m. . . .

In the snakepit, everyone was instantly aware of what was going on and no one had to be looked for when they were needed. We ate at a Greek restaurant which had survived on the ground floor, but the food was so awful that we soon resorted to K-rations and occasional delicacies provided by Steve Cuomo.

F. T. Liu, trilingual in Chinese, French, and English, specialized in liaison with Lumumba, Vice Prime Minister Antoine Gizenga, and Justin Bomboko, the foreign minister. (To accommodate the main tribes the Congo government had twenty-seven ministers.) His animated telephone conversations with these and others were favorite listening in the snakepit.

Despite the endless hours, the occasional dangers and physical harassments, and the frustrations of dealing with Lumumba and his colleagues, our spirits were high in July and August. We felt we were doing something both important and unique and were proud of it. In spite of initial difficulties with the Soviets, the Americans, the Belgians, and sundry others in Leopoldville, we were not yet aware of the gulf that was about to open beneath our feet.

In our first weeks in the Congo we got a very good press in the outside world, and the UN under Hammarskjold's dynamic leadership seemed to be on the crest of the wave. "This UN enterprise," Walter Lippmann wrote of the Congo operation, "is the most advanced and most sophisticated experiment in international co-operation ever attempted. Among all that is so sad and so mean and so sour in world politics, it is heartening to think that something so good and so pure in its purpose is possible." In the *New York Times* of August 9, in a piece entitled "United Nations—A Refuge of Sanity in a Silly World," James Reston wrote of Hammarskjold's success in filling the gap caused by the disagreements of the great powers and in devising a means of avoiding a confrontation of the great powers over the control of the Congo. "This remarkable man," Reston wrote, "is proving to be one of the great natural resources in the world today. . . ." Heady words. I doubt if Hammarskjold, who was skeptical of praise, took much notice, but in the Congo we were encouraged when these encomiums trickled through to us.

In Leopoldville, we were conscious from the beginning that the Soviet Embassy was large and active, but then so were several others. We were aware of a Mr. Fomin from the Soviet Embassy, who seemed to be ubiquitous and far too keen on "liaison" with United Nations contingents. We were constantly warned by the U.S. and British embassies of alleged Soviet moves, efforts to take over the police station, convoys of Soviet trucks at night, etc. Western embassies were obsessed by the imminence of a Soviet takeover. An embassy wife actually asked Bunche when "the Reds were coming," to which he replied, "My dear lady, they are already here."

The American Ambassador, Claire Timberlake, and his British colleague, Ian Scott, seemed irritated by what they regarded as our lackadaisical attitude toward the Soviet threat and were constantly rushing in with new evidence of sinister Soviet doings. Scott breathlessly described a planned rebellion of the army, and I asked him the source of his information. "My military attaché," he replied, "is moving inconspicuously among the Congolese rebels." I couldn't help laughing. The military attaché was a Scottish colonel, over six feet tall, with red hair and a kilt. Obviously the Soviet Union and the United States each feared a takeover by the other, and each was working inside the Congo to prevent it. Certainly the CIA was as, if not more, active in the Congo as its Soviet counterpart.

The Congolese were largely oblivious of the outside world and interested only in getting help and support for their own purposes and causes. I doubt if a single one of them was ideologically motivated, and when the Soviet Embassy thoughtfully made available in large quantities a 600-page French version of Khrushchev's speeches entitled "Bas les Mains au Congo! (Hands off the Congo!)," their boredom and lack of interest were palpable. I strongly doubt that the Soviet Union seriously intended to try to take the tumultuous country over. The Soviets were already having trouble in Ghana, and Lumumba was the kind of loose cannon whom they could not possibly have tolerated as a puppet for long. Certainly they, for their part, feared a United States takeover and would do everything possible to impede it.

In Leopoldville we became dimly aware of something amiss when we received an order that U.S. transport aircraft could bring UN troops to the Congo from *outside* but could not move them about *inside* the country. Since at that time we had no aircraft of our own, this was a serious limitation. The use of American aircraft to evacuate the Belgian troops was also barred. The Russians were already complaining to Hammarskjold of excessive American involvement in the UN operation, and he felt compelled to limit the risk. In New York the Russians began to echo Lumumba's charge that we were disarming the ANC while allowing the Belgian troops to stay, and accused ONUC, though not yet Hammarskjold, of all sorts of failings and misdemeanors. A main Soviet accusation was that we had refused to advance into Katanga to fight Tshombe's secessionist forces, to which Hammarskjold replied, "I do not believe personally that we help the Congolese people by actions in which Africans kill Africans and Congolese kill Congolese."

Certainly in August the storm-clouds were gathering. To give the assistance we felt was needed in the Congo and yet stay within the bleak political realities of the United Nations, to stay afloat amidst all the cross currents, idiocies, and conflicting interests that were soon to emerge in that benighted country, were tasks for angels, labors of vast complexity. Soon our every move would be questioned, every action criticized, every failure to act castigated. The simplest and most humane measures would be misinterpreted, and daily a choice would have to be made between acting in impossible conditions or not acting at all. Other extraneous conflicts would be superimposed on our efforts—East-West, black-white, commercial opportunism against national management, even the internal struggles of emerging Africa.

Hammarskjold came out twice to see us and to try to deal with the Katanga secession, which was becoming an obsession with Lumumba's government. Here we faced a typical Congolese dilemma. We were neither authorized nor equipped to deal with the Katanga secession by force, and Lumumba's army was quite incapable of doing so. In fact when, against all advice, he launched it southward in late August, it got stuck in Kasai and massacred thousands of innocent Baluba tribesmen. Nor, if we were to persuade Moise Tshombe to abandon secession, could Lumumba be associated with the enterprise in any way. In Katanga, Lumumba was regarded with terror and loathing and would have been resisted by all possible means. Hammarskjold therefore had to proceed by a roundabout route, knowing well that this would infuriate Lumumba. (Lumumba had recently visited New York, after which Hammarskjold cabled Bunche that he now understood better what we were up against in Leopoldville.)

On his first visit to the Congo in late July, Hammarskjold gained a first-hand knowledge of the madhouse. When he landed in Brazzaville, his welcome was taken over by the Abbé Fulbert Youlou of the French Congo who, white Dior soutane streaming in the wind, insisted on bringing him across the river to Leopoldville in his own speedboat. At a reception in Hammarskjold's honor, Vice Prime Minister Antoine Gizenga made a long and insulting speech while members of the Soviet Embassy circulated among the guests distributing anti-UN propaganda. At Hammarskjold's meeting with the Congolese cabinet, which arrived two hours late, a curtain was suddenly raised revealing the entire Leopoldville press corps. He observed the rudimentary nature of our office and the clownish disarray of von Horn's staff.

Hammarskjold greatly enjoyed the unexpectedness of it all and was at his best. I spent two late nights discussing with him the politics and the organization of our operation. He was firm that we should do nothing that could be done by the Congolese themselves, but that we should provide the crutch for them to learn to walk on. We must not become the new Belgians. He was already extremely clear about the Cold War complications that were threatening the entire operation. He described our efforts in the Congo as trying to give first aid to a rattlesnake. It was, he said, a political bordello with a number of foreign madams. I never liked Hammarskjold as much as I did on this visit.

After his talks with the Congolese government, Hammarskjold concluded that the time had come to eliminate any ambiguity about Katanga. On August 4, therefore, Bunche was sent by air to Elisabethville, accompanied by F. T. Liu, to establish whether UN troops could be landed in Elisabethville to replace the Belgian troops there. When, after a very rough welcome, Bunche decided that it would be out of the question to land peacekeeping troops in unarmed transport planes in Katanga, Hammarskjold immediately referred the matter to the Security Council and returned to New York to get new authority to deal with Katanga.

The situation in Leopoldville was distinctly tense as a result of all this activity. Lumumba was still abroad, but Gizenga, who in a later crisis entrusted his saxophone to the United Nations for safekeeping, did his utmost to fan anti-UN feeling with all sorts of rumors about Bunche's "negotiations" in Katanga. As a result, a great anti-UN demonstration was planned and then called off. Ironically, the Belgians were equally resentful of the UN for making moves to take over from *them* in Katanga, although it was increasingly clear that only their speedy withdrawal could prevent a new disaster.

At this tense time we were much preoccupied with the safety of the Belgian Ambassador. He should have left long before, but, for Belgian internal political reasons, could not depart until he received an expulsion order. Without this order he had to fly the Belgian flag outside his embassy, which caused angry demonstrations, which we had to control, which caused Gizenga to say we were collaborating with the Belgians, which caused the Soviet Ambassador in New York to make attacks on the ONUC leadership, which led to outspoken support for us from the United States and West Europeans, which led to allegations that ONUC was a

NATO plot, which embarrassed our excellent contingents which were predominantly African, which started Nkrumah off on another public homily to Hammarskjold, which increased the threat to the Belgian Ambassador, which—and so on. A typical Congo vicious circle.

Bunche and I had endless problems with General von Horn. The general—or "Supremo," as he liked to be called—having been asked by Hammarskjold to produce a standby plan for the move into Katanga, produced instead a list of reasons why this could not be done. When I rejected his list, he said that civilians did not understand military operations. After reminding him that I had spent six years in the Army in World War II, I wrote the plan myself. Von Horn sulked for several days and seemed to be on the edge of a breakdown.

When I got back to Leopoldville from a trip up the Congo River, von Horn was still sulking and Hammarskjold was expected back at any minute. He arrived in a bad mood. This was, I suspect, because he was going to have to do something which in other circumstances he would have considered wrong. He was going to install the UN troops in Katanga himself, and to do this without bloodshed it was essential to stay clear of Lumumba, the prime minister. He had therefore written, on the journey from New York, a very complex interpretation of the Security Council's decision on Katanga, which Bunche and I were to give to Lumumba after Hammarskjold had left Leopoldville for Elisabethville. He had written this Byzantine document in English, and it had to be translated to his own satisfaction into French. Being an operational headquarters, not a translation section, we had none of the resources to do this. When I explained this to Hammarskjold, he was furious.

Translating Hammarskjold's nuanced English into nuanced French was a daunting task even for a professional translator. We were at it all night with the help of whatever French speakers we could muster, and Hammarskjold, who insisted on supervising the process, made it very clear that he would be departing on his historic mission exhausted because of our incompetence. I got fed up with this at about 4:00 a.m. and spoke my mind. To my surprise things went much better after this, and when I took him to the airport he was cheerful and friendly.

Hammarskjold was indeed taking a very great risk. He was to land in Elisabethville and insist that the UN troops, all Swedes, land immediately after him. In the face of a lot of bluster from Tshombe in the Elisabethville control tower, he put this plan through. He deserved all possible credit for his courage and skill in doing it.

At our end in Leopoldville, it was Lumumba's turn to be furious.

When Bunche and I saw him that afternoon, he raged on about Hammarskjold going through Leopoldville without seeing him, our connivance with Tshombe, and our control of the airport, and he demanded that the UN leave the Congo at once. He ignored Hammarskjold's carefully phrased memorandum, the sophisticated nuances of which were completely lost on him. And then as always, after a two-hour meeting interrupted by innumerable unsatisfactory telephone calls, he began talking as a "man of peace" and seemed friendly and reconciled.

Hammarskjold's introduction of UN troops into Katanga, far from pleasing Lumumba, humiliated and infuriated him, and our relations with him for the brief remainder of his tenure were never the same again. When Hammarskjold returned from Elisabethville to Leopoldville, Lumumba refused to see him and instead discharged salvo after salvo of insulting letters which brought out the cold, unbending side of Hammarskjold's nature. Lumumba rounded off this display by asking Hammarskjold to delay his departure for New York for twenty-four hours so that four Congolese ministers could travel on his plane. The request was sharply refused, and Hammarskjold left on schedule. The next day opened with the arrest of sixteen of our staff and a military confrontation with Lumumba's army at the airport. Lumumba made a series of inflammatory speeches on the radio against Hammarskjold, which led to more violence against UN personnel.

Getting people out of jail and keeping the airport under control took much of our time. Common sense was a rare commodity in Leopoldville. Three Belgians who went around the town photographing the soldiers, the police, and Kasavubu's and Lumumba's guards, were, predictably enough, arrested. When we got them out, they came to me and made a furious protest at the United Nations allowing them to be arrested in the first place. The Swiss colonel whom we had acquired to organize the training of the army lost his nerve and had to be evacuated by helicopter to Brazzaville for repatriation.

In all this turmoil and silliness the journalists were a great standby. They included my old friend from Oxford, Patrick O'Donovan, and Gavin Young, both from the *Observer*, Henry Tanner and David Halberstam, the latter on his first foreign assignment for the *New York Times*, and David Holden and Jim Bishop of the London *Times*. Drinks and meals with them are my happiest memories of that time. Later on David Halberstam and I intended to co-author a column entitled "Social Notes from the Congo," but we never seemed to get the time to do it.

There were some odd personalities among the press corps. In my first days in Leopoldville, on an early morning walk, I heard pistol shots and came upon an elderly Briton holding a smoking revolver. He introduced himself as the London *Times* resident "stringer" and said he was shooting stray dogs. "I've lost my faith in the Belgians," he said. "They left their dogs behind."

We had a constant problem of mob control in Leopoldville, where riotous crowds could materialize from one moment to the next. The Ghanaian police were an invaluable asset and their commissioner a resourceful man of great common sense. We were particularly concerned at the possibility of massive clashes in Leopoldville itself between the rival youth movements of the various leaders. The "Jeunesse Lumumba" were particularly feared because of their leader's demagogic powers. The Ghanaian police commissioner said he had an idea for dealing with this problem without using force.

He let it be known that his police company would give a demonstration of crowd control in the Leopoldville soccer stadium. As there had been no soccer or any other spectacle since independence, this attracted a huge local audience. On the field the Ghana Police Company was divided into two—one end representing the police and the other disguised as rioters. The commissioner controlled the demonstration by whistle and gave a running commentary translated into Lingala. The teams advanced on each other and clashed violently. The police divided the rioters and searched for ringleaders. "They have now identified the ringleader," said the commissioner. At this point a shot rang out and the ringleader fell most convincingly to the ground. The rioters began to disintegrate. In total silence the audience began to make their way out as rapidly and unobtrusively as possible, taking their story to the townships of Leopoldville. The Ghanaian police enjoyed extraordinary respect after this.

Our problem with the Congolese Army over control of the airport highlighted one of the most difficult issues of peacekeeping, the question of the use of force. We had many arguments about this, some of the military favoring a fight with the ANC, others opposing it. For the UN to kill soldiers of the Congolese National Army was totally unacceptable, and in any case we were outnumbered everywhere in the Congo. Bunche ruled that our troops at the airport should resist the ANC by any possible means short of firing, and meanwhile we redoubled our efforts on the political side with Lumumba, Mobutu, and General Victor Lundula, the commander of the ANC. In the end this approach worked, but, not for the first or last time, it made Bunche and me unpopular with our soldiers. They simply did not want to understand either the principle involved or the bottomless morass into which they would sink if they descended from the high ground of a non-violent international peacekeeping force, which only used its weapons in self-defense, to fighting it out with the far more numerous locals.

Ralph Bunche had been in Leopoldville working night and day for over two months. He was exhausted and far from well. Being a diabetic in the uncertain dietary situation in Leopoldville was awkward, and an old football injury, a varicose ulcer on one leg, had flared up to a dangerous state. He was also anxious to get home to fulfill a long-standing promise to take his son Ralph to visit colleges. But the main reason for his asking to be relieved was the deterioration of his relationship with Lumumba, which made his task virtually impossible.

I have never forgotten Bunche in the Congo. He remained calm, humorous, kindly, and firm in every sort of impossible situation, and was the main source of whatever common sense and compassion there was in that madhouse. He sat imperturbably in the snakepit hour after hour, day and night, receiving a constantly changing and usually pathetic cast of visitors and supplicants, writing directives, cables to Hammarskjold, letters to the government, or instructions to our different sectors in the Congo. He was never excited or nervous, even when the mutineers arrested him early on in July, baffling them on this occasion by continuing calmly to write the cable he had been writing when he was arrested. He did not mind taking unpopular decisions and being regarded as obstinate, for he was determined to do what he thought best in a situation which became daily more confused.

Hammarskjold consented in late August to Bunche's return to New York and selected Rajeshwar Dayal, who had been Indian Ambassador to the UN, to succeed him. He sent Andy Cordier to Leopoldville to take Bunche's place in the meanwhile. Bunche left on August 30 saying that the Congo had been his richest, if not his most pleasant, international experience and that no problem was too great for an organized international community to tackle. In the light of what happened next, these words have a slightly quixotic ring.

Behind all the fuss and fury in Leopoldville a catastrophe had begun to unfold in the Kasai province where Lumumba was flying in detachments of the ANC, supposedly to sweep triumphantly into Katanga. Supported by no logistics or other plans, the soldiers took to living off the country and were soon massacring the resident Baluba, the most successful and richest tribe in the Congo. The first details of these atrocities came from G. C. Senn, the International Red Cross representative in the Congo.

G. C. Senn was a German Swiss who had lived in Africa since 1938. He was outspoken, determined, and always put his own safety and comfort second to the pursuit of his humanitarian vocation. He was short and barrel-shaped, with a bullet head, thick eyeglasses, and a drooping white mustache. He was peppery and sometimes extremely funny. He was deeply religious in a rough-tongued way, and honest and direct as a child. He was terrified of women. I became greatly attached to him and remained in touch with him for many years after he had gone back to his sawmill in southern Rhodesia.

G.C. was not enthusiastic about decolonization—or at least about the way in which it was being carried out—and he was critical of the United Nations, believing us to be a well-meaning but misguided group of liberals, besotted with the heady wine of self-determination and independence and far too lenient with Africans. He also despised the fact that in all our actions, civil and military, we constantly stressed the importance of non-interference. He believed that this pusillanimity on our part caused more confusion and bloodshed than a tougher, less principled approach. His views were summed up in one of his long letters four years later:

> In 1944 nobody thought of the possibility that after 20 years the majority of the UN members were to be a kind of political Teddyboys . . . for judging these representatives of the new independent states by their maturity, they are indeed political Teddyboys: As long as there is no proportional representation, according, e.g., to the number of people in a country, the present bedlam will happily or unhappily go on, and you are in the middle of it, frustrated and/or paralysed. When I could not sleep recently, I pondered over the UNO generally and the Secretariat particularly, and found the parable that you are very like a bicycle rider who is riding without the chain: he cannot ride uphill or on level ground, but only downward. I fear that you are already going downward, and I wonder when the brake will be removed as well, in order to accelerate the speed to disaster—i.e. to the disintegration of UN.

G.C. could never understand that serving an intergovernmental political organization like the UN was different from being the representative of a purely humanitarian non-governmental organization like the International Committee of the Red Cross, but he was an excellent antidote to the kind of self-deception which so easily overcomes bureaucrats with a mission. Whatever his views about the UN, he worked very closely and helpfully with us and was often dependent on us for supplies, transport and, if he would ever accept it, protection.

G.C. first came into my life during the Baluba massacre. He was fearless and believed that his appearance and temperament would protect him. When a journalist said that if G.C. went to Bakwanga, the center of the Baluba massacre, he would be eaten, he commented, "Too old, too tough and too ugly." I came back to my room one day to find a typical penciled note from G.C.: "I am going tomorrow to Bakwanga and return after having had a look at the place and shown my figure and face to the Europeans." When he came back he had, as usual, terrible accounts of what was going on and, in company with Cordier and the rest of us, raised hell with Lumumba and Kasavubu.

On September 1, I decided to go to Kasai myself. I had a good excuse since several visiting Tunisian ministers wanted to visit the UN Tunisian troops stationed in Luluabourg, the provincial capital of Kasai, and needed an escort. Our departure from Leopoldville was typical. We had chartered an Air Congo plane (run by Sabena) for the trip, but the crew, when they heard of the destination, vanished, so we had to postpone our departure until the following day.

We finally reached Luluabourg without incident. My friend Gustavo Duran was our civilian representative there and seemed, in these exotic but unpredictable surroundings, to be enjoying himself immensely. The local ANC commander, Colonel Ndjoku, was evidently appalled at the massacre of the Baluba, and we took him back to Leopoldville to try to help in stopping it. My efforts to go on to Bakwanga, however, were unavailing. No one would fly me there, and when I tried again the following day, all available aircraft had vanished. I was not altogether sorry about this.

Kasai was the "Diamond State" of the Congo, and Luluabourg had been a rather fancy, pretentious, middle-class European town with boutiques, restaurants, and comfortable villas. It was now almost completely deserted but still in perfect condition. It had no relation to the current situation and would soon fall into decay. This made me wonder what economic and social objectives our large civilian assistance program ought to be pursuing.

I returned to a heightened state of tension in Leopoldville. In late August ten Soviet transport aircraft—Ilyushin-14s—painted with the Congolese colors had been put at Lumumba's personal disposal. They operated from Stanleyville in the northeast of the country, Lumumba's political and tribal base. Rumors about Soviet intervention had markedly increased due to the troop-ferrying activities of these aircraft, which were flying the ANC into Kasai. Western embassies were apprehensive that Lumumba would start flying troops from Stanleyville to Leopoldville to tilt the balance in the capital in his favor. I was sent to Stanleyville to see what was going on.

On the surface Stanleyville was far more pleasant and normal than Luluabourg, although our civilian staff there were constantly being arrested or harassed by the ANC on suspicion of being Belgians. Our troops in Stanleyville were Ethiopians who believed in moving slowly and not making waves. They had direct orders from Emperor Haile Selassie not to come to blows with the Congolese. They had just been ordered by ONUC Headquarters to prevent any more troops taking off for the massacre in Kasai by closing the Stanleyville airport, and were convinced this was the wrong thing to do. One of my tasks was to persuade them to do it.

The main source of tension in Stanleyville was the ANC, but an additional complication was the Soviet personnel, "doctors," and other *soi-disant* experts, who were attached to the Soviet transport aircraft. A strong propaganda effort was under way to promote Soviet prestige and undercut United Nations activities, and this in turn made the remaining Europeans uneasy. They were especially fearful that Lumumba might turn up in Stanleyville in person.

On the morning of September 6 I was woken very early by our representative in Stanleyville, Pierre Dufour. Kasavubu had just dismissed Lumumba, and Dufour expected a violent local reaction. He urged me to come to the UN office as quickly as possible. Thirty minutes after Kasavubu had gone on the radio to dismiss Lumumba for plunging the country into civil war, Lumumba made a highly emotional broadcast declaring that Kasavubu was no longer chief of state, and called upon the people to rise up and upon the army to die with him. In spite of all this, Stanleyville seemed ominously calm.

This was a completely new kind of threat to what was left of civil and military order in the Congo, and Cordier decided, apparently with Hammarskjold's acquiescence, that he must react to limit the danger of complete chaos. He therefore ordered the closing of all airports and radio stations. To all of us actually in the Congo this decision seemed to be a responsible and necessary action, but because East and West had now taken sides, the East backing Lumumba and the West Kasavubu, it had far wider international implications than we realized and was highly controversial.

In Stanleyville we were ordered to close down the airport immediately, and I spent most of the day urging our Ethiopian commander to block the runway and thereby prevent further movements of troops to

Kasai in the Soviet IL-14s. To avoid a fight with the Congolese Army over this, we arranged a distribution of beer to the 3,000 Congolese soldiers at the airport and put oil barrels across the runways during the night while they were sleeping it off.

I was supposed to get back to Leopoldville the next day, but the Ethiopians were reluctant to clear the runway again even for one aircraft, the Ethiopian DC-3 in which I was travelling. The airport situation was very tense in spite of our efforts to explain the reasons for blocking the runway.

At this point we had a stroke of luck. General Victor Lundula, the commander of the ANC, was also stuck in Stanleyville and was naturally anxious, in this time of national crisis, to get back to the capital. He asked me if I could take him, and I cordially agreed. The ANC could not very well object to their own commander going back to his headquarters. After a talk with the head of the Soviet aircraft group, who was getting worried about the security of his men and aircraft, I commended him to the special care of the Ethiopians, the barrels were rolled back, and we took off. Everyone, especially General Lundula and his staff, was vastly relieved. The Soviets had given the general a copy of *Bas les Mains au Congo!*, and he quickly dozed off after takeoff.

Our relief was short-lived, for after forty minutes we ran into the worst electrical storm I have ever experienced. The aircraft tumbled about the sky, and the Ethiopian pilot told me he could find no way under, over, or around the massive atmospheric disturbance. I believed him and agreed, with a heavy heart, that the only thing to do was to return to Stanleyville. I did not look forward to our unexpected return to that unhappy city. The runway would have to be unblocked again by the Ethiopians, and the ANC, already highly suspicious, might react badly.

When we landed there was an ominous-looking mob on the tarmac, the soldiers with their guns at the ready and a number of Soviets milling around. I told General Lundula that, as their commander, he had better get out first and make the best speech of his life. Greatly to his credit he rose to the occasion. In fact he did almost too well.

In our brief absence a rumor had been spread among the Congolese soldiers that I had kidnapped their general. They were therefore in an extremely hostile mood. But as Victor Lundula, although he had been air-sick and looked terrible, stood on the aircraft steps and delivered a long speech in Lingala, the mood of the soldiers changed. What he apparently said was that the United Nations in general, and I in particular, were their friends, and they should not listen to rumors put about by mischief-makers who were false friends of the Congo. Whatever he meant by this, the troops understood him to be referring to the Soviets, and the pattern of relationships in Stanleyville changed suddenly and dramatically.

I found myself staying the night in a very pretty small hotel called the "Pourquoi Pas," but I didn't have much time to enjoy it. The Soviet detachment were now anxious to leave as soon as possible, and again we were up against the difficulty of opening the runway. The Congolese soldiers had developed a strong proprietary feeling for the ten IL-14s, which had, perhaps unwisely, been adorned with the Congo colors and the notation *République du Congo*, and they were unlikely to be pleased at their mass departure.

The Ethiopian colonel and I considered the problem and then, advising the Soviet head man of the risks involved, suggested that a mass takeoff at dawn after another late-night delivery of beer to the ANC would probably be the best plan. The Soviets apparently did not get authority to employ this stratagem until several days later. Lundula and I took off for Leopoldville the next day, and this time arrived without incident.

The situation in the capital was lively. Dayal had taken over and was not at all happy with the decision to close the airfields and radio station, all of which he was determined to open again as soon as possible. In the meanwhile F. T. Liu and I spent much of our time rushing to one or other of these facilities to talk down efforts from various quarters to take them over by force. We found that, as so often in the Congo when disaster seemed inevitable, the Congolese soldiers, after an initial show of aggressiveness, would melt away for reasons that could not be determined—suppertime perhaps, or just a general sense of futility. In any case actual fighting was avoided.

The diplomatic corps remained extremely active, everyone wanting us to do what *they* wanted, and all—Kasavubu, Lumumba, the British and American ambassadors, the Soviets, and the various Congolese factions—being equally irritated when we did what *we* thought was right. Our cramped offices were full of ministers, diplomats, foreign residents, and others seeking protection from the storm they were sure was coming. Everyone seemed to be scared stiff. The radio stations and airports were reopened, the latter for non-military flights, on September 12.

Our excitements were by no means over. On September 12 Joseph Mobutu, who was still theoretically Lumumba's chief of staff, appeared at our headquarters in civilian clothes and said he was going to resign because of political interference with the army. Dayal, Liu, and I urged him to stay at his post for the good of the country. In retrospect it seems possible that this well-meant advice may have been misconstrued.

Mobutu returned to our headquarters on the evening of September 14. He seemed anxious to linger and said he was nervous. As we were busy with all the other visitors, F.T. and I put him in our bedroom and gave him a bottle of whiskey. He asked to listen to the radio, which seemed harmless enough. The Leopoldville radio in those days mostly played the cha-cha-cha. Every now and then we checked on our uninvited guest, and during one of these visits the cha-cha-cha suddenly ceased and a voice was heard proclaiming that he had neutralized the chief of state and was taking over the government with a "Council of Technicians." "C'est moi!" Mobutu exclaimed proudly, pointing at the radio, "C'est moi!" After briefly consulting Dayal, we told Mobutu that we could have nothing to do with his coup and that he must leave at once. As he was escorted out of the building he looked disappointed and evidently felt we had let him down.

A third dimension had now been added to the already convoluted constitutional and political situation, putting ONUC in an even more difficult position than before, for Colonel Mobutu had no constitutional basis for his action. Moreover, one of his first moves, apparently in an off-the-cuff reply to a press question, had been to give the Soviet and Soviet-bloc embassies in Leopoldville forty-eight hours to leave. Understandably enough these embassies were deeply worried about their security and haunted our offices at all hours until, despite efforts by Hammarskjold and Dayal to have their expulsion rescinded, we escorted them to the airport on September 17 to be flown out of the country.

Lumumba had become wilder and more irrational during this period and was alleged to be on drugs. We had to rescue him from the main military camp where he had gone to look for Mobutu and had been attacked by Baluba soldiers seeking revenge. He reviled the Ghanaian colonel who, at considerable personal risk, had rescued him. He seemed to resent being protected and also to resent not being protected. Although we did not know until many years later of the CIA's plans to assassinate Lumumba, we stationed a large guard of Tunisian troops round his house.

Mobutu, although he had been Lumumba's man, contrived to bring Kasavubu along with him in the days after his coup. Mobutu was deeply offended at our reserved attitude to him in the new position which he had assumed. He told us that he could reconcile everyone, but the Ghanaian and Guinean UN contingents were preventing it. If they left the Congo, he would be the conciliator. The astute Moroccan General Kettani asked him, "Do you mean conciliator or dictator?"

In the outside world the battle lines were already drawn up. The Soviet Union violently attacked Hammarskjold and ONUC for refusing to give preference to Lumumba, while the Americans, and to a lesser extent the British and the French, were deeply critical of our not giving wholesale support to Kasavubu and Mobutu. De Gaulle expressed lofty contempt and disapproval for all our efforts. The Africans were divided on the issue. It was a dispiriting situation.

My time in the Congo was drawing to a close. Bunche wanted me back in New York where he had no staff at all, and I was more than ready to go. My last chore was to draft a progress report for the Secretary-General. This report was a description of the tumultuous two months we had spent in the Congo. A section entitled "Political Instability and the Problems of Non-Intervention" stated the dilemma in which we had so often found ourselves in trying to keep the lid on the poisonous inanities and intrigues of the country. The report ended with an upbeat conclusion which looks naive in the light of subsequent events:

> There is yet time for the Congolese leaders and people to take stock of the situation, to put an end to factional and party strife, to reconcile political and sectional interests and to embark on the path of national unity. . . . This mission is in the Congo to help but not to intervene, to advise but not to order, to conciliate but not to take sides. While it is not part of its functions to get involved in any way in the political crises which have been constantly erupting, it is hoped that before it is too late, the political leadership will make its choice, both wisely and well.

In September Patrick O'Donovan, on his return to England from the Congo, wrote in the *Observer*,

> The UN operation in Korea was in fact an American operation. In the Congo it is a United Nations operation. No Power dominates it. The UN secretariat is wholly in charge. The nations are more or less at its disposal. Almost unnoticed, a great precedent has been created. What is happening in the Congo is deplorable; what is being done for the Congo is one of the most hopeful events of our time.

This was, alas, the epitaph to a brief and glorious period—a time when for once we could try to do what we thought fit. That time was now very definitely over and would not come again. In the last week of September I left Leopoldville for New York.

XIII

The Loss of Hammarskjold

THE FALL OF 1960 was a turning point. The balance in the General Assembly was radically changing, reflecting a new and very different world from the polarized East-West state of affairs of the 1940s and 1950s. New interests and new forces were coming into play. Power vacuums were occurring in sensitive areas of the world in the wake of decolonization.

A constituency was emerging which had little direct interest in European affairs, disarmament, or in the East-West relationship. It was a radical, angry constituency, in which newly acquired independence had only served to accentuate the feeling of vital time and opportunities lost through colonial status. It was a constituency which strongly resented the established, profitably industrialized, dominant Old World. Neither the West nor the Soviet Union was comfortable in this new environment.

This was also the point at which Hammarskjold's extraordinary show of leadership, innovation, and initiative had run into serious difficulties. For the first time he himself was being openly criticized, not only by Khrushchev and de Gaulle, but even by some of the newly independent states of which he had seen himself as the champion and mentor. The Congo operation, starting with such promise, had not only become a heavy liability, it had also precipitated other, hitherto submerged resentments and rivalries, not the least of which was East-West competition in postcolonial Africa. The prospect of a new and more constructive role for the Secretary-General had suffered a severe setback.

Returning from the Congo to New York should have been like leaving a lunatic asylum for the normal world, but the antics in the 1960 session of the General Assembly did much to blur this contrast.

Nikita Khrushchev had arrived in New York on September 20, his temper perhaps soured by the long Atlantic crossing on the small steamer *Baltika*, and two days later he unleashed his offensive on Hammarskjold by formally proposing the abolition of the office of Secretary-General and its replacement by a troika representing the main power blocs of the world. Hammarskjold was determined to block this wrecking move.

This fifteenth session of the Assembly was perhaps the greatest circus in the history of the UN. It was attended by, among others, Khrushchev, Castro, Nkrumah, Nehru, Sukarno, King Hussein of Jordan, Nasser, Sekou Touré, Macmillan, Eisenhower, and Tito, and their contrasting styles and reactions to each other were fine dramatic material. Khrushchev, for example, made the mistake of trying to heckle Harold Macmillan in Russian. Macmillan stopped his speech and gazed out benevolently at the audience over his glasses, as if searching for the source of the noise. "Oh dear," he said finally, "I'm afraid I'll have to get a translation of that." There was also the famous Khrushchev shoe-banging episode—the unresolved question being whether Khrushchev had used one of his own shoes, borrowed one of Gromyko's, or kept an extra shoe in his briefcase for banging purposes. This question has never, to my knowledge, been satisfactorily cleared up, although there is alleged to be a photograph of the incident taken from the side and showing both of Khrushchev's feet fully shod.

The UN was of course facing a very serious crisis, but in the end Hammarskjold's strength and dignity, his manifest integrity, and the support of the Third World, including its more radical leaders, Nkrumah, Castro, and Sekou Touré, won out. It seemed clear to most people that in the Congo the UN was doing its best and that the collapse of ONUC would spell disaster. The turning point was Hammarskjold's reply on October 3 to Khrushchev's demand that he resign, a moving and compelling statement which brought the Assembly, except for the Soviet bloc, to its feet in a standing ovation that lasted for several minutes. ". . . The Representative of the Soviet Union," Hammarskjold concluded,

> spoke of courage. It is very easy to resign; it is not so easy to stay on. It is very easy to bow to the wish of a big power. It is another matter to resist. As is well known to all Members of this Assembly, I have done so before on many occasions and in many directions. If it is the wish of those nations who see in the Organization their best protection in the present world, I shall now do so again.

Hammarskjold had staked out a lonely eminence in his championship of the integrity and independence of the Secretary-General and the Secretariat and his determination that the UN should play an active role in keeping the peace. He was to spend what remained of his life actively defending this position, not only in the Congo, but in Tunisia against de Gaulle, and also briefly in South Africa on the question of apartheid. His public differences with Khrushchev, however, tended to overshadow his very considerable disagreements with the United States, Britain, France, and other powers. Thus, to his chagrin, he achieved heroic status in the West for his supposed anti-Soviet attitude, when what he was actually fighting for was independence and impartiality.

I was a mere onlooker at this struggle of giants and was mostly occupied in backstopping and directing the continuing complications of the Congo operation, as well as overseeing our peacekeeping operations in the Middle East. On top of the frustrations and pressures of work, my marriage was breaking up. This was a profoundly depressing time.

As so often happens, once the first bloom was off the Congo operation virtually everyone—not just the Soviets—began to attack the UN. The Americans, being for Mobutu and Kasavubu, were furious with our attempts to protect Lumumba. The British, Belgians, and French, with their large financial involvement in Katanga, were strongly opposed to our efforts to put an end to the secession of their hero, Moise Tshombe. The Africans were hopelessly divided among themselves on the Congo issue.

Walter Lippmann, in the *Herald Tribune,* later put our dilemma well:

> The cause of the opposition from East and West is a determination not to have the UN succeed in what it is attempting to do. For if the UN succeeds, there will not be a communist government in the Congo. That is what Khrushchev hated about Hammarskjold and the Secretary-General's office. And if the UN succeeds, there will not be a restoration of white supremacy in the Congo, and that is why money, propaganda, and clandestine intervention are being employed to frustrate the UN.

In February 1961, Lumumba's brutal murder under mysterious circumstances created a new and horrible dimension to the Congo problem. Physical brutality had always been part of that country's sad history, but Lumumba's gruesome death set off a wave of vengeance and ideological exploitation. Those of us who had first-hand experience of the Congo felt compromised, disgusted, and, worst of all, powerless to control the destructive forces that had been unleashed.

Hammarskjold was deeply disturbed, and his normally Olympian control and demeanor at times lapsed into shrill indignation. We spent our days and nights in efforts to deal with the seemingly inexhaustible inanities of the Congo, often in late-night meetings in Hammarskjold's office of a group which, for convenience, became known as "the Congo Club." Later on this harmless appellation achieved, through the writings of Conor Cruise O'Brien, and, later still, in the speeches of Soviet delegates and in Soviet newspaper articles, a sinister connotation—a conspiracy by the United States to take over the UN Congo operation. This meretricious nonsense was particularly ironical in the light of Hammarskjold's and Bunche's continuous disagreements with the United States and their strong reaction to *any* government which attempted to tell them what to do.

By midsummer there seemed to be a chance of improvement. Hammarskjold's persistence had paid off, and the Congolese parliament had, with infinite difficulty, been mustered under UN protection in the Lovanium University outside Leopoldville. It elected a prime minister, the moderate and sensible Cyrille Adoula. Thus, at last, there was again a legitimate Congolese government to deal with and some hope that we might be moving into calmer waters.

The problem of the Katanga secession, the key to the Congo puzzle, dominated our summer. In June, Hammarskjold appointed Conor Cruise O'Brien, an Irish diplomat whom he knew largely through his literary works, to be his representative in Katanga. I knew Conor and liked him very much, but thought him an improbable choice for this ghastly job. He was a brilliant and creative man, but not necessarily suited to the task of superintendent in a lunatic asylum.

In early September, Hammarskjold decided to make another visit to the Congo. He did this in the belief that he must personally try to resolve the Katanga secession problem, which would otherwise poison the forthcoming session of the General Assembly as it had the previous one. His intention was to bring Prime Minister Adoula and Tshombe together in an act of national reconciliation. I believe that he then intended to resign from his post as Secretary-General.

In retrospect, it is clear that, in taking on this praiseworthy course, Hammarskjold made two mistakes. He did not give his representatives in the Congo any clear idea of his intentions. And he did not categorically tell them to abstain from action pending his arrival, sending instead complicated instructions which could be, and were, misunderstood by people under the pressure of a violent and frustrating local situation. Thus, while Hammarskjold was actually en route to the Congo, the United Nations command in Elisabethville initiated a military move against the European mercenaries who led Tshombe's forces. The action went disastrously wrong and degenerated into a squalid battle in and around Elisabethville. On his arrival in Leopoldville Hammarskjold decided that he would meet Tshombe in person to arrange a cease-fire. On September 17, he took off for Ndola in Northern Rhodesia. On its landing approach to Ndola his aircraft crashed, killing everyone aboard.

I had arrived back in New York late that Sunday from a weekend in Massachusetts. At 3:00 a.m. I got a call from Ralph Bunche asking me to come in to the office at once. Hammarskjold's plane had been unaccounted for for several hours and must long since have run out of fuel. A period of unbearable tension and foreboding followed until 10:00 a.m. on Monday, when we got word that the smoking wreckage had been sighted from the air less than ten miles from the Ndola airport. There was no sign of survivors.

I have had news of the death of many friends in my life, but none has affected me as this did, and I believe that others had the same experience. The death of Hammarskjold was not only an appalling blow to the UN and to all who had worked with him. There was also an agonizing sense of irreparable personal loss which I still find hard to account for. None of us knew Hammarskjold really well, but he had come to occupy a unique place in our lives, thoughts, and affections by the nature of his leadership and his character. For a long time it was hard to think of him without tears, not least because one would never see his like again. To this day I can see and hear him in my mind as if I had only just left his presence.

Hammarskjold's death left an aching void at the United Nations. He had been the life and soul of the institution even in the last year of criticism and violence, and without him there was a terrible feeling of emptiness. Ralph Bunche, Andy Cordier, and the rest of us set out to try to fill this void as best we could until a successor could be appointed. When the funerals of the crash victims, in Stockholm, Geneva, and New York, were at last over, a numbing sadness set in. In an effort at catharsis I suggested a memorial ceremony in the General Assembly Hall, where Hammarskjold had delighted in arranging the annual concerts. We got Eugene Ormandy to bring the Philadelphia Orchestra, breaking a long strike for the occasion. Hammarskjold had initiated the tradition of playing Beethoven's Ninth Symphony on United Nations Day, and in the previous year, at a time of severe crisis, had introduced the symphony with a statement beginning "It is difficult to say anything, knowing that the words spoken will be followed by this enormous confession of faith in the victorious human spirit and in human brotherhood, a confession valid for all times and with a depth and wealth of expression never surpassed. . . ."

The program was built around this statement. It started with a eulogy by the President of the General Assembly, Hammarskjold's friend, Mongi Slim of Tunisia, and continued with the final chorus of the St. Matthew Passion ("Here Laid to Rest"). Then Hammarskjold's voice spoke again his commentary on the Ninth Symphony. This was an unbearably emotional moment, ended only by the first notes of the symphony, which Ormandy conducted with tears streaming down his face.

I like to think that after this ceremony we got down to business again with perhaps a new sense of purpose and, in my case at any rate, a sense of profound indignation. I cannot explain this feeling better than by quoting from a letter I wrote on September 19 to a journalist who, three days before Hammarskjold's death, had written to ask whether there was "a case for the UN action in Katanga."

> You ask if there is a case for the UN action in Katanga, which seems to me, in my present state of mind, to be an irritating question. . . . The principal fault of the UN action in Katanga, in my view, has been that we have been much too lenient and leisurely. . . .
>
> I am sorry, in this very hurried letter, to sound bitter, but I am impressed by the fact that it has taken Hammarskjold's death to get the cooperation we needed from the British and American Governments to carry out an operation which is largely designed to put the whole Congo on its feet, to remove from Central Africa a standing invitation to the Russians and others to meddle and intervene, and, incidentally, to carry out a Security Council resolution for which they [the British and Americans] voted.

Hammarskjold, in a codcil to his will, had left instructions that Per Lind, his friend and first Swedish assistant, should go through his papers and decide what should go into his personal archive in the Swedish Royal Library and what should be retained in the UN archives in New York. Per coopted me to help in this task, which we carried out during October with the help of Hammarskjold's chief secretary, Hannah Platz. I was amazed at these papers, exiguous but full of meaning, and resolved one day to try to explain Hammarskjold to a public which had little or no idea of who or what he was.

Hammarskjold's bedside table had contained a very personal account of his inner life. The manuscript was left to his great friend Leif Belfrage, the head of the Swedish Foreign Office, who was to determine whether it should be published. Leif, with considerable misgivings, decided to publish it in Swedish and asked me if I could help to get it translated and published in English. Publishers were lukewarm about the somewhat eccentric personal notes of a Swedish intellectual/diplomat, but we finally got a commitment on condition that a famous literary figure would take over the English translation. I approached W. H. Auden, whom Hammarskjold had known slightly. Auden said he was busy, but finally agreed to give his name and supervision to a translation by the reader in Swedish at Columbia University. No one seemed to have much confidence that the book would sell. The small first printing of *Markings* sold out almost instantly. It subsequently became a perennial best-seller. I wrote a long review of *Markings* in *The New Yorker* which prompted a group of publishers to ask me to write a full biography of Hammarskjold.

I wonder why some people so much prefer their heroes to be assassinated than to die accidentally. Various conspiracy theories about Hammarskjold's death are still current, but after extensively exploring the circumstances, I am convinced that his plane crashed accidentally as a result of human error. No one had any interest in killing Hammarskjold at that particular point—quite the contrary—although quite a lot of people had an interest in blaming others for his death.

There was no mercenary aircraft in that part of Africa with the range, the ground control, or the night-flying capacity to shoot down a plane at night, and there was no evidence of action from the ground against Hammarskjold's plane. Absolutely no sign of foul play was found during the exhaustive examination of the wreckage. Hammarskjold's DC-6, in its landing approach to Ndola with wheels and airbrakes lowered, was a few feet too low to clear a tree-covered hill. The crew had been flying across Africa, largely in radio silence, for more than six hours. They had never landed at Ndola before.

Hammarskjold had changed planes in Leopoldville at the very last minute, giving his own plane to Lord Lansdowne to go ahead and arrange his reception in Rhodesia, then a British territory. In fact the press at Ndola mistook Lansdowne for Hammarskjold, and on the day after his death the *New York Times* actually reported Hammarskjold's arrival in Ndola. If there had been an assassination attempt it would have been directed at Lansdowne's aircraft, not Hammarskjold's. No serious evidence of a conspiracy has ever been produced, nor has anyone been named as a suspect. Nevertheless, people who claim to have been Hammarskjold's friends continue to hint at inside knowledge of a murder plot. This seems to me contemptible.

XIV

Aftermath in Katanga

IN THE WEEKS AFTER Hammarskjold's death the situation in Katanga deteriorated still further. Tshombe's European mercenaries evidently believed that they had scored a victory over the UN, both in Elisabethville and in the outside world. Conor Cruise O'Brien, who had made a brave show of doing an impossible job, took the brunt of a wave of hostility to the United Nations not only in Katanga but also in the Western press, where he was shamelessly attacked and abused. There were also threats to his life which could not be ignored, and in any case he had become so controversial a figure that it was judged impossible for him to continue his job in Katanga. I was therefore designated to replace him. This was not very flattering. In November 1961 no one in his right mind wanted to be United Nations Representative in Katanga.

I left New York in mid-November with a considerable sense of foreboding. I had been told to spend a few days in Leopoldville on my way to Katanga in order to get a feeling for the situation there. It was appalling. Hammarskjold's death had evidently had a traumatic effect both on the civilian UN leadership and on the military command.

After the September disaster, we had at last acquired some military aircraft—Swedish Saab fighters, Indian Canberra bombers, and some Ethiopian fighters which never became operational. I was uneasy that such weapons should be at the disposal of a peacekeeping force, and particularly of one as indifferently led as the UN operation in the Congo.

Although military commanders often want them, I have always been strongly opposed to UN peacekeeping operations having offensive or heavy weapons. The real strength of a peacekeeping operation lies not in its capacity to use force, but precisely in its *not* using force and thereby remaining above the conflict and preserving its unique position and prestige. The moment a peacekeeping force starts killing people it becomes a part of the conflict it is supposed to be controlling, and therefore a part of the problem. It loses the one quality which distinguishes it from, and sets it above, the people it is dealing with. This is what had happened to us briefly in Katanga in September 1961, and tragically, more than twenty years later, to the United States–sponsored multinational force in Beirut.

A peacekeeping force can never use unrestricted force, and the moment it gets into a fight, governments and the press will hasten to tie its hands behind its back. This had happened in Katanga in September 1961 and was about to happen again. Although in Katanga we had been authorized by the Security Council to use force to deal with mercenaries and to prevent civil war, our capacity actually to do so was extremely limited. I learned more about this problem in the weeks that followed.

On my first day in Leopoldville we discovered by chance that the commander of the Swedish fighter squadron had taken off to bomb Kindu, apparently in retaliation for an atrocity committed against some United Nations Italian airmen many days before. The fighter bombers were recalled with some difficulty, having fortunately been delayed by bad weather. This episode gave me a foretaste of what life might be like in the even more volatile atmosphere of Elisabethville. I flew there at the end of November with George Ivan Smith, my old Australian friend, who had been holding the fort until my arrival. We took David Halberstam of the *New York Times* with us as there was no regular air service to Katanga. David got a lot of copy in the next few weeks.

Our arrival in Elisabethville coincided with a visit of Senator Thomas Dodd of Connecticut, the self-appointed American patron of Tshombe. This vain and silly man knew nothing of Africa and had hitched onto, or been recruited by, Tshombe's public relations campaign. He had been active and vocal in Washington in behalf of the Katangese secession and was run by a staff assistant who maintained that Tshombe was fighting Soviet communism in Africa. Tshombe told me later, with a fine show of indignation, that he was paying Dodd a large monthly stipend. I do not know whether this was true. In any case if you had a serious job to do in Katanga, Dodd was just about the last person you wanted to see there.

That first evening in Elisabethville the American Consul, Lewis Hoffacker, gave a reception for Senator Dodd. I and the senior UN military officers attended this function in the perhaps mistaken belief that we should do everything possible to open a new chapter in our relations with Tshombe with a view to persuading him to make his peace with the central government. The reception was a weird occasion, with the Tshombe establishment—European, African, and mercenary alike—making an effort to be civil to the United Nations people whom they hated and routinely spat at in the street. Shady-looking white characters hovered on the fringe of the party, and I noticed that several of them appeared to be identifying me to the Katangese soldiers who were also hanging around. Tshombe was, as usual, charming and effusive.

George Ivan Smith and I left this affair with Maire McEntee of the Irish Foreign Office and Fitzhugh Greene of the U.S. Embassy to go to a dinner given in Dodd's honor by an American businessman in a residential suburb. As our car approached the house a squad of evidently stimulated Katangese "paracommandos" blocked the road, triumphantly identified the UN numberplate, and demanded at gunpoint that we all get out. They accused us of coming to assassinate their general who lived in the area. It was a fatal mistake in the Congo to get out of a car at night unless absolutely necessary, so we argued until the paracommandos got tired of it and let us go on to our destination thirty yards up the road. They loped along behind us.

In the suburban villa the party was already assembled—foreign consuls and their wives and members of the European community. They were apprehensive at the disturbance which had marked our arrival, and one of them, a banker, started to telephone a Katangese minister for help. At this point a wave of thirty or so paracommandos burst through the front door. The squad leader ripped the telephone from the wall and directed his men to George Ivan Smith and myself. Thus, in front of the *crème de la crème* of Elisabethville honoring Tshombe's American patron, we found ourselves being savagely beaten up. One soldier seized me by the collar and rammed his head into my face, breaking my nose, which began to spurt blood; others pounded us with rifle butts. Maire McEntee made a courageous attempt to intervene and got sprayed with my blood before being swept aside. The helpful banker protested in Swahili and French and was beaten for his pains. "*Macaques!*" our assailants screamed, using the Belgian colonial pejorative for Africans, and "ONU assassins!"

The intention was clearly to get us out of the house and into a waiting truck, and, for fear of the conflict spreading to the other guests, we did not resist until we got outside. Once there we hung on, slithered, and evaded for as long as possible in the hope that the guest of honor, Senator Dodd, would arrive. One cause for satisfaction was that among the shrubs and bushes in the dark our assailants managed to hit each other nearly as often as they hit us.

As we reached the gate, I saw the lights and outriders of the Dodd convoy approaching and was then knocked unconscious by a rifle butt. My account of the next few minutes is therefore second-hand. I was dumped into the back of a troop-carrying truck, and George and the banker, both still conscious, were also thrown in. At this moment, Tshombe's car, containing the Dodds and Hoffacker, pulled up behind us. In the headlights George's mustached face could be seen over the tailboard, and Mrs. Dodd is alleged to have said, "Why, there's that nice Mr. Smith," before being ordered by Hoffacker to lie on the floor. Hoffacker then charged into the paracommandos in a rage yelling "Consul Américain," and managed to pull George and the banker off the truck. The paracommandos, nonplussed at this turn of events and impressed by the presence of Tshombe's motorcycle escort, evidently decided to clear out, and took off with me still on board. Hoffacker, being responsible for the Dodds, also decided to leave as rapidly as possible, for the Katangese soldiers were excitedly cocking and uncocking their weapons. The Dodd party drove off at high speed, heads down.

I regained consciousness to find myself lying on the floor of the truck between two benches, the soldiers kicking and stomping me from time to time. We were driving under trees, and there was a smell of woodsmoke. The situation seemed unpromising. After a while I grabbed the nearest boot and twisted it. This was a lucky move as it belonged to the squad commander, to whom I suggested that I be allowed off the floor as I had something important to tell him. This request started a violent argument among the soldiers, punctuated by much kicking and shouts of "Assassin!", "Macaque!", and so on, and a new and dirgelike refrain, "On te tuera ce soir et pas demain. (We will kill you this evening, not tomorrow.)" But eventually the squad leader won out, and I found myself seated beside him. As we drove along, I started to convert the abjectly defensive nature of my position into an offensive one. It was heavy going, accompanied by much shouting and many blows. I was not as impressive a disputant as I would have wished, having lost much of my clothing and streaming with blood.

My first aim was to convince them that I was a civilian—("Mais de quel pays?" "De l'Écosse"—a useful move giving rise to much internal discussion)—that I knew Tshombe, who would be furious at my abduction, and that I was the only person who could protect the Katangese soldiers from the revenge of the UN Gurkha troops, who would be even more furious than Tshombe. When we at last got to this point, the mood of the soldiers changed, and they became quiet and anxious. The Gurkhas were one of the legends of Elisabethville. They were said, for example, to have thrown people off the roof of the post office and hacked off their limbs with their *kukris* as they fell through the air. My captors arrived at their camp in an apprehensive mood. "Si les Gurkhas arrivent . . . ," they kept muttering as they helped me down from the truck.

Unfortunately all this good work had to be repeated on the troops in the camp, who were still in a pre-Gurkha mood and anxious to take their turn at beating me up. When my new friend, the squad leader, tried to stop them they beat him up too, and it took him some time to explain the Gurkha threat they were all facing. This gave rise to a frenzy of weapon-cocking, threat-shouting, and unpleasantness, but soon a more somber mood prevailed. I persuaded them to let me telephone UN Headquarters to call off the Gurkhas, but the phone didn't work, which made them even more suspicious. When headlights appeared on the road that passed the camp, panic set in, all lights were switched off, two submachine guns were put to my temples, and a new refrain was taken up. "Si les Gurkhas arrivent, on te tue."

It took some time to convince my captors that, if the Gurkhas *did* arrive, I was their only hope. It took even longer to get everyone to agree that if vehicles approached the camp, the squad leader and I would go together, and alone, to the gate. The beer and chanvre had now worn off, and the soldiers were dispirited and sleepy. The squad leader became solicitous for my welfare and found some cotton wool and iodine with which he made excruciating efforts to clean up my wounds and stop the flow of blood. Fortunately he was interrupted by a babble of excited voices which heralded the arrival of Tshombe's own car. It contained the captain of Tshombe's personal guard, Captain Yav, resplendent in the gold trimmings of a presidential aide. Yav was extremely nervous, and one look at me made him more nervous still. A new character now suddenly burst upon the scene, Lieutenant Ngoye of the paracommandos, an odious little thug, drunk and in a violent rage. Ngoye threatened Yav with his machine pistol. Yav was in a quandary. The Gurkhas had given him a deadline for my release, after which they would storm Tshombe's residence. But if he tried to take me away, the drunken Ngoye would probably shoot the lot of us.

I had got to the point of discomfort and fatigue where I did not care too much what happened, and such a state of mind provides a degree of clarity and detachment one does not normally enjoy. After letting the argument reach an impasse, I suggested that Yav return to Tshombe with my identity card and a message saying I was alive and more or less well. Yav left gratefully. When he returned with four companions an hour later, Ngoye, in a frenzy, covered Yav with his machine pistol and shouted, "Si quelqu'un prend mon prisonnier, je tire." I suggested that Yav go back again and ask Tshombe, or his interior minister, Godefroid Munongo, to come and talk to Ngoye. He went off again as fast as he could.

By now almost everyone, including Ngoye, was struggling with sleep, and I persuaded the squad leader to move me to a storeroom away from the stench of the barrack room. Here we settled down to a pleasant chat. It emerged that his ambition was to be a ballet dancer, and we discussed how this might be achieved. After another hour there was a new disturbance, and my friend came back to inform me, with great respect, that Ministers Munongo and Kimba had come to fetch me, and President Tshombe was waiting in his car outside. The ministers, in white tuxedos, were extremely nervous and hustled me out, cutting short my grateful farewell to the squad leader. We greeted Tshombe sitting in his white convertible.

As I drove back to town with Munongo and Kimba, I noticed with satisfaction that I was bleeding all over the white upholstery. I insisted on being delivered to the American Consulate because I was anxious to see Senator Dodd, who had always proclaimed that Katanga was the only peaceful and orderly place in the Congo, and, more important, to have him see me. We were overtaken by a jeep driving very fast, and I thought I identified Ngoye. Later that night a Gurkha officer on patrol near Tshombe's residence, Major Ajeet Singh, was killed with his driver. No one was ever charged with the murders, but Ngoye unaccountably disappeared from Elisabethville. The press were waiting at the U.S. Consulate and asked me how I felt. "Better beaten than eaten," I said.

The scene in the consulate at 3:00 a.m. was lively. The house was surrounded by Gurkhas in full battle rig. Hoffacker, George, and Colonel S. S. Maitra of the Gurkhas welcomed me back, and there was Senator Dodd, kneeling, apparently praying into an armchair. I tapped him on the shoulder and told him to cheer up. After a few drinks, efforts were made to clean me up. I borrowed a shirt and a pair of slacks from Hoffacker before going to our headquarters to report to New York. Then I went to our Italian military hospital for X-rays and to be stitched and bandaged up.

I got out next morning in time to give lunch to Senator Dodd as had been previously arranged, but he had thought better of it and left Elisabethville early that morning without a word. I never did find out why. Much trouble had been taken to scrounge up a decent meal for him, and George and I and Colonel Maitra enjoyed eating it.

Nor did I find out to my satisfaction what the significance of this episode was. Later on, when I established a reasonably friendly relationship with Munongo in late-night drinking sessions, he apologized, saying that the French mercenaries had talked him into it and that if he had realized what a good chap I was he would never have allowed it to happen. Munongo, whose grandfather, the Emperor Msiri, had been framed by the Belgians, had become strongly pro-Scottish after I had explained that Scotland was an early victim of colonialism. He even asked me to arrange for the Katanga Gendarmerie to be trained to play the bagpipes, a temptation which I resisted.

In Katangese circles it became fashionable later on to blame the French mercenaries for everything that went wrong in Katanga. Probably someone had the idea of kidnapping, and perhaps killing, the local UN leadership in the muddled hope of provoking a new round of fighting in which Tshombe's mercenary-led forces would be decisively victorious. The mercenaries were quite addled enough to have dreamed up such a fatuous scenario.

*   *   *

The idea that our night out could be used to improve the situation soon proved to be unrealistic. There was outrage and protest in the world outside, and Tshombe grudgingly apologized, saying darkly that "enemies of Katanga" had provoked the incident to disgrace him in the eyes of Dodd. He then left the country for a Moral Rearmament meeting in Brazil. Tshombe was a charismatic but fundamentally weak figure who was constantly being manipulated by other people for their own ends. His money made him a popular target for adventurers of all sorts whom he rewarded handsomely. Of this group Colonel Hubert Fauntleroy Julian, the "Black Eagle of Harlem," confidence man and international arms dealer, was outstanding, and later on we arrested him on his arrival in Elisabethville.

Tshombe was proud of his vast wardrobe of European suits and his presidential guard dressed in Third Empire uniforms. In the fighting that soon followed these uniforms and helmets were lost, and Tshombe asked me to help replace them. I learned, from UNESCO, that Third Empire uniforms, being all the rage in the opera houses of the world, were not available. However, UNESCO helpfully added, due to the new uncostumed productions of the *Ring*, there was a global surplus of Wagnerian helmets and costumes.

Tshombe was an accomplished hypochondriac, using feigned ill-health to escape awkward questions. "J'ai mal à la gorge, Monsieur Urquhart. Je dois prendre immédiatement une piqûre," he would whisper, having been perfectly normal two minutes before. His public relations firm in Geneva did a wonderful job of presenting him to the world as a civilized, popular, successful, anti-Communist, pro-European African leader. He was nothing of the kind even in Katanga, where his treatment of the Baluba was abominable, but his propaganda deceived a surprising number of people in the United States and Western Europe. As far as he stuck to any line, he tended to be against the use of force, and his departure during this period of high tension left Katanga in the charge of more extreme elements, Munongo and the French mercenaries led by Colonel René Faulques, whom Tshombe later expelled.

The harassment of UN troops now increased, and we began to take serious casualties. Katangese roadblocks cut us off from the airport, UN vehicles and their passengers were hijacked and some shot, and it began to look as if UN hostages were being taken in preparation for a trial of strength. I had increasing difficulty in restraining our military command from strong counteraction and I sympathized with them. A series of protests to Évariste Kimba, who was theoretically in charge in Tshombe's absence, produced undertakings which were never honored. The last straw came on December 5 when the roadblock on the airport road was not removed as promised but reinforced during the night. I told Kimba that unless it was removed by noon, *we* would remove it by force. He stalled, and nothing happened, so at noon we moved in. The battle soon spread all over Elisabethville.

Because my residence was isolated and costly to defend, I had moved into our military headquarters, a depressing property called "Le Clair Manoir." As soon as the fighting started, this house became a target for mortar fire which swiftly made the roof a sieve, a great nuisance in the rainy season. On the first day a mortar bomb killed two of the Gurkha guards. When I went down to sympathize with the soldiers, the Subhadar Major restrained me, saying, "Sir, it is our duty to die in battle."

I was not at all happy with the military situation. We had to try to keep the fighting out of the city while restoring our own security and freedom of movement. This would have been difficult enough with a well-integrated, disciplined force. As it was we had a weak Indian commander who was not respected by his subordinates, and there were strong per-

sonal animosities among the senior officers. We had two Indian battalions
(Gurkhas and Dogras), two Ethiopian battalions, an Irish and a Swedish
battalion. It was in no sense a homogeneous command. The Indians,
being professionals, tended to be patronizing toward the others. The
Swedes resented the Indians, and the Ethiopians, very low-grade units,
were undisciplined, paranoid, and dangerous. Only the Irish seemed to
get on with everyone. In two weeks of messy fighting twenty-one of our
soldiers were killed and eighty-four wounded.

As I had foreseen, our Indian Canberra squadron proved to be a
menace, and it was only after they had demolished the post office—a
great inconvenience for all concerned—that I managed to get the aircraft
grounded.

I spent much of my time trying, from our beleaguered headquarters,
to restrain our soldiers in the face of endless provocations. Not least of
these were the reports of their doings by the Western press corps. Having
ordered our troops to stay clear of the center of town, we were at a
considerable disadvantage with the press, who resided there and could
not reach our headquarters. Meanwhile the mercenaries and Tshombe's
people had a field day circulating atrocity stories about the UN. David
Halberstam made a courageous effort to reach us and got stuck under fire
halfway in a cellar from which we had to rescue him. The first civilians
to reach us, after four days of fighting, were a Red Cross team led by my
old friend G. C. Senn, carrying an enormous Red Cross flag.

The person who sticks in my mind from this wretched time is Colonel
S. S. Maitra, the commander of the Gurkhas. S.S. became my greatest
helper and friend at this period. He was not only a good soldier but a
humanitarian of the highest order. He instructed his troops, the best we
had, to make the protection of civilians their first duty even when it meant
tangling with the Ethiopians, and if things got really bad he would show
up on the scene himself. S.S in full battle rig was a formidable sight, shod
in patrol sneakers and festooned with hand grenades, his helmet at a
rakish angle, his mustache bristling, and his eyes shining through his
steel-rimmed glasses with the light of battle. He was blind as a bat, and
being driven by him in a jeep was much more frightening than the enemy's
ill-aimed fire. He was a terrific soldier. He was also a mathematician,
stamp collector, and music lover. His letters to me from India were a
constant source of pleasure until he was killed in a motor accident five
years later.

I loathed the battle in Elisabethville, from which no good came for
anyone. Many innocent people were killed or hurt and neither the UN

nor the mercenaries nor Tshombe came out of it with any credit. When the fighting ground to a halt it was surprisingly easy to reestablish contact with Tshombe and Munongo, who seemed anxious to come to terms. They were impressed that I came to see them driving myself and without a military escort. We discussed all sorts of domestic matters, the return of Tshombe's white convertible, the refurbishing of his presidential guard, and Munongo's new passion for Scottish tradition. Tshombe proudly imprisoned his French military adviser, Colonel Faulques, and boasted to me that he would have him shot for profiteering over arms shipments. I strongly advised against this, and Faulques was expelled into Rhodesia. When domestic concerns allowed, I kept urging Tshombe to make his peace with the central government. He could even become prime minister in due course, I explained, and in fact he did just that two years later. In the meantime he agreed to send the Katangese members of parliament to Leopoldville to take part in the national parliament.

As the fighting died down, we began to get organized again. There was much to be done. We had, for example, a camp on the outskirts of Elisabethville for 75,000 Baluba refugees, victims of Tshombe. The Baluba camp was policed by fifty Swedish soldiers and run with genius by one of those miracles which occur for no reason, a Swedish Major Forslund. This square kilometer of red clay, constantly rained upon, was a microcosm of the urban problems of the world. Almost everything could be found in the Baluba camp—politics, mysterious cults, crime, witch doctors, bicycle chain gangs, and tribal rivalries. I made one useful contribution. After visiting the camp several times I noticed that the people lining up for the day's ration of manioc lived with the certainty that around the corner a youth gang would be waiting to rob them of their food. The Swedes had a dog platoon wasting its time at the airport. We transferred these stalwart German Shepherds and their handlers to the Baluba camp to supervise the food distribution and make a show of escorting people home. The predatory gangs vanished.

I instructed everyone to do their utmost to heal the scars of war and foster an atmosphere in which Tshombe would make his peace with the central government. I might have known that S. S Maitra would go too far. He organized a party in the Gurkha mess for Tshombe. It was a splendid occasion, the mess silver gleaming and the pipers playing. S.S. got up and asked for silence while he greeted Tshombe, who also rose. S.S. then proposed a blood oath and slashed his own hand with a Gurkha knife so that it spurted blood. Tshombe, horrified, fainted dead away.

I was feeling worse and worse. I had been sickened by the ridiculous situation we found ourselves in, and had virtually no help, my only two civilian assistants having faded away during the fighting. The hours were endless since everyone with problems came to me, and I found it difficult to concentrate on my real job, which was to get Tshombe back to legitimacy. Various well-meaning associates had reported that I was exhausted and looked awful. When I learned about this, I riposted angrily that there was nothing wrong that a serious effort to provide the minimum staff would not cure. I flew to Leopoldville early in January 1962 to discuss the problem and believed I had solved it.

The only way of getting back to Elisabethville quickly was on a UN-chartered Lockheed Lodestar carrying a cargo of dried fish for the Baluba refugees. Clambering aboard at 4:00 a.m. in a tropical rainstorm, I was called forward to the cockpit, where the captain asked me to sit in the co-pilot's seat. Forestalling my unspoken question, he said that, for reasons of economy, they did not carry a co-pilot. We took off into the downpour and eventually emerged above the clouds. The captain was affable and relaxed, but two hours into the five-hour flight he produced a hypodermic syringe and gave himself an injection. I could not resist asking him about this, and he explained that he suffered from a deficiency disease and passed out if he didn't take shots regularly. I looked at the banks of switches and controls and at the boiling clouds concealing the African waste below and counted the minutes for three hours until we landed in Elisabethville.

Once a bureaucracy gets into action it is difficult to stop it. The idea had reached New York that my survival depended on my being replaced instantly, and it was announced that I would be relieved by my colleague Jose Rolz-Bennett. The fact that the situation in Elisabethville was now calm and I had, for the first time, an adequate staff made no difference. I was angry that I was to be removed just as I had begun to make progress with Tshombe.

My last duty in Katanga was a macabre one. During the fighting, a representative of the International Red Cross, Georges Olivet, and his two companions, had disappeared. I had last seen him heading, against my advice, toward the Ethiopian sector, and I feared the worst. I had therefore asked for an independent international inquiry. This inquiry, in which I assisted, determined that the Red Cross party had been killed during the battle by our Ethiopian troops, who had then tried to disguise the evidence.

I got back to New York in March 1962 to meet for the first time the new Secretary-General, U Thant.

XV

U Thant

U THANT HAS, in the West at any rate, been virtually written out of history. Very few people seem to remember his nobility of character, his integrity, or his courageous efforts over the Cuban missile crisis, the Vietnam War, and other international convulsions. His memoirs, which contain much original and interesting material, went virtually unreviewed and unnoticed. He is, in the popular Western memory, responsible for the 1967 war in the Middle East, a disaster which, virtually alone among world statesmen, he tried desperately to prevent. He proved on that occasion a useful scapegoat, but even so it is difficult to discern why such scant justice has been done to a decent, brave, and responsible man.

U Thant came to the Secretary-General's office at a catastrophic moment in the organization's history. The Secretary-General's authority to direct peacekeeping operations in critical situations had been challenged by the Soviet Union, and to a lesser extent by France, in a way which threatened to bring the work of the United Nations to a halt. This crisis was especially associated with the UN's Congo operation, but it also had deeper roots in perennial suspicions harbored by the Soviet Union, and also by de Gaulle, of any activity by the Secretary-General which was too independent or hinted at supranationalism. U Thant managed to pull the organization together and, by quiet but firm leadership, to bring it back onto a steady course at a time of storm and change.

U Thant was a devout Buddhist who had played an important role, as assistant and friend of U Nu, in Burma's accession to independence. For several years he had been Burma's Ambassador to the UN and was one of two people—Mongi Slim of Tunisia being the other—whom Hammarskjold had thought of as possible successors.

At first sight U Thant appeared emotionless and moon-faced, and he was, by Western standards, in some ways rather simple-minded. He enjoyed, for example, excruciating schoolboy jokes in which he had laboriously become word-perfect. His approach to issues was also simple. He had strong views of right and wrong. If he took advice, he followed it and took complete responsibility for his actions, regardless of their outcome. He accepted success and failure as part of life and was remarkably free of the desire to take credit, to justify himself, or to blame others when things went wrong.

All of this, and his strong Buddhist self-discipline, concealed his emotions and the irritation and frustration he must often, as Secretary-General, have felt. He never lost his temper. In moments of unusual stress he would go so far as to tap his foot rhythmically, but his emotions were disciplined and turned inwards. He was a martyr to ulcers and other stress ailments in his last years.

U Thant's moral sense overrode his political sense and caused him to do what he believed right, even if it was politically disadvantageous to him. His stewardship had none of the flair or high personal style of Hammarskjold, but his undertakings were just as courageous. He regarded the Vietnam War as a moral, and to some extent even a racial, issue, and was appalled at the almost casual toll of Vietnamese as well as American lives. He doggedly pursued his efforts to find a way to end it long after the resentment of President Lyndon Johnson and Secretary of State Dean Rusk was publicly evident and they had rejected his proposal for talks in Rangoon which North Vietnam had already accepted. Dean Rusk, in a patronizing and sarcastic public speech which the subsequent tragedy in Vietnam renders even more grotesque, implied that in his efforts over Vietnam U Thant was working for the Nobel Peace Prize. It would have been hard to make a more vulgar or erroneous judgment of U Thant's character, or indeed a more foolish dismissal of a possible opportunity to reach an early end to the tragedy of Indochina. Ironically, U Thant's line of approach to ending the Vietnam War was taken up with ultimate success, four years and hundreds of thousands of casualties later, by Henry Kissinger.

U Thant showed courage and firmness in the Cuban missile crisis, the India-Pakistan war of 1965, the Bangladesh crisis, and on many other occasions. He spoke his mind quietly and unpretentiously, his words often being much stronger than his tone. When he called Tshombe and his associates a "bunch of clowns," or told the Soviet public, on Moscow

Radio, that the Soviet people were misinformed about the Congo, he meant it.

He was addicted to strong cigars, especially Burmese cheroots, and strong sauces, including a knockout Burmese concoction made of dried fish which seemed to change his complexion. I worked with him closely and became very fond of him. I wrote the bulk of his political speeches and reports.

U Thant was a family man and liked to go home at the end of the working day and read. He was an omnivorous reader of newspapers and journals. He was not involved in the social or artistic life of New York, which held no interest for him, nor he for it. He travelled far less than other Secretaries-General. He was very quiet, unobtrusive, and unostentatious.

* * *

In 1962, quite apart from the unresolved problem of the Congo and the deep split which it had created in the United Nations, the organization was going through a time of tempestuous change and gestation, the birth of the Third World. The newly independent countries, which had been flocking to their seats in the General Assembly for the past two years, raised the membership, in October 1962, to 110.

This was a turning point in the history of the organization. The General Assembly, where the Western countries had for so long enjoyed an automatic majority, would no longer be their preferred battleground against the Soviet Union. They would therefore be less inclined in future to see the United Nations as a major instrument of foreign policy. The Third World countries were mostly determinedly non-aligned, which provided a welcome dilution of the East-West polarization that had bedeviled the UN since its earliest years. Their main interests were in decolonization and economic development, so that the agenda of the UN shifted and widened to include subjects scarcely dreamed of at its inception—development, population, food, environment, water, and other global problems.

The new shape of the organization tilted it in new political directions—against Israel and for the Arabs, for example—which were unwelcome to Western countries and further eroded their support of the UN. The tilt on the Middle East question had a particularly radical effect on the UN's standing in the United States. On the other hand, it was a far more representative organization than before, and its new agenda was more realistic in terms of confronting the real problems and preoccupations of the majority of the earth's inhabitants. These tendencies were not always viewed with favor by the older and well-established members. A difficult period of adjustment had started.

*   *   *

In October 1962 the world faced the most potentially dangerous international situation since World War II. The Cuban missile crisis was a classic example of how non-communication and brinkmanship between the superpowers, and the situation in a small but key country, can quickly and unexpectedly bring the world to the edge of the nuclear abyss. I realized how far things had gone when a number of rich New Yorkers who hardly knew me and normally had little use for the United Nations called up to inquire about the situation, in some cases asking for advice as to whether to remove themselves, their valuables, and so on, from the New York target area. We had dramatic debates in the Security Council in which Adlai Stevenson, using aerial photos and maps, shone as the prosecuting attorney against the Soviet Union, represented by that dour hatchet man, Valerian Zorin. I had always liked and admired Stevenson but had been disappointed by his performance as Ambassador to the UN. Perhaps because of lack of rapport with the Kennedys, he too often seemed unsure of, or sorry for, himself and made lackluster wisecracks—"Diplomacy is three parts—protocol, alcohol, and Geritol"—which did no credit to his view of his responsibilities. On this occasion, however, he put on a brave show.

Brave show or not, the confrontation of nuclear giants caused universal alarm, and U Thant became very active. He called, in the Security Council, for urgent negotiations between the parties directly involved. He sent messages to Chairman Khrushchev and President Kennedy asking for a moratorium involving, on the one hand, the voluntary suspension of all arms shipments to Cuba, and on the other, the voluntary suspension of the U.S. Navy's quarantine measures against Soviet ships bound for Cuba. He publicly asked "that good sense and understanding will be placed above the anger of the moment or the pride of nations. The path of negotiation and compromise is the only course by which the peace of the world can be secured at this critical moment."

Zorin strongly criticized U Thant's statement and the next day came to lecture him about his failure to condemn the United States. U Thant replied that his appeal to both parties represented his considered position and that Zorin had better condemn him publicly. Half an hour later, to

Zorin's rage, U Thant received Khrushchev's reply welcoming his initiative and agreeing to his proposal. Kennedy's reply was appreciative but less definite than Khrushchev's, saying that Stevenson would be prepared to discuss the arrangements that U Thant had mentioned.

U Thant then turned to Castro, asking him to suspend construction of the missile sites. Castro responded pugnaciously but asked U Thant to visit Cuba to discuss the situation directly. U Thant's visit to Cuba dealt mainly with the possibility of verification by UN Observers of the dismantling of the missile sites. Khrushchev had already agreed to this arrangement, which was the American condition for lifting the blockade on Soviet ships, but Castro angrily rejected it as a humiliating derogation of Cuban sovereignty. However, the Soviet Ambassador and a Soviet general visited U Thant in Havana to assure him that the dismantling process had already begun. This was, from a practical point of view, the most important part of the visit and further angered Castro, who said that the Cuban government alone had the right to give such assurances. The crisis was finally resolved in mid-December with the withdrawal of Soviet missiles and bombers from Cuba and the lifting of the U.S. naval quarantine.

In this most dangerous of international crises, U Thant provided an impartial central point of reference to which both sides could respond positively without the appearance of weakness or surrender. He got very little recognition for this service, but he would not have minded. His morning discipline of meditation included practicing "metta" (good will) and "karuna" (compassion). He tells us in his memoirs that while in Havana he managed to practice these, but "it was difficult to shut off my mind, even for a brief moment, and feel inner peace."

*   *   *

On the Congo front, we had spent most of 1962 trying to get Tshombe to follow up on the promises he had given after the fighting in Elisabethville and to reconcile himself with the central government. To this end U Thant had proposed a National Reconciliation Plan to the central government and the Katangese authorities, but getting Tshombe to follow up on it was like trying to get an eel into a bottle. He was a master of procrastination and of the reinterpretation of agreements. After all the other agonies of the Congo affair this was a uniquely frustrating time, and no end seemed to be in sight. Then suddenly, as had happened before in the Congo, a completely illogical and unexpected development solved the problem.

Late in December, for no discernible reason, our troops in Elisabethville and other towns in Katanga were fired on by Tshombe's soldiers for four successive days, and on Christmas Eve a UN helicopter was shot down. This was followed up by an assault on our positions in Elisabethville. It seemed that Tshombe, for heaven knows what reason, was determined to precipitate the final act of his long-drawn-out secession drama.

We had, at last, a magnificent military command in Katanga, perhaps the best I have ever encountered in the United Nations. The commander was Major-General Dewan Prem Chand, a soft-spoken, serious-minded Indian officer who had started his military career in my old regiment, the Dorsets. His operational deputy was the commander of the Indian Brigade, Brigadier Reggie Noronha, a cavalry officer, fast, stylish, decisive, and with a capacity for the grand gesture. I could have told Tshombe that it was very foolish to mess about with two such formidable professionals. However, mess about he did, and on December 28 U Thant, in response to the attacks on UN soldiers, authorized a military action to remove Tshombe's mercenaries and gendarmerie from Elisabethville and to establish freedom of movement for the UN troops all over Katanga.

Tshombe threatened to destroy the mines of the Union Minière and other installations if the UN counterattacked, knowing that the British and Belgian governments, seeing a threat to their assets, would frantically try to get U Thant to change his decision. If the UN moved across the Lufira River, these governments assured us, all the great mining installations of Jadotville and Kolwezi would be blown up by Tshombe's mercenaries. U Thant cautioned Prem Chand not to move until we had pinned Tshombe down on this score. Meanwhile Prem Chand and Noronha, finding little or no resistance, had pushed on across the river and entered Jadotville to the cheers of the populace and a warm welcome from the manager and staff of the Union Minière. Events proved them right, for what they achieved was the peaceful end of the Katanga secession and the removal of the main obstacle to a united and stable Congo. When they were rebuked for disobeying orders, a miraculous breakdown of communications was revealed. They had failed to receive U Thant's orders in time.

Tshombe finally ended the secession and accepted the National Conciliation Plan on January 14, 1963. He became Prime Minister of the Congo eighteen months later and faced, in his turn, the secession of the Orientale Province and a rebellion led by European mercenaries. He went into exile in Madrid in 1965 and conspired against his successor, Joseph Mobutu. He was kidnapped in mid-air in June 1967 by a French soldier of fortune and taken to Algeria, where he died two years later. After his death there was an unseemly quarrel over his Swiss bank account.

Our unexpected good fortune in resolving the Katanga problem had left some considerable questions, and being a bureaucracy we had to account for what had happened. The inadequacy of our antiquated communications system, limited by the perennial financial stringency of the UN, had paid off well in practice, so it was decided to improve the system. With the Katanga problem out of the way, we also needed to reduce the military strength of the UN operation in the Congo. I was sent to the Congo in early February 1963 with the Military Adviser, General Indar Rikhye, to review the situation and to suggest what should be done next.

This was a light-hearted and enjoyable mission. For once I was not directly responsible for anything except listening, giving advice, and revisiting the scenes of many former tribulations. I prepared suggestions on the future of the UN Force in the Congo and enjoyed watching others at work and seeing old friends.

When I got back to New York in March 1963, the prospects in the Congo seemed encouraging for the first time since 1960, and we could begin to phase out the Congo operation which had filled our days and nights for nearly three years. The moment this intention became clear, urgent appeals to stay on were received from many quarters which had, in the past, been consistently critical of our efforts. This seemed as good a way as any to validate what we had been trying to do.

We had gone into the Congo at a time of anarchy and collapse to secure the territorial integrity of that country and to help its newly independent government to take over responsibilities for which it had had no preparation whatsoever. Our presence had also prevented the East-West struggle for the Congo from actually taking place on the ground. At last there was a government whose writ ran in the entire country. The Congo retained the borders it had had at independence, in spite of three major secessionist movements. It was time to take the UN troops out and let the Congo government take over its responsibilities. U Thant's June 1964 report on this move, which I wrote, concluded: "The United Nations cannot permanently protect the Congo, or any other country, from the internal tensions and disturbances created by its own organic growth toward unity and nationhood. This is an undertaking which henceforth must be carried out only by the Government and the people of the Congo." The last United Nations troops left the Congo on June 30, 1964, four years to the day after its independence.

The United Nations Congo operation is sometimes used as a synonym for failure and for the sort of involvement to be avoided at all costs in the future. A dispassionate study of the record—do such studies ever reach the public?—points to a very different conclusion. What we managed to do in the Congo, at great cost and in the face of enormous difficulties and dangers, seems rather to show that the UN can tackle situations which no one else can tackle. If the Congo had broken up or become an East-West battleground, would the Congolese, or world peace for that matter, have been better served? I doubt it. And many more people would certainly have been killed.

*   *   *

My own personal affairs had at last begun to be straightened out. Alfreda remarried in March, and I married Sidney Canfield in April 1963. After three years of misery, much of it self-induced, the clouds suddenly dispersed and great vistas of happiness opened up.

I had learned a great deal in the ups and downs of the Congo operation, and had gained a much clearer idea of what we could and could not do. I had flung myself into the United Nations after the war with a highly romanticized idea about what an international civil servant might be able to achieve in a world of sovereign states and of virtually unbridled nationalism. As a result I had often ended up angry, bruised, and resentful through assuming that what *ought* to be done *could* be done. In the early days in the Congo we had had, due to the impossible and exotic nature of the situation, remarkable freedom to improvise. Later on the operation had become a painful round of drudgery and frustration.

Reason, justice, and compassion are small cards to play in the world of politics, whether international, national, or tribal, but someone has to go on playing them. If you hold on to your belief in reason and compassion despite all political maneuvering, your efforts may in the end produce results. A determined effort to do what seems objectively right may sometimes eventually transcend the vicissitudes of politics. After the Congo experience I became less upset by outside criticism but more cautious in assessing the validity of what we were trying to do. I also learned that immediate success often has very little to do with lasting achievement, and that the judgment of history on many controversial issues will be very different from the fashionable judgment of the time.

I began, too, to understand the power of mythology as created and propagated by skillful public relations. The Tshombe episode was an outstanding example of well-packaged mythology which we, with very little success, were at pains to dispel. The United Nations is, and always has been, hopeless at public relations. Our earnest and pedestrian efforts were no match for Tshombe's well-financed professional public relations machine, abetted by aficionados like Senator Thomas Dodd and other, perhaps well-meaning but misinformed, Americans and Europeans.

* * *

After the settlement of the Katanga problem the pace and tension of our daily work relaxed, and there was more time for private life and for other interests. One of these was to devise a fitting memorial for Dag Hammarskjold. The new UN Library, which he had so much enjoyed planning and which the Ford Foundation financed, had been named after him. Chagall had executed, at the request of the staff, a glorious stained-glass window in his memory. Hammarskjold had greatly admired the British sculptor Barbara Hepworth, whom he had got to know just before his death. They had much in common, each having a penchant for the abstract and austere.

Hammarskjold had enjoyed walking around the UN Headquarters in New York thinking of ways to enhance its appearance. On one of these walks he had suggested to Ralph Bunche that a sculpture by Barbara Hepworth would give elevation and style to the lackluster forecourt of the Secretariat Building with its dreary pool and fountain. After his death, Bunche and I pursued this idea with Barbara Hepworth. She had originally planned a sculpture ten feet high, but when we tried a mock-up of it it was completely dwarfed by the scale of the surrounding buildings. *Single Form*, which now dominates the forecourt, is nearly thirty feet high. It was unveiled in June 1964.

* * *

My own country, Great Britain, has a unique record of bequeathing insoluble problems to the United Nations. The British government had constantly proclaimed that it would never leave Cyprus and, as in Palestine, only did so when, in 1960, British efforts to control the violence in the island had become impossible to sustain. Unfortunately, British rule in Cyprus had not only engendered a burning desire for independence, but had also stimulated the latent rivalry between the Greek and Turkish communities. Independence did not, therefore, bring peace to Cyprus in spite of complex constitutional arrangements, a Treaty of Guarantee, and a Treaty of Alliance, and violent intercommunal strife broke out at the end of 1963. A large British peacekeeping force found itself in an increasingly impossible position. The Cyprus government came to the

UN for help, insisting that a United Nations peacekeeping force replace the British.

It was a familiar situation. A long-standing feud having been allowed to get out of hand, the protagonists had dumped their problem on the world organization, demanding that we solve it and beginning almost immediately to criticize and denigrate our efforts to do so. The British press, and some British politicians, as befitted the main begetters of the problem, tended to be particularly patronizing.

This is not the place to go into the Byzantine complications of the Cyprus imbroglio. I know of no problem more frustrating or more bedeviled by mean-spiritedness and lack of mutual confidence, nor of a problem where all concerned would so obviously gain from a reasonable settlement.

The year 1964 was an awkward one in which to try to set up a new peacekeeping operation. The repercussions, constitutional and financial, of the Congo operation had virtually paralyzed the General Assembly. At the height of the dispute over the authority of the Secretary-General in running peacekeeping operations, the setting up of a new peacekeeping force in Cyprus might well have run into Soviet opposition. However, the Soviets merely stipulated that the financial basis of the operation must be strictly voluntary. Neither the Soviets nor France, among many others, have ever paid a penny toward the Cyprus operation, which, as a result, has run steadily deeper into debt.

The arrival, at the end of March 1964, of the UN peacekeeping force, initially from Canada, Finland, Ireland, and Sweden, and the beginning of the UN mediation effort, had an almost immediate calming effect. The fighting gradually died down throughout the island, although the war of words continued. Like all UN peacekeeping operations, the UN Force in Cyprus was supposed to be a temporary measure to calm the situation and let reason prevail so that a settlement could be agreed upon. Initially a period of three months was allotted for this purpose. Twenty-two years later the UN Force is still there, and the negotiations continue.

Cyprus is the seat of an ancient civilization, the legendary birthplace of Venus, and a treasure house of historical memories—Iron Age, Greek and Roman remains, Crusaders' castles, great Venetian ports and fortifications, Othello's headquarters in Famagusta, Turkish mosques and towns. There are also the visible relicts of British rule, law courts, an efficient civil service and police force, and the two remaining British Sovereign Base Areas. The frequent pettiness of Cyprus politics stood out sadly against this historical background.

The Cypriots, both Greek and Turkish, are talented and charming people. Unfortunately, however, the elements of compromise, good faith, live-and-let-live, and belief in a common interest in the future, which are the basis of civilized politics, seem to be virtually nonexistent in Cyprus. Instead there is a relentless point-scoring through vitriolic public statements and assertions, a hyperactive local press, and an almost paranoid refusal to take any good will gesture at face value. The most insignificant event tends to be interpreted as part of a conspiracy or parlayed into a threat or a deception. Both confidence and confidentiality are absent, the most confidential papers or suggestions invariably being leaked to the press, often in distorted form. The past has bequeathed to the leaders in Cyprus a bitter legacy of mutual distrust and hatred which makes them extremely difficult to help.

In Cyprus, the local question is an obsession to the exclusion of virtually all other topics or interests. If World War III were to occur, the headline in the Cyprus *Mail* might well read: "Third World War Interrupts Consideration of Cyprus Problem." It is no wonder that outside powers, great and small, have happily consigned it to the United Nations and to the Secretary-General.

On the peacekeeping side, the United Nations has been outstandingly successful in Cyprus. Since the end of 1964 there has been virtually no loss of life except in one incident in 1967 and during the tragic Greek-inspired coup against Makarios and the resulting Turkish intervention of 1974, an event completely outside the mandate of our peacekeeping operation. Critics of the UN have sometimes decried the UN's success in keeping the peace in Cyprus as a deterrent to solving the problem. The trouble with this argument is that the breakdown of peace in Cyprus cannot be an isolated event. Turkey and Greece are inevitably involved, and with them the whole delicate strategic balance of the eastern Mediterranean and the southeast flank of NATO. Cyprus is wired like a detonator to other, larger problems.

During their tenure in Cyprus, the British did not always resist the temptation to divide and rule. The contentious relationship of Greece and Turkey is also reflected in the attitudes of the two communities in Cyprus, both of which have close ties to their motherlands. The Greek Cypriots, being the large majority, did not extend to their Turkish compatriots the kind of magnanimity that might, at independence, have created a united nation of Cyprus. Instead the Turks were treated as an unfavored minority, and the complex constitutional arrangements devised at independence soon broke down. The activities of the Greek general

Grivas, the EOKA leader who had fought the British and who remained on the island to fight the Turks until 1967, were another negative factor.

The president, Archbishop Makarios, was not the type of leader to command the confidence of the Turkish Cypriots. Makarios was a Byzantine prelate, clever and devious, with a propensity for brinkmanship which was often self-defeating. He was unquestionably the father of his own people, and one could only admire his determination and physical courage. He seemed to have many lives, surviving all plots and assassination attempts, including being shot down in a helicopter and having his palace destroyed by tank fire. The Turkish Cypriot leader, Fazil Kuçuk, was no match for Makarios in charisma, eloquence, or international repute.

Our peacekeepers were for the most part considerable innocents in the tortuous world of Cyprus. Their task was difficult and exasperating, and their patience and compassion were often taxed to the limit. Their function, according to the Security Council Mandate, was to "use their best efforts to prevent a recurrence of fighting and, as necessary, to contribute to the maintenance of law and order and a return to normal conditions." It sounded simple enough in New York, but in the agonizing convolutions of Cyprus what, and how much, were "best efforts"? What did "as necessary" mean? What on earth were "normal conditions" in a place where if one side agreed to something the other almost automatically disagreed? We were to learn a great deal about these questions in succeeding years and to listen to much unearned criticism and abuse from both sides. In the meantime we did our best to flesh out the carefully worded simplicities of the Security Council with adequate directives.

As soon as the UN Force (UNFICYP) was established, we tried to concentrate on constructive tasks that would bring the Greek and Turkish Cypriots together. Unfortunately, in Cyprus reason and common sense all too easily gave way to hatred, fear, and fantasy, which often spilled over in preposterous accusations against United Nations personnel who were in any case limited in the nature and scope of the actions they could take. They could not take over the functions of government or local authorities. They could not disarm either regular or irregular forces. They could not dictate or enforce solutions. They could only help those who really wished to find a peaceful solution to their problems, and sometimes such people seemed few and far between.

Peacekeeping forces do not solve political or constitutional problems. This, under the March 1964 decision of the Security Council, was the function of the UN Mediator. Our first Cyprus Mediator, Sakari Tuomioja, the jovial and extrovert Finn who had been Hammarskjold's representative in Laos, died of a heart attack in September 1964; he was succeeded by another delightful extrovert, Galo Plaza Lasso, a former President of Ecuador who had served Hammarskjold in the 1958 Observation Group in Lebanon and also in the Congo.

Galo's experience was typical of the fate of those who try to solve the Cyprus problem. After laboring assiduously in a maze of Byzantine twists and turns, he finally came forward, in 1965, with a plan that seemed to most outsiders as fair and as reasonable as possible in a situation where there was no ideal solution. He was promptly denounced by Turkey and the Turkish Cypriots, who vowed never to accept Galo Plaza's mediation again. The Greek Cypriot side equally promptly responded that they would never accept a mediator *other* than Galo Plaza. The function of mediator thus lapsed. The Turkish reaction seems to indicate that the side in Cyprus which regards itself, at any given time, as the underdog is unlikely to have the confidence to accept any permanent solution which is acceptable to the other side.

After the demise of the mediator's office the search for a basic solution continued in "inter-communal talks" conducted by the Secretary-General's Special Representative, the civilian head of the Cyprus operation. At various times between 1967 and the disaster of 1974 these marathon talks had achieved an overall package deal, only to have one side or the other pull the rug out from under it. They were, as it turned out, the last opportunity to secure a unified state of Cyprus in which Turks and Greeks would actually live together and revive their former mutual tolerance. The opportunity was missed, with results with which the United Nations is still trying to cope. The coup against Makarios sponsored in 1974 by the Athens colonels radically changed both the situation in Cyprus and, through the military intervention of Turkey, the balance of power, so that a divided Cyprus became inevitable. After twelve more years of intensive negotiation by the Secretary-General of the United Nations, it remains to be seen whether a constitutional and territorial arrangement can be found to encompass this new reality.

*   *   *

The celebration of the twentieth anniversary of the signing of the UN Charter in San Francisco in June 1965 took place in the San Francisco Opera House, at a particularly sensitive time in the evolution of the

Vietnam War. The fact that President Lyndon Johnson was to be the keynote speaker tended to overshadow, in the media at any rate, the significance of the occasion. There had been speculation in the American press that the president would use the occasion for a dramatic reversal of American policy in Vietnam, a possibility which had been publicly hinted at, to the evident rage of Johnson, by Adlai Stevenson, the U.S. Ambassador to the United Nations.

Johnson had only reluctantly and belatedly decided to appear, and his speech, far from announcing any new direction on Vietnam, was a confection of vapid and high-minded generalities delivered in a lackluster style apparently intended to display his lack of enthusiasm for the occasion. After his speech Johnson requested U Thant to visit him in his temporary quarters in the tenor's dressing room. When Bunche and I finally succeeded in making our way through the president's security detail to join U Thant at the meeting, we met Adlai coming out, red in the face with indignation and humiliation. "He has thrown me out," he said, and Bunche, an old friend, said, "Then I won't attend either." We tried instead to cheer Stevenson up. It was the last time either of us saw him. Two weeks later he dropped dead in the street in London.

*   *   *

The war which broke out between India and Pakistan in the late summer of 1965 was a major threat to world peace. Since the partition of the Indian subcontinent in 1947, the Kashmir problem had been the subject of many negotiating efforts by the United Nations, and there was a permanent UN Military Observer Group (UNMOGIP) stationed on the cease-fire line in Kashmir. India had always refused any international action, such as a supervised plebiscite, which questioned its claim to Kashmir. Pakistan adamantly refused to recognize the legitimacy of India's claim to the territory. This stalemate was the source of much tension between the two countries.

Throughout 1965 there had been a sharp increase in violations of the cease-fire line in Kashmir by both sides, and irregulars began to infiltrate from the Pakistan side across the line in increasing numbers. India reacted with a counteroffensive into Pakistan, and by the first days of September, with Indian and Pakistani troops crossing the cease-fire line in both directions, a full-scale war was under way. Both sides captured territory and both carried out air strikes against airfields and military targets.

A war between the two great countries of the subcontinent was bad enough in itself, but Pakistan's relationship with China and India's with the Soviet Union added a dangerous dimension to the struggle. There was also the terrible possibility that the war would give rise once again to communal violence between Hindus and Muslims. On September 4, at the urging of U Thant, the United States requested a meeting of the Security Council, which called for a cease-fire and for both armies to withdraw to their original positions. Despite the Council's appeal, the conflict continued to broaden and spread to the border between India and Pakistan south of Kashmir. On September 6, the Security Council, in some desperation, requested U Thant "to extend every possible effort" to stop the hostilities.

I was taking a week's leave at our house in Massachusetts and with my sister-in-law, Maggie Howard, had got to the finals in our local tennis tournament when I was recalled urgently to New York to accompany U Thant to India and Pakistan. We left on the evening of Tuesday, September 7, via London and Teheran. All commercial flights to the subcontinent had been suspended because of the war and the bombing of airfields, so our outward progress was uncertain. We were met in Teheran by my former Secretariat colleague, Amir Abbas Hoveyda, the Shah's prime minister, who was to be executed in the Iranian revolution. He was kindness itself and entertained us in the Shah's special pavilion at the airport while we sought a means of getting to Pakistan. The reports of bombing and parachute attacks on airfields had been much exaggerated in New York and London, and we finally got to Karachi and thence to Rawalpindi without too much difficulty. It is a curious fact of life that the reported degree of violence in foreign parts usually increases in direct ratio to the distance from the scene.

Although there was nothing easy about his mission, U Thant, as usual, was completely calm. He showed no interest in the frantic discussions of his entourage about his travel plans and safety. He was interested in getting there, but didn't mind how. President Johnson had offered Air Force One, but U Thant said he would feel awkward with a party of only five in such a big plane. Getting from Rawalpindi to Delhi reasonably quickly was obviously going to be a problem, and we were finally offered the aircraft of the American air attaché in Teheran, a Convair which did about 200 miles per hour. Both sides routed it on immense detours to avoid military installations in the belief that it had a CIA crew. Thus it took nearly two days to get to Delhi from Rawalpindi.

This urgent and important trip, where the distances were great, revealed once again the UN's lack of adequate and up-to-date communications equipment. As I wrote later, "we were compelled to conduct this mission in a horse-and-buggy manner when what was required was timing, flexibility and mobility. The present nineteenth century method is also extremely exhausting." Any idea of shuttling between India and Pakistan was practically out of the question, so that our negotiations, after the preliminary talks in both countries, had to be conducted by cable and through messengers, which was highly unsatisfactory.

Arriving at the bomb-damaged airfield at Rawalpindi, we went immediately into conference with the foreign minister, Zulfikar Ali Bhutto. Bhutto had been to Christ Church, Oxford, and he reminded me of those stylish, slightly raffish sons of Whig noblemen whom I had admired in my youth. He was intelligent, arrogant, charming, and unpredictable. He would pay dearly for these characteristics later on.

Bhutto urged the necessity of dealing with the basic problem of Kashmir, accusing the Indians of trying to make their occupation a fait accompli. He complained bitterly of the Security Council's lack of understanding of Pakistan's position and of its failure to fulfill its moral and political obligations to the people of Kashmir. He maintained, with an air of injured innocence, that the infiltrators had acted entirely on their own out of a sense of frustration at an intolerable situation and that, short of shooting them, Pakistan could not restrain them. In fact the Pakistani infiltration of irregulars into Kashmir which had started the war had been designed precisely to prevent Kashmir from becoming a dead issue. Bhutto was a past master at playing the injured, outraged party.

We had luncheon with President Ayub Khan. Ayub was the quintessential field marshal, a splendid presence, with the mustache and masterful clipped accent of a British general and a vast natural authority and self-confidence. He had, I remember, the best and most expensive-looking shoes I have ever seen. Ayub claimed that Pakistan was fighting for its life against an Indian attempt to sever its vital north-south arteries of communication. He could not, he said, accept an unconditional cease-fire which gave no guarantees on the settlement of the Kashmir question. He evidently felt that Pakistan's case on Kashmir was being ignored and sidetracked, and had a strong sense of grievance against the Security Council, the Soviet Union, and the United States, which had cut off military aid to Pakistan.

The immediate purpose of our trip was to get a cease-fire and withdrawal of forces. U Thant intended to propose a time and date for this as soon as he had seen the Indian leaders in Delhi. The best reason for hoping for a cease-fire was that neither side could expect a military victory and both were reported already to be low on fuel, ammunition, and spare parts.

U Thant urged again and again that if there was no cease-fire the fighting would escalate and, quite apart from wider disasters, there would be total economic disruption which would be devastating for Pakistan. Bhutto and Ayub insisted that a cease-fire had to be linked to a plebiscite to settle the Kashmir question.

We left Rawalpindi for Delhi in our ancient Convair at 8:00 a.m. on September 11. Bhutto had evidently taken a liking to U Thant, and when we arrived at the airport, heavily ringed by anti-aircraft guns, we found that he had put on board a beautiful Taxila sculpture of the Buddha, a miraculous mixture of classical Greek and Buddhist art. No gift could have meant more to U Thant. The sculpture was not the only offering, for Burmese embassies along the route had apparently been alerted to U Thant's wife's weakness for mango jam, and a first consignment of this explosive substance had been put on the aircraft. Later on, in Bombay, one of the cases of jam began to hiss and tick, and our American pilot declared a bomb emergency until the source of the trouble had been traced. The whole lot was then thrown out.

I enjoyed these trips, the heavier side of which was always balanced by less serious matters. I also enjoyed being able to organize things on my own. I found U Thant very receptive to ideas, and at all points during our mission we had communications, plans, and statements ready in advance, so that he was never in any doubt of what he was going to do next.

We refueled in Karachi and were then routed out hundreds of miles out over the Indian Ocean, arriving in the late afternoon in Bombay, where we stayed overnight with the Governor of Maharashtra.

Delhi was on a war footing, and the fountains and pools of the Rashtrapati Bhavan, the enormous Lutyens vice-regal/presidential palace where we were staying, had been drained as being too conspicuous from the air. But the atmosphere was relaxed, and the war seemed far away.

The Indian foreign minister, Swaran Singh, also struck an attitude of indignation and injured innocence. Did a cease-fire, he asked, include the Pakistani infiltrators? How could there be a plebiscite in Kashmir when there had already been three general elections? The Security Council must deal with the new problem of a war started by infiltrators who weren't even in uniform. India's duty was to defend Jammu and Kashmir, which were part of India.

Late in the evening we went to the modest house of the prime minister, Lal Bahadur Shastri. It reminded me of a Bedouin encampment with old wise men, gurus, fires, and lamplight everywhere. Small and austerely simple, Shastri was a refreshingly straightforward man. He had had, he said, a terrible day in the parliament, but he wanted to stop the fighting and would do what he could.

Our appeal for an unconditional cease-fire and withdrawal of forces evoked long replies from both sides, each imposing conditions and qualifications which they knew perfectly well the other would not accept. Each obviously had to let the situation run down a little further and feel more pressure from outside before the war could stop. Both were facing a crippling and potentially disastrous situation, both were making similar accusations against the other, and both felt betrayed by their erstwhile allies, who now stood by in bewilderment. Both believed that only outside support had made it possible for the other to commit aggression. Both were linked in an intricate way with the mainstream of world politics. In fact the unaccustomed unanimity of the Security Council on this crisis was an indication of how serious a threat it posed to world peace, but more time and more pressure would obviously be required before the fighting could be stopped.

It was clearly time to turn the matter back to the Security Council, and I devoted much of the flight home to drafting U Thant's report so that no time would be lost when we got back to New York. Before leaving Delhi for New York we made two more urgent appeals for a cease-fire, knowing very well that they would meet the same resistance. In one of these we suggested a meeting of the leaders of India and Pakistan to talk directly about a settlement. It was such a meeting, at Tashkent under the chairmanship of Kosygin, that later finally resolved the crisis.

U Thant suggested that the Council might consider ordering India and Pakistan to stop fighting under Chapter VII, the enforcement chapter of the Charter. The only precedent for this was the Council's order in July 1948, which stopped the fighting in the first Arab-Israeli War at a desperate moment for Israel. He also suggested various practical forms of UN assistance in observing the cease-fire and the withdrawal of troops, for which we had already drawn up contingency plans during the trip. He again suggested a meeting of the two heads of government.

In deference to the exceptional gravity of the situation, we were met at Kennedy Airport by Arthur Goldberg of the United States, the President of the Security Council, and all the members of the Council—an unprecedented happening. For the moment, however, the fighting in the subcontinent only intensified, and on September 18 it was reported that

Chinese troops were massing on the Indian border. In the media there was even talk of the possibility of World War III, and when, late on a Saturday afternoon, Arthur Goldberg summoned a press conference, the press flocked to it in anticipation of a historic announcement. They were disappointed when Goldberg's main item of news was the engagement of his daughter.

The Council finally demanded that a cease-fire should take effect on September 22, and the Indians agreed. Bhutto came to New York in a highly emotional mood, at one point throwing his papers in the air and stalking out of the Council chamber, before announcing that Ayub Khan too had ordered his troops to stop fighting.

In addition to the existing Observer Group in Kashmir, we set up a new observer mission on the border between India and Pakistan, but the cease-fire ordered by the Council did not hold, and bickering and re-crimination between the two governments continued. The Soviets started to criticize U Thant for exceeding his authority in setting up the new observation machinery, but they had picked on the wrong man, for he stood his ground and the other Council members rallied to his support. In the end it was the efforts of the Soviet premier, Alexei Kosygin, and not the decisions of the Security Council, which achieved, at Tashkent in January 1966, a complete cease-fire and withdrawal of forces.

*   *   *

In December, U Thant was reelected as Secretary-General. He had wished to leave but finally gave in to the unanimous demand that he stay. This posed a serious problem for Ralph Bunche. Ralph had told U Thant in August 1966 that he would definitely be leaving at the end of the year, mentioning that he had resigned as early as June 1961 but had been talked out of it by Hammarskjold. Bunche was sixty-two and already in failing health. He felt that the day-to-day demands and pressures of his job were too much for his enfeebled state and that he could no longer function with "the intensity and quality of work that my standards call for and which the job itself requires." He was, I think, also influenced by a feeling that his commitment to the United Nations had precluded work on civil rights in the United States, a subject about which he was passionately concerned. When U Thant was reelected, his first move was to insist that Bunche should stay. Bunche at first reaffirmed his intention to retire, adducing personal reasons as well as his dismay at the "lack of compre-hension and cynicism" which had characterized the General Assembly's recent discussion of peacekeeping. However, U Thant finally prevailed, and Bunche, mentioning "the abandonment of plans and dreams which I (and Mrs. Bunche as well) have been cultivating over the past six years," finally agreed to stay on.

I was delighted with this decision, but for Ralph it was a grave mistake. He was already suffering the effects of diabetes—failing eyesight and a host of other symptoms—and a lighter workload and new interests would certainly have given him more of a chance to resist the onset of physical debility. As it was, he stayed on, and his physical condition steadily deteriorated.

*   *   *

In 1967 I was agonizing over a personal decision. Ever since I had reviewed Hammarskjold's *Markings* in *The New Yorker* I had been repeatedly asked by publishers, as well as by Hammarskjold's family and Swedish friends, to write a book about him. Early in 1967 Hammarskjold's family and trustees gave me sole access to his personal papers in the Swedish Royal Library, and, with great reluctance and lack of self-confidence, I agreed to go ahead. I had never written a book before and was not at all sure I was capable of the task, especially with such a complex and elusive subject as Dag Hammarskjold. Moreover, as a member of the Secretariat I was shackled by discretion, or believed that I was. Bunche in particular was emphatic that my status as a member of the Secretariat would make it impossible for me to publish such a book. On the other hand, I felt strongly that few people understood Hammarskjold's work at the United Nations and that someone ought to do something about it. I arranged, therefore, to spend my summer vacation going through Hammarskjold's papers in the Royal Library in Stockholm, and planned to leave New York on June 12. This plan was soon swept aside.

XVI

The Six-Day War

ON THE EVENING OF May 16, 1967, General Indar Rikhye, Commander of the UN Force in the Sinai (UNEF), received, at his HQ in Gaza, a request from General Fawzi, the Egyptian chief of staff:

> For the sake of complete security of all UN troops which install OP's [observation posts] along our borders . . . that you issue your orders to withdraw all these troops immediately.

This request was apparently in preparation for action by the Egyptian Army to deter a supposed Israeli threat to Syria. Rikhye rightly responded that he had no authority to act in such a serious matter and referred Fawzi's strangely worded request to New York. U Thant called in the Egyptian Ambassador, who was, I remember, dressed for a formal dinner at the Asia Society, and asked him to convey to Cairo his concern at this request and its probable consequences.

The next day Fawzi's request was repeated, this time specifying the withdrawal of the UN Yugoslav contingent in Sinai within twenty-four hours and the UN troops from Sharm el Sheikh in forty-eight hours. Egyptian troops moved into UNEF positions in Sinai and surrounded Sharm el Sheikh at the southern end of the Sinai peninsula. U Thant protested these actions and called the Egyptian government's attention to the "Good Faith" accord which had been personally negotiated with Nasser by Hammarskjold and was the basis for UNEF's presence in Egypt. In Cairo, Nasser informed the ambassadors of the countries providing troops for UNEF that the force must leave Egypt and the Gaza Strip forthwith. When this position was put to U Thant, he again warned of the disastrous consequences likely to ensue from such a move.

The official request for the complete withdrawal of UNEF arrived on May 18. U Thant consulted the Advisory Committee on UNEF, which consisted of the governments which had originally supplied the troops for the Force. Although the Western members—Canada, Denmark, Norway, and Sweden—were acutely unhappy at U Thant's contention that he was obliged, under Hammarskjold's previous agreement, to honor the Egyptian request, they made no move to try to get the General Assembly to consider the matter. It was already clear that the majority of member states, which was required to convene the Assembly, would be against considering the matter, as Egypt's legal rights were not in doubt. U Thant told the Committee, and they had little option but to agree, that if Nasser persisted in his requests, he would be obliged to concur in the withdrawal of the UN Force from Egyptian territory. All shared U Thant's misgivings as to the consequences of the Egyptian decision. They wrung their hands and were deeply disturbed, but no one was able to suggest a way out.

Bunche and I devoted ourselves to the search for a solution to this dilemma. On May 17 I had drafted an appeal to Nasser, stating that our Military Observers could find no evidence of Israeli troop concentrations against Syria, stressing the dangers of an armed confrontation in Sinai and Gaza after the withdrawal of UNEF, and urging him to reconsider his decision on UNEF. U Thant had been warned by Cairo that any appeal to Nasser would be sternly rebuffed and he decided not to send this appeal. Although subsequent events seemed to show that Cairo's warning was not just a bluff, U Thant's historical position would have been stronger if he had gone ahead and made the appeal anyway.

The appeal was shelved, and U Thant decided to go to Cairo himself. He took neither Bunche nor me with him, apparently because he had been advised that American or British nationals would not be welcome. In the light of our long relationship with the Egyptians this was absurd, but it is now clear that no amount of argument would have changed Nasser's mind.

U Thant left New York on May 22, stopping over in Paris, where I called him to tell him that Nasser had just announced that he had closed the Strait of Tiran—the access to Israel's southern port of Eilat—to Israeli shipping. U Thant decided to go on to Cairo anyway. Nasser's public announcement of the closure of the Strait of Tiran showed dramatically how committed he was to his self-destructive course, for he knew—and U Thant pointed it out again on his arrival in Cairo—that his action made war with Israel a certainty. Israel had long ago made it clear that the closing of the Strait would be regarded as a *casus belli*. Nasser explained to U Thant that he had made his decisive statement *before* U Thant's arrival, because to make it after his arrival would have been an insult to the Secretary-General. U Thant failed to dissuade Nasser, who had already committed himself publicly beyond the point of no return, but he was the only world statesman even to attempt directly to do so.

These were the opening gambits of an episode which would prove disastrous for Egypt and the countries of the Middle East, and also for the United Nations and for U Thant personally.

Ever since the establishment of UNEF in 1956 Nasser had been subjected to periodic criticism and ridicule from other Arab countries for hiding behind UNEF in Sinai instead of confronting the Israeli enemy. In May 1967 Israeli hints during an election campaign about possible operations against Syria had triggered panic reactions in Damascus, and Nasser, with a misplaced confidence partly inspired by his new Soviet weaponry, had decided to confront Israel.

Bunche and I, since we were responsible for UNEF, were from the beginning intimately involved in this dismal affair. One of our main problems arose from the great and unexpected success of UNEF in securing ten years of peace on the formerly bloody Egyptian-Israeli border. A dramatic innovation in 1956, UNEF had come, over the years of unaccustomed peace, to be taken totally for granted. UNEF attracted attention largely as a budgetary problem, and I had been sent out several times to streamline and reduce it. I found on these occasions a considerable ignorance in the United States and Britain, two countries which paid much of the bill, of the nature of the effectiveness of UNEF, which was its physical presence symbolizing the will of the world community. UNEF's success had led to an unfortunate assumption not only that it was permanent but that it was a far more powerful arrangement than the largely symbolic deployment of only 1,400 lightly armed soldiers on a 300-mile front.

The essence of UNEF's function was to maintain a buffer on the border, 500 yards wide in the Gaza Strip and 2,000 yards wide in Sinai, in which, by a local agreement with the Egyptian Army, there were no Egyptian troops. UNEF was not deployed at all on the Israeli side of the line, because Ben-Gurion had refused its presence in 1957 on the grounds that it would be an infringement of Israeli sovereignty.

The moment Egyptian troops moved into the buffer zone, up to the line and into Sharm el Sheikh, as they did on May 17, the main point of

UNEF and its basis of operation evaporated. Since no one could control or influence Nasser, it was convenient to pretend that the tiny symbolic UN Force *could*, and *should*, have resisted the Egyptian Army, some 80,000 strong, on Egyptian soil, and that everything would have been all right if U Thant had had the courage to take the "right decision." This hypocritical and escapist nonsense is still remarkably prevalent in Western folklore.

We were faced from the start of the crisis with a cruel and insoluble dilemma. There was no doubt of Egypt's sovereign legal right to request the withdrawal of UNEF from Egyptian soil. This was the basis on which Hammarskjold had persuaded Nasser to accept UNEF in 1956. When Ben-Gurion had asserted the same right ten years before in refusing to allow UNEF to be stationed on the Israeli side of the line, no one had challenged Israel. Nor could there be any question of UNEF resisting the Egyptian Army on Egyptian territory. On the other hand, we knew from the start that if Nasser maintained his course, the Israelis would react with devastating force.

The way UNEF had been set up added to U Thant's problem. Because of the British and French vetoes in the Security Council at the time of Suez, the request to the Secretary-General to set up UNEF came from the General Assembly. It was therefore impossible to refer the problem to the Security Council, which had nothing to do with UNEF. To put the matter on the agenda of the General Assembly would have required an affirmative decision by two thirds of the member states, and it was known that a large majority would support Egypt's position and would therefore not agree to the Assembly even considering the question. The sole responsibility for an unavoidable and fateful decision therefore fell on U Thant.

There *was* one way in which U Thant could have escaped this responsibility. This was for the Secretary-General to summon the Security Council under Article 99 of the Charter to consider the situation as a threat to international peace and security. U Thant knew that if he did this, the Council's proceedings would decline into an undignified brawl along East-West lines, as indeed it later did when the Council met at the request of Denmark and Canada. He declined to take this way out. In retrospect I for one greatly regret U Thant's refusal to pass the buck, and I wish we had pressed him harder to do so.

In all my years at the UN I can recall no situation in which humbug, escapism, and a resolute determination *not* to consider the real facts of the situation were so prevalent. Western governments especially were unwilling to recognize Nasser's obsessive determination or to do anything practical to restrain it. The Soviets, who had just provided Nasser with his impressive-looking new armaments, would certainly not do so. Nor in those days was the United States able, or likely, to restrain Israel, which was still getting the bulk of its armaments from France. It was much easier to criticize U Thant and to lecture the Secretariat about our alleged pusillanimity.

When actually challenged by Nasser, Western governments tended to cave in quickly. Bunche and I had decided that the best way to try to redeem the situation would be to take the maximum time to make withdrawal arrangements. These should be orderly, deliberate, and dignified. Thus we would maintain UNEF in situ for as long as possible and use the time to try to talk Nasser round. The Egyptian government was deeply provoked by an announcement from Ottawa that two Canadian warships were being moved to the eastern Mediterranean and by bellicose Canadian statements insisting on UNEF's right to stay in Egypt, as if it was an occupation force. When Egypt riposted by declaring that, because of these statements, it could no longer assure the security of Canadian soldiers in UNEF and demanded their withdrawal, the Canadian contingent was withdrawn in forty-eight hours, leaving UNEF with no logistic units or aircraft.

We received lectures from Arthur Goldberg, the American Ambassador to the UN, about "precipitous" decisions, although the United States did little or nothing either to put pressure on Nasser or to restrain Israel. George Brown, the emotional British Foreign Secretary, was also vocally critical and later gave a fatuous version of the affair in his memoirs.

The general line of criticism was that we were caving in to the Egyptian dictator. In a situation where the West simply did not want to, or could not, face up to the truth, U Thant provided a perfect scapegoat. Words like "poltroonery" and phrases like "U Thant's war," "a thief in the night," or comparing U Thant to "a wet noodle" were freely used. Abba Eban referred to UNEF as an umbrella that folds up when it starts to rain. This kind of public abuse successfully concealed the fact that none of the accusers could suggest any way out of the dilemma. Neither Britain nor the United States, for example, took the situation to the Security Council. They knew all too well that nothing could be done and therefore wished to take no responsibility.

When U Thant returned empty-handed from Cairo, we set about trying to devise ways of slowing down the onrush of events and defusing the tensions and suspicions which were making the situation so explosive.

U Thant, seeking a breathing spell, suggested the revival, at least as a temporary measure, of the Egypt-Israel Armistice machinery which Israel had denounced in 1956 at the time of the Suez crisis. He also suggested the appointment of a Special Representative to act as a go-between and to allay the rumors and suspicions that were causing so much of the tension, and the stationing of UNEF temporarily on the Israeli side of the line. Israel, no doubt having already decided on military action, turned down these ideas.

Many of the reactions to the situation seemed to be designed to *increase* the tension. The United States and Britain were rumored to be discussing means to assert by force the right of passage through the Strait of Tiran. Nasser and King Hussein of Jordan signed a mutual defense pact, which proved to be a disaster for Jordan. Syria and Iraq signed a military cooperation agreement in case of war with Israel. De Gaulle's proposal for a Big Four meeting was refused by the USSR. The Security Council totally failed to reach agreement on any course of action whatever.

At 2:40 a.m. (New York time) on June 5 we received the first news of war from General Rikhye in Gaza. The Israelis had struck at breakfast time by air and land with devastating effect, advancing through Gaza and simultaneously attacking and virtually destroying the Egyptian and Syrian air forces on the ground. Fighting also broke out in Jerusalem, where Jordanian forces moved forward despite our efforts to persuade Jordan, in its own interests, to stay out of the battle. The Israelis had authorized our military representatives in Jerusalem to assure Jordan that there would be no fighting in Jerusalem if Jordan did not attack. By answering Nasser's call to join the battle, Jordan lost, almost at one stroke, Arab Jerusalem and the West Bank, thus creating a problem which the world has been grappling with unsuccessfully ever since.

The Security Council, which had been hopelessly divided in the days before the war, managed to meet at nine-thirty on the morning of June 5, by which time there was nothing it could usefully do. All hope of finding a means to avoid the disastrous consequences of Nasser's ill-starred attempt to assert Egypt's power was now lost, and with it any prospect of reinstating UNEF. Instead, our efforts were devoted to putting an end to the fighting as soon as possible and doing what we could to help the victims, including those Palestinian refugees whose camps had been overrun by the Israelis and who had become refugees for a second time. Our own headquarters in the Middle East, Government House in the no-man's-land of divided Jerusalem, was taken first by the Jordanian Army and then by the Israelis. UNEF found itself in the path of the Israeli advance and suffered serious casualties. By the time a cease-fire took hold on June 11, Israel was in possession of Sinai, Jerusalem, the West Bank, Gaza, and the Golan Heights of Syria, and a terrible new dimension had been added to the problem of Palestine.

U Thant and Bunche, who had tried so hard to head off disaster, were implicitly and explicitly blamed by most Western governments and the Western media for a course of events which no one had been able to control. Egypt and its Arab allies had grotesquely underestimated Israel's capacity, and willingness, to react to a move which it perceived both as a threat to its security and a great historical opportunity. Israel had defeated the forces of Egypt, Syria, and Jordan. The United Nations had been shown to be divided and ineffective, and the new concept of peacekeeping so proudly pioneered by Hammarskjold had suffered a bitter blow with the demise of the original peacekeeping force. The fact that the real cause of the war was the unresolved and bitter conflict between Israel and its Arab neighbors could be safely ignored in favor of an identifiable scapegoat. In the interminable meetings of the Security Council during and after the war, the futility and frequent pettiness of a divided membership made a mockery of the Charter's primary aim of maintaining international peace.

I remember those days as one of the most wretched periods in all my time at the UN. We all labored under a crushing sense of failure. I believe that both U Thant and Bunche suffered irreparable psychological damage from this episode, and the physical health of both steadily declined after it. Bunche was already ailing and was plagued throughout the crisis by a painful and massive neck infection. Immediately after it he suffered progressive hemorrhaging in his eyes.

Could U Thant have acted otherwise and staved off the disaster of the Six-Day War? I have brooded interminably on this question, but I have been unable to think of an alternative course that would have had any better result in the circumstances. Nasser, in the heyday of the concept of the Arab Nation, was unshakable in his determination to plunge over the precipice, which he was legally perfectly entitled to do. Neither from a legal nor from a military point of view was U Thant in a position to challenge him, and it would have made no difference anyway. We could, of course, have refused the original demand for UNEF withdrawal, convoked the Security Council immediately to deal with a threat to the peace, and let the responsibility and blame fall on the members of the Council rather than on the Secretary-General. Disaster would not have been avoided by such a tactic, but the scapegoat would have escaped.

The one thing that *might* have caused Nasser to reconsider before it was too late would have been a united stand by the Security Council, including the United States and the USSR, and some restraining advice from the Arab states. Some hope. The United States and the USSR were abusing each other like schoolboys in the Council, while the Arab states outdid each other in unrealistic rhetoric. The Israelis were not likely to overlook a threat to their security which also provided a historic military opportunity. This not unusual pattern accounts for much of the ineffectiveness of the UN in the Middle East, but the consequences in 1967 were especially grave.

A particularly irritating theme in the criticism of U Thant was the frequent assertion that Hammarskjold would in some way have dealt more effectively with Nasser. It was precisely Hammarskjold's difficulties with Nasser in 1956 that had made Egypt's sovereign right to have UNEF withdrawn at any time the paramount consideration governing UNEF's existence. Lester Pearson, who had been the original inspirer of UNEF, had foreseen the implications clearly at the time. In 1967 Pearson, now Prime Minister of Canada, recalled his forebodings in a speech to the Canadian Parliament on May 24. "I objected to that arrangement at the time," he said, "because I thought it might cause a lot of trouble in the future." It certainly did.

The lesson of the Six-Day War was that peacekeeping operations can be far more important to international stability than their size and scope of activity may suggest when the situation is peaceful. To preserve these operations in stormy times requires the unanimous and active support of the permanent members of the Security Council as well as the cooperation, however reluctant, of those directly involved in the conflict. These essential elements were missing in 1967, and the results are still with us.

XVII

A Desolate Time

THE SUMMER OF 1967 dragged on in endless meetings of the Security Council and a special session of the General Assembly which, with a glittering group of leaders including Kosygin and King Hussein, achieved nothing. Having been defeated decisively in the field, the Arab states were at their most self-destructive and defiant. They banged the door on Israel's offers to restore territory in exchange for peace by insisting on maintaining their belligerency. They appeared, not for the first or last time, to be intent on missing every bus in sight, thus unwittingly serving Israel's purposes and interests.

An uneasy cease-fire was finally achieved on the Suez Canal, the new front line between Israel and Egypt, and in the Golan Heights, a half-hour's drive from Damascus. We installed UN Observers to monitor these volatile arrangements—an unenviable and hazardous duty. The Palestinians had become victims a second time, and their hopes of any reasonable or early settlement were indefinitely deferred.

We were living not only with the normal frustrations of the Arab-Israeli question but also with a deep sense of disgust and failure. There was nothing to do but to try to pick up the bits and stop the bloodshed, to help the stricken refugees, and to get our headquarters, Government House in Jerusalem, back from the Israelis.

In November the Security Council scored one notable achievement in the unanimous adoption of Resolution 242, which has remained the valid and recognized basis for the search for a Middle East settlement. Although the resolution contains expedient ambiguities—"withdrawal from territories occupied," not "from *the* territories occupied" —and treats the

Palestinian question essentially as a refugee problem, it is basically a good and fair document.

The immediate practical result of the adoption of Resolution 242 was the appointment of Gunnar Jarring of Sweden as the Secretary-General's Special Representative in the Middle East. We had suggested such an arrangement in late May 1967 in an effort to defuse the rumors and uncertainties which finally led to the Six-Day War. Now, six months too late, we got what we had suggested.

Gunnar Jarring had been the Swedish Ambassador to the UN in Hammarskjold's time and was currently Swedish Ambassador in Moscow. He was a veteran diplomat with old-fashioned, and distinctly Swedish, virtues. He was a person of the most rigid and controlled integrity, in every sense the opposite of self-seeking or ambitious.

A formidable scholar and linguist, Gunnar did his own thinking and his own work. Although he was always very open with me, he was reticent and discreet to an exceptional degree. Once when he was reported to have said "No comment," U Thant observed, "I'm sure Jarring would never have gone as far as that." When I met him at Kennedy Airport where there were many journalists, he held his hand to his mouth as we were talking. I inquired if he had a toothache. "No," Gunnar replied, "I just want to be sure no one can read my lips."

Gunnar was a man of unflinching honesty, which sometimes slowed things down. After each meeting, he set aside an hour to write his account of what had happened. We suggested that perhaps, in order to simplify the daily program, he could put off writing the record until the end of the day, and then, to save time, could dictate it. Gunnar then explained that if you did not immediately record what had been said, your mind began to adjust your recollections in your own favor—*esprit d'escalier*—and the record would therefore be falsified. Furthermore when dictating there would be a natural temptation to impress your secretary, and the record would be further distorted. Both of these factors certainly play a large part in the way historical events are reported and end up in the history books.

Gunnar Jarring made an enormous effort to carry out the forlorn task of negotiating the Arab-Israeli problem, and it was no fault of his that he did not succeed. As a Special Representative of the UN, he carried no financial, military, or political clout and was dependent solely on the strength of his arguments, his capacity to persuade, and what support he could get from governments. In dealing with the Arabs and the Israelis, this was clearly not enough. In his negotiations he singled out the two critical and interconnected issues on which a settlement would depend —for Israel, peace with the Arabs, and for the Arabs, Israeli withdrawal from the occupied Arab territories. He presented, early in 1971, a proposal to Egypt and Israel designed to get a simultaneous agreement in principle on these two propositions. Although the Egyptian Ambassador received Jarring's memorandum with ill-concealed distaste, it was President Sadat who, a week later, accepted it, and the Israelis who turned it down. Since this was the approach that was to have been followed up later in regard to Israel's relationship with Jordan and Syria, the aborting of the process between Egypt and Israel effectively put an end to Jarring's mission.

Jarring's basic idea was a sound one, and later on, with the United States exerting all of its power and influence, it was the basis of the Camp David Accords. Years later when Moshe Dayan saw Jarring in Stockholm, he told him that, when he had recently read the Jarring memorandum, he recognized it as a dress rehearsal for the Camp David process.

Jarring played an honorable role, but his mission was a further proof that the quiet diplomacy of the United Nations often needs to be harnessed to bilateral efforts, with all their possibilities for bringing pressure to bear, if it is to succeed.

*   *   *

In September 1967 I managed at last to get to Stockholm for two weeks to start on the Hammarskjold papers in the Swedish Royal Library. I went to Sweden with a heavy heart. I did not want to leave home— Sidney, our daughter Rachel, my stepson Thomas Canfield, and our youngest son, Charlie, now eight months old. Weekends at Tyringham in the Berkshires in Massachusetts were a particularly precious part of family life, and I had had all too little of it recently. The summer of 1967 had been extraordinarily demoralizing, and I had none of the spirit of enthusiasm and inquiry which is so important when one is taking on a new and difficult task. To make matters worse, I had little confidence that I would be capable of writing an acceptable book.

I struggled through the days and evenings in the dank basement of the Royal Library and ended up with a far greater comprehension of Hammarskjold than I had expected. In my first effort at writing a book I made a number of initial mistakes. I tried to start writing before I had the material under control. I was far too anxious, even at an early stage, about discretion and confidentiality. I attached too much importance to interviews and found that as the years go by few people remember events accurately, and egotism takes a terrible toll of truth. All in all it was an inauspicious start, but I had already learned something and begun to enjoy the project instead of dreading it.

In 1968 Sidney and I made a private visit to Israel, Egypt, and Tunisia to interview people who had dealt with Hammarskjold. Hammarskjold had treasured the friendship of David Ben-Gurion, the elder statesman and visionary politician of Israel, as much or more than any other. We visited Ben-Gurion at his kibbutz, Sde Boker in the Negev, starting from Jerusalem at dawn on a Saturday morning. Ben-Gurion had just lost his wife, Paula, and I had assumed that he would only wish to see us for a short while. He launched into a fascinating reminiscence of his youth, his time in New York, and his early days in Palestine, and went on to his ideals and his aspirations for his country which, he felt, were now being called in doubt. (Ben-Gurion had just resigned from office for the last time.) I had great difficulty in getting him into the current decade to talk about Hammarskjold. "He was a wonderful man," he said finally, "one of the best friends I ever had." "But according to your correspondence," I said, "you seem to have had a great deal of trouble with Hammarskjold, and he with you." Ben-Gurion laughed and waved his hands above his head. "Who hasn't had trouble with the Jews in the last three thousand years?" he said. We were with him for five hours.

Writing a book was a new interest and, once I became accustomed to the idea that it would take much time and effort, I found that it offered stimulus and comfort at a time when my professional life had become frustrating. For the next two years, apart from working on the Hammarskjold project, I seemed to be going round in circles. The treadmill included Cyprus, the Middle East, and the health of my senior colleagues. Occasionally the routine would be broken by a new crisis.

*   *   *

The Soviet invasion of Czechoslovakia in August 1968 brought out once again the world's need of a scapegoat and U Thant's preeminent availability for this role. The moment the news of the Soviet invasion was confirmed, U Thant called in the Soviet Ambassador, to whom he denounced the invasion. He also called in the despairing Czech Ambassador, who had no instructions, and urged him to speak out before the Security Council. Although there was as yet little reliable information, U Thant immediately issued a public statement deploring the resort to force and denouncing the developments in Czechoslovakia as a "serious blow to the concepts of international order and morality which form the basis of the

Charter. . . ." He had, he said, appealed to the Soviet government, along with its Warsaw Pact allies, to exercise the utmost restraint in regard to Czechoslovakia. He also cancelled an imminent visit to Europe.

Despite all this, U Thant was attacked for timorousness by the *New York Times*, in *The Economist* "Foreign Report," and by other Western oracles, and any attempt to correct the record was strongly resisted. Once again, as in Hungary in 1956 or before the 1967 war in the Middle East, the Western powers were helpless and needed someone else to blame.

I mention this episode because it illuminates the way in which the UN is sometimes used in a crisis which has the potential for precipitating an armed confrontation between the Soviet Union and the West. In such a situation public indignation in the West, as well as a certain sense of guilt, has to be assuaged by other means. Strong denunciations in the UN Security Council may give some illusion of an active stance, but they are not enough, and, in any case, the veto makes it certain that the Council itself will be unable to act in a case against one of its permanent members. It then becomes useful to assign responsibility to the Secretary-General for taking the action the great powers do not dare to take, and subsequently to blame him for ineffectiveness or pusillanimity. This happened to Hammarskjold over the Hungarian crisis, and to U Thant over the Six-Day War and Czechoslovakia.

*   *   *

In the spring of 1971 the tension in East Pakistan (now Bangladesh) began to deteriorate into mob violence and slaughter. The territory had only recently suffered appalling natural disasters by cyclone, famine, and flood. On March 26, after talks with Pakistan had broken down, Sheikh Mujibur Rahman, president of the Awami League, was arrested by Pakistani troops, and the uncertainty of his fate added another explosive element to the situation.

A guerrilla war erupted against Pakistani rule, and President Yahya Khan of Pakistan called in the army to maintain law and order. Millions of refugees began to flood into India, creating an immense humanitarian problem across the border. U Thant and I spent many hours discussing what could be done and we concocted many suggestions and draft communications. The trouble was that neither India nor Pakistan wanted United Nations action at this stage, each insisting for its own reasons that it was an internal affair. Thus, if U Thant himself brought the situation to the Security Council as a threat to the peace under Article 99, he would have no support, and his future usefulness would be seriously impaired. Members of the Security Council showed little enthusiasm for tackling such a thorny problem or trying to preempt further disasters. A war between India and Pakistan had the potential for involving the Soviet Union and China, as well as other powers, and would be a very genuine threat to international peace. In July, therefore, after months of informal contacts, U Thant warned the Security Council, first in a confidential memorandum and then publicly, that a full-scale war lay ahead.

U Thant was determined, in the absence of any responsible action from the Security Council, at least to do something on the humanitarian side. He appealed for help both for the millions of refugees in India and for the relief of the people of East Pakistan, and for the latter purpose, set up the UN Relief Operation in East Pakistan. This well-meaning initiative was hampered by enormous problems. Nothing is more difficult than to distribute relief supplies effectively and fairly in a country where the established authorities are fighting a massive insurrection, and no donor country wished to be accused of giving support to the Pakistani military regime by providing food and other commodities which it might use for its own purposes. It took until November 1971 to get an agreement with the Pakistani government, negotiated by Ismat Kittani, U Thant's Chef de Cabinet, on the conditions under which our relief operation could function, and by that time the situation had degenerated into a full-scale war.

The Indians, confident of eventual victory, resisted any talk of a cease-fire or withdrawal of forces. They were also intolerant of our efforts to maintain in Dacca, the capital of East Pakistan, the headquarters of our relief operation which would certainly report, among other things, on what the Indian Army was doing. U Thant and I had some harsh exchanges with the Indian Ambassador on these matters.

The relief operation in East Pakistan had never achieved its full potential, and our efforts were increasingly devoted to keeping it in place for the next stage and ensuring the security of its personnel. They were a gallant lot, led by Paul-Marc Henry, a fighting Frenchman. I spent many days and nights on the telex with Paul-Marc, listening to his sometimes quixotic ideas for improving the situation, marvelling at his courage and verve, and desperately trying to find a safe means of evacuating most of his staff.

War between India and Pakistan formally broke out in East Pakistan on December 3, and the Security Council met at long last in emergency session. Its efforts showed no early results as veto followed veto, the

Soviets backing India, China and the U.S. "tilting" toward Pakistan. It was a highly confused situation. Pakistan had abrogated the results of the legitimate election which had given Mujibur Rahman a large majority, and as a result more than 5 million refugees had gone into India. The good will India enjoyed due to this vast misfortune had to some extent been offset by the feeling that India had deliberately exploited the crisis in order to dismember Pakistan. Accusations of genocide and aggression were freely exchanged, while the war raged on.

On December 6, when India recognized the People's Republic of Bangla Desh, the Security Council gave up and passed the matter on to the General Assembly. The Assembly, to the chagrin of India, voted for a cease-fire and troop withdrawal. Meanwhile our humanitarian efforts to help the now 10 million refugees in India and the people of East Pakistan were more or less brought to a standstill by the war itself.

Bhutto came to New York to represent Pakistan in the Security Council at this agonizing time for his country. I admired his spirit in a dispiriting task. At 2:00 a.m. one morning in early December I got a message from Paul-Marc Henry, whose radio was the only surviving international station in Dacca. He had received from the commander of the Pakistan Army an instrument of surrender and wanted to know whether he should pass it on to the Indian Command. I called Bhutto at the Pierre Hotel and explained what had happened. He flew into a great passion and said over and over again, "The Pakistan Army will fight to the last man and the last round." I asked Bhutto if he really thought the Pierre Hotel in New York was the best place to fight to the last man and the last round in Dacca. He began to laugh and said that of course we must pass the instrument of surrender to the Indians. On December 9 Pakistan accepted the cease-fire. The nation of Bangladesh was born.

Bhutto did a remarkable job in pulling Pakistan together. He came to New York several times in the following years and seemed to be developing into a charismatic, if arrogant, world statesman. His execution on a capital charge in 1979 came as a severe shock for all of us who had known him.

No one, the United Nations included, emerged with much credit from the East Pakistan war. While the Pakistanis had committed atrocities in trying to maintain their control of East Pakistan and had ignored the results of free elections, the Indians had certainly violated the Charter and international law by interfering by force in the affairs of another state. The Security Council had ignored all U Thant's warnings and, when the war finally dragged it into session, had been paralyzed by the disagreements of its permanent members. All that was left to the world organization was to try to help the new state of Bangladesh to face the disastrous situation it had inherited.

*   *   *

It was after one of my nightly telex exchanges with our people in Dacca and Delhi that I returned home to bed to be awakened almost instantly by a call from Ruth Bunche, who was at New York Hospital. It was 3:00 a.m. on December 9, and Ralph had just died. I went at once to the hospital where Ruth met me and took me to Ralph's room. He looked extraordinarily young and peaceful, and it was impossible to grudge him his release after so long a struggle.

Ralph's death evoked eulogies from all over the world which recalled his achievements and the nobility and integrity of his character. The General Assembly stood for a minute of silence. At his funeral in Riverside Church, Leontyne Price's voice soared high over the congregation in a wild lament. Words of tribute were spoken by U Thant, Roy Wilkins, and myself. After dwelling on his great gifts of intellect and character, I said, "He was the most unpretentious of men, and the grander he got, the nicer and more relaxed he became. I don't think Ralph had any great opinion of himself, but he had a tremendous opinion of the Organization he worked for and the job he was trying to do."

Since he had been visibly dying for more than a year, Ralph's death was hardly a shock. He had obstinately refused to retire, and we had all played along with his obviously vain hope that he would recover his health and return to work.

This refusal to recognize reality was also a convenient pretense for other people. Ralph's position at the UN was a dominant and unique one, and no one knew how to fill it. As his illness became publicly known, there had been much speculation in the press about his successor, but U Thant, whose term of office was ending at the end of the year, did not wish to make such an important appointment on the eve of a new administration. From some of the press stories, the public might have gathered that with Bunche in the hospital his office had completely ceased to function.

My concern with Ralph's health and keeping things going had somewhat blinded me to the oddity of my own position, and it only became fully clear to me after his death. The other Under Secretary-General for Special Political Affairs, Jose Rolz-Bennett, had also been ailing for a year and underwent surgery for a brain tumor in February 1971. On February 4, 1971, I received a note from U Thant:

Dear Brian,
In the absence of Mr. Rolz-Bennett on account of illness, I should be grateful if you would look after matters relating to UNFICYP [the peace-keeping force in Cyprus] as you have been looking after Dr. Bunche's work. Many thanks.

It did not occur to me at the time that this casual increase of my workload was in the least odd. But as article after article appeared in the press lamenting the "vacuum" left by Bunche's absence, canvassing the names of distinguished, and less distinguished, American successors, and even expressing fears of a Soviet takeover of Bunche's work, I began to feel irritated. As Sidney pointed out in exasperation more than once, there are limits to selfless and anonymous service.

After a particularly tiresome piece in the *Christian Science Monitor* about the "inoperative" state of Bunche's office, I felt compelled to point out in a letter to the editor that our office, despite Bunche's absence, continued to originate virtually all of the important political documents put out by the Secretary-General. These included Security Council reports and statements on the Middle East and Cyprus, the documentation on, and overall direction of, the relief operations in East Pakistan and India, all the Secretary-General's major political speeches, and the political part of the Secretary-General's Annual Report. These were, at the time, widely publicized documents, and some—speeches on peacekeeping, on quiet diplomacy, and on the role of the Secretary-General, for example—have since found their way into the permanent literature on international affairs. We also continued to direct, on a twenty-four-hour-a-day basis, the various peacekeeping operations in Cyprus, the Middle East, and the subcontinent. We did all this with a small and experienced staff, who were proud and protective of the tradition and standards which Bunche had established.

In 1969, Max Jakobson of Finland had embarked on a public campaign to succeed U Thant. Although Jakobson was an excellent candidate, this was an unfortunate innovation. Up to that time the search for a Secretary-General had been conducted by the Security Council, and candidates did not present themselves or campaign. Now, however, the quest for the Secretary-Generalship began to deteriorate into a disorderly and often bizarre political struggle. A decision had to be reached before the General Assembly adjourned for Christmas, two weeks after Bunche's death.

Already in January 1970, U Thant had stated publicly that he would not serve another term under any circumstances. His health was deteriorating, and he suffered, among other ailments, from ulcers, hemorrhoids, and acute fatigue. His doctors had advised him to avoid tension and stress, a virtual impossibility for the Secretary-General. Being a highly responsible man, U Thant was concerned that his state of health would seriously affect the discharge of his responsibilities.

The first discussions of the five permanent members on a successor did little to allay U Thant's fears, the candidates of one being infallibly vetoed by another. When the Council met formally to discuss the matter on December 17, Kurt Waldheim of Austria got 10 votes but was vetoed by the United Kingdom and China. At the third try on December 21 China lifted its veto, and Waldheim was elected by 11 votes. On the following day he was unanimously elected by the General Assembly.

XVIII

Kurt Waldheim

I WROTE MOST of the following pages before the great international hue-and-cry about Kurt Waldheim's war record, and I have not changed them. Throughout his ten years at the United Nations, Waldheim's answer to questions about his wartime service was as stated in his two autobiographical books, namely, that he was wounded on the Russian front in late 1941, convalesced, and left the German Army to resume his law studies early in 1942. When from time to time there were unsubstantiated stories or allegations about his past, Waldheim invariably and strongly reaffirmed this story, even claiming that he and his family were anti-Nazi. For lack of evidence to the contrary we all accepted this version and, on the basis of it, reacted strongly to those who, for one purpose or another, questioned it or made allegations about Waldheim's wartime activities.

Waldheim, it has now become clear, lied for nearly forty years about his war record, presumably believing that the truth would stand in the way of his relentless pursuit of public position and office. This seems to me a far greater disqualification for responsible office, either national or international, than the currently available evidence of his doings as an officer in Hitler's army. Waldheim, emerging as a living lie, has done immense damage not only to his own country but to the United Nations and to those who have devoted, and in some cases sacrificed, their lives for it. (I write on the morning of the announcement that our kidnapped colleague, Alec Collett, whom I and many others had made unavailing efforts to rescue, has been hanged by extremists in Beirut in reprisal for the American raid on Libya.)

The Waldheim episode is above all an indictment of the way in which governments, and especially the great powers, select the world's leading

227

international civil servant. Although good men *have* been elected, looking for the person with the qualities best suited to this infinitely demanding and important job seems to hold a very low priority for governments. Rather, political differences dictate a search for a candidate who will not exert any troubling degree of leadership, commitment, originality, or independence. Waldheim was an energetic, ambitious mediocrity. In fact he did rather better as Secretary-General than I had anticipated and demonstrated determination and even, on occasion, courage, but he lacked the qualities of vision, integrity, inspiration, and leadership that the United Nations so desperately needs.

On top of this lackluster selection the permanent members of the Security Council, four of which were members of the Allied War Crimes Commission, apparently never checked either the Commission's files or their own records to discover if there was anything unsuitable or questionable in this German Army officer's past.

When I decided in 1945 that I was going to devote my life to the United Nations, I soon realized that this would mean accepting a number of things that I hadn't bargained for. One of these was the unforeseeable quality of future Secretaries-General. Since we in the Secretariat were stuck with whomever the great powers could agree on and had no say whatsoever in the matter, we either had to give up our vocation or make the best of whomever came along. I chose the latter course and have never regretted it. It is mortifying, however, to discover, years later, that I spent a decade working intensively with, and publicly defending, a man who had deliberately told lies about his past.

To counteract the intermittent irritations and absurdities of working with Waldheim, we had a number of running fantasies about him. We used to speculate on just how far Waldheim would go to get publicity. We saw him as two people: Waldheim Mark I, a scheming, ambitious, duplicitous egomaniac ready to do anything for advantage or public acclaim; and Waldheim Mark II, the statesmanlike leader who kept his head while all about him were losing theirs and was prepared to follow our advice in great international crises. These and other fantasies seem rather less funny now.

In 1970 I knew Kurt Waldheim scarcely at all, but much of what I had heard made me uneasy. I was, in any case, suffering from considerable weariness and disillusion, and the thought of an ambitious, unknown, and untried new boss filled me with gloom.

Waldheim had been the Austrian Ambassador at the UN and then foreign minister of Austria. He had recently run creditably but unsuccessfully for the presidency of Austria and had switched his single-minded ambition like a laser beam from Austrian national politics to the United Nations. I could not help questioning whether he was the right man to remedy the staleness of the Secretariat or to heal the political wounds which the UN had sustained in the previous four years.

My first impressions of, and experiences with, Waldheim tended to bear out this view, but when I got to know him and to work with him closely, I found he had qualities which did not readily present themselves to casual acquaintances or to the public. He was conscientious, hard-working, and had great physical stamina. He was ready to accept ideas and suggestions and follow them up, and he was never too tired or too indifferent to undertake an awkward journey or to make a difficult phone call.

Working with Waldheim could be a grind because he insisted on going over and over the smallest details, often going right back to the beginning and starting all over again, so that meetings and conversations frequently dragged on for hours and late into the night. This was partly due to his innate dislike for coming down firmly on one side or the other, but it was also prudence in a very difficult job in which it was important not to undermine the usefulness of his office as an intermediary. It could, how-ever, drive you crazy. I remember one evening early on, exasperated by hours of dithering over the phrasing of a statement on Vietnam, saying, "We really must make a decision." "There will be no decision," snapped Waldheim. "That is a decision."

Waldheim worried a great deal about his public image, but his efforts to tackle this problem usually made things worse. He was too anxious to be given credit and tended to be too accessible to the media. He fre-quently had to resort to clichés and to bland, noncommittal statements which bored the press. His manner sometimes seemed ingratiating, and he tried too hard with too little to say. Indeed, the discretion imposed upon the Secretary-General by his position as honest broker between governments greatly limits his capacity to interest the media. All in all Waldheim had an unfortunate public personality.

Waldheim tended to make off-the-cuff statements and later to try to retract or alter them. He spent hours editing the transcripts of press conferences he had already given. He occasionally lost his temper with journalists, with disastrous results. He was acutely sensitive to negative press reports, of which the United Nations routinely suffers a great many, and his efforts to deal with them usually made matters worse.

At the outset Waldheim seemed to resent Hammarskjold's almost legendary reputation. He also saw himself as the rescuer of the organi-zation from the fallout of the 1967 Middle East debacle and the debility of U Thant's later years. He apparently believed he would have success-fully avoided the 1967 disaster.

Waldheim succeeded in an effective reallotment of the top political positions, but elsewhere mediocrity and politically expedient appoint-ments predominated. With his critical views about his predecessors, Waldheim was unlikely to regard me with much favor, since I was inti-mately connected with all of them. Nor did I initially feel comfortable with him. When he became Secretary-General, he had little practical idea of the scope or the limitations of his new job and obviously resented advice or suggestions from someone whom he regarded as a loyalist of the old regime. For my part, I was nòt prepared to sit by silently while Hammarskjold and U Thant were patronized and criticized on mistaken premises. Our early relationship was therefore strained.

Waldheim soon discovered that his job was quite unlike being a min-ister in a national government. He also learned which of his Secretariat colleagues were most likely to give him real help and support. As far as I was concerned, I found that his short temper and occasional rudeness were transitory results of the pressures of the job and quickly blew over, often with a generous apology, and I began to respect the wholehearted effort he was making in a difficult office. We thus eventually reached a better working relationship.

Bunche's job had remained open, and I continued to run the Special Political Affairs Office with the other Under Secretary-General, Roberto Guyer, with whom I got on well. In 1974, after we had been through the 1973 Middle East War and its aftermath, Waldheim finally appointed me as Under Secretary-General. I was grateful to him for this. It meant a great deal to me to follow in Bunche's footsteps, and I was also proud to have got to the top in the Secretariat under my own steam, instead of being a political appointee as most of my senior colleagues had been.

*   *   *

When Waldheim became Secretary-General we were engrossed in the aftermath of the war between India and Pakistan. The economic and humanitarian plight of the 100 million people in the new country of Bangladesh was appalling. War, natural disasters, and teeming poverty had plunged the country into the depths of mass misery. The efforts to preempt famine which we had made before the creation of Bangladesh were woefully inadequate, but now the situation was even more pressing.

Ten million refugees were returning from India, and the two main ports—Chittagong and Chalna—were silted up and blocked. The internal transport system was paralyzed, and any hope for the rice harvest depended on the immediate provision of seed and a reestablishment of at least some degree of normality.

An international rescue operation to meet this challenge would require extraordinary leadership and skill. The only person I knew who was capable of such an effort was Sir Robert Jackson, who had been briefly and abrasively associated with Trygve Lie in 1948 and who had recently been responsible for a telling study of the UN system—the Capacity Study. This study had much offended some of the Specialized Agency heads and, in particular, Paul Hoffman, the Administrator of the UN Development Program. This had discouraged U Thant, in spite of my repeated urgings, from assigning Jackson to the East Pakistan (now Bangladesh) problem earlier. Greatly to his credit, Waldheim overrode these objections, and Jackson was persuaded to take charge of the Bangladesh relief operation. At long last in Bangladesh we switched from quixotic amateurism to large-scale professionalism.

Jackson's enormous experience was coupled with imagination, drive, a world view, and a comprehensive approach which covered politics, finance, availability of supplies, shipping, transport and communications, the weather, crop prospects, grain futures, and the morale of all the people he was dealing with. He gave himself totally to the task in hand and seemed to have no other interests.

In Bangladesh there was an urgent need for practically everything. Jackson first got salvage operations going in the main ports, even getting the Soviet Navy's assistance in Chittagong. He chartered the supertanker *Manhattan* for grain storage in the Bay of Bengal until we could provide inflatable warehouses. He procured mini-bulkers—tiny tankers—for internal transport. He made plans for the planting and harvest, worried about the monsoon, badgered the UN Specialized Agencies and the voluntary agencies into cooperating, pursued governments for contributions in cash and kind, and juggled vast quantities of commodities, including grain and rice, to take the maximum advantage of the best market prices. He set target dates and objectives and constantly urged the somewhat bewildered officials of the new state of Bangladesh to keep to them. He insisted on the United Nations system of autonomous agencies and programs speaking, for once, with one voice and acting with a common objective.

I visited Bangladesh with Jacko early in 1972 and saw the beginnings of the results of these labors. I also made the acquaintance of Sheikh Mujibur Rahman, the leader of the independence struggle against Pakistan and head of the new state. He referred to everything Bangladeshi as "my": "my people, my constitution, my salvage vessels," etc. He was assassinated later on. My talks with him centered on trying to help Pakistani prisoners of war and the Biharis, the Urdu-speaking Indian Muslims who had settled in East Pakistan after partition and were supposed to have sided with Pakistan during the civil war. Nobody wanted them. They were eventually resettled in Pakistan.

I returned from Dacca via Kashmir to visit our Military Observers on the cease-fire line. The British had made this beautiful but desperately poor region their pleasure ground. They spent their honeymoons there and stocked the streams with brown trout from Wiltshire which have now multiplied and grown to provide the easiest trout fishing in the world. Even I caught the limit of ten fish in less than one hour.

*   *   *

The United Nations, aside from the personal efforts of U Thant, played no political role in the Vietnam War. Even in the critical situation of 1972 I was skeptical that we could do much good in a ruthless and desperate game of power politics, but Waldheim very much wanted to be involved. We took on, as an informal and undercover intermediary with North Vietnam and the Vietcong, Raymond Aubrac, a famous wartime figure in the French Resistance, who for purposes of secrecy or mystery was referred to officially as "Claude Duval." Raymond knew Ho Chi Minh and had good access to the North Vietnamese government, but in the strained conditions of the last bloody phase of the Vietnam War there was little that the UN could do except to try to arrange for humanitarian relief to all sides and to prepare for the flood of refugees that would inevitably occur when the fighting stopped.

Waldheim was invited to attend the February 1973 Paris Conference on the Agreement on Ending the War and Restoring Peace in Vietnam, presumably to provide some sop to international opinion—a questionably efficacious fig leaf. The conference seemed to be very much a facade for the negotiations between the United States and North Vietnam—"a meeting doomed to succeed," as a member of the British Foreign Office described it.

Waldheim accepted the invitation and took Roberto Guyer and me with him to Paris. We really had very little to do at the conference. Waldheim aspired to the presidency, and there was a half-hearted attempt by Mme Binh, the elegant and charming head of the Vietcong delegation, to bargain with him on the establishment of a Vietcong liaison office at the United Nations, a move strongly opposed by the United States. Quite why it should have been all right for the Vietcong formally to take part in the Paris Conference but all wrong for them to have a liaison office at the United Nations was not made clear. Any illusions that we might have had about a serious United Nations role in ending the war were quickly dispelled. Canada's proposal that the UN should supervise the cease-fire was not even seriously considered by the conference. To the very bitter end the world organization would have no mitigating effect on the tragedy of Indochina.

XIX

The October War

DURING THE SUMMER OF 1973 an intensive series of Security Council meetings on the Middle East problem were held at the instigation of Egypt. In retrospect it seems extraordinary that virtually no one grasped the significance of this Egyptian initiative or took seriously the emotional peroration of the last speech in the Council by the Egyptian representative, Mohammed El Zayyat:

> . . . What do I take back to our people: hope or despair? Strengthening of their belief in a world based on order wherein every country—especially every great country—meets its responsibilities and does not try to evade them, or despair because this world will recognize only force and the results of force?

The general attitude, especially in the West, was that the debates in the Council were meaningless and pointless. This was a great error of judgment. Through these debates Anwar Sadat was setting the stage for the October War, and if nothing came of them, force would remain his only option.

Waldheim had not yet visited the Middle East, and he decided to make a brief trip there before the opening of the 1973 General Assembly. It was not a good time for a Secretary-General of the United Nations to go to the Middle East. The United States had finished off the summer meetings in the Security Council by vetoing a resolution deploring continued Israeli occupation of Arab lands. After virtually aborting the Jarring mission in 1971, the Israelis had made no secret of the fact that they preferred United States mediation. Henry Kissinger had just succeeded William Rogers as Secretary of State. The Israeli attitude to Waldheim personally was also likely to be reserved on account of his wartime service in the German Army.

After visiting Beirut, Damascus, and Cyprus, we arrived in Tel Aviv, to be greeted with full ceremonial by Abba Eban, the foreign minister. I drove to Jerusalem with my old friends Reggie Kidron and Joe Tekoah, the Israeli Ambassador to the UN. As usual there was much talk about what we should *not* say while in Israel. Jarring, for example, should not be mentioned to Golda Meir, and above all no new proposals should be made. I suggested mildly that perhaps what we were going to say was really *our* business.

Before meeting Prime Minister Golda Meir, we had a difficult morning. After resisting an unscheduled wreath-laying ceremony at the monument to Theodore Herzl, the founder of Zionism, we visited Yad Vashem, the most moving and terrible of memorials. Unfortunately Waldheim was not wearing a hat, and at the religious ceremony he was given a cardboard yarmulka which he refused to put on. This misunderstanding was gleefully taken up by the European press.

Golda Meir, as was her habit, delivered a lecture, keeping Waldheim ninety minutes longer than the allotted time and saying graciously, when Eban pointed out that she was running past the schedule, "He's better off listening to me than visiting the holy places." Israeli officials triumphantly told the press of Golda Meir's overbearing attitude—"She more or less gave him a seminar"—but in the long run this boast was ill-judged.

Mrs. Meir was extremely tough. Jarring's memorandum, she said, was a disaster which had created the myth that Egypt had said yes and Israel had said no. She and Eban were also dismissive of Waldheim's statement, in his recently published annual report, that the situation was "highly explosive" and that time was not on the side of peace. I explained that this view was based, among other things, on our observations of what was happening on the Egyptian side of the Suez Canal where a vast army was drawn up. Mrs. Meir told Waldheim that she didn't believe the situation to be explosive, that the Arabs were getting used to the status quo and that in a few years there would be peace. Eban added that Israel's situation in 1973 was much better than in 1970. I respected Mrs. Meir's tough and single-minded devotion to her country, but on this occasion, by dismissing warnings and underestimating the Egyptians, she was in the process of making a colossal misjudgment.

The last event of the day was a dinner given by Eban at his home in Jerusalem. It was billed as a private, informal dinner, but there were about 200 guests. I did not see how anything else could go wrong, but I was mistaken. It had been a long and tiring day, and when Waldheim got up to reply to Eban's welcoming toast, I was dismayed to hear him say in a sort of Pavlovian reaction, "I am very happy to be in your beautiful capital." Although the dinner was supposedly off the record, Eban apparently told the press that "Dr. Waldheim's use of the phrase 'your capital' was not inadvertent," and at 6:00 a.m. next morning the lead story on the BBC World Service was Waldheim's recognition of Jerusalem as the capital of Israel. I wrote a statement for Waldheim saying that he had misspoken and that everyone knew perfectly well the United Nations' position on Jerusalem. There is nothing like a straight admission of human error for killing a press story.

In Cairo Sadat, though welcoming us warmly, was extremely reserved. As he was about to launch his armies across the Canal, this was only natural, but at the time we were puzzled. (After the war, Sadat mentioned the awkward position he had been in and apologized for his reticence.) He did, however, emphasize two things which might have given us a clue to future events. In 1971, he said, in response to Jarring, he had declared that for the first time in twenty-two years Egypt was ready for a peace agreement, but no real Israeli response had been forthcoming; nor had anything come of the Security Council meetings during the past summer. What, then, was Egypt expected to do? The answer came a month later.

*   *   *

On Saturday, October 6, the world awoke with astonishment to the news that the Egyptian Army had crossed the Suez Canal and had confronted the Israelis in Sinai with considerable initial success. Neither Israel nor the United States, both of which maintained regular aerial and intelligence coverage of the area, apparently had any inkling of what was going to happen. Kissinger, when asked, said that both governments had interpreted Egyptian troop concentrations on the west side of the Canal as "regular fall maneuvers." Neither could apparently believe that the Egyptians were capable of an assault crossing of the Canal. They suffered from the same patronizing bias over Egyptian military capacity which had cost the British dearly at Suez in 1956.

After the war Sadat told us that he had been amazed, and also profoundly irritated, at this attitude. The massive Egyptian bridging equipment for crossing the Canal had been out in the open for many days, and there were other signs of impending activity. The Egyptians, for example, had a problem of penetrating the massive sand wall, over fifty feet high in some places, which the Israelis had constructed along their side of the Canal. Bombing and artillery fire were useless against such an obstacle, and concentrations of high-pressure fire hoses were found to be the only effective method of cutting through it. This required a large emergency order of fire hoses and compressor pumps from West Germany, and Sadat told us that he had taken the Egyptian civil airline out of international service to bring the fire hoses from Frankfurt. No national intelligence agency had spotted this puzzling move. Sadat told us bitterly that this lack of interest had caused him to realize how low the reputation of the Egyptian Army had fallen.

The October War, opening on the Sabbath during the observance of Yom Kippur, was a complete surprise at the United Nations. The Canal front had been relatively quiet for some time. Our first news came from UNTSO, whose Observers on the Israeli side of the Canal were quickly overrun by the Egyptian forces. Two of them, at Observation Post Copper, were killed. This news was followed by an early call to Waldheim from Henry Kissinger. There was little we could do but relay to the Security Council whatever we could find out about the course of the battle.

The Council only contrived to meet in the afternoon of Monday, October 8, and as the belligerents were clearly not anxious for a cease-fire, it could do nothing.

The fighting soon spread to include the Golan Heights in Syria, and there were Israeli air raids on Damascus. The Egyptians, having taken the Israelis by surprise, were initially overly confident of success. They peremptorily demanded the withdrawal of all our Military Observers from the front as well as of the UN radio station in Cairo, something they came to regret a little later on. Nearly a week went by with the outside world in complete disarray over a situation which, given United States and Soviet relationships with the respective sides, could all too easily develop into a far wider and more ominous conflict.

It was with this in mind that on October 11 Waldheim made an appeal by television to the combatants. By this time the possibilities for the escalation of the situation had become as clear as the inability of the Security Council to do anything about it. "None of the parties," Waldheim said, "is prepared to concede its objectives, either military or political. They would appear, therefore, to be embarked on a war of attrition with the gravest consequences, not only for the region itself, but for the world community as a whole."

For the following week events took their course with no useful Security Council action, serving only to confirm Waldheim's analysis. The United

States put in an emergency airlift of weapons and stores to the Israeli Army. The Israelis counterattacked and established a salient across the Canal, cutting off the Egyptian Third Army in Sinai and threatening the port city of Suez, which was cut off from Cairo. The Arab states addressed frantic appeals for help to the Soviet Union, where ominous troop movements began to be reported. Waldheim and I had painful encounters with the Egyptian Ambassador, Ismat Meguid, who hysterically demanded that the United Nations put in Observers and forces to stop the Israelis. His tone was very different from that in which he had demanded the withdrawal of our Observers only a week or so before. The Egyptian foreign minister, Ismail Fahmy, frequently called from Cairo in the same vein. Saudi Arabia led the Arab oil states in threatening an oil embargo on the sale of oil to the United States.

On October 12 Kissinger, in one of the press briefings of which he was a master, had already broached the subject of U.S.-Soviet relations as a factor in the crisis. He recognized that each of the great nuclear powers was, from its own perspective, confronting an extremely complex situation in an area so important that there was always a danger that local rivalries might draw them into confrontation, as the Balkans had done with the great powers of the day in 1914 in Europe. He mentioned the special relationships which the United States had with Israel and the Soviet Union had with some Arab states. "The difficulty that both of us have," he pointed out, "is whether while remaining true to our principles we can nevertheless conduct the relationships in such a manner that the larger interests of peace are served."

A week later Kissinger went to Moscow, and as a result the Soviet Union and the United States co-sponsored a resolution which was adopted by the Security Council, at 12:50 a.m. on Monday, October 22, as Resolution 338. It called for an immediate cease-fire and an immediate resumption of negotiations under Security Council Resolution 242. The situation had at last become ripe for Security Council action.

Although the desirability of U.S.-Soviet cooperation is frequently stressed, when it happens, it often causes great resentment. On this occasion the non-aligned members of the Council grumbled audibly about being summoned in haste to rubber-stamp a superpower agreement. The Chinese Ambassador, Huang Hua, protested vigorously and refused to participate in the vote.

Nonetheless, this was an impressive and rare display of statesmanship and great power unanimity. I was not popular, therefore, when I pointed out to John Scali, the U.S. Ambassador, and others, that in our experience self-executing cease-fires, especially in a battle as complicated as the one on the Suez Canal, almost never worked. Some third-party machinery was essential, and the unarmed Observers of UNTSO were obviously not going to be enough to cope with the entangled military situation in Egypt.

This turned out to be all too true. The Israeli forces on the Suez Canal broke the cease-fire on October 23 in order to take new positions. The U.S.-Soviet plan for a cease-fire was in jeopardy, and with it the precarious U.S.-Soviet relationship in the Middle East. Sadat suggested that the United States should intervene, if necessary with force, to guarantee the cease-fire. Brezhnev, citing Israeli "treachery," suggested immediate U.S.-Soviet joint measures. Golda Meir, whose army was trying to make Egypt's military defeat final, accused the United States of joining with the USSR in imposing an ultimatum. The Soviets obviously could not accept that a cease-fire which they had sponsored was turning into a trap for their ally, Egypt.

Although the cease-fire was temporarily restored by the evening of October 23, it broke down again on October 24 as the Israelis fought efforts by the Egyptian Third Army to escape from its encirclement and also strove to collapse the Egyptian bridgehead on the East Bank of the Canal. The Security Council resounded with violent altercations between Jacob Malik, the Soviet Ambassador, and John Scali, the U.S. Ambassador. In the afternoon an effort by Malik to force through another cease-fire resolution almost brought him to blows with the Chinese deputy foreign minister, Chiao Kwan Hua, and the meeting had to be adjourned for ten minutes to allow tempers to cool.

The long-dreaded Soviet–United States confrontation appeared to be becoming inevitable. On the evening of October 24 it became evident that Sadat was about to appeal for Soviet *and* American intervention and that the USSR would support such a move in the Security Council. The United States, being unwilling either to send American troops to deal with Israel or to see Soviet troops installed in the Middle East, was bound to oppose such a move, in which case the Soviets would threaten to intervene unilaterally. The recent cooperation between the United States and the USSR had turned into a very dangerous confrontation.

Reports of massive Soviet troop movements left little doubt that Brezhnev intended to act. Apparently in order to shock the Soviets into abandoning a unilateral move, the United States declared a state of alert, Def Con III, the highest state of alert in peacetime conditions, and buttressed it by additional moves of land and sea forces which soon became public knowledge. The United States rejected Soviet demands for joint action, saying that the United States approved, and would participate in, an expanded United Nations truce supervisory force (UNTSO) which would contain both U.S. and Soviet unarmed Military Observers.

On October 23 Waldheim had called Kissinger to suggest that a UN peacekeeping force should be interposed between the Egyptian and Israeli forces. Early on October 25, at the initiative of Lazar Mosjov, the Yugoslav Ambassador, and its non-aligned members, the Security Council considered setting up a peacekeeping force in Egypt. The United States, determined to exclude the USSR from participating in any military force, insisted, against Soviet, British, and French opposition, on excluding the forces of permanent members of the Council from the UN Force and won this point with the support of the non-aligned members. In the afternoon the Secretary-General was asked to report within twenty-four hours on the setting up of the force. This ended the risk of armed intervention by the Soviets in Egypt, and the extremely dangerous U.S.-Soviet confrontation was defused. The only vestige of the Soviet threat of unilateral intervention was the dispatch, at Kissinger's suggestion, of thirty-six Soviet Observers to join our truce supervisory organization in the Middle East (UNTSO).

As the situation was still very tense, I suggested to Waldheim that we should send troops immediately from Cyprus to pin down the cease-fire and appoint General Ensio Siilasvuo, the Finnish UNTSO Chief of Staff, as the interim commander. The Council quickly agreed to this plan, and we had Austrians, Finns, and Swedes on the ground within twenty-four hours of the Council's decision to set up UNEF II.

Defining the terms of reference of the new force was a more difficult matter. The controversy over peacekeeping, and especially over the relative authority of the Secretary-General and the Security Council for the direction of these operations, had been a long-standing problem, with the Soviet Union on one side and the Western powers on the other. Since 1964 an Assembly Committee of thirty-three members had been discussing this extremely sensitive question but had failed to reach any agreement.

It was a problem to which a solution could not be found in the abstract, but where an emergency might demand a practical working arrangement that could eventually become the generally accepted solution. The very dangerous crisis which had arisen over the war between Israel and Egypt provided just such an emergency. Everyone, including the Soviets, had a deep interest in defusing the crisis and stopping the war in Egypt. If we could get Soviet support for the new peacekeeping force right from the beginning, and could include for the first time an East European contingent, it would be a turning point, for we might avoid the Soviet sniping which had made previous operations so difficult and might also start with all members paying their share of the costs. We would also start with the most desirable basis for such an important operation—the support of *all* the members of the Security Council.

It was with such thoughts in mind that I suggested to Waldheim that we ask the Soviet Under Secretary-General, Arkady Shevchenko, to take part in our discussions of the recommendations he was to make to the Security Council. Four years later Shevchenko created a sensation by defecting to the United States, and, seven years after that, another sensation by announcing that he had been working for the CIA for his last three years at the UN. I was completely surprised by the first of these happenings and mildly skeptical about the second. When he was my Soviet opposite number, it never occurred to me that Shevchenko was anything but the conventional, ambitious, hard-line Soviet apparatchik he appeared to be—a penchant for wine and women perhaps, but no sign at all of unsovietical behavior. In his book *Breaking with Moscow*, Shevchenko makes a big point of Waldheim's including him in the meeting about UNEF II and of his surprise at getting the approval of the Soviet Ambassador, Jacob Malik, to attend.

Our problem was to circumvent the obstacles which had hitherto prevented agreement on the direction of peacekeeping operations and at the same time produce arrangements for the new peacekeeping force which would actually work. We had to preserve the working authority of the Secretary-General while respecting the overall authority of the Security Council to make decisions on basic questions. Thus we could run the force on a day-to-day basis, but the Security Council would have the responsibility for deciding on controversial political matters, and the Secretary-General would be protected from the kind of no-win decisions, such as force withdrawal, which had crushed U Thant in 1967. Fortunately we had very little time. We met with Waldheim about 5:00 p.m. and after three hours were able to send the report for printing and overnight distribution to the Security Council members.

The report was generally well received, although Malik made a show of trying to make changes which were successfully resisted by the other members. After eleven hours of discussion it was unanimously approved.

The setting up of UNEF II was a considerable breakthrough on the constitutional and political problems of peacekeeping. The report we had produced became the standard basis for new operations and has stood up well as a practical working arrangement which is also politically acceptable.

We now had to get agreement on the composition of the force, and to get it organized and into the field. As usual we needed a balanced geographical representation, but also military contingents which were capable of operating in difficult conditions. The countries concerned had to be acceptable to the Security Council as well as to Egypt and Israel. We ended up with Austria, Canada, Finland, Ghana, Ireland, Panama, Peru, Poland, and Sweden, and they mostly performed well. The practical arrangements were, as usual, taken care of by our Field Operations Service, run as always with speed and resource by George Lansky.

The most novel aspect of UNEF II was the inclusion of an Eastern European contingent, from Poland. The resolution setting up the force had specifically excluded the forces of the permanent members of the Security Council, but the Soviet Union objected that Canada, a NATO country, was providing the logistical element of UNEF. After some haggling in the Security Council, it was decided that Poland should share the responsibility for logistics with Canada, which had traditionally provided logistics for UN forces in the Middle East. The Canadian military authorities evidently resented this arrangement, and for me the most difficult part of the organization of UNEF II was to get agreement on which logistical contingent should do what. The Polish military officers who arrived in New York to discuss this matter were open and cooperative, but the Canadian military, who had made such a great contribution to peacekeeping in the past, were obstructive and patronizing. As the umpire, I was embarrassed at this performance. The process of working out agreement dragged on for three weeks while the troops in the field subsisted on improvisation, good luck, and considerable privation.

In the field, UNEF's presence soon made a reality of the cease-fire. General Siilasvuo's men showed drive and ingenuity in stabilizing the situation and preventing moves on either side which were likely to lead to further fighting. They even got into a fist fight with Israeli soldiers who tried to dismantle their checkpoints on the Cairo–Suez road. When we could not solve problems ourselves because of orders which the Israeli or Egyptian troops claimed to have received from their governments, Kissinger was always ready to lend a hand. The beleaguered Egyptian Third Army was supplied by UN convoys driving through the Israeli lines. Our soldiers performed a number of humanitarian tasks, arranging prisoner-of-war exchanges and the transfer of displaced civilians. With the help of dogs supplied by the British, they also recovered the corpses of those who had died in battle.

The cessation of hostilities removed the larger threat to peace and also paved the way for the next steps, the resumption of negotiations at the Middle East Peace Conference in Geneva in December, and the subsequent disengagements and Israeli withdrawals.

Although UN-sponsored meetings between the military representatives of Israel and Egypt in a tent at the 101-kilometer marker on the Cairo–Suez road had dealt with many military matters, Kissinger had always maintained that a peace conference was necessary to discuss the withdrawal and disengagement of forces. The Soviet Union and the United States, as co-chairmen of the conference, finally agreed that the conference would meet in Geneva under United Nations auspices on December 21. Waldheim was asked to convene it.

The conference presented considerable problems. It brought the Arabs and Israelis together for the first time since Bunche's Rhodes negotiations in 1948. With Kissinger and Gromyko on hand as well, security loomed large, and proper arrangements had to be made for a very large turnout of press and television. When the letter from the Soviet Union and the United States asking the Secretary-General to convene the conference on December 21 finally arrived on December 18, it was clear that Egypt, Jordan, and Israel would attend, but Syria, still being wooed by the two co-chairmen, almost certainly would not. Kissinger was still on tour in the Middle East. Waldheim left New York on December 19.

I had gone on ahead to check the arrangements in Geneva. In the previous weeks we had spent a lot of time trying to find out from the two co-chairmen what arrangements were required for this historic meeting and what the procedure would be.

On December 19, with only two days to go before the conference, it seemed to me that we had left things as late as was wise, so I put a series of questions to the United States Mission in Geneva for transmission to Kissinger, who was then on his way from Madrid to Paris. Next day a phone call from the U.S. Assistant Secretary of State, Joseph Sisco, in reply to my inquiries, revealed that co-chairmen Kissinger and Gromyko had not even discussed, let alone agreed upon, vital questions of procedure, agenda, and seating. I therefore made a number of suggestions which Sisco undertook to convey to Kissinger.

The first thing that all the participants asked on arrival in Geneva was what the seating arrangement was to be. For want of any enlightenment from the co-chairmen, I showed them a hexagonal arrangement of separate tables with the two co-chairmen sitting to the right and left of the Secretary-General and the rest in alphabetical order. Thus began an epic game of musical chairs—a different sort of battlefield.

ALPHABETICAL ARRANGEMENT

	Sec.-Gen.
USSR	US
Egypt	Syria (absent)
Israel	Jordan

The Egyptians started it. They were exceedingly sensitive to domestic and Arab criticisms of their talks with Israel at Kilometer 101—Syrian President Assad had called it "the tent of shame"—and in particular about a much published photograph of a cordial handshake between Egypt's General Gamasy and Israel's General Yaariv. They did not want to sit next to Israel, and suggested a "social arrangement":

SOCIAL ARRANGEMENT

	Sec.-Gen.
USSR	US
Egypt	Israel
Jordan	Syria (absent)

When I told the Americans of this problem, Sisco, who was much given to general exhortations, replied that Waldheim should "make the rounds and get agreement." This airy suggestion at least confirmed that Sisco knew that seating the party was not going to be easy.

Gromyko fully supported the Egyptian position, while Prime Minister Zaid Rifai of Jordan asked why Egypt assumed that Jordan would be willing to sit next to Israel (Syria being absent) when Egypt refused to do so. Abba Eban objected to a seating plan which would publicly isolate Israel. With TV crews and photographers all over the place, everyone was hypersensitive about visual impressions.

On the day of the conference Kissinger appeared in our hotel suite at 9:15 a.m., accompanied by Sisco, to see Waldheim. We discussed everything *except* the seating arrangement upon which the opening of the conference depended. On the previous night Waldheim had brusquely dismissed as undiplomatic my suggestion that the Secretary-

General and the two co-chairmen should act as buffers between the participants, but with one hour to go before the opening of the conference, I put it forward again.

BUFFER ARRANGEMENT

Sec.-Gen.

Egypt	Israel
USSR	US
Jordan	Syria (absent)

In the Palais des Nations the delegations were ensconced in different rooms, avoiding one another. Only Gromyko seemed to be at ease and full of bonhomie. Kissinger, arriving last as usual, was consulted about the buffer arrangement. Sisco said Israel would not accept being sidelined with the United States and the empty Syrian chair. Kissinger then suggested switching the U.S. and Soviet seats so that Israel sat next to the USSR. He undertook to talk to Eban about this if Waldheim would speak to Gromyko.

I was dispatched on this errand and broached the matter with Gromyko, waffling about how historically important it was to get the conference started. Gromyko was in his pixie mood and said this was a challenge he had been waiting for for twenty years. When I said that time was short and pressed him to accept, he said, "On one condition. Henry Kissinger must ask me *on his knees.*" I reported this to Kissinger, who came over at once and was greeted with much badinage. Gromyko: "So now you like Egypt better than Israel." Kissinger: "Well, Israel doesn't like me much either," and so on. Gromyko finally accepted. The conference opened at 11:10 a.m., forty minutes late.

FINAL SEATING ARRANGEMENT

Sec.-Gen.

Egypt	Israel
US	USSR
Jordan	Syria (absent)

After all this high-level fuss about seating, the conference was something of an anticlimax. High-minded sentiments were expressed by Waldheim, Kissinger, and to a lesser extent by Gromyko. Tough but civil statements were made by Egypt, Jordan, and Israel. On the following day we had to scramble to write Waldheim's closing statement to end the public part of the meeting (which never resumed) and to open the private military disengagement talks.

The conference, under the auspices of the nuclear superpowers, was a framework which effectively protected the sensibilities of the participants and allowed them to engage without losing face in practical negotiations in the Military Working Groups. It led to the successive disengagement agreements negotiated by Kissinger, under which Israel withdrew in stages from the Suez Canal, as well as to the disengagement of the Syrian and Israeli forces on the Golan Heights. UNEF II, and later UNDOF, played an important practical role as the executors and guarantors of these agreements.

Although the Geneva Conference remained the basic instrument for Middle East negotiations until 1977 when Sadat went to Jerusalem, disagreement over the representation of the Palestinians made it impossible to convene it again. Sadat's surprise 1977 initiative, and later the breakdown of U.S.-USSR detente, superannuated the conference as a practical means of seeking peace in the Middle East.

Kissinger wrote a gracious letter thanking Waldheim and the rest of us for our part in what he called "the success of this historic occasion." At the time he seemed to have discerned the value of the multilateral capacity of the UN and the Secretary-General as an adjunct to his brilliant bilateral diplomacy.

*   *   *

When I visited UNEF II in Egypt in January 1974, its arrangements were still provisional. General Siilasvuo's headquarters was near the Cairo airport, much too far from the troops. The Polish and Canadian logistics units were in the mud on the Cairo racetrack. I inspected these installations with some skepticism but was encouraged by the Poles, who were determined to show me everything actually working. Thus when I arrived forty-five minutes behind schedule, the bakers were baking, the welders welding, and the water purifiers water-purifying. The bathers assigned to demonstrate the mobile bath unit had been under the shower for an hour and were completely waterlogged.

On the Canal and in Suez confusion was slowly giving way to order, although in Suez near to the Israeli forward positions we were desultorily shelled by Egyptian artillery. As so often, road conditions and defective driving skills were more lethal than hostile action. The Egyptian military trucks our soldiers were driving to feed the surrounded Egyptian Third Army in Sinai suffered from frequent brake failure on the hazardous Cairo–Suez road.

I drove across the Canal and through the battlefields of Sinai to Jerusalem, visiting our troops along the way. In Jerusalem it snowed heavily, but I had good talks with the Israelis who, chastened by the 1973 war, were no longer so patronizing about UN peacekeeping.

Kissinger was continuing his follow-up of the Geneva Conference in his usual masterly manner, using the framework of the conference and his co-chairmanship with Gromyko as the umbrella for his diplomatic efforts. In mid-January he got Egyptian and Israeli agreement to the first disengagement, which was carried out under the supervision of UNEF II and took the Israeli forces back across the Canal, stabilizing the line between Egypt and Israel.

*   *   *

The relationship of the United Nations with Israel is a complex one. Israel came into existence through the UN. My predecessor, Ralph Bunche, wrote the first draft of the partition plan which created the Jewish State and which the Arabs went to war to obstruct. When that war threatened the very survival of Israel in July 1948, it was Bunche and the Security Council who persuaded the Arabs to agree to a cease-fire, effectively throwing away their last chance of destroying Israel on the battlefield. Bunche then negotiated the Armistice Agreements between Israel and its Arab neighbors and set up the machinery to supervise them. As the fledgling State of Israel gained strength in later years, various UN peacekeeping arrangements were an important element in whatever peace Israel enjoyed on its borders.

Whatever they may think of the UN as an intergovernmental political organization, Israeli governments have usually appreciated UN peacekeeping, and they certainly complained loudly enough when the first UN Force in Sinai was removed in 1967. But over the years the balance in the UN membership has shifted, creating an enormous automatic majority against Israel. The UN is a place where anti-Israeli demonstrations can be orchestrated on a global level by the Palestinians and the Arab states who regard Israel as the enemy and the usurper. The Israelis, understandably, resent this development, and it has colored their attitude to most UN activity.

Violent partisanship in the outside world has been the bane of efforts to solve the Arab-Israeli problem. Both Israelis and Palestinians have suffered, at different times, a great historical tragedy and diaspora—symbolized on the one side by the Holocaust memorial of Yad Vashem, and on the other by the teeming Palestinian refugee camps. It is impossible to say objectively that either ancient people is right or wrong, only that historical fate has made the Israelis and the Palestinians compete for the same small, precious homeland. The polarization of this problem in the United Nations is a disaster for both peoples as well as for the world organization. Personally I have always been pro-Palestinian *and* pro-Israeli, believing that, since they cannot avoid each other, they must eventually learn to live together.

Much of my career at the United Nations was involved in peacekeeping, especially in the Middle East. Peacekeeping depends on the non-use of force and on political symbolism. It is the projection of the principle of non-violence onto the military plane. It requires discipline, initiative, objectivity, and leadership, as well as ceaseless supervision and political direction. It takes time to develop the full effectiveness of a peacekeeping operation and to secure the confidence and cooperation of the conflicting parties with which it is dealing. For soldiers, peacekeeping can be a thankless and unglamorous task, and yet we have found that most of the soldiers value the experience and volunteer for additional tours of duty.

A peacekeeping force is like a family friend who has moved into a household stricken by disaster. It must conciliate, console, and discreetly run the household without ever appearing to dominate or usurp the natural rights of those it is helping. There have been times when the peacekeeping function was more like that of an attendant in a lunatic asylum, and the soldiers had to accept abuse and harassment without getting into physical conflict or emotional involvement with the inmates. The feelings and reactions of peacekeepers must be kept under rigid control and must always come second to those of the afflicted. Thus they must often turn the other cheek, and never, except in the most extreme circumstances, use their weapons or shoot their way out of a situation. But they must also be firm and assert their authority in violent situations.

In the scores of visits I have paid to peacekeeping operations in different parts of the world, they have seemed to me to be a microcosm of what a reasonable, cooperative international community might be. The soldiers from every corner of the world, with their different racial backgrounds, customs, languages, and military traditions, work together in an atmosphere of friendship, dedication, and mutual support which is deeply moving. If the armies of the great nuclear powers could participate in this civilizing experience—and why not?—we might make an important step toward the realization that in our hazardous times common endeavor must supersede old antagonisms. At present, unfortunately, ideological rivalry makes this development unlikely.

*   *   *

After the first disengagement between the Israeli and Egyptian forces had been carried out, Kissinger turned his attention to making similar arrangements between Israel and Syria. He arrived in the area in late February, emphasizing that it would be unrealistic to expect agreement in a short time. Kissinger took pains to keep us informed of his progress. He told us that although the Syrians did not want a repetition of the UNEF arrangement in Egypt, they had agreed to some form of buffer zone, although not as yet to how it would be manned. The presence in our Truce Supervision Organization (UNTSO) of Soviet Observers—part of the defusing process of the crisis in October 1973—made it unacceptable to Israel, while a copy of UNEF II was not acceptable to the Syrians. Kissinger hoped that he might get a disengagement agreement sometime in June and that the Geneva Conference could resume in July. Israel, he noted with amusement, which had originally refused any UN involvement, was now threatening to break off negotiations if the UN was *not* involved.

In a marathon five-week shuttle between Israel and Syria, Kissinger finally hammered out an agreement for a "UN Disengagement Observer Force" (UNDOF) on the Golan Heights. This convoluted title, a compromise between the Syrian insistence that the UN presence be merely an Observer Group and the Israeli desire for a UN Force, symbolized the difficulty of the enterprise. It was an extraordinary feat of ingenuity, endurance, and persistence on Kissinger's part and resulted in a detailed arrangement for an almost perfect peacekeeping operation, which both parties not only agreed to but desperately needed.

The UNDOF arrangement on the Golan Heights provides for a buffer zone occupied solely by UN forces, padded on each side by a limited armaments zone where there is an agreed limit on the stationing of offensive weapons. This zone is inspected regularly by UN Observers, who report any violations to both sides. As long as this international regime for preempting their natural battlefield is advantageous to both Syria and Israel, it seems likely that the UNDOF arrangement will work well.

At the end of the Kissinger shuttle on May 30, the United States Ambassador, John Scali, informed us of the terms of the agreement.

Early that day I had written the following program:

ACTION TO BE TAKEN

1. Consult Israel and Syria on initial composition of UNDOF. Suggest Austria, Peru; logistics Canada, Poland. In interim phase at least, UNMOs [UN Military Observers] already deployed in the area will be included, except for nationals of Permanent Members of the Security Council.

2. Consult above Governments on their willingness to provide contingents for UNDOF.

3. Report to Security Council on proposed interim organisation of UNDOF. This might be done after adoption of resolution in the form of a statement which could be read out to the Council by the Secretary-General.

4. Inform Siilasvuo [Commander of UNEF II] and Liljestrand [Chief of Staff of UNTSO] of proposed interim arrangements and ask for their urgent comments.

In the afternoon there were Security Council consultations, during which Waldheim explained our proposed arrangements for organizing the United Nations Disengagement Observer Force.

When the Security Council formally approved the plan for UNDOF on May 31, 1974—the same day that the agreement itself was signed by the parties in Geneva in the Military Working Group of the Geneva Conference—we were able to move very quickly. All the troops could be temporarily supplied from existing operations in the Middle East, so delays would be minimal.

On the following day Waldheim and I went to Washington to consult with Kissinger, fresh from his triumphant shuttle. Before meeting with Kissinger, we met briefly with President Nixon, then at the climax of the Watergate crisis. He seemed both broken and, for some reason, sunburnt. He looked terrible, but was very friendly and thanked Waldheim profusely for his excellent work in the Middle East. He said that he felt the United States made too many bilateral efforts and that the keystone of its policy must be to keep the UN informed and to maintain good working relations with the USSR, especially in the Middle East where some degree of cooperation with the USSR was essential to success. The United States, he said, needed the United Nations in many situations, of which the Middle East was a typical example.

Kissinger seemed touchingly enthusiastic about his shuttle and he had every right to be proud of it. He was particularly fascinated by the personality of Hafez el-Assad of Syria, and the arduous achievement of gaining his assent to the agreement. He briefed us on the specific sensitivities of the Syrians and the Israelis and urged us to stick firmly to the exact details of the plan he had so painstakingly worked out.

Waldheim had long planned to leave New York at the end of May for a visit to UNEF II and UNTSO, and the setting up of UNDOF gave additional point to the trip. In Geneva we sent the orders for the preliminary move of troops to the Golan Heights, and then visited Beirut for two days. On arrival in Damascus, we went immediately to the Golan Heights to greet the incoming Austrians and Peruvians. We lunched in the ruins of Kuneitra, a market town which the Israeli Army had completely and scientifically demolished before withdrawing, a foolish and spiteful act. The Syrians have preserved the ruins as a monument and a reminder.

The troops for UNDOF all came from UNEF II in Sinai. By far the quickest and easiest way for them to get to the Golan Heights was by road through Israel. This presented a problem for the Poles, whose government had no diplomatic relations with Israel. The Israelis did not want the Poles to go through Israel and even cautioned that the population might make hostile demonstrations against them. We needed the Poles urgently and eventually succeeded in persuading the Israelis to let them through. The Poles were more than a day late in arriving in the Golan, and we feared the worst, only to learn from the exhausted soldiers that their warm welcome in Israel by Israelis of Polish origin had completely disrupted their timetable.

Next day in Jerusalem we met with Prime Minister Golda Meir and Foreign Minister Yigal Allon. There was an extraordinary change in the Israeli attitude since the previous September, and Allon went out of his way to stress the value Israel attached to the work of the Secretary-General and of United Nations peacekeeping forces. The Israelis made a distinction between the Secretariat and the fundamentally anti-Israeli intergovernmental bodies of the UN. This was understandable enough for them but a dangerous game for us.

We went on to see the troops on the Suez Canal, lunching in Ismailia with the Poles, and visiting the Ghanaians and Swedes in the desert, ending up with the Austrians in Suez for the night. Next morning the commander of the Egyptian Third Army took us on a tour of the ruins of Port Tewfik. The conditions were very different from my last visit five months before when the hostile armies were face to face and the artillery was still firing.

After inspecting the Finns and Senegalese in the desert, we rushed to Cairo, and thence by helicopter to Sadat's seaside residence in Alexandria. Sadat was far more relaxed than he had been the previous September. Puffing away at his pipe, he was urbane and communicative, and apologized for having been so taciturn during the last visit, just before the Egyptian assault across the Canal. He said he was surprised that no one had anticipated his military move after his years of searching for a peaceful solution through Jarring and in the Security Council. He seemed optimistic that the peace process would now go forward in the framework of the Geneva Conference.

From Cairo we flew to Khartoum, where, despite the heat, British colonial cuisine survives almost unmodified. Mulligatawny soup, porridge, kippers, Irish stew, and cakes of all kinds, often accompanied by champagne, were pressed on us at every turn. President Nimeiry gave a formal tea party on the lawn of the president's house where General Gordon was transfixed with a spear on the staircase. The band played "The Colonel Bogey March." We went for a cruise in the last surviving troop steamer of Kitchener's rescue mission. The bossy Victorian notices were still in place—"Passengers accompanied by small children are advised not to let their charges out of sight." Delayed by a sandstorm, we finally took off for Nairobi, where I left Waldheim to go on to Australia for a speaking tour.

*   *   *

The UNDOF arrangement settled down slowly. The Syrians, who had been persuaded only with the greatest difficulty by Kissinger, took a long time to get used to UNDOF and there were many problems—our blowing up of unused fortifications in the buffer zone, discrepancies between Israeli and Syrian maps, and objections to our checkpoints monitoring Syrian traffic. UNDOF also had a formidable and virtually endless task of clearing its area of the mines and explosives of several wars in order to safeguard shepherds and their flocks.

The Syrians were anxious to show that in accepting UNDOF they were not accepting the status quo on the Golan Heights. Thus the renewal

of the UNDOF Mandate every six months was a cliff-hanging affair, requiring Waldheim to make a special trip to Damascus to give Assad the
pretext to agree. Assad seemed to enjoy playing Waldheim off against
Kissinger in their efforts to get UNDOF renewed. Later on the question
was resolved by reciting a routine formula to the effect that the situation
remained unpredictable as long as no just and lasting peace was reached,
but that UNDOF was needed in the meantime. This formula was, and
still is, repeated word for word every six months in the Security Council.

XX

War in Cyprus

WHEN SIDNEY AND I returned to New York from Australia and Tahiti in late June, I was looking forward to a quiet summer. With the successful installation of UNEF II and UNDOF the situation in the Middle East had quieted down, and we all felt we deserved a rest. We were soon disappointed.

Since the previous year there had been signs within the Greek Cypriot community of active opposition to Makarios. "EOKA B," a revival of the Grivas underground, which favored *enosis*, or union with Greece, was supported by the military junta in Athens, which also disliked Makarios's allegedly left-wing tendencies. Many of the Greek officers in the Cyprus National Guard were closely linked to this movement. Acts of sabotage, attacks on post offices and police stations, were on the increase, and the Greek government made no secret of its distaste for Makarios. On one of his visits earlier in the year I had mentioned these ominous portents to Kissinger, and he had replied that he had given instructions in the State Department that if he himself showed signs of getting into the Cyprus problem he should be put in a straitjacket. Unfortunately, as shortly became clear, the Cyprus problem is set in a context of larger interests which makes it impossible to ignore.

In July, Makarios challenged the Greek junta, accusing it of trying to assassinate him and demanding the removal of 650 Greek officers in the Cyprus National Guard. The response was swift. On July 15 the officers, led by an extremist EOKA gunman, Nicos Sampson, revolted, and the National Guard attacked and destroyed the Presidential Palace. Sampson was proclaimed President, and Makarios was reported killed. When the attack on the palace started, Makarios had been receiving a group of

Egyptian schoolchildren. He had hurried them to safety, put his famous archiepiscopal headgear on the back of a chair in a window, and left the palace by a back door, flagging down a car which took him to Paphos. (Makarios without his hat was a different personality, bald and quite insignificant-looking.) Later in the day, learning of the archbishop's successful hitch-hike, we provided a helicopter to take him from Paphos to the British base at Akrotiri, whence he was flown to London.

The treachery, and the stupidity, of the coup against Makarios were stunning. Sampson was an unsavory thug, notorious for his anti-Turkish fanaticism. Although the Turkish Cypriots remained calm, they were evidently nervous, and only quick and positive action could avert an intervention from the Turkish mainland, something that a raid by Grivas had nearly triggered in 1967. Waldheim called for a meeting of the Security Council and appealed to Greece and Turkey to exercise the utmost restraint. He encountered considerable reluctance to act among the members, especially the United States. Waldheim also urged the British, through the Foreign Secretary, James Callaghan, who was passing through New York, to act jointly with Turkey under the Treaty of Guarantee to safeguard the Turkish Cypriot community. The British had a commando carrier, the *Hermes*, standing off Kyrenia, but Callaghan was reluctant, mentioning the trauma caused by the Suez expedition and the unwillingness of his party to get into foreign involvements. Prime Minister Bulent Ecevit of Turkey, who went to London with the same objective, had no luck with the British either. The course was set for disaster.

We instructed UNFICYP to do what it could to protect endangered civilians, especially the Turkish Cypriots, and not to recognize the new government. On July 18 Makarios, risen from the dead, arrived in New York evidently shaken but full of fight. "How did you like the obituaries?" he asked, when we inquired how he was feeling. He told us that he was determined to return to Cyprus. He was received at the United Nations as the lawful President of Cyprus and addressed the Security Council next day. He denounced the coup, called for an end of the Greek invasion of Cyprus, and was in his turn denounced by the Representative of Greece. Turkey announced that it felt free to act under the Treaties to protect the Turkish Cypriots.

On July 20, before dawn, the Turkish Ambassador in Cyprus informed General Prem Chand, our commander, that Turkish troops would be landing on the north coast of the island at any moment. Up to this point international indignation and disapproval had been directed entirely against Greece and the leaders of the coup. Even the Turks had demanded the return to Cyprus of Makarios, whom they detested. The pendulum of odium now began to swing rapidly toward the Turkish Army and Turkey.

The arrival in its area of a large fighting army which it is neither equipped nor authorized to resist creates an impossible situation for a peacekeeping force. All we could do was to tell Prem Chand to "play it by ear" and do his best to limit violence and protect civilians. The Security Council met immediately, called for a cease-fire and an end to foreign military intervention, and called on Greece, Turkey, and Britain, the three guarantor powers, to start negotiations at once to restore peace and constitutional government on the Island. We set about reinforcing UNFICYP.

Once the Turks had landed in Cyprus, it was obvious that they were going to be very difficult to stop. After a brief pause on July 22, the day on which the Greek junta collapsed and was replaced by Constantine Caramanlis, and Nicos Sampson resigned to be replaced as acting president of Cyprus by Glafcos Clerides, the Turkish Army was on the move again and we were soon involved in a major showdown with them.

On July 23 Waldheim and I were in Washington to see Kissinger. Our meeting was interrupted by a call from my colleague George Sherry in New York. The Turkish Army had advanced toward the Nicosia International Airport which was held by the National Guard. In order to avoid fighting and civilian casualties in this populated area, Prem Chand had arranged with the Turkish and Greek Cypriot local commanders that UNFICYP would take over the airport. No sooner was this done and the National Guard withdrawn than the Turkish Command announced that it would take over the airfield, by force if necessary. For UNFICYP to give in to such an ultimatum after the Greek Cypriot forces had withdrawn would have been a gross breach of faith. We told Prem Chand to stand his ground, and Waldheim called Ecevit in Ankara.

Ecevit was under the impression that his army had already taken the airport and seemed mystified, but said he would inquire and get back to us. In the meanwhile Prem Chand manned the airport with a force representing all the nationalities of UNFICYP. The British sent up some tanks from the Sovereign Base Areas and organized overflights by RAF fighter bombers. Kissinger too was very supportive. We hurried back to New York to mobilize the Security Council in support of our action, and later in the evening the Turkish Ambassador proudly informed the Council that Turkey had settled the matter peacefully. It seemed cheap at the price to let him take the credit. For a lightly armed peacekeeping force, it had been a dangerous moment.

Although the Turkish advance was continuing, the delicate relationship of the Western powers with Turkey made them unwilling to put pressure on Turkey to halt its army. Waldheim, to his credit, felt strongly about this and, in an unusual meeting on July 26 with the ambassadors of France, Britain, and the United States, he asked what could be done to deal with the dangers of the expanding Turkish bridgehead. The three ambassadors were extremely reserved in their response. Waldheim was indignant. The Turks, he said, were happy in the knowledge that no one would lift a finger to save a small country caught in the turmoil of history. Without a clearer mandate from the Security Council, UNFICYP was in an impossible situation, and one of the results would inevitably be a steady erosion of the efficacy of UN peacekeeping operations. A firmer lead from the Security Council was essential. This outburst pinpointed a central weakness of the UN, the frequent lack of leadership or consensus in the Security Council at critical times.

The guarantor powers in Geneva declared on July 30 that no party should extend its area of occupation. UNFICYP was to establish a buffer zone, to police mixed villages, and to protect Turkish Cypriot enclaves. On August 8 at a second, abortive, meeting in Geneva, the Turks declared that their aim was a Cyprus of two autonomous regions and that they were ready to use force to get it. They denounced the July 30 cease-fire because the Cypriot National Guard had not evacuated all the Turkish Cypriot enclaves, and demanded 34 percent of the territory of the island. After four days of desperate negotiation at Geneva the Turkish Army resumed its advance and reached the lines on which it has rested ever since.

Cyprus was divided in two. There were atrocities on both sides, many missing persons and prisoners, and a large Greek Cypriot refugee problem. UNFICYP did its best to limit the disaster, to help the helpless, to protect the civilian population, and to evacuate foreign nationals. It eventually established a buffer zone across the island and maintained complete peace between the opposing armies. In all this Prem Chand was outstanding. In an impossible situation he was fair, compassionate, and firm.

The fighting dragged to a halt on August 17. On August 19 a Greek Cypriot mob, believing the United States to have supported Turkey, attacked the U.S. Embassy in Nicosia. UNFICYP dispersed the mob, but not in time to save the life of Ambassador Rodger Davies.

It was increasingly frustrating to be giving instructions and advice from New York to our hard-pressed people in Cyprus. Waldheim and I therefore decided to visit the island. The Greek Cypriot and Turkish

Cypriot leaders were anxious to meet with us, and this provided the possibility of restoring direct contact between the two communities.

Clerides was by far the most realistic and far-sighted of the Cypriot leaders. The tragedy inflicted by the Greek junta on the Greek Cypriots had not blinded him to the needs of the future. He saw, even in 1974, that a federal solution to the Cyprus problem would be the only feasible one in the conditions that now prevailed. Such a view was anathema to Makarios and to Athens, and it took nearly ten years of lost time and tortuous negotiations under UN auspices for other Greek Cypriots to accept it. The Turkish side, which now held nearly 37 percent of the island, was still prepared to consider reducing its zone of occupation. It was important therefore to establish contact between Glafcos Clerides and Rauf Denktash, the leaders of the two communities, as soon as possible.

We went first to Athens to see Prime Minister Constantine Caramanlis. Caramanlis, who was in the throes of trying to restore democracy in Greece, was impressive and direct. He felt that while the first Turkish intervention had been justified by the idiocies of the Greek junta, the second Turkish advance, in August, was inexcusable. Greece would not therefore return to the negotiations in Geneva unless there was a Turkish withdrawal and the Greek Cypriot refugees were allowed to return home. He asked the Secretary-General to look for ways to a peaceful solution of the problem.

In Cyprus, we had extensive discussions with our civilian and military people as well as with the UN High Commissioner for Refugees, Sadruddin Aga Khan, whom we had asked to come to Cyprus. Seven UNFICYP men had been killed and sixty-two wounded in the course of the fighting, and we visited all the military units. We talked, at first separately, with Clerides and Denktash. Like the military top dog in any situation, the Turks and Turkish Cypriots resented the scrutiny of the UN peacekeeping force and its humanitarian efforts, and Denktash was both defensive and arrogant. Later in the day we brought Clerides and Denktash together for the first time since the war to discuss the island's humanitarian problems as a starting point for wider discussions on a political settlement. This meeting launched the intercommunal talks which still continue fifteen years later.

The next stop was Ankara. Prime Minister Ecevit, a poet and intellectual, slight and sensitive-looking, did not seem to fit the Attila-the-Hun image of Greek propaganda. He was polite but extremely firm. He conceded that the Turkish-controlled area would have to be reduced in a final settlement, although it would also have to be self-supporting and defensible. He would not agree, however, for security reasons, to any immediate withdrawal of Turkish forces or to the return of Greek Cypriot refugees.

We returned to Athens early on August 27, but in further talks with Caramanlis it became clear that Greece would not agree to more negotiations in Geneva under these conditions. We were facing the beginning of a long and frustrating stalemate. On the plane to London I wrote the statement that Waldheim would make to the Council on his return. In urging the necessity of negotiating a peaceful solution, he said, "All the people of Cyprus have suffered enough. Already their losses and the dislocation of their lives are tragic. It is vital to make real progress towards peace and to avoid a recurrence of fighting." Over the years we have succeeded in the latter task but failed in the former.

The subsequent Cyprus talks rank as the most frustrating negotiations in my experience. Perhaps the best that can so far be said of them is that they are like the gyroscopic stabilizer on a ship in a storm. They go round and round and produce a certain stability, even if they do not produce forward motion.

The fact that Clerides and Denktash were old friends and both extremely able lawyers made the situation even more tantalizing. Sometimes during our subsequent meetings in Vienna, at the end of an agreeable and informal dinner, the two *bons vivants* would go off into the night together saying they were going to work things out. I remember Waldheim saying as he watched them go, "I hope it lasts into tomorrow." It never did.

There were moments when it seemed as if progress was in sight— when Denktash produced a map of Turkish Cypriot concessions, or when it was agreed that the Turkish population remaining in the South should settle in the Turkish sector in the North. But always a new complication, or an outburst of mutual suspicion, or a betrayal of confidence made the situation as tangled as ever. A breach of confidence on the Turkish Cypriot side finally put an end to Clerides's tenure as Greek Cypriot negotiator, and after that the talks became even more complicated and frustrating.

To keep one's sense of proportion in such negotiations, one must never forget that each negotiator feels the betrayals of the past and the weight of responsibility for his own people and is reluctant to make any move which may be irrevocable. Although this is understandable from the human point of view, it is an almost certain formula for deadlock.

During one of the later Cyprus meetings I happened to read a passage

by P. G. Wodehouse that seemed instantly familiar—a discussion between Gussie Fink-Nottle and Bertie Wooster:

—. . . "During the courting season the male newt is brilliantly coloured.
It helps him a lot. . . ."
—"But if you were a male newt, Madeline Bassett wouldn't look at you.
Not with the eye of love, I mean."
—"She would, if she were a female newt."
—"But she isn't a female newt."
—"No, but suppose she was."
—"Well, if she was, you wouldn't be in love with her."
—"Yes, I would, if I were a male newt."
A slight throbbing about the temples told me that this discussion had
reached saturation point.

The throbbing at the temples over Cyprus has continued and intensified over the succeeding years.

*   *   *

Kissinger continued his efforts to bring about further progress in Middle East negotiations, and in September 1975, achieved another, more
far-reaching disengagement agreement between Egypt and Israel under
the umbrella of the Geneva Peace Conference. This time the Israelis gave
up the oil fields on the Red Sea and handed over the Giddi and Mitla
passes in Sinai.

Kissinger came to New York to explain the new arrangement. The
area covered by UNEF II was now doubled, going as far south as the oil
wells at Abu Rudeis on the Red Sea. We needed additional troops and
helicopters for this task as well as patrol boats in the Gulf of Suez. (The
Shah of Iran undertook to supply these and gave us the names of the
ships and of their captains, but it transpired after some months that the
ships had not yet been built.)

The new arrangements were complicated, including control of roads
to be used on alternate days by the Egyptians and the Israelis. The
Egyptians were extremely touchy about sovereignty, the Israelis about
security. The task of UNEF was crucial to the succes of the plan. Kissinger told us that in spite of his earlier skepticism he was now convinced
of the crucial importance of the United Nations, provided the balance
could be maintained between the West and the Third World, and provided the latter did not become misled by its voting majority into rhetorical efforts against the West and especially the United States, which

would infuriate American domestic constituencies. This was a very accurate prognostication of the problems of future years.

The extravaganza surrounding Yasir Arafat's address to the General Assembly in 1974 was an early example of the tendencies Kissinger had warned about. The Algerian President of the Assembly, Abdelaziz Bouteflika, tried to give Arafat Head of State status by ordering the special chair for heads of state to be installed during the luncheon break. By the time Waldheim discovered this move, it was too late to remove the chair without gravely insulting Bouteflika—nor was it acceptable for Arafat to enjoy the status which the chair symbolizes. An awkward compromise was reached by which Arafat did not sit in the chair but merely stood by it. Another flap occurred when Arafat, in a flight of oratory, raised his arms and revealed a holster in his belt. The pistol had been removed, but the photographs did not make this clear.

At the end of September I went out to survey the new arrangements in Egypt. I flew to Abu Rudeis, an oil field on the Red Sea backed by the great cliffs of the desert. We flew by helicopter to the various future positions of UNEF along the virtually uninhabited coast—a wild and mountainous desert by the sea. One of the positions was on a peak so precipitous that the helicopter had only a narrow ledge to land on with sheer drops of a thousand feet on each side. In another at Ras Sudar, the oil came straight up through the sand and there was a natural hot-water fountain. You could have a steam bath by simply standing downwind.

From the coast we flew to the Sinai passes, where we landed hurriedly at Um Keshiba, the main Israeli electronic surveillance station, bristling with antennae on a high bluff looking 40 kilometers across the desert to the Canal and beyond. Our helicopter engine had overheated. We arrived for lunch in El Tasa, one of our Observation Posts in the middle of the Sinai Desert, a place of blinding heat and flies, and finished the day inspecting a large and scruffy Israeli camp at Ramani on the coast.

I have often wondered why generals, though estimable individually, can become such a bore when there are more than one of them. The rivalry between our chief coordinator in the Middle East, General Ensio Siilasvuo, and General Bengt Liljestrand, who had succeeded him as commander of UNEF II, was palpable, although both were dedicated UN soldiers and each had quite enough to do on his own. At dinner at Liljestrand's headquarters at Ismailia, I persuaded them to sing duets in Finnish and Swedish. However, this improvement was only temporary.

In Cairo the Egyptians were in a desperate hurry to move into the oil fields immediately in order to show that practical advantages had resulted from the Sinai agreement, which was under strong attack in the Arab world. This was awkward, as the Security Council had not yet approved UNEF's part in the new scheme and the U.S. Senate hadn't approved the participation of American experts for the new surveillance station in the Sinai passes. I finally arranged to send UN Observers with the Egyptian technical teams to the oil fields.

From Cairo I flew to Akrotiri in Cyprus for a brief tour of inspection with my old friend General Prem Chand. We flew by helicopter all along the buffer zone which had been established after the 1974 fighting, from the ruined citrus groves of Lefka in the west to Famagusta in the east. We finished the day in the eerie silence of Varosha, the seaside tourist city completed in 1973 and now totally deserted. The tables in the seaside restaurants were still laid for tourists who never came, and the boutiques displayed last year's fashions to empty streets. The grass had begun to grow through the paving stones. Varosha has remained a ghost city to this day, a monument to the foolishness of international politics.

On my way to the Larnaca airport next day, I stopped to pay my respects at the roadside memorial to three Austrian soldiers who were killed by the Turkish Air Force in 1974—three blue helmets and a plaque reading simply

"In Dienst des Friedens."*

---

*In the Service of Peace.

XXI

Watershed

THE MID-SEVENTIES were a watershed in the fortunes of the United Nations, as one development after another glaringly illuminated the loss of control of the organization by its traditional leaders, the Western powers led by the United States. Gone were the days when the West regarded the General Assembly as a safe and convenient refuge from the Soviet veto in the Security Council. The Assembly had become, more often than not, the enemy. This trend was sometimes interpreted on the American side, mistakenly in my view, as a triumph of Soviet manipulation.

The American reaction to this situation was embodied in the striking figure of Daniel Patrick Moynihan, the Permanent Representative of the United States at the United Nations for the second Nixon administration. Pat was something new and very different from his predecessors, Charles Yost, George Bush, and William Scranton. Yost, Bush, and Scranton were more traditional ambassadors who commanded respect by their restraint and patrician style. Pat Moynihan was scrappy and confrontational. In colorful oratory he defied the forces of the Third World, inspired, it was sometimes said, by the radical gurus of the London School of Economics. Pat set a fashion for confrontation which was emulated later on with strong ideological overtones by Jeane Kirkpatrick and the representatives of the Reagan administration. Both were extremely successful with the American public, but it has always seemed to me that, in the United Nations at any rate, rhetorical confrontation is primarily the weapon of the weak, while serenity and a sense of proportion work better for the strong. In the long run the aristocratic embrace is more powerful than a slap in the face.

Whether at that time another response would have brought down to earth the wilder Third World elements who tended to call the tune in the bloc-voting of UN resolutions, I do not know. Certainly some Western governments thought so. The British Ambassador, Ivor Richard, commented:

> We regard it [the UN] as a place in which and from which we can extend British influence, and defend British interests. I do not see it as a forum in which to argue my own particular brand of political theology. Certainly do I not see it as a confrontational arena in which to "take on" those countries whose political systems and ideology are different from mine. I spend a lot of time preventing rows at the UN—not looking for them. Whatever else the place is, it is not the OK Corral and I am hardly Wyatt Earp. . . . I see little to be gained by attacking the institution of the UN because of the idiocies of some of its members. It is rather like complaining about Parliament when you lose a vote in the House of Commons.

These comments caused great ill-feeling on the American side.

In 1975 the Third World majority in the General Assembly was prevailed upon by the PLO to adopt a resolution declaring that Zionism was a form of racism and racial discrimination. This piece of mindless and counterproductive provocation was a turning point in United Nations affairs, especially in the United States, without in any way helping the Palestinians. Kissinger commented to us that a few more votes like that would put an end to U.S. foreign aid.

This episode highlighted the new circumstances in which the United Nations was operating. By the mid-1970s Israel and the defense of Israel had become an indissoluble part of United States foreign policy. The hostility of the Third World to Israel and the attack on Zionism were therefore seen as a thinly veiled attack on the United States. On top of this, in manifestoes such as the New International Economic Order, the Third World, impatient to make up for time lost by colonial status, was demanding radical economic concessions and changes from the United States and other industrialized countries. A particular irony was that the United States had been the moving spirit in the rapid postwar decolonization which had given rise to the Third World in the first place. The net result was indignant outrage in the U.S. Congress and public. The closest and easiest target for this sense of outrage was the United Nations, conveniently situated in New York. The strident reaction first popularized by Pat Moynihan struck a xenophobic chord across large sections of the American public. A few years later this reaction was neatly encapsulated for the assault on the United Nations and multilateralism by the unilaterist ideologues of the Reagan administration. The United Nations had entered a period of deep trouble.

I greatly liked Pat Moynihan even if I didn't believe that his approach was always a productive one. He was highly intelligent, if unpredictable, and he was never dull. I never had the feeling that he felt really comfortable at the United Nations, about which he wrote a book called *A Dangerous Place*. Moynihan left in February 1976 after a difference with Kissinger and shortly thereafter became Democratic Senator from New York.

*   *   *

In 1975 it became clear that further early progress on the Middle East problem was unlikely. Sadat was impatiently asking for a UN conference on the Middle East, which was blocked by the problem of Palestinian representation and overshadowed by the fighting and massive Syrian intervention in Lebanon. The imminent election in the United States also made the time inauspicious for new American efforts in the Middle East. As Kissinger commented to us after one of the Ford-Carter television debates, "After last night's debate it is certainly impossible to deny that Israel is an important country."

The other main subject of Kissinger's visits was Cyprus. The Greek lobby in Washington is powerful, and in 1976, without movement on the Cyprus problem, the Congress would not vote for military aid appropriations for Turkey, which was an essential member of NATO. Thus, the Secretary-General's negotiations on the Cyprus problem, and their perceived success, were, and are, important to Washington. Kissinger said that the U.S. Congress made the Turks more obstinate and the Greeks more hopeful. He urged us to press on with the negotiations, but even he was unable to bring enough pressure to bear on the parties to achieve substantial results.

Already in May 1976 Kissinger had expressed appreciation for Waldheim's "unfailingly constructive role" and had told him that the United States would fully support his reelection. The U.S. presidential election and the election of the Secretary-General more or less coincided, and Kissinger paid us his last visit as Secretary of State on December 16. "Well, Kurt," he said, "you certainly manage your elections here much better than we manage ours in Washington."

Kissinger was a fascinating phenomenon. His extraordinary skill and reputation created a momentum of their own which was a very important factor in critical international issues. He had a coherent and highly articulate view of the world and of American foreign policy, as well as an extraordinary grasp of situations and personalities. Although sometimes late to recognize the imminence of a crisis—as in the 1973 Middle East War or in the 1974 Cyprus disaster—he quickly developed policies which dominated the scene. He was unquestionably a superstar. This in itself created difficulties, because problems had to wait in line until he was ready to deal with them—Southern Africa, for example—and efforts by other, lesser Americans tended to languish. But at his best, as in the negotiations after the 1973 Middle East War, he was truly remarkable.

*   *   *

Mao Tse-tung died on September 9, 1976. It is strange that this historical colossus should have become such a shadowy figure even before his death. Throughout the 1950s and 1960s the United States had successfully kept the People's Republic of China out of the United Nations, a myopic course dictated by ideologically anti-communist considerations and exploited by a lobby which had little in common with the real interests of the United States. The China Lobby's policy certainly contributed to an unreal view of the world and to many disasters, including the Korean and Vietnam wars. At the United Nations, United States policy on China had created a sense of unease and unreality, especially at the time of the annual vote when the United States, with increasing difficulty, mustered the necessary support to postpone the decision on China's credentials to the next session, leaving Taiwan in the triumphant, but largely meaningless, possession of China's seat. This farce finally played itself out in the Assembly session of 1971. George Bush, as representative of the U.S., fought valiantly to the end, suffering the indignity of the famous "dancing in the aisles" incident when the vote went against the United States. His position was made even odder by the fact that Henry Kissinger had already been on a secret mission to Peking to work on the "opening to China."

The long-awaited arrival of the mainland Chinese at the United Nations created much excitement. New York City took to them immediately, but at the UN we had a large permanent Chinese staff of interpreters and other officials, including my colleague F. T. Liu, and there was, at first, some anxiety as to how they would be treated by their now triumphant Communist compatriots. It soon became clear that the Chinese did such things with style. Huang Hua, veteran of the Long March, came to the United Nations as the new ambassador and began at once to reassure our Chinese secretariat staff. While no vestige of recognition for Taiwan could remain, individual Chinese were assured that the new Chinese

Mission was looking forward to making their acquaintance and that they should continue their work. It was up to them to decide if they wished to take Chinese passports, and they would be welcome in China if a visit would help them to make up their minds.

Huang Hua and our new Chinese Under Secretary-General, Tang Ming Chao, set up headquarters in the former Lincoln Center Motor Inn. Their hospitality and cuisine soon became famous, and we all made great efforts to help them take their rightful place in the organization. In the early years they moved slowly and cautiously, not participating in votes on difficult subjects like peacekeeping, and remaining politely aloof from involvement. Their statements were festooned with Maoist clichés and simplicities.

Sidney and I saw a lot of Tang Ming Chao and his charming wife (their daughter Nancy was Mao's interpreter), and they were insistent that we should visit China. The early seventies had been a very busy time for me, but in March 1976 we finally made it, visiting Peking, Shanghai, Yenan, and Soochow. We were given a fabulous welcome in an amazing and exotic world, one part of which, Maoist dogmatism, was about to come to an end. We got back to Peking in good time for our departure on April 4.

We spent the day in the Tien-An'men Square where a great demonstration was getting under way. April 4 in China is traditionally the day to honor the dead, and the hundreds of thousands of people now converging on Tien-An'men Square, piling up wreaths and inscriptions on the Martyrs' Memorial and around any available lamppost, were spontaneously honoring the memory of Chou En-lai. Although that evening the police broke up the demonstration and cleared up all the wreaths, the swing to moderation had begun.

*   *   *

There was never very much doubt about Waldheim's reelection. Personally I felt that second terms did not seem to have been very happy for either Hammarskjold or U Thant and were probably not very good for the United Nations either. At the very least it was a mistake to *try* to be reelected. This view was not welcomed by Waldheim. He had the support of the United States, the Soviet Union, the Western powers, and the African group, which could not agree on an acceptable African candidate. The Latin American group proved less tractable and conducted some ineffective spoiling maneuvers, President Echeverria of Mexico at one point announcing his candidacy. The Chinese were also less than enthusiastic, saying there was no hurry about the election and evidently hoping that a viable Third World candidate would surface.

These uncertainties gave rise, in the fall of 1976, to several tiresome weeks of rumor and intrigue which brought out the worst in Waldheim and drove him to woo the press and governments in the most assiduous manner. This was a far cry from the dignity and restraint of Hammarskjold and U Thant when faced with similar situations, and my doubts about Waldheim surfaced strongly once more. He seemed to be a man without real substance, quality, or character, swept along by an insatiable thirst for public office. In fact Waldheim had little to worry about and was reelected in early December 1976. China vetoed him in the first vote as a gesture to the Third World and finally abstained. His triumph was greeted with general restraint.

In the post-election euphoria and the between-administrations vacuum in Washington, Waldheim gave a number of interviews on the Middle East question. In one of these he implied that the United States and USSR had authorized him "to run with the Middle East settlement ball," a statement which presented great possibilities for cheap jokes and caused Americans, Soviets, and Israelis alike to express their concern to everyone except Waldheim.

The Secretary-General of the United Nations has none of the sovereign powers or economic and military influence of a government, so that his negotiating efforts are often frustrating unless governments are desperate for assistance. He does, however, provide a useful way of filling in gaps and maintaining momentum, especially in transitional periods such as the time between U.S. administrations or the dead period before a national election. (An Israeli election was due in May 1977.)

Waldheim had been active throughout the doldrums of 1976 in trying to find possible ways of resuming the Middle East negotiating process. Like everyone else, he had run up against the obstacle of Palestinian representation, the Arabs insisting on the PLO's participation, the United States and Israel rejecting it, at least until the PLO recognized the existence of Israel by publicly accepting Resolution 242. Waldheim resumed his efforts early in 1977, announcing that he would go to the Middle East to contact all the parties on the possibility of reconvening the Middle East Peace Conference.

Before our departure, we had a working lunch with the new Secretary of State, Cyrus Vance, in Washington. Vance was also planning on an early trip to the Middle East. The relationship between Vance and his colleagues—Philip Habib, Andrew Young, and Roy Atherton—seemed much more natural and down-to-earth than in his predecessor's time, when the entourage all seemed to be dancing attendance on the star. Vance himself was experienced, straightforward, and friendly, and he was extraordinarily helpful and accessible to us throughout his time as Secretary of State.

During lunch we covered Cyprus, Southern Africa, and other topics, but the main message was on the Middle East. Vance made it very clear that Waldheim should not make commitments on anything to do with the Middle East Conference without checking with the United States. The Israeli hand in this gratuitous advice was made clear when Andy Young, refreshingly unversed in the virtues of diplomatic discretion, said that the administration would have great difficulties with Jewish groups in New York if the Geneva Middle East Conference was reconvened prematurely.

His reelection had given Waldheim grander ideas about travel, and his desire for a larger aircraft intensified. He clearly wished to emulate Kissinger's practice of taking the press corps with him as a captive audience. I was strongly against this. For one thing, Waldheim was not Kissinger. In any case the Secretary-General cannot usually speak out interestingly on controversial issues. The press would therefore become bored, and the importation of correspondents from the UN Headquarters in New York would irritate their far more knowledgeable colleagues in the Middle East. In the end Waldheim reluctantly agreed that we should travel in two small Falcon jets and that we should pick up five correspondents in the Middle East and take them with us. They didn't get much of a story.

Travelling with Waldheim entailed late nights, grossly overcrowded schedules, and last-minute rushes to the airport at dangerously high speeds. There was always one interview too many to be fitted in. When we arrived in Geneva from New York hoping to have a good night's sleep before going on to Cairo, we found a request for an urgent meeting from the PLO's Farouk Kaddoumi, who was arriving in Geneva for the purpose at the convenient hour of 11:00 p.m. He was with us until 1:00 a.m. in one of those now-you-see-it-now-you-don't expositions of the PLO's position on current problems, where flexibility and moderation are proclaimed but the horse always jibs at the main fence—the acceptance of UN Resolution 242 and the existence of Israel.

In Cairo we had exhaustive and exhausting conversations with Foreign Minister Ismail Fahmy, who seemed to have assumed the role of main spokesman of the Arab position. Waldheim was extraordinarily polite to him; I felt increasingly inclined to homicide, or at the very least instant departure. Sadat, by contrast, was urbane and helpful.

Meetings with Arafat are always shrouded in mystery until the last minute, presumably for security reasons. We had not expected to see him in Damascus but he appeared at the Syrian Government Guest House, where we were staying, on our first evening.

Arafat, for all his unshaven and dumpy appearance, had a certain feline charm and a mind like a grasshopper. This may well have been his strongest instrument of survival. I admired his courage and resilience, but he seemed to be trapped by the violent opposing forces which surrounded him. Thus he was never able to stick to a consistent line and build up support behind it, much as he personally may have wished to do so. Nor was he able to opt decisively either for moderation or for violence. He was reasonable in Europe but outrageous in the Arab world. He had an incurable tendency to make exaggerated public statements, and his credibility suffered accordingly. He also had a quixotic streak. In Beirut he made the protection of small and beleaguered communities a duty, kept an eye on the security of the American Embassy, and often responded with considerable effect to humanitarian requests. His people were extraordinarily generous with their large store of sensitive information. At our suggestion, since he was at that time close to the Ayatollah Khomeini, he went immediately to Teheran in 1979 to try to do something about the American hostages. But the image he presented to the world, with his unkempt appearance, his Castro jacket and pistol, and his wild and contradictory pronouncements, was not one to inspire confidence or sympathy in those who have never experienced the anguish or the cruel dilemmas of a leader in exile.

In Damascus Arafat's answers to all Waldheim's questions about the Middle East Conference had qualifying clauses, so that the PLO's freedom of action—and of reaction to its own various components—could be maintained. He objected to Security Council Resolutions 242 and 338 as the basis of the conference but said that the PLO would attend the conference anyway. On the other hand, he needed to know the agenda before he agreed to attend. He ignored the fact that the PLO's attendance was the main obstacle to convening the conference. He said, as if it were a great concession, that he would consider the establishment of a Palestinian state in Gaza and the West Bank instead of insisting on a secular state for Muslims, Christians, and Jews in the whole of Palestine. Waldheim later told the press about this and was rebuked by the PLO for embarrassing Arafat and causing an outburst of fighting among the Palestinian factions in Beirut.

Leaders of liberation movements have to live to a large extent in a world of make-believe if they are to survive and keep their supporters with them. They have to believe that all their demands can and will be met, that right is entirely on their side, and that therefore all right-thinking persons and governments will be on their side too. They tend to ignore awkward realities by shows of moral indignation. They are allergic to compromise or pragmatic accommodations. They live in an unending series of Intercontinental Hotels. However much one may sympathize with them, the world is not like that. Thus serious opportunities are often missed, and frustration and disappointment beget increasing violence and extremism.

The Syrians were curious as to the position Arafat had taken—a tribute to that master chameleon's capacity for a constant change of coloring. Foreign Minister Khaddam had recently escaped assassination, being hit by five bullets, and was more subdued than usual. President Assad, on the other hand, was at the top of his form, making incisive and intransigent statements which were logically extremely hard to challenge. His position, unanswerable in principle, made the prospect of a negotiated settlement of the Middle East question seem infinitely remote.

In Riyadh most of our conversations were with the young foreign minister, Prince Saud bin Feisal, an eminently sane and agreeable person. We paid a ceremonial call on the ailing King Khaled, who was unable to rise but spoke forceful words in a voice so low as to be almost inaudible above the air conditioning. The king's court is a strange mixture of such modern attributes and the vestigial remnants of a Bedouin encampment—elders and Bedouin guards and attendants in traditional garb surrounding their chieftain in elaborate air-conditioned buildings constructed by Western architects and contractors. We stayed in what was then the most grandiose of these, King Ibn Saud's palace that had been made into the Royal Guest House, waited on hand and foot by servants directed by an English butler out of the pages of P. G. Wodehouse.

In 1860, in *The Lebanon*, David Urquhart wrote: "The Emirs, the Sheiks and the people of Lebanon had proved alike their inability to defend and to govern themselves. Their wealth and weakness invited, whilst their lawlessness seemed to require, the extension over them of the general administration of the empire." In 1975, after thirty years of independence, civil war engulfed Lebanon.

The Lebanese like to say that they are paying the bill for the troubles and ambitions of others—the Palestinians, the Israelis, the Americans, the Syrians, according to which faction your Lebanese interlocutor belongs. It is certainly true that outside forces intensify and complicate traditional Lebanese internal feuds and struggles. In my last ten years at the United Nations I had much to do with this wonderful, terrible country and made many friends there. Often I found myself watching helplessly and with anguish their courageous efforts to extricate themselves from a self-perpetuating morass of treachery and violence—efforts which, more often than not, seemed to make things worse and to precipitate new disasters.

In 1977 the Lebanese had more than enough problems of their own, so that reconstruction and other assistance took priority over the Peace Conference in our talks with them. Unfortunately, neither at that time nor since was there the political, military, or administrative basis for an assistance program of the kind we had undertaken in other countries. Beirut itself was already ravaged by war, although in good shape by comparison with the shell it has now become. After the fighting, large numbers of refugees from the ruined center had built shanty towns on the outskirts and on the corniche, transforming what had been one of the most beautiful of Mediterranean cities into a slum. The newest hotels in the center, as well as the famous St. Georges, had been put out of action, although the Vendôme next to them, where we were staying, was still functioning at Parisian standards.

The government of President Sarkis, Prime Minister Selim Al Hoss, and Foreign Minister Fouad Boutros was determined to redeem the country from the disaster which had befallen it. They were all, in their different ways, able, courageous, and patriotic men, but they were faced with a situation so daunting, a series of interlocking vicious circles so unbreakable, that one could only wonder at their courage in daring to take on responsibility at all. Being patriotic in Lebanon was then, as now, the most discouraging of roles, and every move seemed to be negated by outside forces or by the factional and confessional divisions of the country.

After being expelled from Jordan during Black September in 1970, the PLO had moved its headquarters and its armed fighters to Beirut. It had become a state within the Lebanese state, and its activities, especially in the south, threatened increasingly to involve Lebanon in a war with Israel, a war which Lebanon had neither the army nor any inclination to fight. The Arab peacekeeping force, which had come into being to end the factional fighting in 1975 and had brutally curbed the military power of the PLO in Beirut, was predominantly Syrian, although President Sarkis was nominally its commander. It signified the new and overwhelming influence of Syria in Lebanese affairs, an influence which stopped well short of being able to solve the problem. The advance of this force southward had, at the time of our visit, caused extreme concern in Israel, and the United States was mediating to put a stop to the southward movement. This was acutely embarrassing for Sarkis, the titular commander of the Arab peacekeeping force.

In Amman, King Hussein, Crown Prince Hassan, and the government showed their usual pragmatism and common sense, and we had cause again to admire the quality of their leadership and the spectacular efforts of the Crown Prince in economic development and adapted technology. Hussein told us in his quiet way that he was asked more and more frequently what advantages his policy of moderation had brought. He was finding this question increasingly hard to answer, especially considering the changes taking place in the West Bank, which in another year or two would leave precious little to negotiate about.

Our stay in Amman coincided with a great personal tragedy. We lunched with King Hussein, on a day of fog, wind, and pouring rain, in the newly constructed Hashemeyah Palace on the hills outside Amman with a view, on a clear day, of Jerusalem. The radiant and beautiful Queen Alia was absent, having gone by helicopter to visit a hospital in southern Jordan. On the return flight the helicopter crashed, and she was killed. We only learned of this disaster after a very silent and constrained dinner at which the Jordanians present had wished to keep the news from the queen's uncle, who was one of the guests.

The Israeli press had done its best to play down Waldheim's visit to Israel, *The Jerusalem Post* greeting us on our arrival in Jerusalem with an editorial entitled "A Visit with No Purpose." This was par for the course. The Israelis, for various reasons, don't much like the United Nations as an intermediary and they certainly had their reservations about Waldheim personally. Foreign Minister Yigal Allon and Mayor Teddy Kollek, who met us at the Jerusalem airport, were evidently keen to dispel this impression. The meetings covered the subject of the Peace Conference fully enough although they were a little stilted because the Israeli participants, Prime Minister Rabin, Allon, and Defense Minister Shimon Peres, were all potential competitors for the Labor Party nomination in the forthcoming election. There was little or no give in the Israeli position on the conference.

We returned to Cairo for another, more amiable round with Fahmy.

Fahmy hoped that the forthcoming Arab summit might provide a suitable opportunity for the PLO to change the Palestine Covenant, which demanded a secular state in all of former Palestine, and to accept Resolution 242, thus becoming an accepted interlocutor in the peace negotiations.

All of this seemed wildly optimistic to me, and so it proved. At the end of the Middle East part of the trip, as a basis for writing Waldheim's report to the Security Council, I made a summary of the positions of all the parties on the conference. It is as good an account as any of why a Middle East settlement, which all in the long run desperately need, is so difficult even to approach, let alone to reach.

SUMMARY OF POSITIONS

EGYPT

A Palestinian state must be accepted (this, not Palestinian participation, is main issue).

Against unified delegation

Against two-stage conference

Against ceremonial meeting: PLO must be invited.

Secretary-General must send invitations.

Co-Chairmen to provide basic security guarantees.

Insists on UN umbrella

Working group under Secretary-General as interim measure.

PLO Covenant might be changed, and even Rabat declaration.

SYRIA

Basis is 338, 344 and 381 [Security Council Resolutions] and all other relevant resolutions.

One Arab delegation unless PLO wants to go independently, but separate invitations.

If two-stage, PLO must attend both.

Against Secretariat working group.

JORDAN

Three conditions: Withdrawal, restoration of Palestinians' rights, appropriate and adequate guarantees.

Palestinian rights and territories are responsibility of PLO.

PLO must participate independently as sole Palestinian representative.

Close ties with future Palestinian state. PLO wants "formalized link."

Conference at earliest possible date.

Working groups should be functional rather than geographical and composed of all parties.

Accept unified Arab delegation and form of invitation if Arab States agree.

ISRAEL

Resolution 338 is basis.

Will go to Geneva at once on previous basis (December 1973).

Geneva an ongoing process which will continue till peace established.

Framework for negotiations anywhere (e.g. KM 101).

No preconditions.

Does not accept unified Arab delegation. Will deal with Governments separately.

Israel will only deal with *Jordan* on Palestinian question. Palestinians should be in Jordan delegation.

Negotiations must be on peace in the Middle East.

Israel will *not* accept independent Palestinian state, but will not oppose federation with Jordan, provided independent state *not* established prior to federation.

Israel will never believe PLO unless it changes Covenant.

Israel not opposed to Lebanon participating, provided Lebanon is independent.

Responsibility for negotiations must be on parties to conference.

The object of our brief visit to Cyprus at the end of the Middle East trip was to get the Greek Cypriot and Turkish Cypriot leaders together to agree on guidelines for their negotiators in the intercommunal talks. Javier Perez de Cuellar, then United Nations Special Representative in Cyprus, had devoted many weeks of meticulous effort to preparing an elaborate scenario for this event. It was like one of those pocket games where you have to get six silver balls into six slots simultaneously. He had been extremely skillful.

The meeting was held in the United Nations Force Headquarters officers' mess near the disused Nicosia International Airport. The president/archbishop arrived first for fifteen minutes alone with Waldheim. On Denktash's arrival the group assembled for photographs in the jovial, joshing atmosphere that often characterizes the beginning, but very seldom the end, of negotiations in Cyprus.

The meetings themselves lasted nearly four hours. After two hours Denktash complained that if he was hungry he could not think, and a large platter of sandwiches was brought, most of which he consumed himself. The archbishop neither ate nor drank, but smoked incessantly. He divested himself of his archiepiscopal hat and robe for greater ease and concentration. (One could write a monograph on the importance of headgear for public figures—Arafat would be another subject here.)

The two leaders had not met for thirteen years, but the atmosphere was almost friendly except when the wrenching problem of missing persons was discussed. There were many somewhat labored jokes. We finally got agreement on four points which would constitute guidelines for their negotiators.

1. We are seeking an independent, non-aligned, bi-communal Federal Republic.

2. The territory under the administration of each community should be discussed in the light of economic viability or productivity and land ownership.

3. Questions of principles like freedom of movement, freedom of settlement, the right of property and other specific matters, are open for discussion taking into consideration the fundamental basis of a bi-communal federal system and certain practical difficulties which may arise for the Turkish Cypriot community.

4. The powers and functions of the Central Federal Government will be such as to safeguard the unity of the country, having regard to the bi-communal character of the State.

For those unfamiliar with the Byzantine nature of negotiations on Cyprus, these anodyne phrases may seem unimpressive and virtually unintelligible. They were considered by experts at the time, however, to be a considerable achievement, and at least the two principals had met again face to face. Unfortunately Makarios died on August 3, and his departure from the scene left the Greek Cypriot side with no leader strong enough to take essential decisions.

Makarios was a courageous man, but not a far-sighted one. He had the shrewdness of a village priest and an obsession for interminable bargaining. Thus he had missed the chance to get an advantageous constitutional settlement through our negotiations in 1972 and again in early 1974—chances that will never recur. He was the father of his people, but also the progenitor of implacable animosities.

February 13, 1977, was an unusually full day for me. I had breakfast in Cyprus with the British 1st Parachute Battalion with which I had been closely associated in its first years during World War II. The officers helped me in and out of vehicles and up and down stairs, as befitted a relic of minor historical interest. At 10:00 a.m. Waldheim gave a press conference at Nicosia Airport, and we then flew in the Falcon to Corfu to refuel and have lunch. We arrived in Geneva in time for me to catch a flight to Paris, in time to catch the 8:00 p.m. Concorde to Washington where I arrived at 5:50 p.m. (Washington time) in time for drinks and dinner at the British Embassy with Peter Ramsbotham, then British Ambassador in Washington. It's wonderful how much you can do in a day if the time difference and the Concorde are with you.

I had been sent to Washington to brief the United States government as one of the co-chairmen of the Middle East Conference. Roberto Guyer went to Moscow on a similar errand. I saw Cyrus Vance, who was leaving that evening for the Middle East, as well as Roy Atherton, Philip Habib, Harold Saunders, Andy Young, and Bill Maynes, the Assistant Secretary of State for International Organizations. I also saw Clark Clifford on Cyprus. I did my best to explain concisely the ramifications of our talks and the uncertain gleams of hope that we had glimpsed. It seemed to all of us that the Arabs and the PLO had an opportunity to assume the initiative in negotiations with Israel. Indeed, such a move on their part would have posed considerable problems for Israel. Once again the bus was missed.

*   *   *

Contemporary popular memory is amazingly short in the United States, and by 1986 the Jimmy Carter administration might almost never have existed. Although it had many substantial successes, especially in foreign policy, only the long trauma of the hostages in Iran seemed to be widely remembered. In 1977, however, a honeymoon atmosphere prevailed, and enthusiasm for the new administration was equally disproportionate. Carter was credited with fabulous qualities of mind and character and was even reported to have read, and liked, the poetry of Dylan Thomas. Why this unexceptional fact should have got such prominence is hard to say. Carter had nominated a friend, Andrew Young, as his Ambassador to the UN (and therefore a member of the cabinet). Here again hyperbole was the order of the day in the media, and Andy was often greeted as if he were one of the Beatles.

From our point of view at the UN, the actual truth was far more impressive. Carter had an ambitious and original list of foreign policy objectives, and we had close and frequent contacts on the Middle East, Cyprus, Rhodesia, Namibia, and other problems with Secretary of State Cyrus Vance and his colleagues.

Carter was anxious to appear before the United Nations as early as possible in his presidency and arrived for that purpose on the evening of March 17, 1977. He came straight to Waldheim's office for a pleasant but fairly inconsequential talk, including an exchange on Dylan Thomas with me, since Waldheim was not well versed in that department.

The bureaucrats had been having a field day with the details of the Carter visit and particularly over the question of how, at the reception to be given by the Secretary-General in his honor, he would escape the terrible pitfall of shaking hands with the representative of the PLO, who, as an Observer in good standing at the UN, would have to be invited. At our meeting in Waldheim's office one of his party informed Carter that it had been decided that he would *not* be in the receiving line but would be stationed at the other end of the room, where carefully screened persons would be presented to him. Carter seemed unimpressed with this pusillanimous scheme, but he merely remarked cryptically that perhaps through the accidents of United Nations protocol great international problems might be solved. He then went off to address a packed house in the General Assembly hall.

As he was walking from the hall to the Delegates Lounge where the reception was held, Carter suddenly announced that he saw no reason why he should not be in the receiving line to greet *all* the guests, since he was, after all, the guest of honor. This caused a great frisson among the journalists, but the well-known PLO representative, Zehdi Labib Terzi, with his unmistakable white goatee, was away from New York, and virtually no one knew his deputy by sight. Thus somewhere in a huge procession of guests, watched anxiously by the press, American diplomats, the Ambassador of Israel, and other inquisitive persons, the President of the United States shook the dreaded hand, and no one knew which hand it was. Later on the young man representing the PLO told me he was more nervous than anyone else. The sky did not fall.

Carter was remarkably well informed and with strong views on matters of principle. He was not a good public speaker, but his unusual personality came through, and his pragmatic, down-to-earth approach impressed the anxious diplomats, including the Arabs who had been prepared to walk out if he ignored the PLO and the Israelis who would have been outraged if he did not. Virtually everyone was highly optimistic about his impact on the future and especially on the Middle East.

There was great initial optimism in Washington about doing something in Cyprus as well as in the Middle East. The president had appointed the veteran lawyer and Truman associate Clark Clifford to take charge of

European mercenaries—
Katanga, 1961.

New Year 1962 with Moise
Tshombe—Elizabethville,
Katanga.

With Sidney—1964.

Arthur Goldberg and Security Council members at Kennedy Airport to greet U Thant on return from peace mission to India and Pakistan—September 1965. (Ralph Bunche and BU on left; Lord Caradon on right.)

Sidney with David Ben-Gurion—Sde Boker, Israel, 1968.)

Ralph Bunche, 1968.

Before the October War—Waldheim talks with Golda Meir August 1973.—Jerusalem,

The Kilometre 101 handshake—General Yaariv (Israel) and General El-Gamasy (Egypt), November 14, 1973. UN General Ensio Siilasvuo (blurred) and James Jonah in background.

With Sidney, Rachel, Thomas Canfield, and Charlie—Tyringham, Massachusetts, 1972.

The symbolism of peace-keeping—Akya Bridge, southern Lebanon, 1978.

Talks with President Makarios and Rauf Denktash—Cyprus, February 1977.

A South African view of our negotiations on Namibia—October 1980. (Cartoon in the *Daily Mail*.)

"Which ball are we going to play with, ref?"   The Daily Mail

United Nations Observer Colonel Thomas Leverette of the U.S. Rangers gives a briefing—southern Lebanon, April 1978.

Yasir Arafat explains the situation—Beirut, April 1981. (General William Callaghan and Jean Claude Aimé in background.)

Working lunch with President Reagan—September 1984. (Left to right: George Shultz, the President, Jeane Kirkpatrick, Edwin Meese, Bud McFarlane, Gregory Newell, Bill Buffum, Secretary-General Javier Perez de Cuellar, BU.)

Farewell to the Danish contingent—Cyprus, February 1986.

the Cyprus problem, and high hopes were placed on the distinguished new broom. Clifford went to the island, got on well with the personalities there, and let it be known that there was a radical change in their attitudes. In fact the Cypriots on both sides were on their best behavior because they wished to have the support of the new American administration, but that was about as far as it went. Clark Clifford, like his American predecessors and successors in the Cyprus game, soon tired of it and reverted to other less frustrating activities, leaving the Secretary-General alone to continue the intercommunal talks.

The year 1977 was a big season for fig leaves. Apart from Cyprus, we were called on to produce one for Sadat's Cairo Conference, which was violently disapproved of by the Arabs and Russians. Later in the year Andy Young and David Owen, the dynamic young British Foreign Secretary, got together—they were known as the "Terrible Twins"—to try to do something about Rhodesia. They put together a package, consisting of a transitional government under a British Resident Commissioner, Lord Carver, pending elections, the writing of a constitution, etc. One of the many problems with this idea was that it was not acceptable either to Rhodesian Prime Minister Ian Smith or to the insurgent Patriotic Front, and the twins therefore suggested to the Security Council that the Secretary-General should send a Special Representative to talk to all the parties in advance about a cease-fire and the disposition of all military forces. This essential task was described as a preliminary first step. My old friend Prem Chand was mobilized to be the Secretary-General's Representative to carry out this patently impossible mission. Waldheim, as always, was delighted to be involved, but only Prem Chand's tact and golden personality saved the arrangement from being a great embarrassment. A fig leaf is all very well if it covers a respectable organ; otherwise it tends to be farcical.

*　　*　　*

In June 1977, Menachem Begin became Prime Minister of Israel after nearly thirty years in the political wilderness. Up to this time he was mainly known for his ruthlessness and fanaticism as leader of the Irgun Zvai Leumi during the British Mandate. His name was especially linked with the blowing up of a wing of the King David Hotel toward the end of the British Mandate in Palestine, and there was no doubt that his terrorist exploits had been an important factor in hastening the British departure. His election supposedly ushered in a new era of intransigence in Israeli policy and was viewed with considerable gloom at the United

Nations. Begin had violently opposed the 1947 partition plan, which provided for a Palestinian as well as a Jewish State. His prime ministership signified the point where Israel would be far more reluctant to relinquish the West Bank and Gaza to the Palestinians.

Begin visited the United States in July 1977. He seemed determined to overcome his sinister reputation and to show that he was charming, urbane, and reasonable. In conversation he was grave and courteous in a rather old-fashioned way. But behind this facade there remained the old Begin—a closed mind, a fanatical intransigence, and a dangerous propensity for taking risks with widespread implications for other people.

I saw Begin quite often while he was prime minister and came to respect him as an extraordinarily single-minded and consistent leader. Although I agreed with him about almost nothing, I found that he would sometimes respond to appeals for common sense, and if he said he would do something, he did it. He left public life a broken man in 1983—I do not know how much his wife's death had to do with it, but certainly the disastrous Israeli invasion of Lebanon and his own failure to control events there were an important contribution to his decline.

Begin's first meeting with Waldheim was a masterly exercise in oneupmanship. At all such official visits there is a prelude when the photographers come in and the principals talk about the weather, jet lag, or how long it takes to get from their capital to New York. Begin had a different idea. As the photographers entered, he unrolled a large map of southern Lebanon with Christian villages heavily circled in red and began to lecture Waldheim about the threat to the Maronite Christians in the south and Israel's duty to protect them. I murmured to Vivien Herzog, the Israeli Ambassador, that this was an interesting new ploy but not exactly the height of courtesy. Begin's emphasis on southern Lebanon should have alerted us that we would shortly be spending much time, effort, and blood there as a result of his preoccupations.

After this the conversation proceeded on predictable lines. Begin proposed a political truce until the Geneva Conference met in October and asked Waldheim to make this proposal to the Arab leaders. He perceived the Peace Conference solely as a place where separate peace treaties would be negotiated. The possibility of a United Nations Force in South Lebanon was briefly discussed. The PLO were simply genocidal murderers and worse than the Nazis. Everything was negotiable, but Israel would never accept negotiations with the PLO; if the Arabs didn't come to Geneva in October, it would be their fault; a Palestinian state would be a mortal danger to Israel and would mean permanent bloodshed;

the Western Europeans, who had just issued a communiqué on the Middle East, should remember that the rivers of Europe were red with Jewish blood; the Zionism-Racism resolution was an obscenity; terrorism was the ugliest phenomenon of our time. I had some difficulty in maintaining a suitably serious expression at this last remark from someone who, in his earlier days, had made so many innovative contributions to this form of political activism. All of Begin's remarks were repeated afterwards to the press.

Waldheim, for once at a loss for words, finally, at my prompting, said politely that while Begin's views were of great interest, they seemed to diverge widely from UN resolutions, and this broke the flow. Begin was impressive but filled me with forebodings for the future. Beneath his urbanity lay unscrupulousness, recklessness, and fanaticism, and he evidently had no idea of, and no interest in, what the Arabs and Palestinians were like or felt like. In fact he seemed scarcely to recognize them as human beings at all.

For all the talk, there was no advance toward Geneva for the rest of the summer despite the good intentions and dynamism of the Carter administration. On October 1 there was a short-lived surprise, a Soviet-American statement on the Middle East appealing for negotiations within the framework of the Geneva Peace Conference, "specially convened for these purposes, with participation in its work of the representatives of all the parties involved, including those of the Palestinian people, and legal and contractual formalization of the decisions reached at the Conference."

The statement called for the reconvening of the conference not later than December 1977. This eminently sensible and constructive declaration, sponsored by the two most influential powers, was denounced by Israel as an effort to impose a superpower settlement and was quickly withdrawn by the United States, and Sadat decided to look for alternative means for a breakthrough in the Middle East. That, effectively, was the end of the Middle East Peace Conference.

On November 9, a day on which Israeli jets attacked PLO targets in southern Lebanon for the first time in two years, Sadat declared that he was ready to make an all-out effort to overcome obstacles to peace in the Middle East. Two days later Begin emotionally welcomed Sadat's statement. On November 20 Sadat flew to Jerusalem and addressed the Knesset. Sadat and Begin met again on December 26 in Egypt.

Sadat's move was violently denounced in the Arab world and by the Soviet Union. As usual we in the Secretariat were compelled to sit on the fence, although I managed to persuade Waldheim to say that it was a historic event, adding that he hoped it would contribute to peace and to removing the remaining obstacles to the Peace Conference. Even this tepid comment was harshly criticized by the Arabs.

In late November, Sadat, without any warning whatsoever, invited Israel, the Arab States, the PLO, the Soviet Union, the United States, and the Secretary-General to a conference in Cairo. If the Arab governments had accepted this invitation, Israel would have had to decide whether or not to turn up and negotiate with the PLO, but there was never any chance that the Arabs, the PLO, or the Soviet Union would grasp the nettle and turn it to their advantage. Their rejection caused Egypt and Israel to put even more pressure on others to come to the meeting. The Israeli Lobby in the United States began denouncing Carter for hesitating, and the *Washington Post* prematurely abused Waldheim for the same reason. The United States was eventually represented "at the expert level" in Cairo.

Waldheim, like others, was in a quandary as to how to respond to the Egyptian invitation. I had suggested that we should at least send General Siilasvuo, our most senior representative in the Middle East, as an observer. Waldheim came up with a further idea. The statement which announced that he was sending Siilasvuo to be present at the meeting in Cairo proposed, as a follow-up, a preparatory meeting at the United Nations of all those invited to the Cairo meeting to facilitate the convening of an early and constructive conference in Geneva.

This proposal was a common-sense attempt to use Sadat's initiative to break the impasse on the Peace Conference, but logic and common sense have little relevance in the Middle East. The Israelis and the lobby in the United States professed themselves outraged at a conference to which the PLO would be invited, although they apparently thought Sadat's conference, to which the PLO were also invited, a splendid idea, presumably because they knew the PLO would not accept Sadat's invitation. The Russians grumbled that they had not been consulted by Waldheim. The Arabs were deeply suspicious of anything remotely connected with the Cairo invitation. Only the Jordanians, sensible and down-to-earth as usual, enthusiastically endorsed Waldheim's idea. Egypt also, more cautiously, expressed approval.

One of Waldheim's problems, which was brought out on occasions like this, was that the public image rather than the substance of a question tended to be the reality in his mind. He seemed to believe that a good proposal or performance had no validity unless it was publicly reported. Thus he talked optimistically and incessantly to reluctant journalists about his suggestion for a follow-up meeting. I begged him to leave his initiative in the ground to see if it would grow, instead of digging it up every few minutes to show it to passers-by. This need for constant public recognition deprived Waldheim's office of two qualities which, in his lack of real power, are essential for the Secretary-General—dignity and mystery. I once told Waldheim that if the Loch Ness Monster came ashore and gave a press conference it would never be heard of again, but he didn't get the point.

*   *   *

The Iranians, who had been very active in the UN, had been trying for years to get the Secretary-General to make an official visit. U Thant had refused the Shah's 1971 invitation to the 3,000th anniversary extravaganza at Persepolis on the grounds that such a show of affluence was inappropriate in a world where millions were near to starvation. Waldheim also was reluctant to pay an official visit to Imperial Iran, which was then under increasing attack in the West for violations of human rights; but in January 1978 he had to visit Turkey, Greece, and Cyprus, and it was difficult to refuse to go next door and visit Iran.

We arrived in Teheran from Ankara on January 10, less than a year before the revolution and the departure of the Shah. We drove incessantly across Teheran to our various engagements, escorted by aggressive outriders and police cars with bullhorns which charged the oncoming traffic, thundering at them to get out of the way. The two landmarks we always seemed to pass were the desolate area on which, with great fanfare, was to be built the greatest piazza in the world, the center of the new Imperial City of Teheran, and a cinema where the movie was *Love on a Horse*.

It was at lunch with Princess Ashraf, the Shah's twin sister, that I began to feel acutely uncomfortable. There was an overwhelming atmosphere of nouveau-riche, meretricious chi-chi and sycophancy. The food was excellent; the conversation nonexistent. There was an overheated, overstuffed atmosphere in those super deluxe mini-palaces in the imperial compound which left one gasping for air.

When we arrived in Teheran we had, as usual, received numerous requests and petitions from the opposition. When I said that it was the normal practice for the Secretary-General to see representatives of the opposition, I was told brusquely that on no account should we receive any petitioners and delegations. I replied that this was unacceptable and that we would pursue the matter. When we saw Foreign Minister Kholatbari on the following day, I was surprised that he opened the meeting by reversing the ruling, saying how glad he would be if we would receive and judge for ourselves the sort of people the government was up against. This was a good ploy because by that time the official program was already so full that there was no time for meetings with opposition groups, even supposing we were able to contact them. I told Waldheim that he must say something about this to the Shah.

We struggled through heavy snow to meet the Shah and at last reached the audience building where the Shah awaited us on the steps. He was small in stature, and seemed intensely egocentric and humorless. When Waldheim complained of our inability to meet representatives of the opposition, the Shah, vastly irritated, remarked, "I will not have any guest of mine waste a single minute on these ridiculous people." Even at the time this remark seemed both intemperate and unrealistic.

The Shah was highly opinionated and plainly unaccustomed to argument. As an absolute monarch he had a view of the world which was all of one piece, not admitting of modification, but he was clearly apprehensive of any radical boat-rocking. His political stance was reactionary, and the word "left" his worst term of abuse. Our meeting was essentially a monologue.

After ninety minutes we migrated to another building for lunch, the Shah driving Waldheim in his own Mercedes. The food was marvelous —caviar and prodigious Persian rice and lamb—the conversation mostly another monologue by the Shah, interrupted occasionally by his half brother Prince Reza. The latter engaged me on the subject of conservation and his life and times with the World Wildlife Fund. After lunch we descended to the foyer where the Shah and my former Secretariat colleague, Amir Hoveyda, now Minister of the Court, suddenly disappeared heavenwards in an elevator, leaving us to find our way back to the Imperial Hilton. It was the last time I saw Hoveyda. He was arrested while the Shah was still in power, as a sop to the opposition. He behaved with great dignity in appalling and humiliating circumstances and was executed soon after the revolution.

I escaped yet another protocol meal to have a quiet supper with my old friend Tony Parsons, who had been British Ambassador for the last three years. He had a passion for the country and its amazing history and archeology, but evidently found the ruling clique cynical and living in a never-never-land of grandiose schemes, like the new city of Teheran, which never progressed unless the Shah flew over them in his helicopter and then cut through the intrigue and infighting. Like everyone else, Tony still had little inkling of what was shortly to happen.

We were glad to leave the suffocating atmosphere of Teheran for the relative freedom of Cyprus. With great difficulty we had persuaded Kyprianou to meet with Denktash at lunch, the understanding that this was a purely social occasion being underscored by also inviting the wives of the two leaders. This grisly affair took place, as usual, in the UN Officers' Mess. There was a photographic session dominated by Denktash, who kept booming at Kyprianou, "Smile, Spyrou, smile," to which Kyprianou glumly responded, "I smiled once already." In this unequal confrontation Waldheim played the role of ringmaster.

XXII

Lebanon 1978

LEBANON HAD BEEN the most tractable of all Israel's Arab neighbors. There had been little or no trouble on the border with Israel since the 1949 Armistice Agreement until the early 1970s, when the mainstream element of the PLO, Fatah, moved into Lebanon after the Black September showdown in Jordan.

In the early 1970s the situation on the border steadily deteriorated into a war between factions and villages, the Maronite Christians supported by Israel on the one side and the PLO and assorted Muslim factions on the other. The PLO was evidently preparing to use southern Lebanon as a base for attacks on Israel, evoking heavy Israeli reprisals. We had set up UN Observer Posts in southern Lebanon in 1972 to monitor this situation and violations of the Armistice Demarcation Line. Our unarmed Observers were constantly in the line of fire and, having no means of protection, were subjected to all the risks of the anarchy of the region. I had visited them from time to time and had finally concluded that we should not, in an area where there was no civil authority and constant violence, continue to risk their lives. The Observers themselves, however, were emphatic that they should continue their duties in spite of the risks. They were proud of their position as the only impartial source of detailed information on the almost daily shootouts among the many factions. They were also getting a unique political and military education.

Involvement with southern Lebanon was nothing new in Israeli history. The Book of Kings describes how King Solomon gave twenty towns in the region of Galilee to Hiram, King of Tyre, in exchange for cedar and cypress wood to build the Temple in Jerusalem. This deal did not please Hiram, who commented, "My brother, what sort of towns are these you have given me?" So they were named "the land of Cabul," meaning "as nothing." At the Peace Conference in 1919 there had been an abortive move to incorporate Lebanon south of the Litani River and up to the slopes of Mount Hermon into the territory of Palestine. More recently, in 1954, southern Lebanon had come up in discussions between Ben-Gurion, Moshe Dayan, then Israeli Chief of Staff, and Moshe Sharett, the first Foreign Minister of Israel. Dayan had put forward an ingenious plan for the Israeli annexation of Lebanon south of the Litani River. In Sharett's words,

> According to him [Dayan] the only thing that's necessary is to find an officer, even just a Major. We should either win his heart or buy him with money, to make him agree to declare himself the savior of the Maronite population. Then the Israeli army will enter Lebanon, will occupy the necessary territory and will create a Christian regime which will ally itself with Israel. The territory from the Litani southward will be totally annexed to Israel and everything will be all right. . . .

The presence and activities of the PLO just north of the Israel-Lebanon border were a new and threatening development for the Israelis, and it became increasingly clear that the Israeli defense establishment would welcome any credible pretext for a military strike to do away with the PLO in South Lebanon.

That pretext presented itself in a grisly and tragic form on March 11, 1978. A PLO squad landed on the Israeli coast north of Tel Aviv and commandeered a bus on the Haifa–Tel Aviv road. In the subsequent shootout with Israeli security forces, thirty-seven Israelis died. A wave of rage swept over Israel, and Ezer Weizman, the defense minister, ordered the army into southern Lebanon. The Israeli Army launched a massive assault on the night of March 14/15, and quickly overran most of the territory south of the Litani River except for the Tyre pocket, which remained under the control of PLO fighters.

This action occurred just as the Israeli-Egyptian talks under United States auspices had reached a critical phase. Begin himself was expected shortly in Washington, but it was clear that President Sadat could not proceed with the peace process if Israel was seen to have occupied the territory of yet another Arab state. Quite apart from widespread international concern, only urgent action would avert the aborting of the Camp David process. The only place where such action could be taken was in and through the United Nations.

We had given much thought to the situation in southern Lebanon and had considered various ideas, including the possibility of a United Nations force. This had even been discussed briefly with Begin the year before. The hard facts of the situation militated against deploying such a force. Governmental authority, an important condition for successful peace-keeping, did not exist in southern Lebanon, where a tribal, inter-confessional guerrilla war was raging. The terrain of southern Lebanon—hilly, with many ravines and gullies and with citrus groves along the coast—was ideal for guerrilla activity and very difficult for conventional forces. The PLO, a dominating factor in the area, was under no formal authority. Another important element, the Israeli-sponsored Christian militia of the volatile Major Saad Haddad, though illegal, would certainly be strongly supported by Israel. A force of the size and with the mandate necessary for the job was unlikely to be agreed upon by the Security Council. Southern Lebanon would almost certainly be a peacekeeper's nightmare.

I expressed these views to a number of ambassadors who came to discuss the situation, but I only realized the degree of concerted United States pressure for action when the British presented me with a message from Foreign Secretary David Owen. The message was in the head-masterly mode, saying that Owen hoped there would be "no foot-dragging on the 38th Floor" as regards putting a force into southern Lebanon. I brusquely reminded the British of Article 100 of the Charter, in which governments undertake not to seek to influence the Secretariat in the discharge of its responsibilities, and added that I was sure that if the Security Council *were* to decide to put a force into southern Lebanon, the British would be among the first to send a contingent. I explained my concern that once the Security Council, under American pressure, had decided to send a force to southern Lebanon, the United States and others would rapidly lose interest, ignore the problems which our soldiers would inevitably face, and leave us and the troop-contributing countries without the necessary political support to do the job. Subsequent events amply justified this pessimistic evaluation.

At the outset it was believed that the Israelis intended to establish a 7-kilometer security zone north of the border. Perhaps because the PLO fought better than expected, and also because it soon became obvious that a UN peacekeeping force would be set up, the Israeli forces went all the way to the Litani River. Air strikes and artillery caused heavy civilian casualties and massive damage, and 150,000 refugees from the south contributed to the confusion in Beirut itself. On Friday, March 17, Lebanon, stung into action at last, came to the Security Council, which began its meetings in the afternoon.

On the day of the Israeli invasion Cyrus Vance, in a conversation with Waldheim, had said that in his view the only solution would be a United Nations force. Other members of the Security Council were not so enthusiastic. A UN force, unless it had a strong mandate, would be a palliative measure and not a solution because it would not be able to deal with the real problems, the presence of the PLO in southern Lebanon and the Israeli determination to occupy part of southern Lebanon by proxy through Major Haddad. However, United States determination to push through a quick decision swept aside further argument along these lines.

The meetings of the Council were, for once, low-keyed. Ghassan Tueni, the admirable Lebanese Ambassador, in normal life the publisher of the great Lebanese newspaper *An Nahar*, was a sensible man with no inclination for rhetoric. Tueni and his brave and beautiful wife, Nadia, represented the best in Lebanon: courage, intelligence, sensibility, and humor. In a dark time they were a sure and constant light.

The Council proceedings were dominated by the determination of the United States mission to get a resolution demanding Israel's withdrawal and the setting up of a UN force *before* Begin arrived in the United States. An Israeli plea that it would be wise to wait for Begin's arrival in New York was brusquely dismissed. Thus at the very outset Israeli antipathy to the new UN force was assured by the unusually firm stand of the United States vis-à-vis Israel.

While the Council was meeting on Saturday, we prepared contingency plans for the force and the draft of the report of the Secretary-General to the Council on its mandate. We showed this draft to members of the Council as well as to the Lebanese and Israelis on Saturday, which meant that it could be circulated immediately the Council made its decision the following morning. The Council was thus able to adopt the mandate for the United Nations Interim Force in Lebanon (UNIFIL) on Sunday before Begin arrived in New York that evening. No "foot-dragging" there, but our repeated requests for a British contingent remained unanswered until a negative and mumbling excuse came a week later—something about commitments in the Falklands.

The task of UNIFIL was to confirm the withdrawal of Israeli forces, to restore international peace and security, and to assist the government of Lebanon in ensuring the return of its effective authority in the area. It looked good on paper, but had remarkably little to do with the cruel realities.

Already during the discussions of the mandate, one of our main problems became clear. I had included in the draft a provision authorizing UNIFIL to prevent the incursion of any armed personnel into its zone of operations. Lebanon, supported by Kuwait, which was the Arab member of the Council and ably represented by an intelligent realist, Abdullah Bishara, insisted that this provision be taken out on the grounds that the PLO would certainly object to it. The Lebanese had a right to take this position as it was their country, but it indicated the fatal weakness of their relationship with the PLO. Thus at the outset the PLO had been given the right to maintain its presence in southern Lebanon. This would give the Israelis the rationale for insisting on maintaining Major Haddad as a counterbalance. A deadlock was therefore built into the original plan. The Council also failed to define the exact area of operation of UNIFIL.

The Soviets abstained on everything, apparently having been begged by the Arabs not to sabotage the resolution. My Soviet assistant, Nikolai Fochin, and Arkady Shevchenko, the Soviet Under Secretary-General who was now only a few days away from his defection, seemed to be in a twenty-four-hour-a-day competition to be first to relay the output of my office to the Soviet delegation.

The resounding generalities of the mandate had papered over profound disagreements among the members of the Council. The new force was therefore launched upon a sea of ambiguity and controversy. It would be, initially, 4,000 strong. France, Nepal, and Norway had already volunteered contingents, and later on Nigeria and Senegal agreed to provide troops. We took Iranian, Swedish, and Canadian troops from existing operations to achieve the initial deployment. Major General Alexander Erskine of Ghana, the chief of staff of UNTSO, was appointed as the commander.

With the establishment of UNIFIL, the real trouble had only just started. The Israelis seemed to think that our force was in Lebanon primarily to continue the mopping-up operations that their army had been engaged in. They urged that we take over the city of Tyre from the PLO, something they had been unable to do. Since the Security Council had not been able to decide precisely what the area of deployment of UNIFIL was to be, we proceeded on the basis that it would deploy in all areas occupied by the Israeli forces. This excluded Tyre.

A week later the situation looked even less promising. The Israelis had begun to dicker about their withdrawal, trying to make it conditional on *our* completing *their* military operation against the PLO, especially in Tyre. Major Haddad had begun to act up, while to the north a kaleidoscopic range of factions were occupying Tyre and the vital Kashmiye Bridge over the Litani River on the coast road.

Arafat was maintaining his right, under the 1969 Cairo Agreement with the Lebanese government, to maintain the PLO presence in the south which was the immediate cause of all the trouble. The United States showed little inclination to support us with a convincing show of authority in any direction, while Oleg Troyanovsky, the suave and charming Soviet Ambassador, told Waldheim that they were expecting another Congo. In the field our soldiers were outraged by the activities both of the PLO and of Major Haddad and had to be restrained from reacting with force against them. The UN soldiers, at this early stage, had not yet appreciated that the moment they drew blood, their special status of being above the conflict would collapse, and with it their only source of authority. The Lebanese, while anxious to get someone else to pull their chestnuts out of the fire, absolutely refused to stand up to Arafat. No one, especially the United States, seemed to want to take a firm line with Israel.

By the first days of April we had done what we could in New York. We had assembled and deployed the force, organized its logistics, and tried to set down a reasonable series of directives to mitigate the weakness and ambiguity of its mandate. Our main preoccupation was now to get the process of Israeli withdrawal actually started. The members of the Security Council, while urging us to action, evidently preferred to have the Secretary-General tackle the Israelis on this matter than do it themselves. In letters to Begin we argued that we had made immense efforts to deploy a sizable force quickly to allay Israeli fears of a vacuum in southern Lebanon, but that lack of a significant Israeli withdrawal made it impossible for UNIFIL to perform its task.

Begin responded civilly enough, but very little happened on the ground, and it became clear that more direct pressure was required. Waldheim and I therefore decided to go to the area in mid-April. I picked him up on Sunday, April 16, in Vienna, where he had been having an unusually exasperating meeting with the Turkish-Cypriot negotiators, and we arrived in Beirut early on the following day.

Our meetings there revealed, in all its impotence and wretchedness, the Lebanese government's situation. We had to leave the airport through a hole in the security fence and travel by back roads and lanes to the Baabda Palace to meet with President Elias Sarkis, Prime Minister Selim Al Hoss, and Foreign Minister Fouad Boutros. There seemed to be little meeting of minds among these three intelligent men. There was no authority, no serviceable army, and an overwhelming desire to pass the buck. We spent an hour discussing the move of the Lebanese Army to the south to reestablish Lebanese authority, in the full knowledge that there were no units of the army capable of such a move and that Arafat would block the whole thing anyway. I was very conscious that our soldiers were taking risks the Lebanese themselves were not prepared to take, and that this could cause serious trouble in the future.

After an outstanding lunch with the president—the cuisine in Lebanon seems to survive all disasters—there was the usual complication about meeting with Arafat, who insisted, presumably for personal security reasons, that the Secretary-General go to an unspecified rendezvous of *his* choosing. Unfortunately Arafat was the key to many of our problems, and we therefore reluctantly accepted this blind date.

Our departure for the rendezvous from the United Nations Headquarters in Beirut was far from reassuring. There were Lebanese police in jeeps, a detachment of the Arab Deterrent Force, an escort of French paratroops, and the PLO group—a colonel in a battered green Ford sedan and two jeeploads of young, heavily armed Palestinian fighters. Journeys in Beirut often start with a motor accident, and sure enough, the PLO colonel rammed another car while turning around, thus raising the level of emotion at the outset. As usual, once on the road we travelled at unnecessarily high speed.

Our various protectors began to disappear as we neared Arafat's area, leaving us with only the PLO and our own people in squalid streets teeming with armed men. As we arrived at our destination one of the PLO fighters in the escort fired an automatic burst by mistake, which heightened the tension even further and started some luxuriant rumors. We were finally jostled into Arafat's headquarters of the moment through a milling mob of militiamen, photographers, and hangers-on.

Arafat was friendly and ostensibly cooperative, but in fact he was not being helpful at all. He could afford to express his respect for Lebanese sovereignty since it had no reality, but he opposed any move of the Lebanese Army to the south along the coast road and seemed uneasy at the intended increase in the strength of the UN Force—moves which might constrict the PLO groups already in the south. He agreed to our putting Observers into his stronghold at the Château de Beaufort, a crusader castle just north of the Litani which dominates much of the region. It was an unsatisfactory visit, and could only lead to endless trouble with the Israelis and Major Haddad.

The atmosphere of order and control in Tel Aviv was in striking contrast to Beirut. We drove directly to the Ministry of Defense to see Ezer Weizman. Weizman is a large, breezy, and amiable man, sharing with some British generals the technique of jollying people along with jokes and asides which camouflage the very tough position he is taking. He was accompanied by Raphael Eitan, the dour and hard-line chief of staff. Weizman's line was the same as Begin's—much as Israel wanted to get out of Lebanon, we had to prove that we could protect the Christians before any Israeli withdrawal took place. We insisted that withdrawal plans must be produced.

The foreign minister, Moshe Dayan, was reported to have been against the Lebanon invasion, and certainly when we saw him the next morning he was much more positive about UNIFIL than Weizman, but he seemed to be the odd man out in the government, playing, not for the first time, a lone hand. I had always respected Dayan, who was tough, direct, and imaginative. If he agreed to do something, you could be sure he would do it. Begin, whom we saw later, seemed tired and dispirited.

We flew by helicopter from the Knesset to Naqoura, the headquarters of the UN Force in South Lebanon. Naqoura is now an extensive permanent military camp beside the sea, but in 1978 it had only two permanent buildings, the border customs house and an old Turkish cemetery. It was a desolate and beautiful spot on a rocky coastline. Alex Erskine, the Ghanaian Force commander, and Colonel Jean Salvan of the French Parachute Battalion gave us a briefing. Salvan was a magnificent fighting soldier, a glass eye and other disfigurements testifying to his fearless record in Indochina and Algeria. He had, however, not yet fully grasped the nature of, and the necessary attitude for, our form of peacekeeping. (The techniques of UN peacekeeping were not, at that time, a part of the French Army's training program.) Colonel Salvan spoke of "the enemy" in relation to both Major Haddad and the PLO. After the briefing I took him aside and pointed out that our peacekeeping forces had no "enemies," just a series of difficult and sometimes homicidal clients. He responded that the "haute direction" in New York evidently didn't understand "l'esprit des paras." I told him that I didn't accept the relevance of that remark as far as our task in Lebanon was concerned and that anyway I, as a "para" who had been involved in the training of the First Free French Parachute Battalion in 1942, had a fairly good idea of the old "esprit." He turned the tables on me charmingly by saying, "Sir, you look much younger than your age." A few weeks later he was badly shot up and nearly died extricating one of his patrols from a confrontation with the PLO north of Tyre.

General Erskine had decided to take the Secretary-General up the coast road to Tyre past the Palestinian refugee camp of Rachideyeh, which had suffered much from Israeli air strikes. James Jonah, then my principal director on Middle East matters, and I had questioned the wisdom of doing this, but we were assured that there would be no problem, and we set off up the coast road led by a French armored car. We negotiated the last Israeli checkpoint without difficulty and were met by a PLO liaison officer at the first PLO checkpoint which signified the limit of the UN zone. Increasing numbers of heavily armed men and youths now appeared on the road and our pace slowed to a crawl, finally grinding to a halt at the gates of the Rachideyeh refugee camp.

We were engulfed by a large and highly emotional crowd bearing canisters which had contained the cluster bombs dropped on the camp by Israeli aircraft. Some of the demonstrators were brandishing olive green spheres in the windows of our vehicles. I saw the sudden tension in Colonel Salvan's battle-scarred face, but fortunately only learned later that these were unexploded cluster bombs. The crowd jumped on the cars and pounded on the roofs, yelling for immediate Israeli withdrawal. We finally managed to move out in low gear and arrived at the gate of the Tyre Barracks, where there was another large and violent demonstration. The French paratroops had some difficulty getting the Secretary-General's car through the gates and closing them behind it. In the following car I had an awkward time with the crowd before we could get the gates open again. The plan to visit the town of Tyre was obviously out, so we arranged to have a Norwegian helicopter land inside the barracks to take us to our next destination. This enraged the crowd outside.

Arafat later told one of our people that he had been appalled at the decision to take the Secretary-General to Tyre. There was, he said, a conspiracy by an extremist Palestinian group to kill Waldheim as a rejectionist gesture to discredit Arafat. Arafat had rushed his own special guard down to arrest the conspirators, who had been going to use the demonstration organized by "agents provocateurs" as a cover for the assassination. I cannot vouch for this melodramatic story, but certainly our experiences gave some credibility to it.

The rest of our visit was something of an anticlimax. We visited our Iranian Battalion on an idyllic hilltop overlooking the Litani. They seemed to be wonderfully self-confident. Only eight months later the Iranian revolution took them away forever. We flew over a demonstration organized by Major Haddad, who wished to meet with the Secretary-General in order to strengthen his claim to legitimacy. The Norwegian

Headquarters at Ebel es Saki was infested by hundreds of migrating storks. We flew back to Jerusalem in time to get a report from Siilasvuo that the Israelis would withdraw from 65 percent of the territory by April 30—not bad, but not good enough.

We were at this time still living under some illusions about the Lebanese situation. We still believed that by a supreme effort the Lebanese might be able to send a significant body of troops to the south and begin to restore the government's authority. We believed that with American persuasion the Israelis might be induced to withdraw completely and quickly. And we believed that it might be possible to persuade Arafat, for his own good, not to rock the boat by persisting in maintaining PLO groups south of the Litani, even though they had managed to remain there during the Israeli invasion.

These illusions gradually dissolved during the summer. The Israelis carried out their 65 percent withdrawal at the end of April, and pressure soon began building up to get them to relinquish the remaining 35 percent. On June 13 the Israeli Defense Ministry announced the completion of their withdrawal, but they did not hand over the remaining occupied territory to UNIFIL. Instead, with much fanfare, they handed it over to the ineffable Major Haddad, Dayan's 1954 "even just a Major." As usual the Israelis did this with considerable skill. They got Alex Erskine, a decent but credulous man, to confirm their total withdrawal, and on top of that Dayan, in formally telling the Secretary-General of the completion of the Israeli withdrawal, denounced the "return" of the PLO and UNIFIL's alleged assistance to them. He accused Waldheim in insulting terms of going back on what he had said in Jerusalem in April.

Much as I admire the talent of the Israelis for putting up a smokescreen of indignation to cover their own actions by loudly indicting others, this was too much. They were handing over to an Israeli proxy regarded by most Lebanese as a traitor and at the same time accusing us of all sorts of misdemeanors and demanding self-righteously that we mend our ways. Dayan, who was highly intelligent, must have been laughing as he signed this preposterous letter, which had been released to the press before we got it. I got Waldheim to respond strongly.

"In light of the above," he wrote,

I must take exception to the implication and to the context of your statement that the present situation "bodes ill for the future." In extremely difficult circumstances, UNIFIL has made great efforts, and will continue to make great efforts, to carry out all parts of its mandate. . . . Its task has certainly not been facilitated by the decision of the Israeli government not to turn over control of the remainder of the area of operations to UNIFIL, although I am making efforts to deal satisfactorily with the consequences of this development in co-operation with the Lebanese government. . . .

I am sure you will agree with me that in such a situation it would be helpful if those concerned refrain from making unsubstantiated public statements about this or that aspect of an extremely difficult operation.

A considerable period of silence ensued.

We had now arrived at a position which would not substantially change for four years until the Israeli invasion of 1982, and it was a rotten position for UNIFIL. To the south, Major Haddad was greatly puffed up by his formal takeover from the Israeli forces and strongly supported militarily and politically by the Israelis just across the frontier, as well as by Israeli military personnel in his own shaky military set-up. UNIFIL's headquarters in Naqoura was actually in Haddad territory and could be easily harassed and even attacked. To the north and west and in part of UNIFIL's own area were PLO groups and various Lebanese Muslim factions, although these groups were restrained by UNIFIL from trying to launch further cross-border raids against Israel. The PLO had Observer status with the UN and an agreement with the Lebanese government to be deployed in the south, neither of which facts could be ignored by us. The PLO presence was the main pretext for Haddad, and Haddad was the main pretext for the PLO presence. Caught in this violent vicious circle was UNIFIL. Arguments with both groups that the presence of UNIFIL alone in the area would be their best guarantee of peace and security fell on deaf ears. With each faction our force's credibility suffered from its inability to deal effectively with the other.

The Lebanese government, under pressure to show gains in the south to offset its lack of authority elsewhere in the country, was insistent that UNIFIL make progress, and we engaged in many somnambulistic exercises involving four- or five-stage plans by which the Lebanese government would triumphantly establish its authority in the south. This meant a preliminary deployment by the Lebanese Army. The Lebanese Army itself was reluctant to go south; the PLO was against it; the Israelis claimed that any Lebanese Army contingent in the south would be a cat's-paw of Syria; and Major Haddad would violently resist a move which would, among other things, highlight his own illegitimacy.

In view of these obstacles, we were surprised when, in late July, under heavy American pressure, a unit of the Lebanese Army *did* in fact move south. Admittedly it went by an inland back road and only to the eastern sector, but move it did to an obscure village called Kaoukaba. Major Haddad opened fire on it, just as he had said he would, and the unit was pinned down.

This was highly embarrassing for the Lebanese government, which had assumed, wrongly, that the U.S. government had obtained Israeli agreement for the move and that the Israelis would restrain Haddad. At the urging of Ghassan Tueni, the Lebanese Ambassador, and of the United States Mission at the UN, I went to Lebanon in mid-August to see what could be done.

In Beirut, where for once there was no shooting, the Lebanese, as usual, were blaming someone else for their misfortunes, this time the United States and to some extent the United Nations. President Sarkis, alone and isolated in the Baabda Palace, was not normally the most cheerful of heads of state, and on this occasion he was practically lachrymose. I told him that the American move and assurances had surprised us too and that *our* troops were under fire as a result. He was extremely bitter about his position, and seemed relieved to be talking frankly. He thanked me in advance for anything I could do.

I flew south next day to have a look at the situation in Kaoukaba. It seemed to be largely dominated by the antics of Major Haddad. The major's method consisted of opening fire on almost all occasions—to protest the failure of the electric light or the water supply, for example, or in response to some imagined slight. Haddad had much heavier weapons, including tanks and artillery, than UNIFIL. His handlers were from the cowboy wing of the Israeli military establishment.

Haddad came up true to form on my visit to the beleaguered Lebanese unit in Kaoukaba, a village garrisoned by our Nepalese contingent, whose professionalism and soldierly bearing were in distressing contrast to the Lebanese Army. As we arrived, the Nepalese colonel who was accompanying me received over the radio a message from Haddad advising me that I should leave at once, as he was going to start shelling the village in fifteen minutes. I told the colonel to ask Haddad to move the program up a bit, explaining that I was short of time and was anxious to show the journalists with me how a Lebanese officer treated his compatriots. The colonel's mustache bristled with glee as he delivered this message over the radio in clipped Bengal Lancer's English. We heard no more from Haddad, but he later complained that I had insulted him.

The Lebanese soldiers were pathetic and clearly terrified. They were all in shelters when we arrived and had to be coaxed out into the open. Alex Erskine was furious with them, having in mind the risks his own soldiers were running to help these reluctant patriots. Their colonel, one Terezian, was shifty and morose. I was supposed to find a way to move the Lebanese Army into the much more important town of Tibnin, but I couldn't help wondering if it was worth the trouble.

In Israel I learned that the American Ambassador, Sam Lewis, was infuriated that the State Department had not consulted him on the move southward of the Lebanese Army. The Israelis were busy preparing for the Camp David summit meeting. Weizman was amiable but tough. When I said that we could find no evidence of undue Syrian influence in the Lebanese unit in Kaoukaba, General Eitan produced the minutes of a meeting two days before between Haddad, the Israelis, and the same morose Lebanese Colonel Terezian I had seen in Kaoukaba. Colonel Terezian had said his battalion was under the control of the Third Syrian Brigade. So much for Lebanese patriotism and good faith. However, Weizman agreed to ensure that the Lebanese could move to Tibnin without further shelling from Haddad.

In spite of my work on the Namibian question, our force in Lebanon remained my chief preoccupation. The UNIFIL soldiers were in constant danger. Southern Lebanon had a pattern of its own that was singularly careless of human life, and the fact that virtually everyone strong enough to carry a weapon was fully armed and ready to fire on the smallest pretext gave us many anxious days and sleepless nights. The region also had a lunatic quality which can best be described by excerpts from daily reports.

On 29 May, at 1440 LT, Fiji soldiers at Ayn Bal checkpoint confiscated a pistol from a civilian. The civilian was annoyed. He went to his home in Ayn Bal, and to express his annoyance fired five rounds AK-47 into the air and concluded by throwing a hand-grenade to his garden. Slight damage to the garden. He did not get the pistol back.

* * *

Yesterday at 1320 Z, a jeep, presumed to be IDF [Israel Defence Forces], started to approach NORBATT POS [Norwegian Battalion Position] 5-17A in vicinity of DFF [Haddad] BLAT encroachment. UNIFIL Personnel fired a few warning shots, the jeep did not stop, more warning shots were fired with MG, and the DFF position fired on the NORBATT POS with eight rounds. The jeep then stopped and a man (presumed to be IDF but in civilian attire) came forward and stated his purpose as desiring to say hello.

There was an incessant background of gunfire, deepened by artillery and mortar exchanges between the PLO groups and Haddad's people, who were often reinforced by Israeli artillery from across the border. It was a very noisy and nerve-wracking place in which to be caught in an indefinite deadlock.

I went to Lebanon again in February 1979 with a depressing sense of déjà-vu. My arrival in Beirut coincided with the resignation of the moderate Prime Minister Shapur Bhaktiar of Iran. This news was greeted in Beirut with a two-hour feu-de-joie by the Shia'a population, firing all weapons and God knows how many thousands of dollars worth of ammunition. The night sky was full of tracer bullets—very pretty. In Beirut we sleepwalked once again through discussions of phased programs and rational and peaceful outcomes, but in reality none of the elements were there. Arafat was euphoric about the Iranian revolution and kept saying, "Bye-bye USA," echoing Brzezinski's Camp David wisecrack, "Bye-bye PLO."

President Sarkis was tearful as usual, saying life was impossible, that everyone had let him down, and that it was up to us to do something. During my meeting with Prime Minister Al Hoss, lively sniper fire broke out in the street below. When Kamal al-Assad, the Speaker of the Assembly and absentee landlord from the south, accused us of failing in our duties, I told him that, since he was so dissatisfied, we should perhaps pull out of his home territory, which he had not visited for years.

Things were no better in Israel. Weizman was sour and intransigent about Lebanon and even boastful about killing Palestinians, referring to the recent assassination in Beirut of Abu Hassan. The Iranian revolution seemed to have induced an irritable mood in Israel. I cut the meeting short and went to see Begin who, though courteous and conciliatory, was full of misinformation which I was at pains to correct. He said, for example, that the PLO artillery was firing into Israel from the UN zone and that the PLO had killed seventeen United Nations soldiers. The source of much of this misinformation was the Israel liaison officer who was sitting on my right, and he blushed becomingly when I begged him to stop misinforming his own prime minister. Begin was obviously worried by the Iranian revolution and Israel's increasing isolation, but ended by assuring me that he would seriously consider my suggestions on southern Lebanon.

At UNIFIL the main change was in the Iranian Battalion. After the Iranian revolution the men had arrested their commander, who was a Bahai, and two of his officers, and we had rescued them with some difficulty. The soldiers, awaiting repatriation, were a smoldering threat to order in the whole area and were sitting on 75 tons of explosives and ammunition which they apparently wished to give to the local PLO. This was stopped, and we evacuated the Iranians by truck. All in all this was a depressing visit, well symbolized by a full-page cartoon in a Lebanese newspaper showing me with a head wound and a stream of blood reading "South Lebanon."

*   *   *

In March 1979 the Egyptian-Israeli Peace Treaty was signed, a triumph for President Carter and his colleagues which was received with hostility and indignation by the rest of the Arab world and the Soviet Union. The Arabs, understandably, resented Sadat's separate peace, but I wonder what would have happened if they had, with United States support, really pushed on with the talks about Palestinian autonomy, a feature of Camp David which Begin did not like at all. Since 1979 no progress whatsoever has been made on the Palestinian issue, and the Israelis have consolidated their grip on Gaza and the West Bank. The autonomy talks, skillfully pursued, might have produced better practical results for the Palestinians.

The treaty provided among other things for an international force and observers in Sinai and stated a preference that the United Nations should provide them. As the Soviets and Arabs were dead set against this, there was no possibility of the Security Council agreeing to it. The Israelis also were not keen on a United Nations force, and a substitute would have to be primarily from the United States, thereby introducing a sizable American force into the region, something the Soviet Union didn't want. I tried this impeccable piece of logic on the Soviet Ambassador, Oleg Troyanovsky, but he only smiled politely.

Thus we set about dismantling UNEF II, the force which had played such an important role in the 1973 crisis and ever since. I flew out to say goodbye, addressing a farewell parade of each contingent. We flew from one to the other along the shore of the Gulf of Suez and to the moon landscape of the Mitla Pass in a Skyvan, a sort of flying shoe box, piloted by Malaysians. At the Swedish parade, in a temperature of 110 degrees, the dogs of the dog platoon seemed to follow my speech with much more interest than the men, and I had to resist the temptation to say a heartfelt "Woof, woof." It was sad to say goodbye to the excellent soldiers from Canada, Indonesia, Sweden, Ghana, Australia, and Finland who had served so well in this desolate region. They too seemed sad to go and had evidently enjoyed their brief peacekeeping career.

There was a farewell dinner in Cairo at which I sat next to General Magdoub, who had just been put in charge of normalizing relations with Israel. I asked him how often he had been to Israel. "Never," he replied, "and I shall never go to that place." Not a promising attitude for a normalizer.

*   *   *

Nothing in our problems over southern Lebanon changed substantially for nearly two years. I went to the area every few months to talk to all concerned and visit the troops, but with regrettably little effect. The Lebanese in their impotence continued to make impossible demands and criticisms of UNIFIL which was, unlike the Lebanese Army, actually being shot at. Arafat remained friendly but elusive and given to flights of fancy. At one meeting he told me dramatically that the Israelis were using *nerve* gas in South Lebanon. "This is very, very important," he insisted. I agreed that, if true, it certainly was, but I doubted that such a historical first could take place without anyone else, our soldiers included, noticing it. He repeated the charge periodically throughout the meeting, and at the end I asked his military adviser for more information. A long colloquy in Arabic ensued, after which the adviser said, "It is quite true what the Chairman says. The Israelis *are* using *tear* gas in southern Lebanon."

In Israel I made the acquaintance of the new foreign minister, Yitzhak Shamir. I viewed this meeting with considerable distaste, for Shamir, as a member of the Stern Gang, had played a key role in the 1948 assassination of our Mediator, Count Folke Bernadotte. I felt, against the strong advice of the Israeli Foreign Office, that I must say something about Bernadotte before proceeding to business, but was perplexed as to how to do it without bringing the meeting to an abrupt end. As it was, Shamir helped me by saying that I was the first United Nations person he had ever dealt with. I recalled Bernadotte's short-lived efforts in 1948 and his confidence that he could achieve a settlement acceptable to both Jews and Arabs. Shamir said what a tragedy and misunderstanding that whole episode had been. We had an equally unsatisfactory, but equally courteous, talk about the current agenda.

A visit to Damascus was an important part of these trips, not so much for any palpable gain but for avoiding the danger of seeming to ignore the Syrians. In the Middle East especially, it is essential to invite the fairy godmother to the christening. These Syrian visits followed a uniform pattern, a lavish welcome and great kindness but little, if any, substantive progress. The Alawite regime of Hafez al-Assad is a formidable and secretive autocracy sustained by pragmatic ruthlessness. Security was very tight, and tough plainclothes security men were ubiquitous. Shootouts with the Muslim Brotherhood and other dissidents were common. (Sidney and I found ourselves in the middle of one in Aleppo in 1980.) A rigid dogmatism guided the Syrian government's foreign policy. Damascus is a wonderful city, and the Syrians themselves are charming and hospitable people.

On visits to Abdel Halim Khaddam, who was foreign minister until he became vice-president in 1984, I came to enjoy his abrasive, all-or-nothing style. "We shall cut off the hand of neocolonialism at the wrist," he would say matter-of-factly, à propos of an ill-considered suggestion by the United States Secretary of State Alexander Haig and the French Foreign Minister for action in the region. He often wasn't very polite about the United Nations either. When he called our peacekeeping "merely psychological gymnastics," I replied that if people's psychological state was bad enough, as in the Middle East, psychological gymnastics were quite healthy. Khaddam's view of events tended to be the mirror image of the Israeli view. From Damascus I would also visit the troops of UN-DOF in the Golan Heights, an operation which performs its buffer and inspection function perfectly.

The advent, in January 1981, of the Reagan administration signalled a major emotional and ideological shift in United States policy in the Middle East as in other areas. We had a foretaste of this in March 1981 when three of our Nigerian soldiers in southern Lebanon were killed by Haddad's mortar fire and it took the Security Council four and a half days to agree on a statement deploring the tragedy. There was no doubt about the facts or that Israel made Haddad's extravagances possible. However, Jeane Kirkpatrick, the new United States Ambassador, was determined that Israel should not be mentioned in this statement. The Soviet Ambassador, Troyanovsky, was equally determined that Israel *should* be mentioned. The matter was resolved somewhat mystifyingly late in the night of the fifth day when Ambassador Kirkpatrick agreed that the statement could quote the original resolution on UNIFIL, which happens to mention Israel no less than four times.

I visited Lebanon shortly after this episode at a time when the battle was raging both in Beirut and in the Christian town of Zahle, both highly emotional situations in areas where we had no authority. Most of the government were living in the relative safety of Baabda, to which we had to go by helicopter. During my talk with President Sarkis, artillery and small-arms fire came nearer and nearer, until aides ushered us into a less exposed room. At the Defense Ministry we were taken up to the roof to watch an intensive Syrian bombardment of downtown Beirut, the Lebanese officers arguing about what type of artillery was firing, as if it was a sporting event and not the destruction of their own capital city. Our excellent Ghanaian military adviser, Timothy Dibuama, who was accompanying me, was deeply shocked at this cynicism. At 2:00 p.m. a ceasefire gradually took hold, allowing us to go downtown to see the new prime minister, Shafik Wazzan. There was no traffic at all and our motorcycle escort mistakenly took us through the Galérie Seeman, then the most active sniping area between East and West Beirut.

Arafat, whom we visited later in the night, explained the disastrous situation as the beginning of Operation "Accordion," which he said was an Israeli plan designed to crush the PLO between the Christian militias of the north and the Israelis in the south. He claimed that the bombardment of Beirut was the first stage of this plan.

At the parliament the next day I was having my routine talk with Speaker Kamel el-Assad just as shelling of that area started in earnest. We both gloomily observed the soldiers outside the window jump into their slit trenches and take cover, but neither of us was prepared to take the initiative in following their example. It was a rather stilted conversation.

I took a helicopter across the bay to the Christian port of Jounieh to lunch with Bashir Gemayel. The once limpid bay was thick with the city's garbage, but the Jounieh Yacht Club was in a 1935 time warp, resembling prewar Eden Roc at Antibes. While the guns thundered in the distance, people lazed on yachts and girls in bikinis sunbathed and swam in the pool. I was greeted by Bashir's father, Pierre Gemayel, and former President Camille Chamoun, whom I had first met in London in 1945. The *King Lear/Macbeth* syndrome here assumed also a touch of *The Godfather*. The two old chieftains were behaving like loving brothers and capping each other's lines less than a year after the Gemayel militia had annihilated Dany Chamoun's Tigers on a blood-soaked afternoon in Beirut. Now they were telling me in unison that they belonged to Western Europe and that the United Nations must save them. When he was president during the crisis of 1958, Chamoun had surprised Hammarskjold by producing in front of the press a vast iced cake with the inscription: "ONU, Sauvez Le Liban." Evidently nothing had changed.

Bashir Gemayel arrived from the fighting front in full battle rig with pistols and hand grenades—a cinematically good-looking, tough young man with considerable charm. He let the old men do most of the talking.

Pierre Gemayel, incidentally, must have been the last person in the world whose role model was Mussolini, of whom he spoke warmly during lunch. It was an interesting expedition into the past, but not a reassuring one.

Nor was driving to dinner in the evening with the Druse leader, Walid Jumblatt, over a potholed road with my feet resting on a box of hand grenades and a bodyguard with his finger on the trigger perched in the back seat.

Secretary of State Alexander Haig's first visit to the area was having strange repercussions. His first requirement appeared to be for everyone to declare themselves anti-Soviet crusaders, so he had got gloomy reviews everywhere except Israel. His denunciation of Syria over Zahle stiffened the Syrian position and greatly stimulated the military efforts of the Syrian Army, while his reported remark that Israel might have to come in to defend the Lebanese Christians there had vastly encouraged the Christian militias, so that the battle had greatly intensified.

The situation in southern Lebanon came to a head during the summer of 1981. There had been an ominous development in May when Israeli fighters shot down two Syrian helicopters over the Beka'a Valley in eastern Lebanon, and Syria riposted by moving in SAM-6 ground-to-air missiles. At the same time Israeli reprisal raids against Palestinian targets in Lebanon, including attacks on traffic and bridges on the coast road, and PLO efforts to respond with rocket attacks and long-range shelling of northern Israeli settlements, opened a new and appalling chapter of violence in southern Lebanon. On July 17, Israeli planes bombed Beirut, causing massive damage and killing 300 people in an effort to hit Palestinian targets. They also destroyed eleven bridges on the coast road to the south.

President Reagan dispatched the veteran troubleshooter Philip Habib to the area to try to stem this deadly tide of violence. Waldheim made public appeals to one and all for a return to the cease-fire, and I spent much time urging the PLO, in spite of the Israeli attacks on them all over Lebanon, to refrain from firing rockets and artillery into Israel in reprisal, in order to avoid civilian casualties and to halt the escalation of violence. The PLO were dubious, believing that the long-promised all-out Israeli attack on them had started. It is very difficult to argue for moderation with people who believe they are facing extinction.

On July 17 the Security Council appealed for a general cease-fire, and this gave us a better basis for asking the PLO to desist from firing. U.S. policy did not permit Habib, who was doing his best with the Israelis, to talk to the PLO. The Israelis, although they were launching a major assault on the PLO, would not communicate with them either. Communications with the PLO on establishing the essential elements of a cease-fire therefore had to go through me, usually in the form of telephone calls from my bed at home in the early hours of the morning. We again urged Arafat to stop all firing into northern Israel as a basis for Habib requiring Israel to stop its by now almost incessant air strikes. We also urged Arafat to respond to the call of the Security Council, which provided an excellent face-saver for him as it implied no show of weakness on his part. Our UNIFIL commander, Bill Callaghan, followed up these appeals with the PLO at the local level and on July 20 met with Arafat in Beirut.

After initial reluctance, Arafat accepted Waldheim's call for a de facto cease-fire, provided Israel also accepted it. All of this was passed on to Habib.

The Israelis attempted to use the situation to pin the PLO down to a much wider restriction on its activities, but this would have inevitably opened up an endless and futile debate between parties who were not in direct touch at all, and I did what I could through the Americans to discourage the idea. We ended, on July 24, with a plain statement that there would be no hostile military activity either from Lebanon on targets in Israel or from Israel on targets in Lebanon, this arrangement including Haddad's area. Habib in Jerusalem announced that at 1330 hours on July 24 all hostile military action in both directions would cease. Israel said the agreement had been negotiated by the United States. The PLO said it had been negotiated by the United Nations. Honor was saved all round.

This strange arrangement, after initial efforts to disrupt it by dissident PLO elements, ushered in a period of almost complete calm in southern Lebanon. The breathing space was supervised by UNIFIL and lasted until the Israeli invasion of the following year.

XXIII

Namibia

IN THE LATE SEVENTIES and early eighties there were extensive changes of cast and script. On February 1, 1979, the Ayatollah Khomeini arrived, to a tumultuous welcome, in Teheran, and in November of that year the long agony of the American hostages began. In December 1979, the Soviet Union occupied Afghanistan. In September 1980, Iraq invaded Iran, starting one of the longest and bloodiest wars of the twentieth century. During all this period China was swinging from doctrinaire Maoist Marxism toward a freer economy and a more open relationship with the West and the Third World.

Changes in personalities and political trends were no less striking. In May 1979, Margaret Thatcher became Prime Minister of the United Kingdom, signalling among other things the Western swing to doctrinaire conservatism which reached a peak with the election of President Ronald Reagan in November 1980. In October 1981, President Anwar Sadat was assassinated by fundamentalist Egyptian soldiers at a military parade. The year 1981 also saw assassination attempts on President Reagan and Pope John Paul II.

In July 1979, I went to London with Waldheim to make the acquaintance of the new British government. At first glance Mrs. Thatcher seemed to combine characteristics of La Pasionaria, the girls of St. Trinians, and Mrs. Miniver. She seemed to believe that the United Nations was, or should be, primarily the instrument for asserting Western values in the world. Lord Carrington, the new Secretary of State, a man of outstanding wisdom, common sense, and humor, provided an excellent foil for the new prime minister. Mrs. Thatcher, who had been answering questions in the House of Commons about the Vietnamese boat people, was anxious to point the finger of condemnation at Vietnam, although we suggested that this might well limit our capacity to do anything helpful about the refugee situation, on which we were already undertaking active operations. When I pointed out that the Cambodian refugees were probably in worse shape than the Vietnamese boat people, she said, "Is that the Pol Pot lot? I don't care for that lot." Lord Carrington covered his face with his hands. But Mrs. Thatcher also gave the impression of a strong and forthright person, hardworking and well informed.

There was little doubt about Mrs. Thatcher's effect on the emerging conservative trend in the United States. Her visit to the United States in December 1979 coincided with the triumphant conclusion of the Lancaster House conference on the independence of Rhodesia, and she swept all before her as the Joan of Arc of free enterprise capitalism and no-nonsense-from-foreigners. At a dinner of the banking and foreign policy establishment given by David Rockefeller in New York, she evoked an almost revivalist atmosphere with a ringing assault on socialism and on generally unsatisfactory behavior throughout the world. When she was done, ancient bankers staggered to their feet to forswear 1776 and suggest that she ought to be President of the United States. She was urged to tell the United States, then in the early throes of the hostage crisis, where it had gone wrong. Along with the other Brits present, I was acutely embarrassed.

There were other changes. Since his arrival at the United Nations in 1977, Andy Young had become famous for his off-the-cuff remarks, for he expressed, mixed up with a lot of loose thinking, refreshingly individual and sometimes perceptive views about important issues. Indulgence ran out, however, when he became involved in one of the touchiest areas of United States foreign policy, the relationship of the United States and the Palestine Liberation Organization. Either by accident or on purpose, Young went to the house of Ambassador Bishara of Kuwait on Beekman Place in New York and there met the representative of the PLO. The Israelis soon heard about it and tipped off *Newsweek*, which began to ask questions in Washington. Andy Young thereupon felt that he must tell the whole truth to the Israeli Ambassador to the UN, Yehuda Blum, who in turn felt he could not remain silent on such a key issue. Israel protested, and Young had to resign. Just before he left I had a long talk with Young about the dangers, for a great power, of a moralistic refusal to recognize, or talk to, governments or groups it disapproved of ideologically. Much of his farewell speech to the Security Council was on this theme.

Andy Young's successor, Donald McHenry, who was already in the

United States Mission, served for the rest of the Carter administration and performed brilliantly. He was a tough and realistic professional with great experience and intelligence and a strong point of view of his own. He was immensely helpful on the whole range of issues we dealt with, but I particularly associate him with the question of Namibia.

*　　　*　　　*

The mandate for German South West Africa was assigned by the League of Nations to South Africa after World War I. After World War II, in spite of General Assembly resolutions, a ruling of the International Court of Justice, and decisions of the Security Council, South Africa doggedly hung on to control of this territory, now called Namibia, in defiance of all international opinion. Namibia is the last surviving significant colonial problem and as such is an important symbol with the African group and in many other parts of the world. It is also a source of violence and disruption in southern Africa, where a liberation movement, the South West African People's Organization (SWAPO), based in various African countries, has kept the Namibia issue alive by desultory guerrilla activity, which in turn triggers reprisal actions by South Africa. The future of Namibia is intimately connected with the situation in Angola, the relations of the African front-line states with South Africa, and also with the domestic political situation in South Africa. Nowhere has the South African talent for delay and obfuscation been deployed with such skill.

The South African government's way of facing its problems often seems to be an exercise in schizophrenia. On the one hand, South Africa agrees in principle that a problem must be solved; on the other hand, every possible obstacle is put in the way of solving it. Its domestic politics, an unusual history, and a considerable paranoia about the outside world all contribute to the South African state of mind, and the results can be terrible. They are bad enough as far as Namibia is concerned, tragic and catastrophic for the far more complex and deep-rooted question of apartheid.

In 1977 the Western members of the Security Council, the United States, France, Britain, Canada, and West Germany, constituted themselves as a "Contact Group" to make a determined effort to achieve the long-overdue solution of the Namibia problem. This was very much an initiative of the Carter administration, and Don McHenry was the leader of the group. It was at that time generally considered that the Namibian problem would be easier to resolve than the Rhodesian problem.

The basic idea of the Western Five Contact Group was a plan for

Namibia's transition to independence through elections for a constituent assembly supervised by a UN Special Representative and a large United Nations civilian and military operation, working with the South African Administrator-General to ensure that the elections were free and fair. Nothing could have been more sensible, and nothing more difficult to achieve. By the summer of 1978 there was agreement in principle for a UN operation of 1,000 civilians, 350 police, and 7,500 soldiers. Both South Africa and SWAPO objected to parts of the plan, which contained a number of uncertainties and ambiguities.

Pik Botha, the South African foreign minister, and Brand Fourie, the head of the South African Foreign Office, came to New York to discuss further steps at the end of November, at Waldheim's invitation. Pik Botha tended to start talks with a twenty-minute warm-up of grievances. He was misunderstood; he had been bending over backwards, and look how the United Nations had rewarded him for jeopardizing his political career; the Western Five had tricked him; the Africans hated him; he was a martyr to his own good intentions; he was fed up with it all and might as well leave for home now; etc., etc. All this was said with an actor's delivery, dramatic crescendos and diminuendos, and much flashing of the eyes. I always enjoyed these performances and felt like applauding. The fact was, of course, that the South Africans had no intention of allowing any election in Namibia which might put SWAPO into power. Their strategy, therefore, was to give the appearance of cooperation but to block actual progress. This Penelope's web exercise was the story of the next two years.

The original Western proposal on Namibia, like most products of diplomatic negotiation, was full of ambiguities and places where different interpretations could, and would, be made by the different parties. In February 1979, Waldheim issued a report designed to give a central interpretation of controversial questions and to ask everyone to accept it in the interests of progress. In this report we suggested March 15, 1979, as the day that the cease-fire would come into effect and the whole process of independence would start.

The report got a rousing reception. The South Africans, in their perennial search for a new and insurmountable obstacle to progress, grumbled darkly about double-dealing and the suppression of vital information. They were particularly indignant over our suggestion that the fighting members of SWAPO actually in Namibia when the cease-fire went into force should be assembled in special locations, a provision we had made at the urging of the South African military.

SWAPO was not to be outdone by the South Africans. Its President, Sam Nujoma, announced from Addis Ababa that he could no longer cooperate with the Secretary-General, that he would not accept any NATO country in the UN Force, and that he disagreed with a number of the Secretary-General's interpretations.

The summer of 1979 went by in futile exchanges of letters, but in November I found myself in Geneva presiding over "high-level simultaneous consultations on Namibia." These talks included the Western Five; the front-line states, including the foreign ministers of Tanzania and Zambia; South Africa, represented by Brand Fourie and General Johannes Geldenhuys, the South African commander in Namibia; and Sam Nujoma. Ostensibly we were discussing the establishment of a Demilitarized Zone in northern Namibia and southern Angola. This new idea provided South Africa with a heaven-sent new pretext for delay.

As the oldest Secretariat hand, I was supposed, at Geneva, to inspire confidence and a desire for progress, but knowing the reluctance of both South Africa and SWAPO to agree to anything sensible, I felt more like the priest at a shotgun wedding arranged by the Western Five and the front-line states. I wanted to show the South Africans that our group in the Secretariat, which would run the Namibia operation, were impartial, serious, and objective. I wanted to show the Africans that we would not put up with delays and evasions from South Africa and would work with the front-line states to get agreement to proceed.

Sam Nujoma was not a very helpful interlocutor, and his habitual obstinacy could only be overcome by massive pressure from the front-line states. The front-line states, sensible as always, said they could bring SWAPO into line, provided the South Africans accepted the Demilitarized Zone. It was the worst kind of chicken and egg situation.

I had known Brand Fourie since 1945. He was a decent and honorable man, personally dedicated to finding a proper solution for the Namibian problem, but constricted by the policy and politics of South Africa. General Geldenhuys, too, was straightforward, a first-rate soldier and also someone who saw that Namibia must become independent and wanted, within his limits, to help us find the solution.

Fourie and Geldenhuys professed themselves highly satisfied with both the tone and substance of our Geneva meetings. Nonetheless, the reply they had promised on the Demilitarized Zone was long delayed after they got back to Pretoria, and a few weeks later Pik Botha, seizing triumphantly on Sam Nujoma's aggressive statements in Geneva, disowned the Geneva consultations altogether. This in turn made it impossible for the front-line states to rein in Nujoma. We had achieved a perfect vicious circle.

In early March 1980, in another attempt to break the impasse on the Demilitarized Zone, I took a team consisting of Martti Ahtisaari, our designated representative in Namibia, and Prem Chand, whom we had put in charge of the military side, to Capetown for technical and military discussions. Early on the day after our arrival I went to the Foreign Office to talk to Brand Fourie. At 9:00 a.m. the Rhodesian election results—a landslide for Mugabe—came over the radio. This was evidently a severe shock to the South Africans who had invested much emotional and other capital in Bishop Muzorewa, who only got 3 seats to Mugabe's 77.

The immediate South African reaction was that Mugabe's triumph was the result of intimidation and that any decisions on Namibia would have to wait while South Africa digested the Rhodesian results. I argued, with no success, that the change in Rhodesia made progress on Namibia all the more urgent and desirable.

Our talks on the Demilitarized Zone were particularly frustrating, and the South African generals wanted—the perfect blocking stratagem—to have absolute assurances in advance that nothing would go wrong, a manifest absurdity. There was a great deal of obfuscation and gamesmanship.

Fourie and Geldenhuys appeared embarrassed at these goings-on, and the British Ambassador later told me that Fourie had said to him that if the South African government could not negotiate an agreement on Namibia with our delegation, they certainly wouldn't be able to do it with anyone else. This backhanded compliment represented the basic truth. There was no real intention of reaching an agreement, and the negotiations were a game of procrastination.

This became even clearer when I saw Foreign Minister Pik Botha. For once there was no twenty-minute overture of grievances, Botha simply saying they needed two or three months to digest the Rhodesian experience and they might then "make gestures that would surprise us." An irresistibly comic picture of this contingency arose in my mind, but the ostensibly forthcoming words were anything but encouraging.

Prime Minister P. W. Botha, one of the world's preeminent preachers, lectured me on the childishness of the international community, and said that if he had to choose between international popularity and stability in Namibia, he would choose the latter. Not having asked him to make any such choice, I replied mildly enough that our whole aim was for him to have both international popularity *and* stability in Namibia, which in any case most people did not regard as South African territory, and I hoped we could cooperate in achieving this aim. P. W. Botha was not receptive. Rhodesia and the threat from the South African right were evidently on his mind, and I knew we had been staved off again.

On my way home I spent two days in Namibia's capital, Windhoek, a monument to German colonialism. I received representatives of seventeen of the internal political parties of Namibia, a country of less than 1 million people. With one or two exceptions, gracelessness was the order of the day. To be a politician of any party in Namibia must inevitably be an exercise in total frustration as long as the independence question remains unsolved, and I felt very sorry for all of them. A visit, strongly opposed by the Administrator-General, to the African township of Katatura where the non-white inhabitants of Windhoek live, only served to remind us of the urgent necessity for change.

It was a relief to get back to the front-line states. In Botswana, Zambia, and Tanzania the knowledge and understanding of South Africa were striking, and they were prepared to do anything within reason to meet outstanding South African difficulties on the implementation of the Namibian settlement plan. I could not help wondering what would happen if the Arabs were to start talking like this.

Luanda was rather different. We landed on an airfield crowded with Soviet transports, helicopters, and MiG-21 fighters, and had the usual People's Republic press conference, where a correspondent asks one prescribed question, receives one answer, and everyone leaves. The SWAPO representatives from New York were wandering about in the Panorama Hotel improbably dressed up as Castro-style guerrillas. They were effusively polite to me, and I discovered why when I received a copy of a three-page SWAPO press release excoriating me personally and our mission in general for going to South Africa and for having been to Windhoek and seen the internal political parties there. The style was Marxist-Liberation-Movement abuse. I told Sam Nujoma that, not for the first time, he had been duped by South African propaganda.

After my return to New York there was no more talk of "gestures that would surprise us," and in August Pik Botha, in a letter making a number of assumptions about the DMZ and castigating the United Nations for its so-called partiality, suggested further talks in Pretoria to clarify matters.

It was with a heavy heart that I set off for Pretoria at the end of October. During the summer Angola, in its desperation over the Namibia situation, had held secret bilateral talks with South Africa with a view to arranging direct talks between South Africa and SWAPO on the desolate island of Sal (Salt) in the Cape Verde Islands. The front-line states believed we should visit Pretoria before these talks took place, to see if we could not at least establish a time frame and a starting date for the independence process. The Namibian problem was damaging them militarily, financially, and economically. Moreover, the presence of SWAPO in Angola and Zambia, like the presence of the PLO in Lebanon, had become a costly and dangerous moral obligation, and they desperately needed to see the end of it. The South Africans were under no such pressure.

*   *   *

Over the years whenever I went through Geneva, I invariably went to the Hôtel Beau Rivage at Ouchy on the lake below Lausanne to see Rowland Burdon-Muller. I did this on my way to South Africa in October 1980 and realized, with deep sadness, that I was seeing Rowland for the last time. Although at eighty-nine he still made a valiant effort to talk and to give me "a decent meal" in the excellent hotel restaurant, he was breathless, weak, and evidently anticipating death.

Rowland came into my life at a Sunday luncheon in New York in 1948. His lifelong partner, Charles Hoyt, an eminent collector of Chinese and Korean ceramics, had suddenly and unexpectedly died, and he was lonely and distraught. From that day on I received a regular flow of letters, for Rowland had the Edwardian habit of putting aside the hours between tea and dinner for letter writing. His letters were long and full of social reporting as well as expositions on matters which he felt strongly about —the Republicans, Senator McCarthy and his attendant clowns Cohn and Schine, John Foster Dulles, Vietnam, the Middle East. He tended to become obsessed and rather shrill on such matters.

Rowland described himself as "liberal in thought but conservative in habit," and he was a strong opponent of hypocrisy, reaction, humbug, or anything that he conceived of as wrong-headedness or injustice. He had a strong moral sense about politics and was surprisingly shrewd and often very funny.

Rowland was the last surviving true Edwardian in my experience. He had an extraordinary visual and verbal memory, and his reminiscences of the personalities and lifestyle of his youth were fascinating. Rowland went to Eton and Oxford where his motorcar was maintained by "that nice Mr. Morris," and where he became a close friend of Prince Felix Yusupoff, who assassinated Rasputin. (Rowland left me the diamond, ruby, and mother-of-pearl Fabergé waistcoat buttons Yusupoff gave him for Christmas in St. Petersburg in 1911.) As soon as he could get his inheritance he went to Boston, where he eventually settled down with Charles Hoyt.

The key to many of Rowland's anecdotes was his extraordinary propensity for being on the scene at interesting historical moments. He was present as a young guest—part of his family was German—at the decisive German maneuvers of 1911. He went to Russia soon after the Revolution as a member of the Anglo-Soviet Trade Commission ("the only regular job I ever had") and visited the deserted Yusupoff Palace in Leningrad to inspect the room where Rasputin had been killed. As a guest of the British Ambassador in Cairo in 1921, Rowland had been on the special train to Jerusalem for the installation of the first British High Commissioner of the Mandate of Palestine, Herbert Samuel, in company with the Winston Churchills, Lawrence of Arabia, and Mrs. Greville, a leading social figure of the day. The train stopped at Gaza to refill the engine boiler and to let the ADCs walk the numerous dogs without which no British imperial party was complete. The travellers walked into the town where, as still happens in that gritty and fly-blown place, a large and excited crowd soon gathered. The ADCs nervously shepherded the distinguished visitors onto the steps of the Anglican cathedral as the crowd surged past shouting and flashing their teeth. "Isn't it wonderful, Winston," said Mrs. Greville, "how the Arabs love us British." At which Lawrence muttered to Rowland, "It's lucky that I am the only one here who understands Arabic. What they are shouting is 'Death to the Jews' —and they mean the Samuels."

Rowland had no sense of guilt about being a man of leisure, for he worked very hard at leading a civilized life. He looked after himself meticulously. In his eighty-eighth year, seeing me off at the station in Lausanne, he could read without glasses the fine print of the timetable. When I commented on this, he said, "My dear, I have always made it a rule—and you should too—*never* to read when I am tired."

Rowland was a strong believer in getting the best out of life, and he did everything he could to ensure that his friends did the same. Whenever we met—in New York, or Boston, or Camden, Maine, where he had a house beside the sea, or in Europe—his first concern was to give me a "decent meal" at the best possible restaurant or at home. Late in his life he helped in setting up the restaurant in the Hôtel de Ville in Crissier, outside Lausanne, where Freddy Girardet presides over what many people believe to be the best restaurant in Europe.

Rowland loved shopping and going to exhibitions and galleries and concerts, and he never failed to buy things he thought you might like.

He was an incredibly kind and generous man, and his friends were always in his thoughts. When he left the United States in the early seventies he worked out (he was extremely astute financially) what it would cost him, with inflation, to live at the Hôtel Beau Rivage at Ouchy until he was ninety. He then sold at auction the less good pictures, books, sculptures, and so on, of his large collection up to the required sum. The rest, the really good things, he gave anonymously to museums or to friends.

Rowland had a high fluting voice that rose to a whoop, or even a shriek, when he was excited or making a point. This caused a considerable stir in public places or restaurants, especially when the subject matter was controversial. At lunch in a Boston restaurant, Stuart Hampshire was listening to Rowland's description of the private lives of Marcel Proust's circle—Rowland had known Proust in Paris—when he suddenly realized that everyone in the restaurant had stopped speaking and eating and was listening too.

Rowland was a unique and wonderful friend who occupied a very special place in all our lives. He kept us in touch by the letters which no one else ever seemed to have the time or the inclination to write. I miss him to this day and often think of him with great pleasure. Soon after I saw him in October 1980, he went into hospital. On Christmas Eve one of his friends brought him her usual combined Christmas and birthday gift—a round of fresh foie gras. Rowland took it and then gave it back saying, "Thank you, my dear, but this year you will have to eat it yourself. It's much too good to waste." These were his last recorded words. He died an hour and a half into his ninetieth birthday, just as he had planned.

*   *   *

The jacaranda trees were flowering in Pretoria, bathing the city in a haze of blue. The basic aim of our mission was to establish a date for starting the independence process. I took this up privately with Pik Botha and Fourie. Botha delivered a positively Wagnerian thirty-minute recitative of self-pity and indignation, saying that he was everyone's scapegoat, he was always responsible for everything, everyone hated him, his life was ruined, and, surprisingly, that he was being threatened by armed persons. I said I hoped we could help. Botha told me that he would rather have "sanctions and the lot" than be responsible for civil war in Namibia. A main problem, therefore, was how the responsibility for going ahead on Namibia could be shared in such a way that recriminations would not fall exclusively on the heads of the two Bothas, who would be fighting a national election in 1982.

I was fed up with the well-worn agenda of talks on the DMZ and "impartiality," and decided to try instead to get at the more fundamental question of sharing responsibility for the consequences of Namibian independence as a possible means of getting South Africa to agree to set a date for starting the independence process. One way of doing this would be a meeting of all the parties, including the internal Namibian political parties, to get acquainted and discuss their differences as a final step before independence.

My suggestion was that we should have a meeting of all the parties who would take part in the Namibian election process, on condition that the meeting would be held in the context of an agreed time frame for independence, starting on March 1, 1981.

The next evening, after a gargantuan cookout at the home of the new Administrator-General for Namibia, Danie Hough, Fourie and I drove somewhat unsteadily to Fourie's home, where, over further drinks, I gave him my suggestion in writing. Fourie, who was in a convivial mood, suggested a number of changes. He seemed highly enthusiastic and said he would consult his government.

The following day passed in a desultory and frustrating discussion of our regular agenda. Fourie told me that he would come to the airport to see us off the next evening, by which time he hoped to have the prime minister's reaction to my suggestion. Meanwhile the press triumphantly proclaimed the failure of the talks.

Next evening Fourie turned up at Jan Smuts Airport and handed me the text of my suggestions with his amendments incorporated into it. I pointed out once again that these would make it very difficult for the front-line states to accept. He said that he had had the greatest difficulty in getting the prime minister to agree to the text and begged me not to change it. The most surprising thing was that the time frame was still included—the first time South Africa had ever committed itself in writing, even tentatively, to a specific date for starting the Namibian independence process.

I anticipated a lot of nonsense from the young activists of the Council for Namibia in New York, but my suggestion, even as changed by Fourie, seemed worth pursuing. Martti Ahtisaari, whom I had come more and more to like and respect, gamely volunteered to set off for the front-line states to sell the idea, while I returned to New York to brief Waldheim and the Security Council. We spent the next month in a highly complex round of parallel negotiations to pin down the actual text of the suggestion and the date and place of the Pre-Implementation Meeting, or PIM, as it was now called.

SWAPO and the front-line states deeply distrusted the internal political parties of Namibia, especially the Democratic Turnhalle Alliance (DTA), which they regarded, with some reason, as a vehicle for an internal settlement along the lines that had been unsuccessfully tried with Bishop Muzorewa in Rhodesia two years before. Their desire for a Namibian settlement finally overcame their skepticism, and they went along with our plan, carrying SWAPO with them. As usual they were refreshingly sensible about the actual details of the proposal. The Western Five were enthusiastic, crediting us with a real breakthrough in Pretoria. After endless exchanges about possible locales and dates, it was agreed that the Pre-Implementation Meeting would open in Geneva on January 7, 1981.

I have no means of knowing whether, in October 1980, the South African government had any real intention of going ahead with a Namibia settlement. Certainly everyone else had, and it was generally conceded that we had, as the title of the meeting implied, pushed the matter further forward than ever before. On November 4, however, with Ronald Reagan's victory over Jimmy Carter, the pressure went out of the enterprise.

One of the concepts which surfaced even before President Reagan's inauguration was the policy of "constructive engagement" in relation to South Africa. An implication of this policy was that a tough adversary attitude, and the impatience of the UN majority, were unproductive approaches to South Africa and that a more understanding and cooperative policy would work wonders. This particularly applied to the Namibia problem, and the new administration appeared to believe that an early solution of the Namibia problem would be the first fruit of the new approach. Six years later, when the prospects of a Namibia settlement are more distant than ever and there is a rising exasperation in the United States and in the rest of the world over South Africa's intransigence on apartheid, one may question the validity of this doubtless well-intended policy. Some of us pointed out at the time that "constructive engagement" implied a very optimistic and innocent view of Afrikaner psychology and politics, but nobody wanted to listen.

The attitude of the incoming Reagan administration deflated both United States support for the Pre-Implementation Meeting and its leadership of the Western Contact group. It also signalled unmistakably to the South Africans that the future U.S. administration would not mind at all if South Africa wrecked the meeting. Any possibility of a breakthrough at Geneva had thus effectively vanished soon after United States Election Day on November 4, 1980.

We had no choice but to press on as best we could, but it was no surprise when just before the meeting the South Africans began to tell us the internal Namibian parties were reluctant to attend. I said that the meeting was largely for their benefit and they were lucky to have been asked to attend at all, but it was up to them. After all, in what other international meeting were the individual political parties of a country (seventeen of them) invited to take part? Eventually the DTA and six others overcame their reluctance.

The SWAPO delegation list included ten people who were still in jail. The Organization of African Unity sent its Secretary-General. The enthusiasm of the Western Five, on the other hand, seemed to have suddenly died after November 4. Don McHenry was particularly pessimistic, and only West Germany sent its foreign minister, Hans-Dietrich Genscher, for the opening. Genscher's presence decided Waldheim, at the last minute, to come to Geneva and open the conference.

I went to Geneva two days in advance to have a look at the practical arrangements. I was anxious to avoid any confusion at the starting line which might allow the horses to balk. Predictably enough, early on the opening day, January 7, the wrecking process began. The South African UN Ambassador, Riaan Ekstein, called me early in the morning to say that the Namibian political parties would not attend unless they had nameplates. I told him that we had been through, and agreed on, all this six weeks before. If they did not attend, everyone would draw their own conclusions. Then he called to say that South Africa wanted to sit on the Observer side with the Africans and leave only the Namibian internal parties in the South African seats, implying that they, and not South Africa, were running Namibia. I refused to agree to the South African delegation sitting with the OAU and the Africans, but finally allotted them a pewlike structure above and behind South Africa's allotted seats. This bizarre arrangement caused much amusement among the African group since the South African representatives, towering sternly above the Namibians, looked more like colonial masters than ever.

These blocking ploys having failed, Fourie arrived at the Palais at 10:00 a.m. to say that South Africa could not attend the opening meeting unless all the internal parties were allowed to make opening statements. Scraping the bottom of the barrel, I thought, but politely replied that we had been discussing the arrangements for two months, and this was obviously impossible. The front-line states had even had a special Foreign Ministers' meeting to persuade Sam Nujoma not to make an opening statement. Fourie didn't seem to have his heart in this ploy and went away.

Although the opening meeting was dignified and impressive, further blocking moves continued, and it took a full twenty-four hours to get the proper meeting started.

The Africans at the Pre-Implementation Meeting were a model of civility and common sense. Sam Nujoma was also on his best behavior and even gave an interview to the *New York Times* on the benefits of free enterprise capitalism in the independent Namibia of the future. His delegation were impeccably dressed in three- piece suits.

In contrast, the representatives of the internal parties put on a deplorable exhibition. They displayed no interest whatsoever in the subject matter of a meeting which was mostly for their benefit and indulged in preposterous diatribes against the United Nations, the front-line states, the Western Five, and SWAPO. I had to call one of them to order when he launched into a scurrilous attack on Nujoma. Nor were the South Africans, for reasons that soon became all too clear, the least interested in discussing the problems they themselves had raised about the future UN operation in Namibia. They were sulky and evasive both in public and in private. They complained about everything and seemed bent only on a negative outcome.

In order to promote contacts and good will, I had asked the Swiss government to arrange a Sunday outing, since the South Africans had told us that for religious reasons they couldn't work on that day. The Swiss provided a special train which took us to Montreux and a bus up to Glion where there was an admirable lunch, although the snowbound Alps were shrouded in mist. At my table were Sam Nujoma's chief deputy; Fourie; Administrator-General Hough and his wife; and the Zambian and Zimbabwean foreign ministers. They got on so well that at the end Mrs. Hough circulated her menu for all to sign, but I fear that this document, with the SWAPO representative's elegant and charming inscription, while undoubtedly a collector's item, will remain unique.

Dirk Mudge, the leader of the DTA delegation, sulked throughout the excursion and in the evening told the Western Five that he was no longer interested in the settlement plan because he knew he could not win the Namibian election. So much for democracy. Much to Fourie's chagrin, Mudge had given away the real South African position.

On Sunday evening, on our return from the Swiss outing, I telephoned Fourie. I found him extremely gloomy. He said that he was sick of dealing with Namibia because he always found himself in the position, after great efforts had been made, of breaking things off, and he was going to have to do it again. He saw no hope of any progress at this meeting and only wished never to have to attend another meeting on Namibia. Fourie was a decent man, and I respected his mood. His news was no surprise.

I presented Fourie with a proposal. South Africa and SWAPO would, in Geneva, initial a declaration of intent for a cease-fire starting on March 30. This would be confirmed in writing by February 10, and in the meanwhile, in order to take care of the main objection of the internal parties, the General Assembly would state that SWAPO would simply be one of the contending parties in the election as soon as the implementation of the independence plan had begun and a situation of legality prevailed. Fourie wanted to hand this paper back to me, saying it was hopeless, but I told him to keep it, at least for the South African archives.

The following day in plenary session I formally asked Administrator-General Hough to agree to the date of March 30 for the start of the independence process. He answered that it would be quite premature. That was that. In my closing statement I thanked the African front-line states and the other observers for the vast effort they had made and regretted that their will to proceed in a civilized manner had not been reciprocated. To the press I said that a great opportunity had been missed (which I believed) and that the word "premature" did not bang the door forever on a Namibian settlement (which I was far less sure about).

Soon after I got back to New York, two meetings threw light on what had happened in Geneva. The first was on a Saturday afternoon in late February with Mrs. Thatcher, who had come from Washington quite intoxicated by the heady new wine of Reaganism. She was going on about not giving ground to the Soviet Union when Waldheim brought up the question of Namibia. Mrs. Thatcher said she would like to play the devil's advocate and expressed anxiety that if the Namibia problem was solved, the African states would turn all of their attention to South Africa and apartheid. She appeared to think, anticipating the Reagan administration's future policy, that the Cubans ought to leave Angola and that the Russians should stop giving aid to the Angolans *before* any Namibian settlement. She ignored the fact that South African raids into Angola from Namibia and South Africa's military support for Savimbi's insurgency were the main reasons for the Cuban presence in Angola.

Two days later the new Secretary of State, Alexander Haig, came to see us. He seemed to see every international problem through the cold warrior's telescope, an instrument which does not contribute to a clear view of issues like Namibia. Haig said the United States had no intention of allowing "the Hammer and Sickle to fly over Windhoek," and would not be a party to installing a Marxist-Leninist government in Namibia. I doubted if Nujoma would know a Marxist-Leninist idea if he met one in the street, but, like most liberation leaders, he would take help from wherever he could get it. According to Haig, the Cubans were in Angola as part of Soviet imperial strategy, and not because the Angolans desperately needed them in their struggle against Savimbi and South African cross-border raids. Like the South Africans, Haig evidently was not prepared to tolerate an internationally supervised election in Namibia which might result in a SWAPO victory. This effectively removed U.S. support for the Western plan for Namibia of which the United States had been a principal author. No wonder the South Africans had so unceremoniously trashed the Geneva meeting.

The United States "reviewed" its policy on Namibia for some time and then pronounced the "linkage" policy, making the departure of the Cubans from Angola a prerequisite for the solution of the Namibia problem. South Africa was thus provided with the perfect self-perpetuating obstacle to progress, since the Cuban presence was directly related to South Africa's activities from Namibia against Angola. "Constructive engagement" has so far provided no progress toward Namibian independence, nor indeed the basis for an effective approach to the deeper problem of apartheid. Meanwhile the African states and the hard-pressed people of Namibia wait patiently but with increasing skepticism.*

*One of the early results of improved East-West relations after 1987 was the successful implementation of the United Nations plan for Namibian independence, which had been stalled since 1978. With the United States and the Soviet Union cooperating, agreement was reached on both the independence plan and the progressive withdrawal of the Cuban forces from Angola. The independence process, supervised by the large United Nations civilian and military operation which we had planned between 1978 and 1980, began on 1 April 1989 and concluded triumphantly with the independence of Namibia in March 1990.

XXIV

Alarms and Excursions
in the Gulf and Middle East

THE CAPTIVITY OF THE American Embassy hostages in Iran lasted from November 4, 1979, until the first day of the Reagan administration in January 1981. On the day the hostages were taken, Cyrus Vance happened to be visiting Waldheim, who asked him if there was anything we could do to help. Vance replied that there were signs that a solution was at hand and politely declined Waldheim's offer. Unfortunately Vance was wrong. The crisis dominated the last year of the Carter administration and crippled Carter in the 1980 presidential election. The zealots of Teheran had discovered that they could punish the head of the most powerful government in the world.

In Iran we were dealing, or trying to deal, with a new phenomenon, a modern theocracy in which no individual took responsibility and where international practice and normal rules of behavior meant little or nothing at all. Waldheim tried very hard to help, immediately sending an appeal to the Ayatollah Khomeini to release the hostages in compliance with international law and the Vienna Convention on diplomats. Two weeks later, when it became clear that no negotiated solution was in sight, Waldheim called for a Security Council meeting under Article 99 of the Charter, which authorizes the Secretary-General to bring to the Council any matter he believes to be a threat to international peace. The Council was held up, first by the delay in the arrival of the Iranian foreign minister, Abolhassan Bani-Sadr, and then by his dismissal by Khomeini. Bani-Sadr was replaced by Sadegh Ghotbzadeh, who lost no time in saying he would *not* be coming to New York. Waldheim was thus reduced to trying, day and night, to reach Ghotbzadeh on the telephone. One of the things I remember from this time is the seemingly limitless variety of pronunciations he gave to the new foreign minister's name.

The Security Council voted for the immediate release of the hostages, but we did not escape the customary rhetoric, in the U.S. Congress and in the media, about the United Nations being on trial in this matter. Quite for what, or for whose mistake, was not specified. Our main preoccupation was to do anything possible to gain the release of the hostages and to avoid a situation in which the United States, in an election year, would feel impelled to use force, a course that might well be fatal for the hostages. The trouble was that no one—not the Secretary-General nor the Islamic States nor the Non-Aligned nor the PLO nor anyone else—could find a way of approaching the Ayatollah Khomeini and the Iranian Revolutionary Council that was likely to have any positive results.

Just before Christmas the United States announced that it would press for sanctions against Iran. Few people believed this would do much for the hostages, but the Carter administration evidently felt obliged to try to show some muscle. This development certainly did not help Waldheim's efforts to create conditions for a useful visit to Teheran. The United States then switched signals and said that it would not press for sanctions immediately but would request Waldheim to intensify his efforts and visit Iran. If that failed, the United States would demand sanctions. This self-defeating proposition, published by the *New York Times* and the BBC, compromised Waldheim's intended visit to Teheran in advance and infuriated the Iranians. However, there was no turning back, and on December 30 a grudging message was received that Waldheim could come to Teheran if he wanted. He left the next day.

The omens for this visit could scarcely have been less favorable, the visit itself even worse, and the reporting on it in the Western press lamentable. I felt very sorry for Waldheim on this occasion. He had no illusions about what he was getting into and could at best hope to open up a reliable channel for negotiations with the Iranians, a hope which United States statements had already put in doubt. Other cards were also stacked against him. It was only two years since his official visit to the Shah, and enlarged photos of Waldheim kissing Princess Ashraf's hand were displayed on placards all over Teheran. Old World Austrian courtesy can be hazardous to your health.

Waldheim had an appalling time in Teheran, being bundled from place to place in a mob of weapon-toting zealots. When visiting a cemetery, as required by his hosts, he was chased by a hostile mob and only just made it to the helicopter. A photograph of this episode showing Waldheim looking alarmed was much criticized. It seemed to me he had every *right* to look scared. His hosts required him to spend much time inspecting amputees and other victims of SAVAK. He saw the Revolutionary Council under chaotic conditions in near darkness and got nowhere with them or anyone else. At the end of it all he was blamed for timidity, opportunism, and, a little later on, for having made concessions unfavorable to the United States position. Carter and Vance publicly supported him and were grateful, but their voices were drowned out by the Iranian mob and the Western media, who seemed delighted to have someone new to blame.

Except as a general adviser I had little to do with the hostage crisis. Waldheim continued to try to find a way into the problem. He appointed a commission which visited Iran to look into the human rights and other abuses of the Shah. The efforts of the Islamic Conference were stymied. The aborted American rescue expedition, Desert I, came and went. The Algerians played a helpful role, and in the end a scenario of great complication, focused on negotiating financial assets, was agreed to. A main Iranian objective seemed to be the humiliation of the incumbent President of the United States, who had mourned and striven and fretted. When that possibility ran out, the hostages were released.

One advantage of the UN in normal times is that it provides a forum where there are considerable possibilities of changing the stand of governments through a process of face-saving. In the hostage crisis we were not dealing with a government in any normal sense of the term; and a militant theocracy does not find face-saving necessary.

*   *   *

On September 22, 1980, Iraq invaded Iran in a dramatic escalation of the long-standing enmity between the two countries. The hostage situation and Islamic revolutionary fervor in Iran were at their height, and few governments were well disposed toward Iran. On the other hand the Iraqi action was a clear and massive violation of the sovereignty of another state which should, if only as a matter of principle, have immediately been denounced as such. As it was, it was impossible to avoid the conclusion that the members of the Security Council, under strong Iraqi pressure, were sitting on their hands hoping that the Iraqi victory would be quick and total. This attitude, apart from being unprincipled, was based on a serious underestimate of the strength, both physical and psychological, of the Khomeini regime.

Waldheim, to his credit, called for Security Council consultations the day after the Iraqi invasion, and again two days later. These informal meetings dragged on in a depressing and undignified way, mostly late at night, as, under Iraqi pressure, the Council put off a public meeting or a vote on the war. The Security Council had seldom seemed less worthy of respect.

In the plummy rhetoric of visiting ministers, a foreign minister had recently referred to the Council as "this awesome organ," and the British Ambassador, Tony Parsons, and I had adopted this appellation in our talks about the business of the Council. In the midst of all the spineless pettifogging, in a meeting one night I wrote:

> We are the Awesome Organ,
> A famous sight to see.
> We cannot meet, we cannot vote;
> What bloody use are we?
> And when we reach the Chamber
> The combatants will say,
> "The war was over long ago,
> So, Organ, go away."

I was wrong in my estimate of the duration of the war, but right about the pusillanimity of the Council. When the Council finally did pass a resolution asking for a cease-fire, it did not demand the withdrawal of the invading Iraqi forces, thus ensuring that Iran would not take the Council seriously in the future.

The early belief in a quick Iraqi triumph soon gave way to a deadly stalemate in which vast numbers of young lives were lost in futile and bloody battles. Efforts to get a cease-fire continued. Olof Palme became the Secretary-General's representative for this purpose and put a series of proposals on the table, where they have lain to this day. The fact was that no negotiating process could curb a war in which the egos and the mutual hatred of the two leaders were decisive factors.

The international community was too divided and too intent on its various short-term national interests to consider using the Charter provisions for dealing with threats to the peace. These include arms embargoes and trade embargoes. It is an interesting reflection on the decline of a sense of common purpose in matters of peace and security, that the Security Council has never even considered the possibility of taking cooperative measures to put an end to a bloody and pointless war in a very sensitive region of the world. Instead, the ball was left in the Secretary-General's court.*

*Only in July 1987 did the five permanent members of the Security Council propound, and the Council unanimously adopt, a resolution demanding the end of the war. The fighting

*   *   *

The triumphant return of the hostages from Iran was the first dramatic event of the Reagan administration. Less enchanting was the ideological approach to internationalism, and to foreign affairs generally, which appeared to inspire the new administration. The effort to construct an international system which will begin to measure up to the daunting realities of the late twentieth century has constantly been assailed and eroded by lesser governments. The Soviet bloc had never shown any real willingness to assist in developing an active and effective international system, and in the Secretariat we had long ago learned not to expect much help or support from the Soviets. The support of the United States in this enterprise, of which it was the principal initiator, had always been taken for granted.

The attitude of the Reagan administration became clear early in 1981. The Western plan for Namibia had already suffered a major setback. The United States disowned the Law of the Sea Treaty, a remarkable feat of international negotiation in which the United States had, for nearly ten years, played a leading role. SALT II was put on hold. The United Nations Charter itself and the International Court of Justice seemed unlikely to be immune to this ideological tide. The attack on UNESCO, an agency which certainly deserved stringent criticism, was thought by some to be a rehearsal for an assault on the United Nations system as a whole. In Reagan's Washington there seemed to be an open season on a variety of multilateral or international arrangements which were the fruit of years of painstaking work and negotiation. Some neo-conservative ideologues even advocated the virtues of "global unilateralism" for the United States.

In the United Nations, as in most large representative bodies, there are many excesses, idiocies, and extravaganzas of bloc voting and logrolling, which tend to obscure the essential constructive work the UN does all over the world. The United States, the richest and most powerful country in the world, is an easy mark for the disgruntled and underprivileged, and rhetoric of a mindless anti-American kind is often the last refuge of the destitute. A large Soviet presence in New York, in the Secretariat as well as in the Soviet Mission, and the abuse of their privileged status for espionage activities by some of its members, were a worry and an irritation which the United States rightly resented, although the use of embassies for espionage is hardly a practice confined to the

---

ceased with a UN-supervised ceasefire in August 1988. In the post–Cold War climate of August 1990, when Iraq swallowed Kuwait, a united Security Council immediately imposed sanctions on Iraq.

Soviet bloc. The anti-Israeli stance of the majority in the United Nations, and such idiocies as the Zionism-Racism Resolution, also provided invaluable ammunition to the ideological enemies of internationalism and the United Nations.

On the other hand, as a global power the United States has an abiding interest in international stability and has traditionally used the United Nations very effectively to deal with international problems it could not easily handle by itself. It also has an abiding interest in establishing an effective international system for peace and security, no matter how frustrating this task may be. The United Nations, and particularly the Security Council and the Secretary-General—although powerful governments do not like to admit it—have proved to be an invaluable last resort, safety net, and face-saving device when the great nuclear powers find themselves on a collision course. The United States also has a long and successful record of using the United Nations to rally and to lead an effective international constituency on a wide range of global problems.

The Reagan administration and its first Ambassador to the United Nations, Jeane Kirkpatrick, were evidently not overly impressed by these considerations. They seemed to view the United Nations as a troublesome sideshow, although Reagan made use of the platform of the General Assembly every year, and the United States was glad enough to have the Secretary-General handle impossible assignments like Afghanistan, the Iran-Iraq War, or Cyprus. The conservative right apparently believed that if the UN was not effectively dominated by the United States, did not respond unquestioningly to United States values or priorities, and failed to function as a bastion against the Soviet Union, it was not the international organization the United States ought to belong to. The perception of a hostile, anti-American Third World majority in the United Nations also militated strongly against the Reagan administration's using the UN to exert leadership and to rally a worldwide constituency on important global problems.

Ambassador Kirkpatrick and her chosen associates in the United States Mission seemed to see themselves primarily as embattled defenders of the faith, venturing out from their fortress in the U.S. Mission mostly to do battle with the infidel, to chastise offenders, and to worry about the loyalty of putative allies. They did not associate with the Third World and other representatives, as George Bush or William Scranton or Andy Young or Don McHenry had done, making friends for the United States and building an international constituency. They seemed to be more preoccupied with punishing reprehensible behavior or trying to score points off the Soviet Union. Certainly the wanton abuse of the United

States by some countries was justly resented in Washington, but a great power needs a more positive and self-confident policy if it is to establish respect for its international leadership and use the international system to its advantage.

Jeane Kirkpatrick had an extraordinarily difficult task, being required as a member of the United States Cabinet to spend much of her time in Washington or on the road making speeches. Of all the ambassadors at the United Nations, she had the least time or opportunity to get to know and work with her colleagues in the diplomatic community. The press seemed determined to portray her as the dragon lady of the extreme right, which was both inaccurate and unhelpful. On some matters, the Middle East, for example, she held rigid and rather extreme views. On many other subjects she was open-minded.

*   *   *

On June 7, 1981, the Israeli Air Force destroyed a nuclear reactor on the outskirts of Baghdad. Even by Israeli standards of military enterprise, this feat set a new and dangerous precedent. Bombing Palestinian targets in Lebanon was one thing; knocking out a nuclear reactor built by the French in Iraq was another. Even the most devoted supporters of Israel had difficulty in accepting the concept of one country demolishing, in another country, an installation which conceivably might, at some unforeseeable point in the future, constitute a threat to its security. Virtually all governments, including the United States, denounced the Israeli action.

Israeli credibility was further eroded by various statements by Begin which were easily shown to be untrue—that Iraq had refused inspection of its reactor by the International Atomic Energy Agency, for example, or that there was in the reactor "a secret underground chamber" for making bombs. Begin also quoted Saddam Hussein as saying that the reactor was for use against Israel, not Iran, a remark which the Iraqi leader had never made.

The Iraqis reacted slowly to this stunning attack, and only five days after the raid did the Iraqi foreign minister, Sa'adoum Hammadi, arrive in New York. Waldheim was still in China, the Chinese vote being crucial for his reelection. The Iraqis were surprisingly moderate in their presentation to the Security Council and evidently did not want an extreme resolution which the United States would veto, an outcome which extremists on all sides would have preferred. When Waldheim finally returned, I suggested that we should at least try to get Hammadi and Ambassador Kirkpatrick together, and I sounded them both out. Jeane

Kirkpatrick called Washington and quickly agreed. Hammadi at first said that he was a foreign minister and didn't deal with ambassadors, but when I pointed out that Ambassador Kirkpatrick was a Cabinet member in the world's most powerful government, he sought for, and finally got, authority to meet with her provided that a third party was present.

The meetings in Waldheim's office went surprisingly well. Both Kirkpatrick and Hammadi were reserved and somewhat shy by nature, but they seemed from the beginning to understand each other. The problem was a paragraph in the draft resolution which demanded an arms embargo on Israel, something the United States would never accept. I had assumed that this difficulty would be insurmountable and was prepared for the Kirkpatrick-Hammadi talks to break down, when Hammadi, as he was getting up to leave, said, "Very well. Since we can't agree on paragraph 2 [sanctions], let's drop it completely." This surprisingly sensible move allowed the resolution to be adopted unanimously.

This outcome was widely interpreted as a considerable triumph for Jeane Kirkpatrick. President Reagan referred to her as one of the greatest diplomats of the age, although muffled explosions were reported from the South Pacific, where Alexander Haig was apparently less impressed. The Soviets didn't like it either, and the Israelis were furious. "Jeane Kirkpatrick: Joining the Jackals," ran *The Jerusalem Post* headline on a story telling the readers that Kirkpatrick "has suddenly become the darling of the Third World." She had "helped to turn an Israeli military triumph into a diplomatic disaster." Ambassador Kirkpatrick said that she was surprised at the violent reactions she had been getting, even from many of her own friends. She was evidently sharing a dismaying experience which is familiar to anyone who has found it necessary to disagree on serious matters with Israel.

*   *   *

The news of President Sadat's assassination at a military parade in Cairo came over the radio early on Tuesday, October 6, 1981. It was first rumored that he was not gravely hurt, and only several hours later did the Egyptian government finally announce his death. He had, in fact, been killed instantly.

The tragedy of Sadat's death, and the reminder of the deadly risks a man of peace runs in the Middle East, brought out the worst in many quarters at the United Nations. A luncheon at the Waldorf by the foreign minister of Bahrain went ahead as if nothing had happened, and during the after-lunch speeches only Waldheim mentioned Sadat's death. The

Arabs tried to prevent any commemorative ceremony in the General Assembly. Ismat Kittani of Iraq, as President of the Assembly, found himself in the middle but decided to have the usual ceremony for the demise of a head of state, in which there are speeches by the Secretary-General, the different regional groups, the host country, and anyone else who wishes to speak. All the Arabs except Tunisia and Oman absented themselves from this occasion. I commented to the Syrians, Saudis, and Lebanese that it seemed ironical that they should not wish to honor a man who was killed at a ceremony commemorating the only time (the October War) when an Arab state had fought successfully to regain territory occupied by Israel. They looked suitably woebegone, and Tueni said that for an Arab ambassador to be photographed in a ceremony commemorating Sadat not only invited assassination but could threaten the stability of his government. Such was the level of rationality in the Middle East.

The Arabs were not alone in unseemly reactions to the tragedy. It is customary on such occasions for the United States as host country to speak first after the representatives of regional groups. On this occasion, however, Yehuda Blum, the Israeli Ambassador, prevailed on Jeane Kirkpatrick to let Israel speak first to emphasize Israel's close relationship to Egypt, a gesture scarcely helpful to Hosni Mubarak, the new President of Egypt.

The arrangements for attending the funeral provided the opportunity for more indecorous behavior. Waldheim decided to send the head of the European Office, Ambassador Luigi Cottafavi; Aly Teymour, our Egyptian Chief of Protocol; and General Alex Erskine, the Chief of Staff of UNTSO. This decision drew fire from all sides. The *New York Post* accused Waldheim of "treachery," presumably for not going himself, while my Soviet colleague called me and objected violently to *anyone* going, especially General Erskine. When I pointed out to him that it would be inconceivable, not to mention indecent, for the Secretary-General not to be represented at the funeral of a head of state and that General Erskine had some thirty Military Observers in Egypt of whom fifteen were Soviet officers, he subsided.

There was nothing half-hearted about the American and Israeli response to the funeral. The United States sent Secretary of State Haig, Secretary of Defense Weinberger, Ambassador Kirkpatrick, ex-presidents Ford, Carter, and Nixon, Henry Kissinger, and a covey of congressmen. Begin also attended. Neither Begin nor the American delegation were shown on Egyptian television. While in Cairo, Alexander Haig emitted a series of "warnings" about the U.S. response to anyone who meddled in Egyptian affairs. In all this posturing, I felt deeply sorry for President Mubarak.

These sad goings-on were a poignant reminder of the bloodthirstiness, pettiness, short-sightedness, and lack of tolerance or understanding which particularly bedevil the Middle East question. I had, and have, considerable respect for all the parties to this infinitely difficult and tragic problem, but affairs like Sadat's assassination and funeral test one's respect to the utmost.

*   *   *

Waldheim's travel program for 1981 left no doubt that he was hellbent on running for a third term. He did not discuss this with me because I had long ago expressed my negative views about a second term, let alone a third one. I therefore continued to deal with Waldheim Mark II, the dedicated, far-seeing public servant and statesman, while my colleagues fretted under Waldheim Mark I, the scheming and obsessively ambitious bureaucrat. During the Assembly session Waldheim's performance became a general joke, as he buttonholed and cajoled and wheedled everyone in sight. Ministers and diplomats scurried nervously along the corridors, dreading the familiar grasp of the Secretary-General's hand on their elbow. We seemed to be in a different century from the time when Dag Hammarskjold was the last person to hear of his own nomination as Secretary-General. Waldheim's blind ambition for public office showed an astonishing lack both of self-respect and of concern for the reputation of the United Nations.

His main opponent, as in 1976, was the foreign minister of Tanzania, Salim Salim. I had a lot of respect for Salim, with whom I had worked for years, especially over Namibia, and I believe he would have made a good Secretary-General, for he was capable of a broad statesmanlike view. I remember his reaction, later on, to the Nkomati agreement between South Africa and Mozambique. We were together at a conference in Arusha, Tanzania, and Western journalists were needling Salim to denounce the pact as a breach of the common African front against South Africa. Salim resolutely refused to do this, saying that while Tanzania might well be against such a move in principle, Mozambique was in a different, and extremely difficult, situation, and if his brothers there felt the pact was necessary, then he fully supported them. I thought of the contrast between this realistic, generous view and the attitude of the Arabs to Sadat.

Salim was subject to the veto of the United States, which was supporting Waldheim. Tanzania was a "radical" African state in Washington's eyes, and Salim was also associated in American folk memory with the alleged "victory dance" in the aisles of the General Assembly which had discomfited George Bush when the United States lost the vote to exclude the People's Republic of China in 1971. The Soviets were also supporting Waldheim, saying, not too flatteringly, that an old shoe often fits best. The British had declared for Waldheim but would not veto Salim. China's support of Salim meant that it would almost certainly maintain its veto against Waldheim, so a long and debilitating deadlock was likely. This only caused the two antagonists to redouble their efforts, while an improbable crop of opportunist candidates also entered the lists. The issue began to monopolize people's attention and became an indecorous bore.

There were other candidates who would have done the job well, but they too were stymied by predictable vetoes. Shridath Ramphal, the Secretary-General of the Commonwealth, had the qualities of intellect, ability, and experience to recommend him for the job, but he came from Guyana, a "radical" Third World country, thus ensuring a U.S. veto, while his association with the British Commonwealth invited a Soviet veto. Sadruddin Aga Khan, who had just finished a long and effective stint as UN High Commissioner for Refugees, also had outstanding qualifications of ability and experience, but apparently had no hope of evading a Soviet veto. Both men would have been independent internationalists in the Hammarskjold tradition—a prospect certainly not welcome to the Soviet Union, and possibly not to other great powers either.

By late October, when it became clear that the Chinese were not going to stop vetoing Waldheim and the Americans were not going to stop vetoing Salim, Waldheim was prevailed on to withdraw from the voting. Salim followed suit a week later. Fortunately for the United Nations, Olara Otunnu, the brilliant young Ugandan Ambassador, was President of the Security Council for December, and he set about solving the impasse in the Council in a dignified and effective way. He conducted a straw poll among the members to discover which of the, by then, nine candidates was a real possibility and then asked the permanent members to indicate which names they would veto. This eliminated some highly unsuitable candidates and soon led to the nomination of Javier Perez de Cuellar of Peru.

I had known Perez de Cuellar well for many years. After a time as Peruvian Ambassador to the UN, he had spent two years as our Special Representative in Cyprus and had then become my opposite number as

Under Secretary-General for Special Political Affairs. He was well qualified by experience and ability—a quiet, highly intelligent, and civilized man with a wide knowledge of the job he was undertaking. Whether he was *too* civilized, or too lacking in ego or cutting edge, remained to be seen. The fact was that out of an apparently hopeless situation, a reasonable and qualified Secretary-General had emerged.

XXV

1982: A Dismal Year

JAVIER PEREZ DE CUELLAR took up his post on January 1, 1982, living at the Waldorf-Astoria for some weeks until his predecessor reluctantly got out of the official residence. I offered Perez de Cuellar my resignation in order to give him a free hand with appointments. I was nearly sixty-three and had had a long run. He refused this offer and said that he counted on me to stay.

Working with Javier was a considerable contrast to the previous ten years. He was a quiet, serious person who knew who he was, had no pretensions or election debts, and wanted to get on with the job, which he already knew a great deal about. He liked short and decisive conversations, and was uninterested (perhaps too much so) in his public "image," which saved a great deal of time. With him I never felt the embarrassment or apprehension I had sometimes experienced when listening to Waldheim talking to visitors. I hoped very much that he would be able to establish general confidence quickly so that he could achieve some progress, especially on Namibia, Afghanistan, Cyprus, and even on the Middle East. He had taken over at an inauspicious point in the history of the United Nations, when the organization was discredited and under attack in the United States and other countries at the very moment that several serious international storms were threatening. The year 1982 was, in every way, one of the most disagreeable I can remember.

Lebanon and the situation of UNIFIL were very much on our minds. Although the cease-fire in southern Lebanon was holding, important elements in the Israeli government obviously still wanted to settle scores with the PLO once and for all, before it became militarily more effective or politically more respectable. Ariel Sharon's Defense Ministry was undoubtedly in an aggressive, opportunistic mood.

Another worry was that it now only seemed possible to get the U.S. government to pay attention to Lebanon for the wrong reasons. We had visited Washington in April 1981, just after the Israelis had shot down two Syrian helicopters in the Beka'a Valley and the Syrians had caused a stir by moving up SAM-6 anti-aircraft missiles. Because virtually all the weapons of the Syrian Army, for lack of other available sources of supply, were Russian, Haig seemed to believe that this was a sinister Soviet move. It was useless to try to explain that the Lebanese situation had terrible imperatives of its own and had very little to do with superpower rivalry.

In December 1981, Israel had announced its annexation of the Golan Heights, thus formally extending its law, jurisdiction, and administration over the territory it had captured from Syria in the 1967 war. In May 1982, Begin declared that Israel would assert its sovereignty over the West Bank at the end of the five-year transitional period specified in the Camp David Accords. There was no question that the mood which had prompted the attack on the Iraqi reactor still prevailed in Israel. Nor was there much doubt that Lebanon had a place in this program. In a speech on Israel's strategic problems in December 1981, Sharon had stated, "We will prevent any violation of the status quo ante in South Lebanon," adding, "The PLO poses a *political* [my italics] threat to the very existence of the State of Israel." There was little doubt about Sharon's intentions. The question was *when*.

At the end of January 1982, I went to the Middle East to see what could be done on our side to preempt a development which would almost certainly be disastrous for all concerned. I had never felt less like undertaking an effort of this kind. I was deeply depressed and was also suffering a paralysis of the vocal chords of undiagnosed origin. I felt awful and could only speak in a whisper.

After two routine days in Cyprus, I arrived in Beirut in torrential rain on February 2. There was little to discuss with Foreign Minister Boutros and the prime minister, Shafik Wazzan. The main object of my trip was in Israel, and the Lebanese could do nothing to influence events. They were mostly anxious that I should insist on the Syrians, the PLO, and the Israelis doing things they had no intention of doing. President Sarkis was his usual mournful self, saying over and over again, "C'est le désespoir, Monsieur Urquhart." I couldn't have agreed with him more. He certainly had one of the world's more impossible jobs.

Sarkis observed that the Lebanese problem could only be resolved in Moscow, Washington, and Tel Aviv, and that no one in any of those places gave a damn about Lebanon. He was right. At a charming dinner given by the Lebanese defense minister, I was told by the British Ambassador, with that air of complete authority which only simpletons and autocrats enjoy, that the only solution to the Lebanese problem was for UNIFIL to "fight its way to the border." He had, he said, made strong recommendations on these lines to "HMG." I said it was a pity there wasn't a British contingent in UNIFIL.

In Damascus it was my habit to escape when possible from the rigors of Syrian official hospitality to the Souk in order to walk around and buy rugs. That ancient rabbit warren of a marketplace, with the great Omayad Mosque and the relics of so many civilizations embalmed in the smell of spices and herbs, is a wonderfully soothing environment. The atmosphere in Damascus was tense and the Souk nearly deserted. It was said that there had been an attempted coup ten days earlier, and the plainclothes security men of Rifat Assad, the president's brother, were everywhere in evidence. Our Force Headquarters was surrounded on three sides by one of Rifat Assad's establishments, which contained, among other things, a veritable showcase of exotic foreign cars—Rolls-Royce, Ferrari, Mercedes, Volvo, Jaguar, and others, side by side. My main job in Damascus was to deal with the chaotic situation in our Golan Heights peacekeeping force (UNDOF) Headquarters. The general was a soggy, drunken disaster, the staff at each other's throats, and the Syrians incredulous. Before I left, I told the general that the situation was intolerable and that he would be recalled immediately.

I had to return to Beirut from Damascus to see Arafat. There was a heavy snowstorm at the airport, and our veteran Swiss pilot, Captain Willi Jetzer, one of the best and most resourceful pilots in the Middle East, was, for once, pessimistic. He was right, for we ran the full length of the runway without lifting off and came to a screeching halt with engines reversed at the very end. In the minutes that we had been taxiing to the takeoff point after receiving clearance, the temperature had dropped below freezing and frozen the snow on the wings. Jetzer summoned the airport fire engine to hose the aircraft down, and we eventually took off. It got colder and colder in the passenger cabin, and Jetzer reported the outside temperature as 40 degrees below zero. Water had frozen in the air ducts of the heating system, and the cabin had no heat. I remembered the cook on the *Titanic*, who had survived the icy ocean by drinking a whole bottle of rum, and mentioned this through chattering teeth to Jean-Claude Aimé, my director for the Middle East. Jean-Claude is a marvelous companion, humorous, calm, and courageous. He is never better than in a tight corner and has been in many all over the world. He produced a large bottle of Canadian Club whiskey, and we arrived in Beirut chilled but in high spirits. I explained to Arafat, a teetotaller, that we had had to choose between arriving drunk or dead.

I had fifty minutes alone with Arafat before our long formal meeting. He seemed cheerful and said he had nothing to lose, although he was expecting to be assassinated any minute by the Syrians. He was at his most forthcoming about South Lebanon and had good reason to be. He asked me to pass on to the Israelis (and to the Americans, if I thought fit) a message consisting of several points. He didn't like violence any more than anyone else, although before the Palestinians took up the gun no one had paid the smallest attention to them; he was totally committed to the cease-fire in southern Lebanon; he had said, at great risk to himself, that the Palestinians would establish their state in the occupied areas Israel withdrew from—why did no one take this seriously? As a Palestinian moderate, his life was now in grave danger, and the Americans and Israelis would certainly find any successor to the leadership of the PLO far more difficult to deal with. I undertook to deliver his message.

Arafat's attitude reflected both his anticipation of dramatic Israeli action to destroy the PLO and his own preference for a peaceful settlement, if only he could survive to negotiate it. Liberation leaders must usually run a double track, on the one hand sincerely desiring to negotiate a settlement, but on the other having to maintain the violent option to rally their followers and to keep the attention of the outside world. I respected Arafat's courage and resilience, however exasperating his double-track activities might be. He was to some extent a play-actor, as exiled liberation leaders have to be, having little but their histrionic talents to work with. His real trouble, if he was ever accepted as a negotiator by the United States and Israel, would be whether he could deliver results. His acceptance as a negotiator by the United States and Israel would in one way strengthen his position, but it would also inevitably strengthen the fanaticism of those who would see him as a traitor to the armed struggle. To accept him as a negotiator would be a gamble—for him and for everyone else. In any case, in February 1982, these thoughts were purely hypothetical.

After a brief visit to Jordan, where King Hussein and my old friends in Amman were deeply worried about Israeli adventurism, the lack of a coherent American policy, and the Gulf War, I drove over the King Hussein Bridge to the West Bank and Jerusalem. After the General Assembly's condemnation, two days before, of Israel's annexation of the Golan Heights, I had expected a cool reception in Israel, but I was welcomed with warmth and friendliness. I have always enjoyed talking to the Israelis even when we disagreed, which was a lot of the time. There is no country where controversy and differences of view are so much a vital part of national life.

I had an informative lunch with David Kimche, the Director-General of the Foreign Office, who was, at this time, the main connection between the visible and the invisible government of Israel, the government itself, and the forces which were pushing it into action. I asked him why on earth the formal annexation of the Golan Heights had been necessary, and he explained that it was a domestic measure designed to disarm the efforts of the extreme-rightist Geula Cohen, and the Gush Emunim, to sabotage the Israeli evacuation of Sinai under the Peace Treaty with Egypt. I commented that other governments might find it hard to understand the annexation of one country's territory in order to justify the relinquishment of another's.

I had the usual courteous but wooden talk with Shamir, who ignored the Palestinian dimension and was pinning all hopes on the Camp David process. I visited Begin for an hour. David Kimche had advised me not to deliver Arafat's message but I saw no reason not to do so. Begin was friendly though obviously in pain, having recently broken his hip. I delivered the substance of Arafat's message, saying that we were all united by our humanity and I felt obliged, as one who knew him, to give a picture of Arafat which Begin was otherwise unlikely to get. I do not know what effect, if any, this had on Begin. He listened to me politely and even with a touch of interest. Such efforts probably have little effect on men who deal in historical absolutes, but at least I had done what I said I would do.

For the rest, Begin praised our peacekeeping operations and even said how useful he thought UNIFIL was. In the light of what subsequently happened I have no idea what this meant. I told Begin, with as much emphasis as I could manage with no voice, that I believed the current situation in southern Lebanon, with the cease-fire being supervised by UNIFIL, was a great deal better than anything else Israel was likely to get on its northern border. I urged him to consider this point of view seriously.

Next day I went to see the defense minister, Ariel Sharon. I had received much cautionary advice on how to deal with Sharon, as if he were some sacred monster who might suddenly bite off your head. Actually Sharon was perfectly reasonable and gave a lucid and masterly exposition of Israeli defense policy. I brought up southern Lebanon and urged that he should consider carefully the advantages of UNIFIL and the cease-fire over other, ostensibly more dashing, approaches which would have unpredictable and bloody results. He said over and over again that Israel had no wish or intention to undertake military operations anywhere. Israel would, however, react strongly if attacked or provoked, because, as a small country, it had no other choice. I mentioned that the present Israeli government, and he especially, were viewed with great apprehension and suspicion on the other side, and that his recent speech on Israel's strategic problems was required reading in Arab capitals as a blueprint for Israeli expansionism. Sharon firmly denied any such intention and even made some positive remarks about UN peacekeeping operations, but I did not have any illusions that my arguments had made much, or indeed any, impression on him.

I was not happy with this trip. Everyone in the Middle East seemed determined to think the worst of everyone else and to ignore the intermediary possibilities of the United Nations. The main powers of East and West were at loggerheads, and no useful restraining action could be expected of them. The Arabs were divided, negative, and self-defeating, the United States incoherent, and the Israelis in an opportunistic and aggressive mood. The outlook in the Middle East was bleak.

*   *   *

On April 2, 1982, the British Ambassador informed us that the Argentinian fleet had left Buenos Aires for the Falkland Islands. Perez de Cuellar immediately called on the Argentinians and the British for restraint. The Argentinians landed at dawn the next day, easily overrunning the tiny British garrison, and the war was on—a war on the time scale of the nineteenth century, fought with twentieth-century weapons. It was inexplicable that the British government, knowing that the unstable junta in Buenos Aires needed a patriotic victory, should have taken no serious measures to protect the Falklands or South Georgia. Successive British governments had certainly been less than enthusiastic about the costly and unrewarding commitment to some 1,800 sheep farmers on these desolate and distant islands, but a determined local lobby had sidetracked all efforts to do a deal with Argentina. Now national honor was involved, and it was too late. Peter Carrington, the best man in the Thatcher government, insisted on resigning as Foreign Secretary because he felt that someone must take public responsibility for a disastrous oversight.

A mood of flag-waving jingoism quickly enveloped both Britain and Argentina. Serious principles, however, were involved—the Charter prohibition on acquiring territory by force and the principles of sovereignty and self-determination. The inhabitants of the Falklands unquestionably wished to remain under the British flag.

The British wisely brought the matter to the Security Council on the very Saturday of the Argentinian landing and secured, by a narrow margin of 10 votes, a resolution calling on Argentina to withdraw immediately and for all sides to refrain from force and enter into negotiations. But for the speed of this action and the brilliant management of the British case in the Council by Sir Anthony Parsons, it is unlikely that the British would have obtained this essential underpinning for their future action. A day or two later the uncertain majority for the British position would have disintegrated. Even United States support was in some doubt, and Ambassador Kirkpatrick had initially told Parsons that she would try to block any effort to bring the question to the Security Council. Sidney and I were staying that weekend with the British Ambassador in Washington, Nicho Henderson, who was engaged in an intensive and ultimately successful effort to pin down United States support for the British position.

The British fleet was seen off by crowds waving Union Jacks. It was to be joined later on by troop-carrying vessels, including the liner *Queen Elizabeth 2*. It was believed that the fleet would take two weeks to reach the Falklands.

Alexander Haig sprang to life as a mediator, but shuttling between Washington, London, and Buenos Aires was very different from the short laps of the Middle East and allowed arrangements to come unstuck while he was in transit to the next point. In any case the jingoistic mood in both countries made it highly unlikely that their leaders would, at this point, be amenable to diplomacy.

The British fleet finally reached the war zone on April 30, the same day that Haig announced that Argentina had rejected the American proposal for a settlement and that the United States would therefore support Britain short of actually intervening in the fighting. Perez de Cuellar took up the mediating function. Being British I excluded myself from this effort, although I remained in close touch with it. Perez de Cuellar was a skillful and experienced negotiator. Since the British had to await the arrival of the troopships *Queen Elizabeth 2* and *Canberra* before they could attempt a landing, there was still some time for negotiation, although skirmishing at sea continued, the British losing several ships to Exocet missiles and Argentina the cruiser *Belgrano*.

By Saturday, May 14, Perez de Cuellar had achieved agreement on important points of a possible settlement and had identified the main sticking points, but time was obviously running out. He therefore decided to put on the table his own suggestion for a solution. Tony Parsons personally took the Secretary-General's proposals to London and went over them point by point with the prime minister and the Cabinet.

Parsons came back, after an intense weekend at Chequers, with a surprisingly reasonable reaction from London, which Perez de Cuellar passed on to Buenos Aires. After two days a reply came back introducing a series of new and obviously unacceptable demands which were rejected out of hand by the British. This was effectively the end of the negotiating effort, although Perez de Cuellar once again put to the parties a memorandum of their agreements and disagreements, suggesting formulae to overcome the latter. The British said their deadline had run out, and there was no reply from Argentina. The one thing that seemed generally agreed was that Perez de Cuellar had made an impressive and skillful effort to settle the matter before the war started in earnest. On the evening of May 20 he stated publicly that his negotiating effort was at an end. On the following day the British Expeditionary Force battled its way ashore in the Falklands.

If ever there was a war that should have been avoided, it was this one. It was aptly described at the time as two bald men fighting over a comb. The Argentinians were expelled after bloody fighting. The junta fell in disgrace, and Argentina soon returned to democratic rule. The British retained the Falklands at colossal expense—a white elephant that now had to be actively defended. The Secretary-General was stuck with the seemingly indefinite task of trying to negotiate a settlement.

*   *   *

Throughout the early months of 1982 there had been signs that the Israeli government was eagerly awaiting a pretext to strike at Palestinian positions in Lebanon. Israel's efforts increasingly to try to apply the 1981 Lebanon cease-fire agreement to acts of violence originated by the PLO from other places or continents than Lebanon was an indication of the Israeli mood. Our efforts to restrain the PLO had worn dangerously thin because of this interpretation.

On June 3, 1982, the Israeli Ambassador in London, Shlomo Argov, was shot and critically injured by agents of the extremist Abu Nidal group. It was almost immediately evident that the provocation which Sharon had spoken of had occurred and that the Israeli operation to destroy the PLO and radically to change the situation in Lebanon would soon be unleashed. The fact that Arafat denounced the shooting and the PLO representative in London was next on Abu Nidal's list of victims made no difference. The long-awaited provocation had been provided.

The day after the attempt on Argov, Israeli planes attacked Palestinian targets in Lebanon. The PLO responded with rockets and artillery fire on some of the northern towns and settlements of Israel. If the shooting of Argov wasn't enough of a provocation, the rockets certainly were. The fat was in the fire.

The Israelis invaded Lebanon in force, in what was called "Operation Peace for Galilee," on the morning of Sunday, June 6. General William Callaghan, the commander of UNIFIL, who had a prearranged meeting in Metulla on the Israeli-Lebanese border at ten-thirty that morning to discuss the Security Council's June 5 call for a cease-fire, was surprised to be informed by General Eitan, the Israeli chief of staff, that the Israeli invasion would start in thirty minutes' time. The meeting ended acrimoniously, and Callaghan hurried back to his headquarters to give orders, as best he could, on how UNIFIL was to face the Israeli invasion.

I had long been preoccupied with what UNIFIL should do in the event of a full-scale Israeli invasion. We had had a similar experience in Cyprus when the Turkish Army landed in 1974, and UNFICYP was criticized in some quarters for not resisting the Turkish forces. A peacekeeping operation is specifically *not* intended to fight the army of a member state and is neither equipped nor authorized to do so. The Security Council would never agree to such a mandate, and no government would provide troops if it were possible that they could become involved in a major shooting war with the army of a sovereign state. The weapons of peacekeeping are presence, consensus, the defusing of tension, and nonviolence. In a great crisis, however, it is all too easy to blame the local peacekeeping force for failing to control a situation which it was neither set up nor equipped to deal with.

The previous year, in an effort to anticipate this problem, I had given General Callaghan some points of guidance for UNIFIL in the event that major hostilities broke out. Protests were to be made, and token resistance, roadblocks, etc., should be maintained as long as possible. Positions should be held, and all possible efforts should be made to prevent UNIFIL's area of operations from being used as a base for offensive action.

I knew all too well that this was largely cosmetic stuff and that the Israeli Army would sweep through UNIFIL with little difficulty. So it did, although token resistance by some units held up its advance for short periods. The PLO protested violently that UNIFIL had failed to check the Israeli advance.

The Israeli forces moved fast and with maximum force, bombing, shelling, and naval bombardment causing heavy casualties and massive destruction. By June 7 they had taken the PLO strongholds of Tyre, Nabatiyeh, and the Château de Beaufort, and were speeding northward with little opposition. By June 10 they had reached the outskirts of Beirut and were in contact with the Syrian forces. On June 11 a cease-fire was announced, but it turned out to be only between Syria and Israel. Sharon announced that the "mopping up" of the PLO would continue.

When it became clear on June 4 that the Israeli invasion was imminent, Perez de Cuellar had appealed urgently to all parties to restore the cease-fire which had been broken by Israeli air attacks and PLO reprisal fire. He also urged President Mitterrand to rally the Western and Japanese heads of state, including President Reagan, who were then attending the Summit Meeting in Versailles, to support his efforts to bring back peace to southern Lebanon before the situation exploded. The summiteers replied with a somewhat muffled communiqúe on June 6 after the Israeli invasion had already started, expressing support for the efforts of the Secretary-General and the Security Council.

The Security Council, as usual in the opening phases of a war, appealed for restraint, called for a cease-fire, and then demanded unconditional withdrawal, all to absolutely no effect. The Arabs and the Soviets seemed to be sitting on their hands, leaving the PLO alone to resist the Israeli advance. The Lebanese Army, true to form, did not fire a shot in defense of its homeland.

On Saturday, June 12, with the Americans working on the Israelis and I on the PLO, we tried to get a cease-fire in and around Beirut for that evening. The PLO, who earlier in the week had been bitterly critical of the UN, now turned to us as their only hope. They were cheerful and fatalistic, and proud of the resistance they had offered to the vastly superior Israeli forces. They said they had nothing to lose and a great capacity for continuing the struggle in Beirut—heroic, no doubt, but bad news for the civilian population of the Lebanese capital.

A self-executing cease-fire seldom works in battle conditions, and it soon became clear that if the cease-fire in Beirut was to have any hope of taking hold, it would have to be monitored by United Nations Military

Observers in large numbers. Over the weekend of June 12–13 I tried to rally support for this idea. The Americans were initially encouraging, and so apparently was Ghassan Tueni, the Ambassador of Lebanon. We even got as far as drafting the letter from Lebanon requesting Military Observers and the Secretary-General's letter to the President of the Security Council asking authority to deploy them in Beirut. During Sunday, however, it became clear that the plan was being sabotaged. Tueni kept delaying his promised call for an urgent meeting of the Security Council, and American enthusiasm evaporated. By Sunday afternoon it emerged that the Israeli forces had vastly improved their position during the cease-fire and now effectively encircled Beirut. Israel obviously had no desire to have UN Observers monitoring and reporting on its military moves in the Beirut area and had so informed the United States. The Lebanese, meanwhile, had been dazzled by another glittering potential prize, the possibility of getting the United States directly involved in Beirut. The letter requesting UN Observers therefore remained in Tueni's pocket.

Tueni finally called for a Security Council meeting late on Sunday evening. I sloshed through the rain with Tony Parsons to this cynical affair, to find that the United States could not vote on the stationing of UN Observers in Beirut that night and needed "time for reflection." The Council held consultations at which Perez de Cuellar told the members that Saturday's cease-fire had not held and that Arafat had just requested that UN Observers monitor the cease-fire. We had the Observers ready, he said, if the Council authorized their deployment. Knowing that the United States, at Israel's urging, would block this move, the Council did not even hold a formal meeting.

I was disgusted by this episode. Of course our Observers would not have solved the problem, but they would have been there as an internationally accepted source of common sense, objective information, and decency which could have been built on in the future. As it was, Lebanon and the United States had become committed to a course, partly dictated by Israel, which in the end was a disaster for everyone.

Begin visited the United Nations the following week to address the Special Session on disarmament. In his talk with us, his self-confidence was breathtaking. He launched into a long exposition to Perez de Cuellar on Latin America and Ladino, a medieval Spanish-Hebrew dialect, and I had difficulty in turning the conversation to Lebanon. Israel had gone into Lebanon to make peace, he said. He wanted a multinational (i.e., American-run, not United Nations) force and the expulsion of the Syrians and Palestinians. He seemed very confident about everything.

On June 18 the Israelis moved into central Beirut and laid siege to the estimated 6,000 PLO fighters in West Beirut. The casualties and damage from Israeli air strikes, artillery, and naval gunfire were appalling. At this point France made a proposal to the Security Council calling for the simultaneous withdrawal of PLO forces from Beirut, for Israeli withdrawal, and the immediate emplacement of UN Observers. During the Council consultations the United States representative, Charles Lichenstein, was ominously silent, and it soon became obvious that he was going to veto the whole thing because it demanded Israeli withdrawal without specifying the disarming of the PLO.

To avert another stalemate I asked Tony Parsons if he could introduce a simple resolution demanding an immediate cease-fire, authorizing the stationing of UN Observers, and asking governments capable of doing so to bring their influence to bear on the fighting parties. We wrote the text quickly, and during one of the endless pauses on Friday night, Tony got the members of the Council, including the United States, to agree to it. Only the French Ambassador, whose own proposal was doomed by the U.S. veto anyway, rejected it in a rage, saying it was an insult to France and that he would veto it. He referred to Tony's resolution as an "American-British maneuver." Tony withdrew the proposal in a fury, saying that unlike the French he would never introduce a resolution which would be vetoed by an ally. Thus at 3:15 a.m. on Saturday, June 26, the United States alone voted against the French resolution. The destruction of Beirut continued, and the United Nations lost any possibility of playing a useful role in the foreseeable future.

I do not remember any time at which I felt such exasperation with diplomats and their governments and so little hope for the United Nations as on that early Saturday morning. The United States, at a time of appalling human tragedy and out of partisanship for Israel, had more or less written off the possibility of using the United Nations and thereby assumed an obligation in Lebanon which it was later bitterly to regret. The French had made it impossible to get the United States off the hook. The Lebanese went on dying.

On June 27 Israel announced a "Peace Proposal" of blinding simplicity. The Lebanese Army should enter West Beirut and disarm the PLO fighters, who would leave Lebanon for Syria. Beirut would be unified, and all foreign forces would leave Lebanon. "This agreement will insure security and peace for the Galilee and its inhabitants, of Israel and its citizens." Israel would "gladly accept" the good offices of the United States.

Philip Habib was already in the field as Special Emissary of President Reagan with the task of trying to end the massacre in Lebanon. We had contacted him to suggest the role which our experienced Military Observers might play, but the United States alone among members of the Council had opposed it, and Habib's hands were tied.

The Israeli bombardment of West Beirut continued relentlessly. It was clear that only the departure of the PLO fighters would stop it, so Habib turned his attention to trying to find a new home for them in the Arab world. On August 1 the Israeli Air Force bombed West Beirut for fourteen hours. Conditions in West Beirut became catastrophic. Sharon's message was all too clear.

That same day the Council again demanded an immediate cease-fire and the immediate stationing of UN Observers. This time the United States supported the demand, but when we ordered the Observers to move up, the Israeli forces blocked them from reaching Beirut. The bombardment continued even after Lebanon announced on August 6 that the PLO had agreed to withdraw peacefully and the United States had presented, on August 10, a plan for PLO withdrawal with the assistance of a multinational (non-UN) force. On August 12 the Israelis bombed Beirut for ten hours. Reagan phoned Begin, and at last the Israeli bombardment ceased.

On August 30 Arafat left for Greece, and the PLO pullout from Beirut was completed on September 1. The United States Marines and the French and Italian contingents of the multinational force all left Beirut on September 10, the former under banners reading "Mission Accomplished." When I queried the United States Mission about the wisdom of this move, since the Palestinian refugees in the camps in West Beirut were now totally vulnerable, I was told not to worry "because the Christians are now in charge." I said that that was precisely why I *was* worried. We were on the sidelines anyway.

Bashir Gemayel had been elected President of Lebanon on August 23. On September 14 he was killed by a bomb planted in one of his headquarters. The next day Israeli troops moved back into West Beirut in force. On September 16 Christian militiamen began a two-day slaughter of Palestinian refugees in the Sabra and Shatila camps. This cold-blooded massacre, even after all the horrors of the summer, shocked the conscience of the world. We had only ten Observers in Beirut at this time, the main body having been blocked by the Israelis, but their reports of what had happened were appalling. Perez de Cuellar reported to the Security Council at once, recalling the blocking of efforts to put UN Observers into Beirut and saying that in the present tragic circumstances unarmed Observers were not enough. He noted that in UNIFIL's area of operations in the south the harassment of the civilian population by militias had been successfully prevented and relative peace prevailed. The Council did not take the hint, but merely authorized the immediate dispatch of fifty more UN Observers and asked the Secretary-General to discuss with the government of Lebanon the possible deployment of UN forces in Beirut. The Lebanese government was not interested, having decided to request the return of the multinational force, 4,000 men of which arrived again by September 30.

The summer had been a prolonged exercise in tragedy, brutality, and futility. Now that the Lebanese government had opted firmly for a multinational rather than a United Nations force, there began, to add to our frustration, a flood of comment to the effect that the UN peacekeeping role, and indeed the whole concept of UN peacekeeping, had been discredited and superseded by the superior skill, force, and wisdom of the United States and its NATO allies, France and Italy. I found this hard to take, particularly since I was convinced that a multinational force led by the United States and consisting solely of NATO countries was bound, however powerful militarily, to come to grief in the volatile and murderous conditions of Beirut. Another heavily armed group using its weapons in Beirut was just about the last thing that was needed.

In a press conference in September, I said that the advantage of United Nations forces was that they represented the will of the whole international community as expressed by the Security Council and thus had a certain durability which a force mounted by one power, or a particular group of powers, was unlikely to have. I admitted that the current inability of the Security Council to agree on such matters was deplorable, but suggested that it might be wise to let a little more time elapse before rushing to judgment on the relative merits of the two methods of peacekeeping. These prophetic words attracted no attention whatsoever.

*   *   *

The dismal year dragged to its end with few compensating features. One of these was the unveiling, on September 17, of the great sculpture of a recumbent figure which Henry Moore had given to the United Nations. I had pursued this idea for many years, and in 1980 Sidney and I had spent a happy day with Moore in England, discussing the sculpture and the way it should be shown. Now at last it was installed in the Secretariat forecourt at the United Nations.

I had been responsible for writing the Secretary-General's Annual Report on the work of the organization since the later years of U Thant, and in the midst of the summer uproar I managed to write the draft of Perez de Cuellar's first report. Although it was a considerable additional burden, I enjoyed the challenge of trying to put a commentary on the whole spectrum of United Nations activity into twenty readable pages. While U Thant had been perfectly happy to go out on a limb on controversial questions, Waldheim had been nervous about taking strong or critical positions, and it had often been a struggle to retain the substance, and especially the punchlines, of the more interesting parts of the report.

Perez de Cuellar was, in his own quiet way, an outspoken man. In 1981 I had written an article in *Foreign Affairs* entitled "International Peace and Security: Thoughts on the Twentieth Anniversary of Dag Hammarskjold's Death," which had analyzed the current capacity of the United Nations Security Council for maintaining international peace and security and had made some suggestions as to how to improve it. I knew that Perez de Cuellar had read this article and agreed with much of it, so I set out—in pauses from the Lebanese crisis—to expand on it and put it in the shape of his Annual Report.

Perez de Cuellar had excellent ideas of his own and had no inhibitions about sticking his neck out. There was no trimming or watering down. The report was extremely well received and was regarded as both constructive and audacious. Unintentionally, however, we contrived to underline the central weakness of the Security Council. The members were so impressed by his report that they decided to review the Secretary-General's ideas in detail with a view to strengthening the Security Council's performance. They discussed the report for more than two years, but could never agree on anything but the mildest and most vacuous comments on it. Our suggestions remained on the printed page, and the Council went on exactly as before. After this experience I concluded that only a complete change of heart among the great powers, which was unlikely, or a devastating international crisis, by which time it might already be too late, would change the Security Council's ways.*

---

*The end of the Cold War encompassed such a "change of heart among the great powers," and much of what Perez de Cuellar had suggested in his 1982 Annual Report became, after 1987, the standard method of operation of the Security Council.

XXVI

Winding Down

AFTER THE HORRORS OF September 1982, a stalemate settled over the Lebanese situation. Israel would not withdraw unless other foreign forces in Lebanon withdrew. Philip Habib took the field once again. The United States was anxious to keep UNIFIL in southern Lebanon as a bastion of peace and decency in a sea of violence and brutality. The Lebanese government, having rejected the possibility of getting a UN operation in Beirut in favor of a United States presence, was now desperately anxious to keep UNIFIL, and wished, it said, to have UNIFIL expanded to assist the government to establish its authority all over Lebanon. This belated recognition presented, for countries providing troops for UNIFIL, the nightmare possibility of being pitchforked into a sort of Levantine Congo situation.

I went to the area in early January 1983 to try to clarify the situation with the Lebanese and the Israelis. Beirut was alive with fantastic rumors. Ambassadors, the Lebanese, and our own people, cooped up in a violent hothouse atmosphere, had all developed varying degrees of localitis, a total obsession with local events and their own supposed role in them, to the exclusion of virtually all other considerations. My old friend Paul-Marc Henry, now the French Ambassador, was particularly voluble. I was bombarded with anticipated assassinations, fantastic plots and conspiracies, and Byzantine explanations of ostensibly simple happenings. Although I reckoned that there was about 15 percent of truth in most of these fantasies, the reality was bad enough. Our Military Observers, who spent their time patrolling, seemed to have a better idea of the situation than anyone else.

The multinational force was already the object of much Lebanese malice. The French were derided for jogging *en masse* through Beirut in the briefest of shorts. The U.S. Marines, dug in at the airport, were mocked for never going into the city and for keeping only one company ashore, the remainder living securely on naval vessels in the bay. The situation was a humiliating one for the Marines, and the helicopter traffic between the airport and the ships was impressive. The Lebanese seemed particularly gratified that a Marine helicopter had inadvertently chopped off a wing of the aircraft of David Kimche, the Israeli negotiator in the withdrawal talks which were going on under American auspices.

Attacks on the occupying Israeli forces were on the increase, the harbinger of the onslaught which finally caused the Israelis to withdraw. The predictable difficulties of occupying Lebanon were about to become embarrassingly clear.

Amin Gemayel, who had succeeded his murdered brother Bashir as President, seemed boyish and energetic by comparison with the gloomy Sarkis. He was putting a bold face on an impossible and extremely hazardous job, and I respected him for it. The Lebanese had fanciful notions of expanding UNIFIL, even suggesting that we take over Baalbek, which had fallen under the control of the Iranian "volunteers" sent to fight the Israelis.

Morris Draper was Habib's deputy in charge of the negotiations. He looked like a Roman pro-consul and was maintaining an admirable calm in the face of the mind-numbing complications which characterize negotiations between Israel and the Lebanese. UNIFIL had now, belatedly, become an important element of stability in everyone's thinking, direct experience of Lebanese conditions having at last opened the eyes of the Americans and Israelis to the difficulties we had been facing with considerable success for the previous four years. The ruins and squalor of West Beirut and the swathe of desolation on each side of the Green Line were an ever-present reminder of the disasters of the summer.

I paid the usual visit to Damascus and then flew to Jerusalem. En route we passed over the aircraft carrier *Nimitz*, surrounded by its support ships like a sow with a brood of piglets. In Israel I found the beginnings of the realization that in Lebanon the Israelis had bitten off more than they could chew. There was a far greater willingness to understand UNIFIL's difficulties, and some of the warnings that I had given a year earlier about the difficulties of operating in Lebanon were ruefully recalled. As there was no possibility of UNIFIL being removed from southern Lebanon in the present situation, I urged the Israelis to learn to live with it. I found Begin very much changed. His wife had just died, and the debacle in Lebanon, something over which he had not been able to exercise full control, had obviously taken its toll. He was sad and low and praised our peacekeepers in UNIFIL, although he thought they should be deployed in the north to deal with the Syrians. He seemed to be a broken man.

In southern Lebanon I addressed all the contingent commanders, urging them to be patient and stoical in the very awkward position in which they were placed. At a ceremonial parade of the Senegalese Battalion, after a display of African dancing, two Israeli jets went over at about fifty feet. The noise was shattering, and all the village children began to cry. It was an unnecessary display of omnipresence. Wherever I went, the Mukhtars and headmen came to beseech me to keep UNIFIL in southern Lebanon. "They are our only hope and our only friends," they said.

While the American-sponsored talks on Israeli withdrawal were going on, there was little we could do to change the situation. Larry Eagleburger, then Under Secretary of State, had finally, on May 12, shown us the article of the agreement which, as "a great Israeli concession," grudgingly allotted UNIFIL vague and unsatisfactory general responsibilities for the security of the Palestinian refugee camps in Tyre and Sidon. I expressed strong reservations both about the practicality of this insulting task and the likelihood of the Security Council, or indeed the troop-contributing countries, ever agreeing to it. There also seemed to be a facile American-Israeli assumption that UNIFIL would be able to leave its area in southern Lebanon and go north to form a *cordon sanitaire* between the Israeli security zone and the Syrians, effectively partitioning Lebanon and sanctioning Israeli occupation of the south. I did my best to point out that, for an organization set up to maintain the sovereign integrity of nations, this was completely unacceptable.

The storm signals were already beginning to fly. On April 18 the American Embassy in Beirut was devastated by a truck bomb. Sixty-three people, including seventeen Americans, were killed. Nonetheless, on May 17 Lebanon and Israel signed an agreement providing for Israeli withdrawal, but also for a continued Israeli security role in southern Lebanon. The implementation of this agreement by Israel was contingent on the simultaneous withdrawal from Lebanon of Syrian forces. Syria had been more or less taken for granted, and only minimal contacts had been made in Damascus during the negotiating process. It was no surprise, therefore, when Syria denounced the agreement, demanded that Lebanon renounce it, and heated up the fighting in Beirut as a gentle hint.

On the afternoon of May 19, two days after the signing of the agreement, Perez de Cuellar received a surprise telephone call from President Gemayel, who asked him to visit Lebanon in the next few days. The weather was good, the president said, and the bathing excellent ("Apportez votre maillot de bain"). We replied politely that the Secretary-General's schedule was already impossibly full. Evidently Gemayel was beginning to feel isolated and lonely. Shultz had refused to return to Beirut, and Damascus had refused to see Philip Habib. Gemayel was apparently looking for moral and international support, but it was a little late to involve the Secretary-General unless we could hope to do something useful in Damascus. Inquiries clearly showed that this was not the case. The scene was changing once again in Lebanon. The Americans had had enough, the Israelis would be withdrawing, the Syrians were breathing down his neck, and Gemayel was looking for new friends. In March 1984, after a year of increasing violence, Lebanon, under Syrian pressure and to the disgust of Washington, renounced the May 17 agreement.

*   *   *

Perez de Cuellar had certainly taken over the Secretary-Generalship at an appallingly difficult time. Administrative and financial arrangements have always been one of the most vulnerable points of the United Nations. It is impossible to make an international civil service based on, and answerable to, 159 governments as efficient as a national civil service. And it is impossible to make a program of activities decided upon by 159 states by majority vote as streamlined and purposeful as a national program. Thus there is always plenty to criticize.

Over the years there had been a serious erosion of the standards of international civil service which we had so jealously guarded at the beginning. Too many top-level officials, political appointments, rotten boroughs, and pointless programs had rendered the Secretariat fat and flabby over the years, and it clearly needed drastic rehabilitation. In our office we had tried very hard to stick to the original standards, and I had kept my staff as small as possible—never more than ten officials in all—in spite of its heavy and varied workload, believing that hard work never killed anyone, and that a large number of posts in a conspicuous political office would only invite undesirable pressures from governments for jobs.

Although, or perhaps because, I had a Soviet assistant, I never had much trouble with the Soviet Mission. The Soviets always provided an intelligent and well-informed official for the post. I made it clear that I would keep confidential information and dealings to myself, but would do my best to include my Soviet colleagues in our work as far as their rather special status permitted. I found that they were usually not anxious to be burdened with awkward or sensitive information, knowing that they would have to report it to the Soviet government and that I would know they had done so.

The task of streamlining and rationalizing the Secretariat is Herculean, because governments in the General Assembly exercise much of the essential control, and vested interests lead to much log-rolling if any change or reduction is suggested. Early in 1983, foreseeing that, in the ideologically hostile climate in Washington, this issue was likely to become a critical one, I suggested to Perez de Cuellar that he get ahead of the game by commissioning one or two respected international figures with experience of large organizations to stalk through the jungles of our administration, put the fear of God into the inhabitants, and recommend serious changes and improvements. I suggested that Robert McNamara, formerly head of the World Bank, the Ford Motor Company, and the U.S. Department of Defense, would be an excellent person for this task. This simple idea scared the timid souls in our administration, and it was shelved.

In late 1985 the full force of the disapproval of the United States, in the form of withholding a large part of its assessed contribution, hit the Secretary-General and the Secretariat, creating a financial crisis and a resulting rush to draconian measures of economy. A default by a major contributor is particularly serious because the UN has never been permitted by its member states to borrow money. This means that, unlike a government, the UN suffers serious and immediate consequences from a major deficit such as the one that arose from the United States defaulting on its assessed payments.

I had put into the Secretary-General's report for 1985 a suggestion that, for everyone's good, no country should pay more than 10 percent of the budget, but the same timid souls in our administration had insisted on taking it out. The United States insisted on continuing to be assessed to pay 25 percent of the UN budget but was, in 1986, actually paying about 12 percent.

The fact was that the U.S. Congress had become strongly anti-United Nations over the years. Its members apparently believed that the United States was assuming too great a financial burden for the world organization and was being victimized by the Third World majority. They ignored the fact that the United States contribution to the UN is a treaty obligation incurred under the UN Charter.

It is true that the majority of governments that vote the UN budget actually pay a very small percentage of it, but other aspects of the United States position in the financial affairs of the UN are less well known. The United States, even at 25 percent of the UN budget, is not paying its fair share as assessed as a percentage of national income, the criterion applied to all member states. Its assessed share under the rules would be about 29 percent of the budget. Moreover, the United States is the largest single financial beneficiary of the UN, which annually spends more than $800 million (four times the U.S. assessed contribution) in New York City alone. The UN budget in recent years, unlike most governmental budgets, had been maintained at zero growth. None of these facts dampened the ardor of those in Washington who wished to "teach the UN a lesson."

The UN "financial crisis," as far as the United States is concerned, is less a financial crisis than the expression of a political and ideological point of view. The sums of money involved are not large by national standards; they are more symbolic. There is no question that administrative and other reforms are badly needed in the UN. Nonetheless it is to be hoped that the mutually destructive phase in the relations between the United States and the United Nations will be short-lived and that the United States, for its own good and everyone else's, will soon resume its natural role of leadership in the world organization. A global power like the United States needs the multilateral machinery which previous administrations had always used so effectively in the United States interest. And the international community needs the constructive participation and leadership of the world's most powerful democracy. The sooner the faults and misconceptions on both sides are remedied, the better for world peace.

*   *   *

In February 1983 I went with Perez de Cuellar to the Summit Meeting of the Non-Aligned Countries in Delhi, stopping for two days on the way in Kuwait, where the main preoccupation was the Iran-Iraq War. Its artillery exchanges were plainly audible in the Kuwaiti capital.

The government of India had put on a tremendous show for the Summit Conference, which was attended by sixty-three heads of state. Indira Gandhi had just taken over the chairmanship of the Non-Aligned Movement from Fidel Castro, to the palpable relief of virtually all the members. This meeting signified the Non-Aligned Movement's new maturity and pragmatism, of which Mrs. Gandhi's opening speech was an excellent example. A great, new, rational constituency was emerging which, with encouragement and the right leadership, could play a vital role in the future, especially in bringing the United Nations back to its essential functions.

One of the main purposes of summit conferences is the series of bilateral talks they make possible, and Perez de Cuellar had an eighteen-hour-a-day round of them. I concluded that there was a possibility of doing something useful about Afghanistan, that there might eventually be a possibility of doing something about the Iran-Iraq War, but that the Middle East and Namibia situations were not susceptible, in the current conditions, either in the areas concerned or in Washington, to any serious negotiating effort. Unfortunately, Afghanistan and the Iran-Iraq War have so far proved just as intractable as the other problems.*

Shortly after our return to New York, I set off again with Perez de Cuellar to Moscow. We had been there to see Brezhnev in September 1982, two months before he died. It had not been a very productive visit. Brezhnev, who had to be supported whenever he moved and was obviously in his last days, had barked, wheezed, and boomed a thirty-minute prepared text to which Perez de Cuellar had intoned a prepared reply. Now we were to repeat the performance with his successor who, in his turn, expired less than a year later. We were to go the following year to talk to Chernenko, who also very shortly died.

Andropov was obviously in frail condition. His hands shook and his voice tended to trail off in an old man's falsetto at the end of sentences. His mind, however, was clear and active, and it was possible for Perez de Cuellar to engage him in a normal dialogue. He was plainly obsessed with President Reagan, and with "Star Wars" and Reagan's "Evil Empire" speech in particular. For all the rivalry between them, the Soviets regard the United States and themselves as the only members of the exclusive superpower club and express outrage if the other member is abusive or rude. When I commented to Oleg Troyanovsky, who accompanied us, that the Soviets had been deluging the West with abusive and jargon-ridden rhetoric for nearly fifty years and shouldn't be too surprised to get some of it back, he just laughed.

Andropov himself raised the subject of Afghanistan, saying that anyone who believed the Soviets *wanted* to be in Afghanistan was crazy and that it caused them nothing but casualties, money, and international complications. They would not be prepared to leave until interference by others in Afghanistan's internal affairs had ceased and there were guarantees that it would not be resumed. There was also the threat to the security of the Soviet Union to be considered. Andropov expressed strong support

---

*In 1988, however, both problems were resolved along the lines of the Secretary-General's proposals, backed by a newly united Security Council.

for the Secretary-General's efforts to negotiate a solution, but said he suspected that the United States liked having Afghanistan as a stick to beat the Soviet Union with. Andropov seemed a cold but highly intelligent and experienced person, less ideological and far more pragmatic than his predecessor.

*   *   *

The relations between the Soviet Union and the United States, the two most powerful permanent members of the Security Council, have a decisive effect on the way the United Nations works or doesn't work. When the Cold War was at its coldest, as in 1983, it was extremely difficult to get sensible or constructive decisions from the Security Council. When, however, the Cold War looks as if it might suddenly become hot, the Council is an indispensable safety valve, and even the superpowers gratefully resort to it.

On September 1, 1983, a Korean Airlines jumbo jet was shot down, and all 269 persons aboard perished. The aircraft had been hundreds of miles off course over the Soviet strategic submarine base at Sakhalin Island and had been dispatched by Soviet fighters. This was a great tragedy, and also a fearful reminder of the dangers of paranoia, non-communication, and Soviet-U.S. tension, but these essential considerations were soon obscured by other, less worthy ones. The Soviet Union was arrogant, abusive, and unwilling to admit error. Although little reliable information on the disaster was yet available, the United States launched a furiously moralistic campaign of denunciation of the Soviet Union for banditry, murder, and worse. They chose the Security Council as the obvious and safest place to do this.

The incident brought the relations of the two superpowers to their nadir just before the 1983 General Assembly session opened. Instead of treating the affair as the appalling human tragedy and ominous multiple mistake that it was, and drawing important conclusions for the future, the world's two most powerful countries became embroiled in a vicious round of name-calling and recrimination, taken up by lower-level authorities on both sides eager not to be less extreme than their leaders. The governors of New York and New Jersey vowed they would deny landing rights to Andrei Gromyko's airplane. The Soviets accused the United States of failing in its responsibilities as host government to the United Nations. Ambassador Kirkpatrick's deputy, Lichenstein, happily sinking to the level of the occasion, was quoted as saying in a UN committee that if the UN chose to leave New York, the members of the

United States Mission would be on the dock to wave them farewell as they sailed into the sunset. Instead of treating this pettish remark with the oblivion it deserved, the press inflated it into a debate about the UN presence in New York. This brought the U.S. administration, ex-presidents, former Secretaries of State, and the New York authorities to the defense of the United Nations, and many helpful and friendly statements were made.

As this macabre flap was dying down, Reagan came to New York to address the General Assembly. We had, as usual, a "working lunch" with him in the Waldorf Towers—Perez de Cuellar, Bill Buffum, the American Under Secretary-General, and I, with the president, George Shultz, Jeane Kirkpatrick, Michael Deaver, and Judge William Clark on the other side of the table. The occasion coincided with an alleged cease-fire in Lebanon and much time was spent on the telephone to a very excited Amin Gemayel in Beirut. Gemayel wanted UN Observers to supervise the cease-fire, and in the general enthusiasm I didn't have the heart to say either that the cease-fire was unlikely to hold (it didn't) or that the Russians, with the Syrians near Beirut, would certainly veto UN Observers just as the United States had vetoed them the year before.

It is absolutely impossible not to like President Reagan. He is patently good-hearted and has great charm. I was surprised, on this occasion, to discover another side to his character. Set off by the discussion of Lebanon and the Korean airliner, he launched into a passionate denunciation of the involvement of civilians in war. Warming to his subject, he invoked youthful memories of Billy Mitchell and of World War II. We must start, he declared, to respect civilians again, and nuclear weapons, above all, must be outlawed. Shultz, perhaps nervous at the implications of his leader's spontaneous outburst, said soothingly that you couldn't separate the problem of armaments from the resolution of conflicts, especially regional conflicts. This was where the UN was so important. The president also observed that the people of Angola should go to the polls to decide on their own form of government and future through the democratic process. I wished he could just see Luanda.

*   *   *

On August 28, 1983, Menachem Begin resigned as Prime Minister of Israel, and a week later Israeli forces withdrew from the Beirut suburbs and the Shouf Mountains. The situation on the southern outskirts of Beirut now became more violent, and the U.S. Marines, stationed at the airport, were on the fringes of the fighting both in the Shouf Mountains and in

West Beirut. On August 29 two Marines were killed by mortar fire, and the next day four members of the French contingent died. The United States, which had not clearly defined the mandate of the multinational force, now increasingly took the position that its function was to support the Lebanese government of President Amin Gemayel. Since to many people in Lebanon the government was just another faction in the civil war, this was a dangerous task, and one which, unless carried out with the maximum restraint and skill, was bound to bring the multinational force, and particularly the U.S. Marines at the airport, into the violent entanglements of the Lebanese conflict.

United States retaliation soon began. On September 16 U.S. naval vessels bombarded "anti-government positions" in the hills around Beirut, and six days later the French followed suit with air strikes. The multinational force was now a fighting party and had become part of the problem, instead of a possible solution to it.

Those of us who had spent nearly thirty years trying to evolve the technique of non-violent peacekeeping were appalled at this development. On September 28 I gave a speech in Washington on "The Work of Peace" at a celebration of the two hundredth anniversary of the Treaty of Paris. I referred to the situation in Lebanon:

> The principles underlying our wide-ranging peacekeeping operations have been relatively simple. They must have broad political support and a broad base in the world community. Force can be used only in self-defense, and therefore our peacekeeping operations are lightly armed. Our peacekeepers must remain above the conflict; they must never become part of it. Their aim should be to ensure the cessation of hostilities and the maintenance of peace between conflicting forces, and, to that end, they should provide the pretext for peaceful conduct and the atmosphere for negotiation. They must have the cooperation of all the parties, however grudging.
>
> In Lebanon we see that older United Nations concept side by side with the newer one of the Multinational Force. The Multinational Force is militarily far more powerful and has far greater fire power than any U.N. operation. At this moment it has the support of at least three aircraft carriers. But it also has much less flexibility, less capacity to act, and is far more vulnerable when things go wrong. This is because it has a narrow political base, being perceived by most people in the Middle East as a Western, NATO operation. Moreover, its four separate contingents have no articulate, unified command structure. This is all right when nothing is happening, but when things go wrong it is a very considerable hazard, because each contingent will go its own way according to its national

instructions and preoccupations. Thus when things go wrong, as they have in recent weeks in Lebanon, the Multinational Force can become very controversial. It can become part of the problem rather than the referee of the problem, and it can come to be viewed as one-sided and partisan. Unfortunately in Lebanon it is now extremely difficult to change course. Last year it was Israel and the United States who objected to a U.N. peace-keeping force or observers in Beirut. Fourteen months later, ironically, it is the United States and Israel and the Government of Lebanon who long for a United Nations force to take over, and Syria and the Soviet Union who object to it. This is very frustrating. We must persist in trying to find a means to balance the situation once more in the interests of the people of Lebanon.

Senator Charles Mathias of Maryland put this speech into the Congressional Record.

Editorials began to appear in the United States press urging that the United Nations ("lately maligned but always invaluable," as one put it) should immediately replace the multinational force. My old friend Joseph Kraft, in arguing this course, recalled that in 1958 UN Observers had replaced the U.S. Marines in Lebanon. This belated sense of realism was particularly ironic because only the concurrence, in the Security Council, of the Soviet Union, which had been systematically excluded from Middle East matters by the Reagan administration, could make this course possible, and the Soviets and the Americans were still at daggers drawn over the Korean airliner disaster.

The wheel had indeed come full circle. In Israel it was widely conceded that the invasion of Lebanon had been a national disaster of the first magnitude. The Israeli Army had just sustained its 800th fatal casualty, including 300 killed since the cease-fire. The Israelis were now talking about a United Nations force between the Syrian and Israeli armies to allow the Israelis to withdraw. The presence of the U.S. Marines in Beirut had become a vast embarrassment for Washington. President Assad and the Syrians, humbled in the field and in the air the previous year, were now in a strong position to play power politics.

The Soviet Union, excluded from this situation for the previous eighteen months, would have nothing to do with a rescue operation in Lebanon involving United Nations forces or Observers, maintaining that as the Israelis had withdrawn, the situation in Beirut was now essentially a civil war situation in which the UN had no place. The recently popular theory that the Israeli invasion, by ridding the Lebanese of the PLO and the Syrians, would make possible a government of national unity in Lebanon which would be friendly to Israel had been totally exploded. Beirut shuddered under rocket and artillery exchanges. The United States, first by brokering the May 17 agreement under which Lebanon would share its sovereignty in the south with Israel, and then by participating in the fighting in Beirut, had become the hated enemy of much of the Lebanese population and an encumbrance for Gemayel's hard-pressed government. Poor Tueni was sent to New York by Gemayel to try to get United Nations intervention, but his efforts to get a UN force and Observers deployed all over Lebanon only strengthened Syrian and Soviet objections and made things worse.

As often before, the only hope of salvaging the situation would have been an agreement among the permanent members of the Security Council to support a United Nations action. There was absolutely no possibility of this, as we found when we tried to discuss the matter with United States and Soviet representatives.

On October 23, two days before United States forces stormed ashore in Grenada, a truck bomb crashed into a U.S. Marine compound at Beirut Airport and killed 241 American servicemen. Simultaneously another truck bomb killed fifty-eight French soldiers. It was a grotesque and terrible protest against American policy and the multinational force. Ten days later a car bomb destroyed an Israeli Army Headquarters in Tyre. Once again the underestimated resistance had turned the tables on supposedly superior forces, and it was a matter of time before the whole multinational force would withdraw. On December 4 two U.S. aircraft were shot down in attacks on Syrian positions in the Beka'a Valley.

In mid-December, Sidney and I went to England for my mother's one hundredth birthday. In the airplane on the way over I wrote an Op-Ed piece for the *New York Times*, trying to define the nature of peacekeeping and the conditions required to pursue it successfully. I pointed out that a perfect peacekeeping operation would need the complete support of both the United States and the Soviet Union, naive though such an idea might seem at the present time.

> After 35 years and some 13 United Nations peace-keeping operations, I have a dream that we shall have peace-keeping operations in which contingents from the United States and Soviet Union join those of other countries under the mandate and directives of the Security Council to keep the peace and contain conflict in crises that threaten international peace and security.
>
> Surely this must eventually happen if we are to have a relatively peaceful world. It is not such a new idea, being very much in the original

spirit of the United Nations Charter. In the Charter, a basic assumption is the unanimity and concerted action of the great powers in the face of threats to international peace and security or acts of aggression. And why should not the lion sometimes lie down with the lion instead of terrifying all the lambs by their mutual hostility?

* * *

My mother's hundredth birthday was a celebration not only of a long life but of someone who had been all too little celebrated. My mother rose to the occasion with enthusiasm and joy. She was manifestly delighted with all the attention and the messages and gifts which poured in from all over the world. She looked wonderful, ate, drank, talked to the sixty or so assembled members of the family, cut the cake, and made a speech. She had evidently been saving all her strength for this occasion and was, for once in her life, radiantly and uninhibitedly happy. After her birthday she seemed to lose interest in living. She died peacefully in her sleep the following summer.

It was impossible to feel sad about the death of one so old who had fought such a hard and lonely struggle throughout most of her time. My mother did not have a happy life in the normal sense, but her particular outlook would have militated against such a notion anyway. What she did have was a devoted family, who respected her and were much in her debt for the example and encouragement she had given and the code of discipline and behavior she had instilled. She also had an admiring extended family in the generations of girls she had taught and the teachers she had worked with. A surprising number of them kept in touch with her to her dying day, and that was her main reward.

My mother certainly had an enormous influence on me, and I think she was proud of her two sons, although it would have been out of the question for her ever to say so. She did not encourage demonstrations of love, admiration, or affection, but with her there was something deeper, less demonstrative but more enduring—an active concern, an abiding interest, an unshakable integrity, a rational belief in the good—which bound us all to her and left us with an immeasurable gift when she died.

* * *

Partly because of the general preoccupation with Lebanon, a dangerous vacuum had developed in the search for a settlement of the wider problems of the Middle East. In early December I suggested to Perez de Cuellar that we put to the permanent members of the Security Council some ideas on how this vacuum might at least partially be filled. The idea was to use the Security Council as a working group to distill, from all the various proposals that had been made, an acceptable basis for future negotiations in the Middle East, as had been done seventeen years before in Resolution 242. Such a process might at least have done something to alleviate the pressures of bitterness and frustration that were building up and to strengthen the beleaguered forces of moderation and peace. Washington's support was essential if this idea was to work, but when we took it up there it got a polite but blank reception.

A more immediate problem was the violent and dramatic deterioration of the situation in Lebanon. The Soviets had made it clear that any agreement to a wider United Nations role in Lebanon would depend primarily on the United States consenting to talk to them as an equal superpower with legitimate interests in the Middle East rather than as a delinquent outlaw. As the presence of the Marines in Lebanon was now a critical problem for the United States, Perez de Cuellar asked me to go to Washington in early January 1984 to discuss the situation. Our idea was to use the UN's peacekeeping capacity to facilitate a cease-fire, Lebanese national reconciliation, and the withdrawal of foreign troops. Since Security Council approval would be needed for such a plan, high-level discussions on the situation between the United States and the Soviet Union would be a necessary preliminary.

George Shultz was, as always, friendly, and listened to me patiently, but he was evidently still wedded to the moribund May 17, 1983, agreement on which he had staked his reputation. This agreement had become an albatross hung round the necks of anyone trying to do something realistic about the Lebanon shambles and the disastrous involvement of the United States and Israel. The presence of the U.S. Marines in Beirut had become a matter of prestige for the U.S. administration and also, apparently, a bone of contention between Shultz and Secretary of Defense Caspar Weinberger. These local facts seemed to distort Washington's view of the grim realities of Lebanon itself. Our suggestion of high-level talks with the Soviets was passed over in silence. Obviously there would be no consensus in the Security Council for a broader United Nations role in Lebanon.

On February 15 President Reagan announced that the Marines would be "redeployed" within thirty days, and France called for a United Nations peacekeeping force to replace the multinational force in Beirut. The Soviets vetoed this proposal on February 29; the United States voted for it. We were back to square one.

Although it was now too late for the UN to play a peacekeeping role in Beirut, UNIFIL in the south could certainly be helpful in facilitating Israeli withdrawal now that the Israelis urgently wanted to pull out. I therefore set out again for the area on March 10. This time I took Sidney, our son Charlie, and my brother-in-law Walter Howard with me for some of the time.

My main purpose was to work out what constructive role our troops could play in the next stage in Lebanon. Everyone concerned, Lebanese, Israelis, and Syrians, had a common interest in resolving the problem of security in southern Lebanon after the Israeli forces left. UNIFIL could be the key to this problem.

When I returned to New York, Perez de Cuellar recommended to the Security Council that UNIFIL should deploy in areas evacuated by the Israeli forces and should temporarily be responsible for the security of the civilian population and the Palestinian refugees in those areas until the Lebanese Army could take over. Meanwhile we would work out with the Lebanese and the Israelis security arrangements in southern Lebanon which, by satisfying their worries over the safety of their northern settlements, would allow the Israelis to withdraw.

I had checked these proposals out with the governments in the area. The Lebanese, delighted at a proposition which, for once, all parties in Lebanon could agree to, formally proposed them in a draft resolution of the Security Council. No one, not even the Soviets, seemed to object. At this point Ambassador Kirkpatrick returned to New York from London and Paris, where she had been reproaching the allies for not supporting the United States in the debate over the CIA's mining of Nicaraguan ports. The United States had already had the Lebanese proposal for five days, but Ambassador Kirkpatrick denounced it because it didn't also demand the withdrawal of the Syrian forces from Lebanon. Since the proposal specifically related to UNIFIL and southern Lebanon, this didn't make much sense. The American debacle in Lebanon had evidently drastically reduced Washington's practical interest in Lebanese affairs. Ambassador Kirkpatrick's insistence on simultaneous withdrawal of the Syrian forces, one of the main factors in the demise of the May 17 agreement, was an empty political gesture and a certain way to wreck the Secretary-General's modest proposals for southern Lebanon. As a result, UNIFIL was simply extended in its existing role, and another opportunity was lost to help both the Lebanese and the Israelis.

Perez de Cuellar himself visited the Middle East in early June at a time of disillusion, drift, and anxiety. Elections were pending in Israel and the United States, the Arabs were disunited and fractious, Lebanon was in chaos, there was no negotiating process on the overall Arab-Israeli problem, the superpowers were at each other's throats, the Iran-Iraq War raged on, and the Palestinian leadership was split. Everyone seemed to be sitting on his own volcano.

We flew by Lebanese helicopter from Damascus to Beirut. I was against this, believing that travelling by the back mountain road was both more scenic and safer, but I was overruled by the local experts. The Baabda Palace had been badly damaged by shellfire since my last visit two months previously, but Gemayel put on a brave show and gave us an excellent lunch. We visited Nabih Berri, the Shi'ite leader, in West Beirut. Berri said he could guarantee the security of the south with his Amal militia working with UNIFIL and that the Israelis "had nothing to fear unless they want South Lebanon to be the North Bank" (i.e., to occupy it). He was prepared to work out security arrangements that were acceptable to the Israelis and said he would never countenance the return of the PLO. Many subsequent battles have confirmed this latter statement. After the meeting with Berri, as we climbed aboard our helicopter, the shelling started in earnest. It continued heavily throughout the night and we had a grandstand view, from our hotel in the hills at Beit Meri, of a once civilized people blowing each other to pieces.

After visiting UNIFIL we were to fly back to the Lebanese Defense Ministry at Yarze to pick up the Lebanese helicopter that was to take us back to Damascus en route to Amman, but as Yarze was being shelled, we went to Jounieh, north of Beirut, instead. On the way to Damascus the Lebanese helicopter flew over two Syrian missile sites. This made me extremely nervous, and, sure enough, when we landed at the Damascus airport, there was a tremendous flap. The Lebanese had failed to clear our flight with the Syrian Air Defense Command, and only a chance phone call from the Syrian Foreign Office asking where the Secretary-General was had, at the very last moment, alerted the Syrian missile sites to our identity. There were sensational press stories. It was all very stupid.

During our visit to Israel, private friendliness and public denunciation of the UN indicated that a national election was in progress.

At the end of August Peres and Shamir formed a national unity government, Peres taking the first two years as prime minister. We all hoped that this might lead to a more forthcoming approach both on the Middle East negotiating process and on Lebanon, and to some extent it did. The immediate situation, however, was bad. On September 6 Ambassador Kirkpatrick had vetoed a Security Council resolution demanding Israeli withdrawal from Lebanon, denouncing it as "unbalanced, selective and myopic." Since lesser powers or groups have little or no legitimate recourse against a great power veto on a matter of urgent concern to them, it was not altogether surprising when another attempt was made, on September 20, to blow up the new U.S. Embassy in East Beirut. This time fourteen people were killed.

I made another brief trip to the area in September. The new Israeli coalition government obviously did have a different attitude about withdrawing from Lebanon. I mentioned to David Kimche that trying to negotiate with the Lebanese the conditions and arrangements for withdrawal might well prove an exercise in total frustration. I suggested that Israel announce unilaterally its unconditional withdrawal in stages and let the Lebanese and others worry about the consequences. Kimche said that was an interesting idea, but I would have to talk to Rabin, the defense minister.

Gemayel welcomed me warmly at his home in Bikfaya and said that the Secretary-General and I were the only people who could help, since we had the confidence of all parties. I was not as pleased with this compliment as I might have been, reflecting that the corridors of recent history were lined with the ruined reputations of people who had tried to help Lebanon. Gemayel's new word was "pragmatic" and he complained that the Israelis were "insufficiently Cartesian." He asked me to tell them that he wished to enter into a new era of peace in the south, with us as the channel of communications. He complained, with some reason, that the Israelis "always publish everything," a reference to Ze'ev Schiff's brilliant *Israel's War in Lebanon*, which recounts Israel's extensive contacts with the Gemayel family before the 1982 invasion.

In Damascus the strain of trying to manage Lebanese affairs was evidently telling, and I found a rare mood of positive pragmatism. Khaddam fully understood the necessity of making proper security arrangements in southern Lebanon, but would not agree to anything which detracted from Lebanese sovereignty or "paid a price" to Israel. He asked me to find out, and let him know, what kind of arrangements and guarantees Israel had in mind, and I undertook to do so.

I also saw Walid Jumblatt, the Lebanese Druse leader, who haunts the Damascus Sheraton. Jumblatt, with his gangling figure, protruding eyes, elegant leather jacket, and offhand charm, has a raffish aristocratic air. He is nothing if not disillusioned. He was deeply suspicious of the Lebanese Army, where the Christian brigades had all the armor and artillery, and commented that it was awkward to be a member of a government in which the president might easily shake hands with you one day and have you assassinated the next. On a later occasion, when I asked what the key to a Lebanese solution was, he instantly replied, "Gemayel in a coffin." A disproportionate amount of the time and energy of Lebanese leaders has to be spent in avoiding assassination.

I went back to Israel in a relatively cheerful mood. Shimon Peres, now prime minister, was at this time largely preoccupied with economic reorganization, so the key man on Lebanon was Defense Minister Rabin. I met Rabin at a private luncheon in President Vivien Herzog's house in Herzliya. As I arrived the news came through of the bombing of the American Embassy in Beirut, shortly followed by a report of a massacre of villagers in southern Lebanon by Druse members of the Israeli-run South Lebanese Army. Rabin gave me his plan for the Israeli withdrawal from Lebanon, a radical departure from the previous government's stone-walling. I checked with him how much of this I could tell the Syrians, and he repeated the official version in a meeting at the Defense Ministry after lunch.

Throughout my trip I had received messages from Sam Lewis, the American Ambassador in Israel, saying how important it was that we should meet. Much as I liked Sam Lewis personally, I was doubtful about his attitude to UNIFIL and southern Lebanon. He was anxious to know what Rabin had told me. I described to him my talks in Syria and Israel, and told him that I was sending someone back to Damascus to give Khaddam the information he had asked for about Israeli requirements and to ask Khaddam for the assurances the Israelis wanted about Syria's not moving its forces in Lebanon southward and controlling infiltration to the south from the Beka'a. Lewis took to wondering heavily whether this would not "cross wires" and whether I should not postpone the whole thing. I replied that both the Israelis and Syrians had asked me to do all this. If I now refused, there really wasn't much point in my being in the Middle East at all. I asked whether by any chance the United States might be sending a special envoy to Damascus soon. Sure enough, it turned out that Assistant Secretary of State Richard Murphy was on his way. Evidently Washington, in an election year and sensing possible progress on Lebanon at last, had no intention of being left out of it. I had nothing against this provided *someone* got results, although past experience indicated that when the United States gets into Middle East bargaining, the price of all the rugs tends to go up, and the prospect of a deal becomes more distant. Murphy was a friend and an excellent man, and I could only wish him luck and trust that the United States irruption would not destroy the hope of a quiet and constructive arrangement in southern Lebanon.

*   *   *

On my way back to New York, I stopped off in Holland for the fortieth anniversary of the Battle of Arnhem. I had always stayed away from the Arnhem commemorations, believing that I would provide a discordant note in the celebrations, but this time the Dutch had urged me to go, and I met my surviving former brother officers for the first time in forty years. After this interval it was evidently possible to separate the heroism of the soldiers from the criminal foolishness of the plan, and I was much moved at the friendship and interest with which I was greeted. Some had aged more than others, but when the band struck up for the march to the Airborne Memorial, even the oldest straightened up and marched like young soldiers.

The Dutch, who had paid a terrible price, had determined to keep the history and the symbolism of the battle alive. The children of Arnhem all took part, and at the wreathlaying at the Airborne Cemetery each grave was attended by a child with a bunch of flowers so that none of the dead were forgotten. Everyone, young and old, knew the history of the operation in detail, as well as the personalities involved. Many of the civilians who had helped the British soldiers during and after the fighting were on hand to meet again with their battlefield friends. Prince Bernhard of the Netherlands attended the ceremonial parachute drop on the main dropping zone of the 1st Airborne Division near Wolfheze, and as I talked to him my mind went back to our meeting before the battle, in another world forty years ago. The celebration, a triumph of the human spirit and of a sense of history, was profoundly moving.

*   *   *

I arrived back in New York just in time for our annual working lunch with President Reagan, accompanied this time by Shultz, Kirkpatrick, Bud McFarlane, and Michael Deaver. Shultz seemed put out when I said that for once the Syrians were positive and that one way or another we already had, as a practical matter, most of the assurances the Israelis wanted. Murphy had evidently not yet reached Damascus.

In Israel, Peres had commented, "With Syria we shall have agreement but no negotiations; with Lebanon we shall have negotiations but no agreement." He was right, but the idea of Israeli-Lebanese negotiations still seemed worth pursuing. The Lebanese insisted that the only framework for such negotiations was the Israel-Lebanon Armistice Agreement, which Israel no longer recognized and which Lebanese Prime Minister Karame had pronounced dead in 1967. In the end we persuaded Gemayel and Karame, who were in New York for the Assembly, and the Israelis, to accept military talks under UN auspices at the UNIFIL Headquarters in Naqoura. We worded this arrangement in such a way that Lebanon could maintain that the talks were under the Armistice Agreement and Israel that they were simply at the invitation of the Secretary-General. The talks began in November and, after twelve meetings, reached a stalemate. I went out after Christmas to see what could be done.

My arrival in Israel coincided with Israel's decision to withdraw from Lebanon unilaterally and without conditions. David Kimche, who met me at the airport, recalled that I had suggested this in September. Rabin and the admirable Chief of Staff, General Moshe Levy, explained their three-phase withdrawal plan to me the following day. They were anxious to hand over in the first instance to UNIFIL to avoid bloodshed, but this would mean UNIFIL going north of the Litani River, a move that required Lebanese agreement. I therefore arranged for the meetings in Naqoura to be resumed so that the Israelis could formally present their withdrawal plan, and then flew to Beirut.

Joint meetings with President Gemayel and Prime Minister Karame were a charade in which neither said what he thought, but only what he thought the Syrians would like to hear that he said. The time was therefore not very well spent. The party line was now that Lebanon couldn't discuss the help it needed from the United Nations until Israel produced a precise timetable and plan for its entire withdrawal. I explained that this was totally impractical and self-defeating. Peres and Rabin had only been able to get the Israeli coalition government to consent to total withdrawal by conceding that it would be in three phases, each dependent on the satisfactory completion of the previous phase, and each subject to a separate decision of the Israeli Cabinet.

After the joint meeting with Karame and Gemayel was over, we worked out with Gemayel's advisers a plan for the use of our forces during the Israeli withdrawal which we hoped would command both Syrian and Lebanese approval, and I left for Damascus.

The Syrians persisted in believing that the Israeli withdrawal was a trick to sow chaos in Lebanon and get the UN deployed in the north so that the Israeli forces and the Israeli-sponsored "South Lebanese Army" could retain their hold over southern Lebanon. They too insisted on a detailed plan and timetable for the Israeli withdrawal before agreeing to any role for UNIFIL. I concluded that the Syrians didn't want UNIFIL any further north because we would protect the Palestinian camps, which Arafat, whom the Syrians now hated, might then use to build up a new power base.

My return to Beirut, after a brief visit to Israel, was delayed by the Hamsin, a hot, sand-laden wind off the Sahara which had closed all airports. When we finally took off, the clouds below emerged out of a sea of airborne sand like floating islands, and we made an unnerving blind landing in Beirut. I visited the American Ambassador, Reg Bartholomew, in the bunker which had once been his residence. I wanted to be sure that Washington, whose support with Israel was vital, got an accurate picture of what we were trying to do. One approached what was left of the United States Embassy through roadblocks, tank traps, knife-rests, dugouts, tank positions, and assorted military checkpoints, at last reaching a house submerged in sandbags. Reg seemed cheerful enough and was enthusiastic about our ideas. Gemayel and Karame were also enthusiastic about our plan for the Israeli withdrawal and had sent an envoy to Damascus to get Syrian approval. This seemed too good to be true, and it was.

The first phase of the Israeli withdrawal, from the Sidon area, was to start on February 18, and the Lebanese had no time to lose if they were to make any sensible arrangements; but in my next meeting with Gemayel and Karame it was obvious that the Syrians had turned down our plan, although naturally no one was so crude as to mention this fact. After a mind-bendingly evasive conversation, Gemayel said, "You must now take this in hand and change the situation. What are you going to do?" "I am going back to New York to get on with my normal work." "How can you do that?" "Easily," I said, "because I have exhausted every option and every sensible course of action here. You have an opportunity, but only you can take it. I can do no more."

On the way back to Jerusalem I stopped in southern Lebanon, largely to present my condolences to the Fiji contingent which had lost three men in an ambush the day before. Not for the first time I felt strongly the contrast between the rational, decent world of a peacekeeping force and the irrational violence and self-destructiveness of the people it was trying to help. An important opportunity had been missed, and there would be a lot more trouble.

XXVII

Leaving

PRESIDENT REAGAN'S landslide reelection in November 1984 was no surprise, and in January Jeane Kirkpatrick finally resigned as United States Permanent Representative at the United Nations. This event, and speculation about her future in the power business in Washington, preoccupied the media for some time and, through no fault of Ambassador Kirkpatrick's, highlighted the somewhat parochial way in which it had become fashionable to view the United Nations in the United States. In Washington the organization sometimes seemed to be seen exclusively as a target of contempt and ridicule and as a minor prop in the ongoing extravaganza of American public life. This point of view was epitomized in a *New York Times* editorial entitled "Who Next for the UN?"

My own feelings on these matters were well expressed in a letter to the *New York Times* from William vanden Heuvel, a former United States Ambassador at the UN.

> In your issue of February 1, I read Ambassador Kirkpatrick's far from grudging assessment of herself ("intellectual in a world of bureaucrats" etc.) and an editorial "Who next for the UN?" which appears to regard the UN solely as an appendage of American domestic policy, patronage and job-swapping. Are we not perhaps in danger of losing our sense of proportion—not to say humor?

> From your editorial the reader could conclude that the UN, "a wordy convention fragmented into voting blocs," "a small pedestal" for large American names, is nothing more than an arena in which this all-American celebrity folk-dance can be conducted.

> Let me say simply, in case your readers might be interested, that there is, with all due respect to Dr. Kirkpatrick, another UN—the UN

of peace-keeping, of negotiation and good offices in Cyprus, Afghanistan, South East Asia, Lebanon, and other conflict areas, of refugee problems, of great and desperate humanitarian enterprises and of economic development. These and other similar activities go on twenty-four hours a day, 365 days a year, year-in, year-out, all over the world.

In the current discussion over the Kirkpatrick succession, it would be nice once in a while to recall that thousands of people with no great personal ambition, and with little chance of acclaim or advancement, are engaged in these tasks of the United Nations in distant and less fortunate lands, as well as at UN Headquarters.

Ambassador Kirkpatrick's successor, General Vernon Walters, reverted to the practice of having qualified professional senior staff in the United States Mission, and it was thus possible once again to discuss the various problems on hand with American representatives who were less preoccupied with ideological matters than with the actual substance of the problem, and to whom issues like the Middle East or Cyprus or Namibia were realities in themselves rather than pawns on the East-West chessboard. The problem, however, of the attitude of the United States government to the United Nations remained and deepened.

The fact that in 1985 we were to celebrate the fortieth anniversary of the world organization only seemed to dramatize this unfortunate situation. At the celebration of the signing of the Charter in San Francisco in June 1985, the "highlight" was a condescending speech by George Shultz in which he spoke of the world organization as if it was a delinquent schoolboy who had flunked his exams. In listing United Nations peace-keeping operations, he pointedly omitted the operation in Lebanon, UNIFIL. It was a depressing performance. In my own speech I said, among other things, that as one who had watched the Security Council from the beginning I sometimes felt that only an invasion from outer space would be a sufficiently non-controversial disaster to bring the Council back to the great power unanimity that the Charter required in order to make the United Nations effective.

The San Francisco celebration coincided with the hijacking of a TWA airliner to Beirut by a Shi'ite group demanding the release of Shi'ites rounded up by Israel in southern Lebanon. We had, as usual, offered to try to help, and the Israelis had asked Jean-Claude Aimé to go to Beirut and talk to Nabih Berri, the leader of the mainline Shi'ite Amal, which he did several times. The problem—a familiar one—was to get the plane and its passengers released and the Shi'ite detainees liberated without appearing to link the two issues, in order to preserve the principle of not negotiating with terrorists. We had made a practical suggestion as to how this might be done. The Israelis seemed interested but were anxious we should not so inform the United States. Shultz, when we talked to him in San Francisco, was definitely *not* interested. Both the TWA passengers and the Shi'ites were eventually released, mainly, apparently, through the efforts of Nabih Berri, the Syrians, and perhaps the Iranians.

*   *   *

In April, after visiting Saudi Arabia and Oman with Perez de Cuellar, I returned to Beirut. After the idiocies of January, I was not optimistic and was largely concerned to try to dissuade the Israelis from establishing a "Security Zone" in southern Lebanon after their withdrawal had technically been completed. I was convinced that this arrangement, apart from being illegal, would eventually create a new crisis. It would inevitably provoke the active hostility of extremist groups in Lebanon and other countries, and would also gradually disaffect and radicalize the sensible and moderate Shi'ia who constitute 80 percent of the population of the area. A proper deployment of UNIFIL seemed to be far more likely to establish the peace on the border which both the inhabitants of southern Lebanon and Israel so desperately wanted. In Israel these arguments fell on deaf ears. I thought this a great mistake and said so.

On June 10, the Israelis announced the withdrawal of their last large combat unit from Lebanon, leaving behind a "Security Zone," manned by General Antoine Lahd's South Lebanese Army, and an undisclosed number of Israeli posts, observers, and advisers. I had little respect for the illegitimate South Lebanese Army (SLA), which was bound to provoke violent reactions as well as to cause endless difficulties to UNIFIL. There was also the danger that UNIFIL would come to be perceived as the shield for the Israeli "Security Zone" and itself become a target for extremists and radical elements in Lebanon. Trouble was not long in coming.

In early June, during a weekend in England, I learned that the South Lebanese Army had kidnapped twenty-three of our Finnish soldiers. Efforts to free the Finns seemed to be dragging, so I left London for Tel Aviv on June 11.

What had apparently happened was a case of Nordic romanticism. A group of Shi'ites in the South Lebanese Army wanted to defect to Amal, the Shi'ite militia. They were afraid of reprisals on their families if they did this directly. They therefore asked our Finnish contingent to stage a mock battle with them after which they would surrender, hand over their weapons to the Finns, and cross over to the Amal. It is always unwise for simple and straightforward people to become involved in Levantine intrigues. The Finns, however, without consulting the UNIFIL commander, enthusiastically agreed to this cock-eyed plan. The Israelis and General Lahd, predictably furious at what was a considerable loss of face for the SLA, retaliated by kidnapping a busload of unarmed Finns returning from leave in Israel. The Israeli story was that the Finns had treacherously disarmed the SLA men and handed them over to their enemies.

When I arrived in Israel, Rabin was self-righteous and indignant. General Levy gave a short lecture on the unsoldierly conduct of the Finns. I said that the kidnapping of UN soldiers by anyone, let alone an illegitimate militia, was totally unacceptable, and in any case we had better find out what had really happened before making judgments.

I instructed UNIFIL to make arrangements with Amal for the International Red Cross to interview the eleven SLA defectors in a neutral place in order to establish whether they had defected of their own free will, and whether they wished to stay with Amal.

As I flew into Beirut by helicopter, a high-jacked Jordanian airliner exploded on the airport. A battle was raging between Amal and the Palestinians in the refugee camps in West Beirut. I gave Gemayel, who had lost his gramophone records in the recent shelling, an album of Beethoven's Piano Concertos played by Alfred Brendel. In response he touched a button on his desk and released a stereophonic blast of Tchaikovsky which quite drowned out the noise of gunfire outside. On our way back to our hotel a burst of automatic fire impacted in the dust on the side of the road just in front of our car. "Tiens," said our French Chief Observer, Colonel Fourrière, and accelerated.

In Damascus Khaddam, referring to the Finns, asked, "Why do your peacekeepers always turn the other cheek?" I commented that while Jesus Christ was still universally remembered after 2000 years, we didn't hear too much nowadays about all his contemporaries who *didn't* turn the other cheek. Khaddam laughed.

All the SLA defectors told the Red Cross they had defected of their own free will and had no wish to return to the SLA. This should have convinced General Lahd and the Israelis that they had no case against the Finns.

The Finns had now been detained for a week and it was Friday, the eve of the Sabbath. When the Israelis told me that General Lahd could not be found to receive the Red Cross report, Jean-Claude Aimé offered to send our French Battalion to look for him, and he magically reappeared.

I told the Israeli Defense Ministry that we had fulfilled our side of the bargain and unless the Finns were released we would have to consider other measures, including, with the greatest regret, the use of force. We did, after all, have some world-class fighting troops in Lebanon, although they had never been allowed to put their skills to the test. Half an hour later the word came through that the Finns would be released at 11:00 a.m. the following day.

There had been a mounting uproar in Finland over this incident, and I went to Helsinki on my way home. I explained to the government and over the television that in Lebanon it took more courage to exercise restraint than to open fire and that the Finns had behaved in a completely soldierly manner. I didn't mention my theory of "Nordic romanticism."

The southern Lebanon situation settled down to an uneasy stalemate punctuated by bursts of violence. When I went there in October, the moderate Amal was up against an extremist coalition of the Communist Party, the Hezbollah (Party of God), and sundry radicals, all clamoring for an assault on the Israeli "Security Zone." Many photographs of the Ayatollah Khomeini had appeared in the villages, and some of the Hezbollah fighters were wearing headbands inscribed "On to Jerusalem." Amal's moderation and its once dominant position were both already heavily eroded.

*   *   *

The main celebration of the fortieth anniversary of the United Nations took place at the session of the General Assembly in October. Some seventy heads of state or government, with the notable exceptions of Gorbachev and Mitterrand, and virtually all foreign ministers attended. Most of the speeches were good and some—those of Olof Palme, Rajiv Gandhi, the prime minister of New Zealand, the president of Burkina Faso, and Julius Nyerere of Tanzania, for example—were outstanding. There were obviously great, but more or less untapped, resources of international leadership, decency, and common sense in the world.

The general view was that among the least inspiring speeches, on what was supposed to be an occasion for reassessment and rededication, were those by President Reagan and Soviet Foreign Minister Eduard Shevardnadze. Reagan spoke on October 24, the official birthday of the UN. His speech was evidently designed to score points at home off the Soviet Union before the upcoming Geneva Summit. He scarcely mentioned the United Nations except to praise the 1950 Korean War and the Office of the High Commissioner for Refugees, and his list of regional conflicts which should be discussed with the Soviet Union omitted the Middle East. He concluded with a tear-jerking story about the rescue of a baby in the recent Mexican earthquake which left his audience writhing with embarrassment. At the conclusion of this performance the main body of the United States Delegation left the hall, leaving only junior officials to listen to Mrs. Thatcher, Rajiv Gandhi, and the prime minister of China. Both statesmanship and good manners took a considerable beating. Shevardnadze's performance was no more appropriate to the occasion. The United Nations fortieth anniversary celebration, if it did nothing else, dramatically highlighted the need for new international leadership.

*   *   *

I had for some years been thinking seriously of retiring. Much as I loved the work and was dedicated to the organization, I had had forty years of fairly continuous pressure and enforced discretion, and I wanted a little freedom of action and speech before I got too old to enjoy it. I was also anxious to hand over in an orderly fashion to a properly designated successor. The fortieth anniversary seemed a suitable time to do this and would avoid the complications of the following year when the election of the Secretary-General would come up.

Early in 1985, I told Perez de Cuellar that I wanted to retire at the end of the year. Some time before, he had given Mrs. Thatcher, who had raised the matter a number of times, an undertaking that, when I left, my successor would be British. It was decided, in March 1985, that Marrack ("Mig") Goulding, currently the British Ambassador in Angola, would take over from me on February 1, 1986.

Although I dreaded leaving the organization I had served for more than forty years, this was a considerable load off my mind. As the year wore on, however, I felt sorry to be leaving at a moment when the United Nations was in increasingly low water both politically and financially. I was also sorry that we had not managed to make progress on the Cyprus problem, the southern Lebanon situation, or Namibia, and that we seemed to have dropped out of the Middle East settlement business almost completely. But forty years was a good, tidy term of service, and it was time to go. Early in January 1986 Sidney and I set out on our farewell tour.

We went first to Delhi for a meeting of the Palme Commission. This was the last time I saw Olof Palme, who was assassinated in Stockholm the next month. Palme was a tremendous loss to the international community as well as to his own country. He was the last of a generation of national politicians who felt passionately about international issues and were prepared to put their reputations on the line for them. His funeral in Stockholm attracted a vast crowd of national leaders and international figures of all persuasions.

After Delhi we made farewell visits to Damascus, Amman, southern Lebanon, Israel, Egypt, and Cyprus. In southern Lebanon we got a particularly warm welcome in the ancient and embattled port of Tyre, where the Amal were anxious to show that Tyre was an example to all Lebanon. "We are all brothers here," they said, "even the Palestinians." At Naqoura a farewell parade awaited us on the parade ground by the sea. I remembered Naqoura in 1978 when there were only two crumbling buildings. Now the encampment stretched as far as the eye could see. Would we ever get out of it, I wondered, and, if so, who would take it over? The Club Med perhaps?

At Government House, our headquarters in Jerusalem, I gave medals to the Observers of the United Nations Truce Supervision Organization, our oldest peacekeeping organization, dating from 1948. In Cyprus for once everyone was relaxed and talked about things other than the Cyprus problem.

Our voyage ended with a final farewell dinner in Government House, Jerusalem, with all our generals—Alex Erskine of Ghana, Gunther Greindl of Austria, Bill Callaghan of Ireland, and Gustav Hägglund of Finland. This emotional occasion was a fitting end to my peacekeeping career. I had loved that part of my job more than any other and felt closer to the soldiers than to anyone else. Although, as their civilian chief, I had often had to prod or to restrain them, we had had, on the whole, the happiest of relationships, and I was very sad to leave them. They were all at the airport to see me off at dawn the next morning and, much to the surprise of Swissair, sang "For He's a Jolly Good Fellow" as I boarded the plane.

My last days in New York were full and mercifully brief. Mig was already installed, and my papers were on their way to the United Nations archives. Everyone was extraordinarily kind and helpful. Contrary to my fears, it was an easy departure.

At such leavetakings many complimentary words are written and spoken. The ones I valued most appeared in *The Jerusalem Post* in an Open Letter to me from its Diplomatic Correspondent, David Landau, urging me to continue to work for peace in the Middle East.

> I need not tell you, nor the readers of this newspaper, that of all the many shuttlers and would-be peacemakers, you have come through with an unblemished record for dispassionate compassion—appreciated in every regional capital.

Nor are you a politician, present or past, concerned with the "place in history."

Although Landau's words were excessively kind, they caught the spirit in which I had tried to work. I only wish that I could have achieved more in the way of practical results.

Epilogue

WE HAVE CREATED unprecedented possibilities for both progress and disaster on our planet without yet assuming the collective responsibility that both those possibilities demand. We already have much of the machinery for this purpose. We must take it out, overhaul it, and get it on the road.

Struggle is the essence of life. The problem is to draw a line between struggle, which is stimulating, and conflict, which is often lethal. Of the United Nations, which embodies the international effort to draw this line, Dag Hammarskjold said that "the constant struggle to close the gap between aspiration and performance now, as always, makes the difference between civilization and chaos." If we tire of this effort, it will be at our extreme peril.

Idealism, which is the distillation of human experience, is far more realistic than ideology, let alone cynicism or defeatism. It takes different forms. My brother Andrew conducts a ceaseless campaign for the general good of his community at a very practical and immediate level. His example has sometimes led me to wonder whether the pursuit of wider ideals and longer-term goals is not really a form of escapism or self-indulgence. But the present tidal wave of irreversible change, the ever-present possibility of a terminal manmade disaster, the complexity, the violence, the sheer numbers, the heedlessness, and the hurry of our times all demand that we manage not only conflict, but also what we used to call progress. If we fail to do this, coming generations will pay a terrible price.

In the United Nations, the only global design we have for this daunting task, the enormity of the challenge, the feebleness of the general will, and the smallness of the means were all too evident. As the years went by, the obstacles often seemed overwhelming and the spirit alarmingly weak. But then a disaster, or a near-disaster, or sometimes even an exceptional leader, would remind the nations once again that they must cooperate or perish. The effort continues. It must be intensified.

Just before he died, Sir Isaac Newton wrote: "I do not know what I may appear to the world, but to myself I seem to have been only like a boy playing on the seashore, and diverting myself in now and then finding a smoother pebble or a prettier shell than ordinary, whilst the great ocean of truth lay all undiscovered before me."

The seashore is more crowded and disorderly now, and the tide is rising. Will we have the courage to take to the ocean together?

Index